Indonesia Betrayed

Indonesia Betrayed

How Development Fails

Elizabeth Fuller Collins

University of Hawai'i Press
Honolulu

Library of Congress Cataloging-in-Publication Data

Collins, Elizabeth Fuller.
    Indonesia betrayed : how development fails /
Elizabeth Fuller Collins.
        p. cm.
    Includes bibliographical references and index.
    ISBN 978-0-8248-3115-8 (hardcover : alk. paper)—
    ISBN 978-0-8248-3183-7 (pbk. : alk. paper)
    1. Economic development projects—Indonesia.
2. Economic assistance—Indonesia. 3. Indonesia—
Economic conditions. I. Title.
    HC450.E44C65 2007
    338.9109598—dc22

                                2007005035

University of Hawai'i Press books are printed on acid-free
paper and meet the guidelines for permanence and durability
of the Council on Library Resources.

Designed by University of Hawai'i Press production staff

Printed by Edwards Brothers, Inc.

Never doubt that a small group of thoughtful committed people can change the world. Indeed it is the only thing that ever has.

— MARGARET MEAD

Contents

ix   *Acknowledgments*

xii   *Abbreviations and Acronyms*

1   Prologue: Paris, France, 1848

7   Chapter 1. Land of the Nine Rivers

28   Chapter 2. *Reformasi* in South Sumatra

53   Chapter 3. Who Owns the Land?

77   Chapter 4. No Forests, No Future

98   Chapter 5. Struggling for Workers' Rights

116   Chapter 6. "Where's My Cut?": The State and Corruption

134   Chapter 7. Local Autonomy: Democracy in Name Only?

152   Chapter 8. Islam and the Quest for Justice

171   Chapter 9. Indonesia in Global Context: Development, Free-Market Capitalism, and Democracy

193   *Chronology: The New Order and Post-Suharto Era, 1965–2004*

195   *Notes*

217   *Glossary*

219   *Bibliography*

255   *Index*

In memory of
Munir Said Thalib
1965—2004

Acknowledgments

MUNIR SAID THALIB was assassinated on September 7, 2004. Arsenic was put in food or drink served to him on a Garuda flight from Jakarta to Singapore. He died on the flight to the Netherlands, where he planned to study for a Ph.D. Four years into the post-Suharto era, Munir said that he needed to learn more about countries in Latin America that had successfully been transformed from a dictatorship to a democracy.

Munir was best known as the head of Kontras. Originally known as the Independent Committee on Human Rights Violations (Komite Independen Pelanggaran HAM or KIPHAM), Kontras was established in May 1997 after the attack on *reformasi* (reformist) activists at the PDI headquarters in July the previous year. In the context of a New Order crackdown on all forms of protest, KIPHAM was to be a "low-profile" organization that educated people about human rights and the role of the military in repression. In January 1998 the military began to kidnap democracy activists, and KIPHAM gave birth to the Commission on the Disappeared and Victims of Violence (Komisi Orang Hilang dan Korban Tindak Kekerasan, which came to be known simply as Kontras). Kontras joined LBH and other *reformasi* NGOs—ELSAM, AJI, PIPHAM, KIP, PMII—leading a high-profile campaign to inform the public about the abduction of democracy activists and violations of human rights by the Indonesian military. Munir worked tirelessly for reforms that would bring the military under civilian control, for the rights of farmers and workers, and for peaceful reform through education. In response the Kontras office was attacked, Munir was accused of being a communist and betraying his country, and his family was threatened. I asked him once how he managed to keep on with the struggle. He thought my question strange. One simply could not give up.

In writing this book, I have been inspired by the courage, integrity, and determination of Munir and other leaders of the nonviolent *reformasi* movement that brought down the New Order. Throughout Indonesia young activists refused to be intimidated by the Indonesian military. In their struggle against injustice they kept alive the hope that human beings could work together to build a more just society. A list of names of activists in South Sumatra alone would be longer than I could include here. I hope that those I do not name will forgive me for the omission. While I alone take responsibility for fact checking and putting together as carefully as possible an account of what happened, this book could not have been written without the work of many activists who helped me collect the stories I relate here: Jamilah Nuh, Nur Kholis, Yeni Rosliani, Abdul Wahib Situmorang, Chairil Syah, Tarech Rasyid, Taufiq Widjaya, Anwar Putra Bayu, Arief Nurhayat Permana, Indra Gunawan, Aidil Fitri, Syamsul Asinar, Untung Saputra, Azimi Asnawi, Robby Puruhita, Djayadi Hanan, Umar Abdullah, Saparuddin, Imelda, Erwita Lista, Sri Lestari, Roseka, Endah Agustiana, Ganda Upaya, Emil Makmud, Helmi Nawawi, Joni Widodo, Imron Supriyadi, and M. Subardin. The farmers and workers who emerged as leaders in villages and settlements, such as Pak Tarto, Pak Jafar, and Tamin Neklikesabe, are extraordinary human beings in the best sense of the word. I mean this book to honor their commitment to a nonviolent struggle against the rich and powerful elites who benefited from the expropriation of their land and other natural resources.

The Ford Foundation in Jakarta provided funding for a research project entitled "Democratic Practice: South Sumatran Field Studies," which was conducted by Yayasan Masyarakat Madani (YMM) under the directorship of Laurel Heydir. Research by YMM in South Sumatra was directed by Professor Zen Zanibar, Zulkifli, MA, and Suharni, MA. In this book I have drawn on reports by Adang Yuliansyah, Widyawati, Dian Novita, and Ahmad Fali Okilas. Faculty at Sriwijaya University were helpful at many different stages of my research. I especially wish to thank Zainab Bakir, Ahmad Nangsari, Rita Hayati, Abdul Aziz Numal, Ridhah Taqwa, Amzulian Rifai, and Amran Halim, Rector (1986–1994). I also wish to thank Junial Komar, Djohan Hanafiah, Arnold Bakara, Abu Arman, Umar Nawawi, H. Husni (mayor of Palembang), Bupati Alex Noerdin, Governor Rosihan Arsyad, and Governor Syahrial Oesman, who agreed to extended interviews.

I also am deeply grateful to friends and colleagues who took precious time to read drafts of my book. All have offered helpful suggestions: Jamila Nuh, Abdul Wahib Situmorang, Nur Kholis, Yeni Rosliani, Mohamad Sirozi, Amran Halim, Zainab Bakir, Amzulian Rifai, Sherri Biegeleisen, Dick McGinn, Rick Kraince, Ann Tickamyer, Christine Fahl, Putut Widjanarko, Susie Sutch, Nicholas Collins, Michael Leaver, David Steward, Emmons Collins, Patricia Black, Barbara de Janvry, and Steve Howard. Ezki Widianti, Nurul Pratiwi, and Erda Handayani all came to my rescue when I needed help in finding information. Finally I thank my editors at the University of Hawai'i Press, Pamela Kelley and Cheri Dunn, and my copy editor, Barbara Folsom.

Indonesian Names and Spelling

I use the modern spelling of Indonesian names rather than Dutch spelling, as in Suharto rather than Soeharto, unless a particular name is consistently spelled with Dutch spelling. Many Indonesians are known by only one name, such as Suharto (although later in life he occasionally used Muhammad Suharto), while others may have three or more names. People with long names are often referred to by an affectionate short name or by their initials. Thus the former president of Indonesia, Abdurrahman Wahid, is known as "Gus Dur," and the present president of Indonesia, Susilo Bambang Yudhoyono, as SBY.

On South Sumatra

In 1994 the province of South Sumatra was divided into eight districts *(kabupaten),* roughly equivalent to a county–Ogan Komering Ulu (OKU), Ogan Komering Ilir (OKI), Lahat, Musi Banyu Asin (MUBA), Muara Enim, Musi Rawas (MURA), Bangka, Belitung–and two metropolitan administrations *(kota madya),* Palembang and Pangkalpinang. The creation of new political and administrative districts in the post-Suharto era led to the creation of a new province, Babel, composed of the former districts of Bangka and Belitung. The process of dividing districts into smaller units is still ongoing. In South Sumatra, MUBA has been divided into two districts, OKU into three, and OKI into two. Pagaralam, Prabamulih, and Lubuk Linggau have been made autonomous metropolitan administrations.

Abbreviations and Acronyms

In Indonesia abbreviations and acronyms are used to refer to political parties, government departments, and nongovernmental organizations. I have tried to keep this alphabet soup under control, but these short forms of names are so ubiquitous in Indonesia that they are impossible to avoid. This list gives both Indonesian and English names in full. In the text, the first time I refer to an organization with an acronym I provide the name in English.

ABRI	Angkatan Bersenjata Republik Indonesia (Armed Forces of the Republic of Indonesia during the New Order, now divided into Tentara Nasional Indonesia [TNI] and the National Police)
AJI	Aliansi Jurnalis Independen (Alliance of Independent Journalists)
Bapedal	Badan Pengendalian Dampak Lingkungan (National Environmental Impact Management Agency)
Bapedalda	Badan Pengendalian Dampak Lingkungan Daerah (Provincial Environmental Impact Management Agency)
BPS	Badan Pusat Stastistik (National Bureau of Statistics)
BPS	Barisan Pemuda Sumsel (South Sumatra Youth Front)
BUMN	Badan Usaha Milik Negara (State-owned Enterprise)
DDII	Dewan Dakwah Islam Indonesia (Indonesian Council for Dakwah)
DPR	Dewan Perwakilan Rakyat (National Legislature)
DPRD	Dewan Perwakilan Rakyat Daerah (Provincial Legislature)
ELSAM	Lembaga Studi dan Advokasi Masyarakat (The Institute for Policy Research and Advocacy)
FITRA	Forum Indonesia Transparansi Anggaran (Indonesia Forum for Budgetary Transparency)
FKBB	Forum Komunikasi Buruh Bersatu (United Workers Communication Forum)
FKPPI	Forum Komunikasi Putra-Putri Purnawirawan Indonesia (Communication Forum of Sons and Daughters of Retired Military Officers)

FOLSIP	Forum Olah Lingkungan Sekitar Industri Palembang (Palembang Community Forum on Industrial Environment)
FORDS	Forum Dakwah Sekolah (Dakwah School Forum)
Gemuis	Generasi Muda Islam (Young Islamic Generation)
GMNI	Gerakan Mahasiswa Nasional Indonesia (National Student Movement of Indonesia), associated with Sukarno
Golkar	Golongan Karya (Functional Groups), the New Order political party
HMI	Himpunan Mahasiswa Islam (Muslim Student Association)
HGU	Hak Guna Usaha (right to use land, land concession granted by the government)
HPH	Hak Penguasaan Hutan (forest concession)
IAIN	Institut Agama Islam Negeri (State Institute for Islamic Studies)
ICMI	Ikatan Cendekiawan Muslim se-Indonesia (Association of Indonesian Muslim Intellectuals)
INSAN	Informasi dan Studi untuk Hak Asasi Manusia (Human Rights Information and Study Network)
IRM	Ikatan Remaja Masjid (Union of Mosque Youth)
ISAI	Institut Studi Arus Informasi (Institute for the Free Flow of Information)
JAMUR	Jaringan Advokasi Masyarakat Urban (Advocacy Network for the Urban Poor)
JPS	Jaring Pengaman Sosial (Social Safety-Net Programs)
KAHMI	Korps Alumni HMI (HMI Alumni Corps)
KAMMI	Kesatuan Aksi Mahasiswa Muslim Indonesia (Action Committee of Indonesian Muslim Students)
KESMADA	Yayasan Kesejahteraan Masyarakat Desa (Foundation for Village Social Welfare)
Keppres	Keputusan President (Presidential Order)
KIPP	Komite Independen Pemantau Pemilu (The Independent Electoral Monitoring Committee)
KISDI	Komite Indonesia untuk Solidaritas Dunia Islam (Indonesian Committee for World Muslim Solidarity)
KNPI	Komite Nasional Pemuda Indonesia (National Committee of Indonesian Youth)
KODAM	Komando Daerah Militer (Regional Military Command)
Komnas HAM	Komisi Nasional Hak Asasi Manusia (National Commission on Human Rights)
KONTRAS	Komisi Orang Hilang dan Korban Tindak Kekerasan (Commission on the Disappeared and Victims of Violence)
Kopassus	Komando Pusakan Khusus (Special Forces Command)
Kostrad	Komando Operasi Pemulihan Keamanan dan Ketertiban (Army Strategic Command)

KSKP	Kesatuan Solidaritas Kesejahteraan Petani (Farmers' Prosperity and Solidarity Union)
KUD	Koperasi Unit Desa (village cooperative)
LBH	Lembaga Bantuan Hukum (Legal Aid Institute)
LDK	Lembaga Dakwah Kampus (Institute for Campus Dakwah)
Lonsum	PT PP [Perusahan Perkebunan (Horticultural Industry)] London Sumatra Indonesia (a multinational corporation producing crude palm oil, rubber, cocoa, coconut, and coffee)
LP3ES	Lembaga Penelitian, Pendidikan dan Penerangan Ekonomi dan Sosial (Institute for Social and Economic Research, Education, and Information)
LSM	Lembaga Swadaya Masyarakat (self-reliant community institution or NGO)
LSP	Lembaga Studi Pembangunan (Institute for Development Studies)
Masyumi	Majelis Syuro Muslimin Indonesia (Islamic political party of modernist Muslims, banned in 1960 by President Sukarno)
MHP	PT Musi Hutan Persada (subsidiary of Prayogo Pangestu's Barito Pacific Group)
Muspida	Musyawarah Pimpinan Daerah (commission composed of government officials from the provincial to the local level)
MUBA	Musi Banyu Asin (district in South Sumatra)
MURA	Musi Rawas (district in South Sumatra)
Muspida Plus	Muspida plus NGO representatives
NU	Nahdlatul Ulama (Islamic Scholars Association)
OKI	Ogan Komering Ilir (district in South Sumatra)
OKU	Ogan Komering Ulu (district in South Sumatra)
PAN	Partai Amanat Nasional (National Mandate Party)
PBB	Partai Bulan Bintang (Islamic Crescent Moon and Star Party)
PDI	Partai Demokrasi Indonesia (Indonesian Democracy Party)
PDI-P	PDI Perjuangan (PDI-Struggle)
PIPHAM	Pusat Informasi dan Pendidikan Hak Asasi Manusia (Human Rights Information and Education Center)
PKI	Partai Komunis Indonesia (Indonesian Communist Party)
PKS	Partai Keadilan Sejahtera (Justice and Prosperity Party, formerly Partai Keadilan)
PMII	Pergerakan Mahasiswa Islam Indonesia (Indonesian Islamic Student Movement, aligned with the NU)
PNI	Partai Nasional Indonesia (Indonesian National Party)
PON	Pekan Olahraga Nasional (National Sports Competition)
PPDD	Pemberdayaan Pemerintahan Desa Dalam (Village Empowerment and Development Program)
PPP	Partai Persatuan Pembangunan (United Development Party)
PRD	Partai Rakyat Demokratik (People's Democratic Party)

PSPKL	Persatuan Solidaritas Pedagang Kaki Lima (Street Vendors Solidarity Union)
PT	Perseroan Terbatas Ltd.
Rohis	Kerohanian Islam (Islamic Spiritual Training)
SBSI	Serikat Buruh Sejahtera Indonesia (Indonesian Prosperity Labor Union)
SPSI	Serikat Pekerja Seluruh Indonesia (All-Indonesia Workers' Union, the government-controlled labor union)
SKEPHI	Sekretariat Kerjasama Pelestarian Hutan Indonesia (Indonesian Network for Forest Conservation)
SSCW	South Sumatra Corruption Watch
TEMPUR	Tim Advokasi untuk Penyelamat Uang Rakyat (Team of Advocates to Save the People's Money)
TNI	Tentara Nasional Indonesia (Indonesian Armed Forces)
VOC	Verenigde Oost-Indische Compagnie (Dutch East Indies Company)
WALHI	Wahana Lingkungan Hidup Indonesia (Indonesian Environment Network)
WCC	Women's Crisis Center
YAHLI	Yayasan Advokasi Hukum Lingkungan Indonesia (Foundation for Environmental Law Advocacy)
YMM	Yayasan Masyarakat Madani (Foundation for Civic Society)

Indonesia Betrayed

Prologue

Paris, France, 1848

How could the poor and inferior and yet powerful classes not have
dreamed of rising up out of their poverty and inferiority by using their
power, especially in a time when the view of the hereafter has become
more obscure and when the miseries of this world are more visible and
seem more intolerable?
  —Alexis de Tocqueville, *Recollections* (1851)

ON THE EVENING of February 21, 1848, all across Paris groups of
students, reporters, and members of workers' guilds gathered to make final
preparations for a demonstration planned for the following day. The democracy movement had started the previous year when a coalition of repub-
lican political leaders introduced a motion in the Chamber of Deputies
extending the vote to all men who paid one hundred francs in direct taxes.
When the Chamber, which had been elected by a limited franchise, rejected
the reform, the democracy activists took their campaign onto the streets.[1]
Alarmed by the growing strength of the democracy movement, Prime Minister Guizot called out the National Guard to confront the demonstrators.
Instead, the guard joined the protestors in chanting, "Long live reform!"
The following day Guizot resigned. As the news spread, people poured into
the streets to celebrate. Unfortunately, on the same day a unit of the guard
panicked and fired into a crowd, killing fifty people, an incident that soon
became known as the massacre of the Boulevard des Capuchines.

As the revolutionary spirit spread throughout Paris, King Louis Philippe,
recalling the fate of a previous monarch, fled. The revolutionaries took over
the Chamber and proclaimed the Second Republic.

The revolutionaries in 1848 were inspired by the spirit of equality and
the "rights of man" as framed by the Marquis de Lafayette in the *Declaration of the Rights of Man and of the Citizen* and adopted by the National
Assembly in 1789. The leaders of the democracy movement sought demo-

1

cratic reforms that could be achieved by an expanded franchise, reforms that would make their government more accountable to its citizens.[2] The fuel that made the revolution flare up, however, was the "social issue" of the day, the problem of poverty. The first half of the nineteenth century witnessed a deepening economic crisis caused by the transfer of land rights from peasants to the state and large landowners. In the countryside where three-quarters of the population lived, peasants relied on traditional rights to pasture animals and gather wood on communal lands. A forestry code, passed at the end of the Restoration, abolished these "usage rights" and established a rural police force charged with enforcing state regulations. Large landowners, who were beginning to engage in commercial agriculture for profit, took advantage of the opportunity to usurp the usage rights of peasants. This led to increasing poverty in the countryside and a steady stream of migration to cities. In the first half of the nineteenth century, the population of Paris nearly doubled.

As this occurred, those who sought work in Paris and other cities were exposed to new ideas. In the first half of the nineteenth century, primary education was extended. People read newspapers where the problems of poverty and the working class were debated in a vocabulary provided by social reformers. Phrases like "exploitation of man by man" and "the right to work" fired the imagination of workers, students, and revolutionaries.[3]

The immediate cause of the revolution was a financial crisis. The potato blight of 1845 followed by a poor wheat harvest in 1846 left up to one-third of the population of France on relief in 1847. Food riots and protests against the high cost of wheat led the government to import foreign grain, depleting French gold reserves. In consequence the value of the franc fell, causing a depression in the domestic market. Businesses curtailed production, and many of the financial elite fled the country. The number of bankruptcies skyrocketed, workers lost their jobs, and wages fell.[4]

In the view of Alexis de Tocqueville, who in 1850 recorded his thoughts on the political events leading to the Revolution in his *Recollections,* the true cause of the outbreak of revolution was a failure of political leadership and corruption in the government. As he wrote in April 1848 to his friend Nassau William Senior:

> The great and real cause of the revolution was the detestable spirit which ani-
> mated the government during its long reign; a spirit of trickery, of baseness,
> and of bribery, which has enervated and degraded the middle classes, destroyed
> their public spirit, and filled them with a selfishness so blind as to induce them
> to separate their interests entirely from those of the lower classes from whence

they sprang, who consequently have been abandoned to the counsels of men who, under pretence of serving the lower orders, have filled their heads with false ideas.[5]

The provisional government established after the fall of the monarchy proclaimed freedom of the press, the right of free assembly and association, and universal suffrage. The response to these freedoms was dramatic. Between February and December of 1848, 479 newspapers were started in Paris. Political organizing appeared in the form of a loose network of associations known as the "club movement." By March 15, 1848, 59 clubs had been formed in Paris; by mid-April there were 203 clubs with over 70,000 members.[6] Because the rich had fled the revolution, the number of businesses in Paris had declined by 54 percent, and small businesses could no longer obtain credit.[7] Because there were no jobs, the number of unemployed increased daily. The chief demand of the clubs was that the "right to work" be recognized. The first step taken by the new government was to limit the workday in factories to ten hours in Paris and eleven hours in the provinces. The unemployed were paid two francs a day to work on the roads and fortifications outside of Paris. By mid-March there were 25,000 men enrolled in the workshops; by mid-June the number had escalated to 120,000.[8]

By providing guaranteed employment, the workshops strengthened the position of workers in negotiating with employers. An article in the newspaper *Le Constitutionnel* described the situation from the perspective of employers: "The men were supported during their strikes by the government which paid them for doing nothing. They were encouraged by speeches that were hostile to the masters. The men's solidarity in their strikes was confirmed, and they became more and more hostile to the employers. As this system developed the alarm increased in industry and commerce. The workers' poverty helped swell what the employers regarded as the army of anarchy."[9] In fear of the army of the poor, the Parisian middle class, which had formerly supported the ideals of the revolution, began to turn against the democracy movement.

The April election brought to power a Constituent Assembly with more landlords, clergymen, and aristocrats than any assembly elected during the July Monarchy. Leaders of the club movement were divided on how to press for further democratic reforms. Encouraged by their success in the February revolution, some favored resorting to violence. Others argued for a long-term campaign for peaceful reform. As one of the reformers assessed the situation, the working class consisted of two groups—skilled workers in the artisan trades and wage laborers driven by anger over their poverty and with nothing to lose: "The [former] are very democratic and understand the proper meaning of the word 'liberty.' The [latter], on the other hand, mistake liberty for license and are apt to commit disorders to avenge their suffering caused by their masters. Thus they are capable of compromising our cause." [10]

A demonstration in support of pro-democracy revolutionaries in Poland was scheduled for May 15. As thirty thousand demonstrators gathered to march on the National Assembly, anxiety about a possible outbreak of violence spread. There were rumors that some demonstrators wanted to force a violent confrontation with the assembly. This caused the crowd of protestors to dwindle to about two thousand. The remaining demonstrators did force their way into the assembly and declare it dissolved, but their audacity was ineffectual. This incident, which came to be known as the "Polish fiasco," led the National Assembly to take action against both the political clubs and the national workshops.

On June 22, 1848, a crowd of a hundred thousand massed at the Hôtel de Ville to protest the closing of the workshops. In the report of the Paris prefect of police, a second revolution appeared imminent: "11:00 a.m. A column of five hundred people, headed by a banner [with the words "National Workshops"] has just marched through the 7th Arrondissement. The men in it say they will not go away to Sologne [a project to drain the marshes] and that they prefer to die here. They add that they will take up arms against the National Assembly, and that the Mobile Guard will support them." [11] By the next day working-class quarters were studded with barricades, many flying the flags of national workshops or National Guard legions. Brutal street fighting between members of the Parisian working class behind the barricades and poor unemployed youths in the Mobile Guard, whom Karl Marx called the "lumpen proletariat" lasted for four days.[12] When the June insurrection was suppressed, three thousand people had been killed and fifteen thousand more arrested and deported to Algeria.

For Marx, the revolution in France was the first against capitalism. He called for the workers of the world to unite in a long struggle for a society in which there would no longer be classes and a division between those who owned property and those who sold their labor. For Tocqueville, too, the revolutionaries of 1848 were inspired by the love of equality. He believed that the ideals of equality and universal human rights would ignite future revolutions to establish democratic governments. The Revolution of 1848 in France stands at the beginning of an era dominated by two great opposing forces: on the one side capitalism, which tends to concentrate wealth and power in the hands of a few; and on the other, a call for democratic government accountable to the people, a more equal distribution of power and wealth, and an end to poverty.

In 1998, one hundred and fifty years after the Revolution of 1848, a democracy movement led by students, reporters, and elements of the middle class emerged to confront the authoritarian regime of Suharto's New Order in Indonesia. There is a striking similarity between the causes and course of the Revolution of 1848 and the *reformasi* movement in Indonesia. Like the democracy activists in Paris who had inherited the tradition of the French Revolution, protestors in Jakarta saw themselves as carrying on the traditions of the "generation of '45" that had fought for independence and the "generation of '65" that had destroyed communism. When the regime of Suharto unexpectedly collapsed overnight as elements of the middle class gave their support to the democracy movement, like the revolutionaries of 1848, *reformasi* leaders found themselves unprepared to establish a new government.

As in France, the democracy movement in Indonesia grew out of an economic crisis. This was precipitated by the spread of capitalism in the guise of export-oriented policies aimed at production for the world market. The transfer of land rights from farmers and indigenous groups to the state and corporations involved in commercial agriculture increased rural poverty and led to urban migration. In Indonesia, as in France, the expansion of education during the New Order, as well as access to newspapers, radio, and television, brought new ideas to many and fueled hopes for political change. As in France, the success of the democracy movement in Indonesia was due in part to a financial crisis that hit Indonesia in 1997; the Indonesian rupiah was reduced to less than one-quarter of its former value. Businesses went bankrupt, the middle classes saw their prosperity erode, and wealthy Chinese Indonesians tried to preserve their fortunes by sending their money out of the country. The loss of jobs plunged many in the urban working class into poverty, and a dramatic rise in the cost of food provoked mass protests.

After the fall of Suharto in 1998, elites associated with the regime tried to retain their grip on power by calling for order, security, and national unity. Supporters of Suharto's authoritarian New Order warned that demonstrations of workers and peasants could lead to mob rule, anarchy, and chaos. They argued that the economy would not revive without foreign investment, and foreign investment would not return to Indonesia until there was order and stability. Many in the government maintained that the people were not ready for democracy. Leaders of the *reformasi* movement were afraid that a military coup would crush their hopes for democratic reform. They feared that if the middle class were convinced that it must choose between the twin threats of anarchy and despotism, it might prefer despotism.

The democratic revolution that took place in Indonesia in 1998 provides an opportunity to take stock of the worldwide struggle for a more just economic order 150 years after the Revolution of 1848. The spread of free-market capitalism as a global system has fueled democratic movements, but the gap between rich and poor continues to grow wider despite fifty years of Western-sponsored "development." This study aims to describe the challenges faced by those who struggle for democratic reforms and social justice and to consider, given the world we live in, what kinds of policies and strategies are most likely to promote more accountable government and justice for the poor.

Chapter 1

Land of the Nine Rivers

as the sun hurries behind the bridge
and the tide rushes away, a flock of kites
fly low across the river, lamps shine
inside the mosque, as he enters his house
he remembers a poem, and writes it
on the back of a card. the poem says
there are twenty moons, gather them together,
don't be shy, God has given you
all of them, take them one by one
from the sapphire sky, roll them into a ball,
and remember to throw me one as well,
God's Word is addressed to both of us.
By the Banks of the Musi River
     —Anwar Putra Bayu[1]

I FIRST WENT TO SUMATRA in 1971 with my husband, who was doing dissertation research on the traditions and ethnic ties of the highland peoples of South Sumatra. We settled on the Pasemah Plateau, a fertile plain below the majestic volcano Gunung Dempo in South Sumatra. At that time there was no electricity or running water, no newspapers, and only one telephone at the post office in the market town of Pagaralam. On our first trip to the highlands cars and trucks had to travel in convoys so one vehicle could be used to help haul another through places where the road had deteriorated to a muddy swamp.

Yet the Pasemah were prosperous. They cultivated rice in fields irrigated by mountain streams, harvested coffee from gardens planted on the slopes of the Barisan mountains, grew vegetables, and raised chickens and water buffalo. Every village had a fishpond. Houses built of forest hardwoods stood on sturdy pillars high above the ground. Marriages, births, deaths, and the harvest were celebrated with lavish feasts of thanksgiving *(sedekah)* to which neighbors and kin from near and far came.

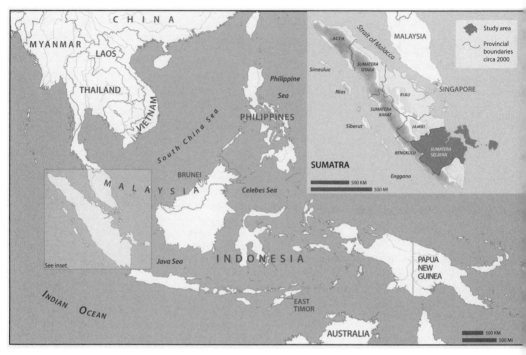

Indonesia. Inset: Sumatra. (Margaret Price)

As the main roads linking the highlands to Palembang were paved and transportation improved, we watched the Pasemah take advantage of new opportunities by raising vegetables and pond fish to sell in Palembang, which was eight hours travel by road. With cash from the sale of coffee, some people were able to buy a car or truck and begin new enterprises.

Over the twenty years between 1973 when I left Sumatra and 1992 when I returned to do my own research, there were many changes. Palembang was ringed by new suburbs accommodating an expanding middle class. This was credited to the policies of Suharto's government, called the "New Order," which had been in power for twenty-five years. Economists and international economic institutions, such as the World Bank, were pointing to Indonesia as a model of successful economic development. More surprising to me were signs that the middle class had become more self-identified and observant Muslims. New mosques had been constructed, and prayer rooms were set aside in public buildings. Going on the hajj, the pilgrimage to Mecca, had become the mark of respectable success. The most striking sign of the new importance of Islam was the number of young women in the universities who now wore the Islamic head-covering called a *jilbab*.

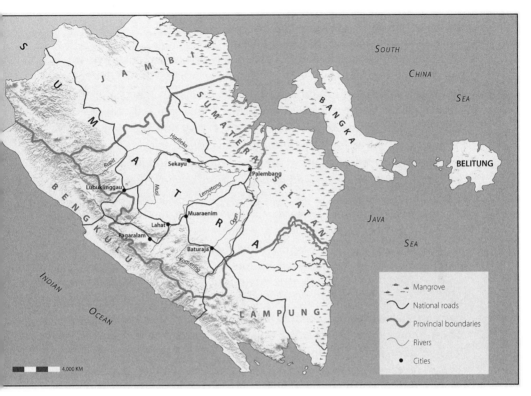

South Sumatra. (Margaret Price)

In 1992, foreign researchers in Indonesia were treated with suspicion. I began my research cautiously by proposing to look into women and social change. That summer I interviewed women at Sriwijaya University, asking them how they came to the decision to wear the *jilbab,* how their families had reacted, and what the implications of this decision was for their future.[2] Many described Islam as a "moral compass," and gradually I came to understand that for students the turn to Islam was a part of a struggle for a more just society based on Islamic values.

In the summer of 1994 I returned to Palembang to find students demonstrating against an increase in tuition outside the office of the rector of Sriwijaya University. The Asian Development Bank had funded construction of a new campus. The tuition increase was attributed to cost overruns and corruption. The students' protests, the like of which had not been seen in twenty-five years in South Sumatra, appeared to be a first crack in the facade of order and harmony erected by the New Order. Nothing in the discussions I had had with students and faculty just two years before had suggested that such demonstrations would occur. The focus of my research shifted to the emerging *reformasi* movement.

Jamila Nuh, a student who had emerged as one of the spokespersons for the demonstrating students, took me to the Palembang Branch of the Legal Aid Institute (LBH), an Indonesian nongovernmental organization (NGO) that campaigns for the rule of law and protection of civil and political rights. In 1994, LBH volunteers in Palembang were busy documenting land conflicts between villagers and corporations given land concessions in South Sumatra. They introduced me to the other side of economic "development" there: people forced off the land, increased rural poverty, flight to the cities, large-scale unemployment, and environmental destruction that eliminates the possibility of future prosperity for the majority and ultimately affects the health and well-being of all Indonesians.

In 1994 there was little reason to think that the small but growing protest movement would bring change soon. Confident that the New Order "development state" had established its legitimacy, in the early 1990s Suharto had announced a new era of "Openness" *(Keterbukaan)*, and restraints on the press were relaxed. Criticism of government policies and accusations of corruption, however, provoked Suharto to crack down in July 1994. The minister of information banned three national news magazines known for critical, investigative reporting: *Tempo,* the respected magazine edited by Goenawan Mohamad, and the tabloids *Monitor* and *Detik.* In Palembang, Jamila was one of a small group of about twenty activists who protested. Carrying a banner, they marched to the South Sumatra legislature. At the time, it did not seem possible that such limited demonstrations could multiply and coalesce into a pro-democracy *reformasi* movement that would force Suharto to step down four years later.

The Asian economic crisis hastened the end of the New Order. In the second half of 1997 and early 1998, prices for basic commodities skyrocketed following a precipitous drop in the value of Indonesia's currency, the rupiah. The student-led democracy movement grew in strength and began to win middle-class support. To suppress the demonstrations, security forces began kidnapping leaders of the movement, but the protests continued. By February 1998, protests had spread to market towns in South Sumatra. In March students in Islamic organizations joined the *reformasi* movement with hopes of reforming society and government in accord with Islamic values.

On May 13, 1998, four student demonstrators were shot and killed on the campus of an elite private university in Jakarta. In both Palembang and Jakarta the response was immediate and dramatic. The protests turned into mob riots that lasted for three days. A week later, President Suharto resigned. The New Order had effectively collapsed. When Vice President B. J. Habibie became president, the *reformasi* movement split into two factions; one demanded democratic reforms and the other called for a government based on Islamic values.

In 1997 I was developing a proposal with colleagues at Sriwijaya University to study the emergence of NGOs in South Sumatra. By the time our proposal was funded in 1998, Suharto was gone.[3] The *reformasi* movement continued as farmers and workers mobilized to reclaim their rights. The focus of our research shifted to the role of civil society organizations in the "democratic transition."

Adam Schwarz had predicted the end in *A Nation in Waiting: Indonesia's Search for Stability* (1994); Douglas Ramage told the story of Muslim activists working for democratic reform in *Politics in Indonesia: Democracy, Islam and the Ideology of Tolerance* (1995); and Anders Uhlin described the emergence of the *reformasi* movement in *Indonesia and the "Third Wave of Democratization": The Indonesian Pro-Democracy Movement in a Changing World* (1997). Nevertheless, experts and democracy activists alike were stunned by the unexpectedly swift fall of Suharto at the end of May 1998.

Like the disintegration of the Soviet Union at the end of the 1980s, the disintegration of the New Order caught people by surprise. Looking back, scholars have described how opposition to Suharto gradually emerged and then coalesced in the early months of 1998. Robert Hefner chronicled the rise of an Islamic pro-democracy movement in *Civil Islam: Muslims and Democratization in Indonesia* (2000), and Kevin O'Rourke provided an engaging account of the jockeying among elites as the end drew near in *Reformasi: The Struggle for Power in Post-Soeharto Indonesia* (2002).[4] Ed Aspinall examined the role of student groups in organizing opposition to the New Order in *Opposing Suharto: Compromise, Resistance, and Regime Change in Indonesia* (2003).

This book adds to this literature an account of the pro-democracy movement at the grassroots level in a province outside Java, showing how New Order development policies deprived small holders in South Sumatra of rights to land and access to the economic resources that had traditionally sustained them. Meanwhile, President Suharto, his family and associates built economic empires, and foreign interests benefited from neoliberal economic policies designed to produce exports for the world market. I also show how an NGO movement arose that helped to lay the foundation for the democracy movement of 1997–1998 by popularizing concepts like human rights and empowerment of the people.

There have been many important studies of the "transition to democracy" in Indonesia, including Arief Budiman, Barbara Hatley, and Damien

Kingsbury, *Reformasi: Crisis and Change in Indonesia* (1999); Damien Kingsbury and Arief Budiman, eds., *Indonesia: The Uncertain Future* (2001); Ed Aspinall and Greg Fealy, eds., *Local Power and Politics in Indonesia: Decentralisation and Democratisation* (2003); and Richard Robison and Vedi R. Hadiz, *Reorganising Power in Indonesia: The Politics of Oligarchy in an Age of Markets* (2004). I add to this literature by describing the challenges faced by *reformasi* activists in the post-Suharto era as national and local elites have established new networks of power in order to maintain control of natural resources and the perquisites of political power.

In this book I examine phenomena like development, civil society, and democracy in a concrete context demonstrating how asymmetries of power lead to outbreaks of violence and corruption. I show how a global economy increases the gap between rich and poor. While argument by illustrative examples may be dismissed as merely anecdotal, it has the virtue of providing an integrated understanding of a complex reality. I take readers behind the abstractions of development, globalization, and neoliberalism so they can make grounded judgments about the claims of those who promote "globalization" or "free-market" economics.

I also draw a distinction between "globalization" and the neoliberal policies that the United States and international organizations such as the International Monetary Fund (IMF), the World Bank, and the World Trade Organizations (WTO) promote in the name of globalization. These policies—market deregulation, fiscal austerity measures, and privatization of state enterprises—are an extension of capitalism or "free-market" economics to countries of the developing world. Supporters of neoliberalism claim that in an ideal world free markets lead to economic growth, the creation of a middle class, and the establishment of democratically accountable government. Critics point to a widening gap between the rich and the poor, the "race to the bottom" as countries compete to win foreign investment, and the effects on the poor of neoliberal structural adjustment programs that restrict funding for health, education, and welfare programs.

Globalization refers to networks of transportation and communication connecting people throughout the world. Globalization has positive and negative aspects, as it includes both the spread of ideas, technology, and goods and the spread of diseases and global environmental problems. The relations of power that are structured by neoliberal economic policies shape a particular form of globalization that increases the wealth and power of rich countries and multinational corporations at the expense of developing or poor countries and smallhold farmers.

Globalization and the Land of the Nine Rivers

Globalization is an old story for the peoples of South Sumatra, who have been engaged in systems of global exchange from their earliest known history. In the Pasemah highlands, carved megaliths depicting warriors wearing helmets and carrying drums and painted stone cist graves dating from the first centuries of the Common Era testify to the exchange of ideas and technology with other societies in Southeast Asia. These monuments are part of a Bronze Age culture known as Dong Song after a site in Vietnam, which spread throughout most of Southeast Asia (except for Borneo and the Philippines).[5] As early as the seventh century, a thriving port on the Musi River became the capital of the maritime kingdom of Sriwijaya, which flourished between the seventh and tenth centuries. The Buddhist pilgrim I Ching, traveling from China to India, reported that over a thousand monks studied in monasteries under the protection of the Sriwijaya ruler.

Muslim traders from India and the Hadramaut coast of Yemen came in the following centuries, bringing Islam. With the establishment of the Palembang sultanate, South Sumatra once again became an important trading kingdom. Muslims from the Hadramaut, known as the Alawiyin, a title for descendants of Ali, son-in-law of the Prophet, settled in Palembang and built mosques and prayer houses, which served as Islamic schools. In the eighteenth and nineteenth centuries Palembang came to be known as a center of Islamic learning. The most famous scholar, Abd al-Shamad (born c. 1700), the son of a Hadrami Sayid and a Palembang noblewoman, was known as al-Palimbani after his birthplace. He went to Arabia to study, where he joined the community of Malay Muslims known as Jawi. Through his writings, al-Palimbani spread Sufi teachings to Southeast Asia and encouraged Muslims to engage in jihad against European colonizers.

The rulers of Sriwijaya and the Palembang sultans drew their prestige, wealth, and power from the trade that passed through the Straits of Malacca. Their capital on the Musi River was a cosmopolitan port that welcomed merchants from China, India, and Arabia. Traditionally known as the Land of the Nine Rivers (Batang Hari Sembilan) for the majestic slow-moving rivers—the Musi, Enim, Lematang, Ogan, Komering, Burnei, Batang Hari Leko, Kelingi Rawas Dalam, and Keramasan—that flow from the Barisan Mountains to mangrove forests that line the east coast, the interior of South Sumatra was organized in ethnic groups *(suku)*, which spoke distinctive dialects and were generally named for the river or area where they lived. The *suku* were organized in clans *(marga)*, which formed political alliances that dominated a particular area. This pattern of small ethnolinguistic groupings, which distinguishes South Sumatra from regions where a single large ethnic group, such as the Acehnese, the Batak, and the Minang Kabau, dominate a large area, made it difficult for rulers in Palembang to control the peoples of the highlands and remote lowland forests and compelled them to treat them with respect as "younger brothers." [6]

In the eighteenth and nineteenth centuries a new pattern developed in which European traders and colonial administrators pressured local rulers to extract valuable resources from South Sumatra through forced labor. People in South Sumatra reacted to the imposition of this new power structure. Members of the sultan's family led rebellions against the Dutch in 1848 and 1881. In the twentieth century, as South Sumatra became important to the colonial power as a source of oil, coal, gas, and rubber, people in South Sumatra adopted ideas from Europe to resist the Dutch domination. They formed new Islamic organizations, established commercial associations, and created their own educational system. In the oil fields laborers from Java joined the Indonesian Communist Party (PKI). By 1937, rising nationalism led the Dutch to set up limited forms of local self-government in the lowland districts close to Palembang. [7]

In February 1941, the Japanese took over Indochina as the first step toward securing supplies of oil from the Netherlands East Indies. Japanese forces landed in Palembang on February 16, 1941, only one day after Singapore fell. The unexpectedly quick defeat of Dutch forces by the Japanese fueled dreams of an independent Indonesia. As the end of the war approached, soldiers trained by the Japanese in South Sumatra organized guerilla forces to resist the return of the Dutch.

Just as South Sumatrans are proud of the legacy of Sriwijaya and the role of the Palembang sultanate in spreading the teachings of Islam, so, too, are they proud of the guerilla forces that harassed Dutch troops defending the oil fields during the revolution (1945–1950). [8] A. K. Gani, governor of South Sumatra throughout the revolution, bragged that he was "the biggest smuggler in Southeast Asia" because he arranged for ships to evade the Dutch blockade of Sumatra ports. [9] With the establishment of the Indonesian Republic on August 17, 1945, South Sumatrans hoped that a new era was beginning in which the people and the land would no longer be exploited for the benefit of foreign rulers.

When the central government of the new republic adopted the colonial pattern of expropriating the lion's share of wealth from natural resources in the province, people in South Sumatra felt betrayed. In 1957 Islamic-oriented separatist rebellions led by dissident military officers erupted in West Sumatra and South Sulawesi. The Indonesian military dispatched Colonel Ibnu Sutowo to suppress support for the rebellion in South Sumatra. The commander of the Palembang garrison and his followers fled into the forests of the Barisan Mountains, where they were hunted down.

Ibnu Sutowo, now a general, was sent to South Sumatra again after a coup attempt on September 30, 1965, in which PKI was implicated.[10] His mission was to secure the oil fields where the PKI-affiliated oil workers' union was strong. In the following months state terror was unleashed against members of the PKI and leftist organizations. Children of prominent families in Palembang were among those targeted. The respected historian Djohan Hanafiah, who was the leader of the Indonesian Nationalist Student Movement in South Sumatra at the time, relates that he narrowly escaped arrest. When the PKI was wiped out, the Indonesian military gave its support to the New Order of General Suharto in exchange for sharing in political power and the economic benefits it brought. During the thirty-two years of authoritarian rule that followed, former activists like Djohan Hanafiah took care to distance themselves from any form of political protest as the New Order (1966–1998) extended its power.

South Sumatra in the New Order "Development" State (1966–1998)

The creeping authoritarianism of Suharto's New Order was supported by a formidable array of laws and institutions dating back to Dutch colonialism and the "Guided Democracy" (1959–1965) of Sukarno, Indonesia's first president.[11] The political parties of the Sukarno period were dissolved and reconstituted into two nominal opposition parties: the United Development Party (PPP), a forced marriage of Islamic parties; and the Indonesian Democratic Party (PDI), a coalition of "nationalist" and Christian parties. Suharto's political vehicle was Golkar (from *golongan karya*), an association of "functional groups" said to represent peasants, labor unions, businessmen, intellectuals, civil servants, and so forth. In the 1971 election Golkar and the military ensured the election of General Suharto as president.

Suharto ruled Indonesia through Golkar and a parallel administration based in the territorial command structure of the Indonesian Armed Forces (ABRI). In South Sumatra the governor was either an active or a retired military officer throughout the New Order. The territorial command Sriwijaya Corps was based in Palembang, and military posts were located strategically throughout the province, generally along highways in the lowlands so that troops could move out at a moment's notice. All this was masked by rhetoric promoting a Javanese version of "Asian Values," emphasizing harmony, order, stability, respect for authority, and commitment to family and nation.

The New Order promulgated the concept of the "floating mass" according to which people would vote once every five years but otherwise refrain from political activity. Nominally democratic elections at the national level were officially described as a "festival of democracy," while a tightly controlled administrative structure extended the absolute authority of Suharto down to the most basic local level of government. Every student and government employee was indoctrinated with Pancasila, the state ideology of national unity.[12] Anyone who criticized the government or resisted its authority could be labeled a communist and banned from any role in civic life. Civil rights to freedom of speech and association and the rights of people to their land and its resources enshrined in the 1945 constitution were ignored on the grounds that the New Order would bring economic development and greater prosperity for all.

At the beginning of the New Order the Indonesian economy was in a state of crisis. In 1965, interest payments on foreign debt exceeded the value of Indonesia's exports, and inflation was over 600 percent. Urgently in need of revenue, the government turned to foreign investors and the rich natural resources of the outer islands. A foreign investment law was passed in 1967 giving generous tax and import duty concessions to foreign companies.

In the 1970s oil revenues provided the government with the greatest part of its income. When oil prices rose to their highest point under the OPEC oil embargo in 1974–1975, oil revenues provided more than half the government's income from domestic sources.[13] They also provided the basis for corruption and massive foreign borrowing. During the oil boom, foreign lenders poured money for development into Indonesia.[14] Table 1 shows the increase in foreign debt.

By relying on foreign loans and income from rents on natural resources, the New Order was able to resist establishing a domestic tax base that might have led to demands for greater accountability from tax-paying citizens. Instead, corruption on the part of well-placed officials flourished.

General Ibnu Sutowo was given the position of director-president of the state-owned oil company Pertamina as a reward for suppressing rebellious troops in South Sumatra in 1957 and his actions against the PKI in 1965. As director of Pertamina, he was in a position to borrow unlimited amounts of money from international banks. He borrowed to build a major oil refining and transshipment center on Batam Island, to establish a tanker fleet for transport of oil, to build plants to produce liquefied natural gas, and to construct the Krakatau Steel plant. Without oversight, Ibnu Sutowo also borrowed to build up a personal economic empire of companies that contracted with foreign oil companies for essential services. (To this day the

Sutowo family remains one of the richest families in Indonesia.) In 1975, Pertamina defaulted on a loan of US$40 million.[15] To preserve the country's credit worthiness and maintain the trust of foreign investors, the Indonesian government was forced to assume responsibility, doubling Indonesia's foreign debt in one day.

Despite the corruption and the funneling of oil revenues to the central government, South Sumatra's oil provided the basis for growing prosperity in Palembang, where the headquarters of Pertamina was located. Pertamina and PT Pusri, a state-owned fertilizer company with a factory in Pelaju, downstream from Palembang, employed a sizeable number of white-collar workers. Together with government officials they constituted a new middle class that demanded higher education for their children. In 1960 the government took over Sriwijaya University, which had been founded by private entrepreneurs. Other institutions of higher education established in Palembang included an Institute of Islamic Studies, IAIN Raden Fatah, a Muhammadiyah University, and eight private professional institutes. Farmers in the Pasemah highlands who grew prosperous selling their coffee and

Table 1

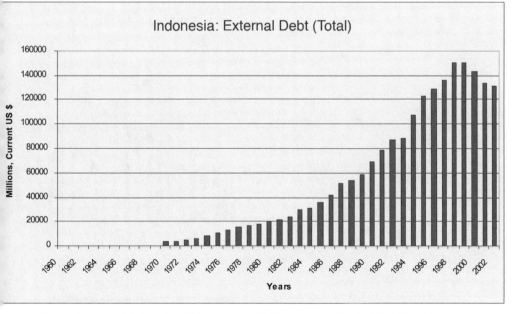

Source: Based on data from World Development Indicators posted by the World Bank Group (2003).

people in lowland villages with rubber holdings began to send their children to university in Palembang. Gradually the middle class expanded into housing developments that ringed the city by 1990.

In 1982 oil prices collapsed, and by 1986 Indonesia's foreign debt began to spiral out of control, as shown in Table 2.

To service its foreign debt, the government of Indonesia, needing a new source of income, turned to the timber resources of the outer islands. State control over forests, established by the Basic Forestry Law of 1967, gave the Forestry Department authority to grant a Right of Forest Exploitation (HPH) to state-owned corporations and private timber companies. These concessions allowed corporations to harvest Indonesia's forests without significant oversight or restraint.[16]

In 1983, the New Order extended its control over forests in South Sumatra by means of an administrative reform that replaced *marga* (a territorial system of administrative units that the Dutch had imposed on the indigenous clan-based system of self-government) with the system of centralized administration used in Java.[17] The *marga* system had preserved much of the

Table 2

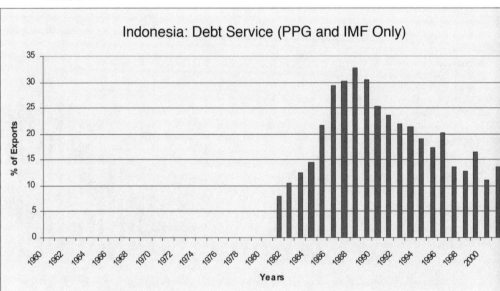

Source: Data from World Development Indicators posted by the World Bank Group (2003).

Note: Data on Indonesia's external debt and debt service is available on the World Bank Group Web page: http://www.worldbank.org/data/

tradition of local rule. The *marga* head *(pasirah)* was generally a traditional clan leader, and at the village and subvillage level, the village head *(kerio)* and kampung leader *(penggawa)* were chosen by popular vote (known as *pancang,* or stake), in which villagers lined up behind a stake representing the candidate they supported. Although hereditary rights influenced the selection of village headman and kampung leader, villagers felt that these local officials were accountable to them.

The administrative reform merged *marga* communities or divided them into different administrative units, thereby undermining traditional patterns of authority and rights to communal forest resources. In the new system the village headman *(kepala desa)* was responsible to the administrative head of the subdistrict *(camat),* who was responsible to the administrative head of the district *(bupati),* who was responsible to the central government. The *camat* and village headman were given authority to recommend concessions of land for industrial forestry and oil palm plantations.

Foreign and Indonesian companies seeking a concession were pressed to form a joint venture with either a member of Suharto's family or a Suharto crony as silent partner. As Vedi Hadiz has observed, "state power gradually evolved into the instrument of a newly ascendant capitalist oligarchy."[18] The Suharto business empire was known as the Cendana Group after the street in Jakarta where the Suharto family lived. Members of the Suharto family and their business associates controlled major monopolies in construction, communication, the automobile industry, and the marketing of lucrative spices, such as cloves. They were also prominent importers, exporters, and distributors of oil and fuel products. In June 1998, the Indonesian Business Data Center estimated the value of Cendana Group holdings to be US$17 billion, including US$3.16 billion equity in joint ventures with foreign partners.[19] According to the Transparency International Global Corruption Report 2004, Suharto bartered his power over Indonesia's natural resources for US$15–35 billion.[20]

Among the most notorious associates of Suharto to benefit from such "development" projects was the Chinese-Indonesian mogul Prayogo Pangestu. In 1989, his company, PT Musi Hutan Persada (MHP), a joint venture with a state-owned enterprise, was granted concessions to almost 300 thousand hectares of forest land in five districts of South Sumatra. The land was to be developed into industrial forests to supply wood for paper and pulp production by another company in Prayogo's corporate empire, the Barito Pacific Group. Suharto's daughter, Siti Hardiyanti Rukmana (known as Tutut), had financial interest in both ventures.

Between 1985 and 1997, the lowland forest of South Sumatra was harvested at an annual rate of 192,834 hectares, a rate exceeded in only East Kalimantan. In just twelve years, 65 percent of South Sumatra's forests were clear-cut under the guise of "development."[21] As Robison and Hadiz (2004) explain: "Special concessionary loans were made available to investors willing to establish forestry plantations, supposedly to create a long-term sustainable supply of logs and ease pressure on the diminishing natural forests. These were seen, however, as opportunities to clear existing native forests without serious intention of replanting, while channeling the subsidized loans into other areas."[22]

The New Order also made land concessions for corporate agriculture. In 1995 Syamsul Nursalim, another notorious Suharto associate, was given a concession of 170,000 hectares of coastal wetlands in South Sumatra to extend the industrial shrimp farms his Gajah Tunggal Group had established in Lampung province to the south. Global demand for palm oil escalated in the 1990s, increasing approximately 7 percent a year between 1992 and 1997, and concessions were given to foreign and Indonesian companies for the development of oil palm plantations. By 2000, the provincial government of South Sumatra recorded ninety-four such concessions.[23]

This corporate development created a facade of prosperity in Palembang. In 1990 the poverty rate in South Sumatra was between 10 and 20 percent, as compared to the neighboring provinces of Lampung and Bengkulu, where the poverty rate was between 20 and 30 percent. The Palembang middle classes and the relatively prosperous smallholders of the Pasemah highlands gave their support to Suharto's party; Golkar increased its share of the vote from 62.6 percent in the 1971 election to 70.2 percent in 1992.[24]

This facade crumbled when the Asian Economic Crisis of 1997 hit Indonesia. The private sector carried US$82 billion in debt.[25] Two of the top three debtors were Prayogo Pangestu and Syamsul Nursalim. In 2000, Economic Minister Kwik Kian Gie described the Barito Group and the Gajah Tunggal Group as "black conglomerates" for their failure to repay debts or cooperate with the government in fulfilling their financial obligations.[26] The debt was passed on to the Indonesian people.

According to 1999 census data, people in South Sumatra, one of the richest provinces in Indonesia with oil fields, coal mines, natural gas, and "development projects" in industrial forestry, palm oil production, and industrial shrimp farming, had the lowest per capita income of any province in Sumatra, as can be seen in Table 3.

These negative effects of "development" were masked by the gloss of official life in Palembang, which fed on corruption and relied on government control over the press and other media and the suppression of protests.

Table 3

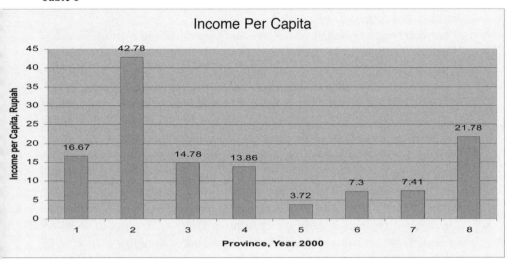

Key: 1. North Sumatra, 2. West Sumatra, 3. Riau, 4. Jambi, 5. South Sumatra, 6. Bengkulu, 7. Lampung, 8. Bangka and Belitung

Corporate Development versus Small Holder Capitalism

Military force and intimidation were used to suppress protests at the expropriation of forest resources. In South Sumatra increasing poverty in rural areas led to urban migration that fueled a population explosion in Palembang, which swelled from half a million in 1961 to three-quarters of a million in 1981, and to over a million in 1990. The gap between the rich and the poor grew as profits went to corporations, government officials, and well-connected associates of Suharto; peoples in the lowland forests were impoverished, and urban migrants struggled to survive in shantytowns at the edge of Palembang and other market towns.

In contrast, access to world markets brought relative prosperity to smallhold farmers in the Pasemah highlands. In 1971, when I first went to Pasemah, we paid our rent in rice because people did not trust paper money. They remembered that when the Japanese came, Dutch money suddenly was worthless; and when the Japanese left, Japanese money became worthless. The Pasemah preferred to store their wealth in the form of gold jewelry and sacks of rice. During the two years I lived in Pasemah with my husband and our young son, the army resurfaced the road linking Pagaralam to Palembang, and our Pasemah neighbors began to grow market crops, such as cabbage, to sell in Palembang. They bought vehicles that could be used for transport of coffee, rice, or other crops, or alternately rented out for transport of people. The signs of growing prosperity were clear.

I returned to Pasemah in 1994 to find electricity and banks with ATM machines. People no longer sat on mats on the floor in the traditional way; they owned chairs, sofas, and refrigerators. Their coffee gardens and fish-ponds were now tended by Javanese employees. Although the price of coffee rose and fell on the world market, the Pasemah had learned how to ride the market, holding their coffee until the price was high if they could and investing profits from good years in new endeavors. They watched the evening news on television, kept track of interest rates, and checked the exchange rate.

The Pasemah used their wealth for their children's education. Our friends of the 1970s who had grown up during the years of guerilla warfare against the Dutch had received only a junior high school education at best. Now the walls of their homes bore photos proudly commemorating the graduations of sons and daughters from the university. Our former neighbor's son was the manager of an oil palm plantation in Java; another son had emigrated (illegally) to New Zealand, where he worked in a factory and sent home glamorous photos of ski outings; their daughter worked in a bank in Pagaralam. Another friend had gone to Japan (illegally) where he worked for three years before returning to Pagaralam to build a house for his family. When I visited again in 1999, before Indonesia's first free election in fifty years, my friends told me, "We Pasemah are not interested in politics, only in earning money."

The Pasemah did not see all the changes in their way of life as being for the best. In the 1970s, people ploughed and harvested their own rice fields and harvested their own coffee, but the seasons gave work a rhythm; no one worked all the time. At the end of the day a man would sit by the side of the road talking with friends or take a walk with his youngest child slung in a sarong on his back while his wife prepared dinner. After dinner no one worked because there was only the light of kerosene lanterns. Now, my friends complained, they worked all the time. Yet, despite the increased pace of life, it seemed to me that the Pasemah had maintained their sense of community and identity. Important events, like a marriage, a baby's first haircut, circumcision, and the harvest, are still celebrated by a ceremonial meal of thanksgiving *(sedekah)* to which neighbors and kin are invited. Everyone brings a contribution; a kilo of rice, a chicken, vegetables or fruit, or money. As in the past, the Pasemah keep a mental accounting of gifts exchanged. Although they joke about how expensive it is to manage such traditional obligations, they seem to understand the importance of maintaining the bonds that make a community strong.

The Pasemah generally do not hold formal title to their land, but individual rights to terraced "wet rice" fields and coffee gardens are recognized because evidence of cultivation is clear. In contrast, villagers in the lowland forests plant rubber and fruit trees in or adjacent to natural forests. To the untrained eye, the rubber gardens blend into forest that is regarded as state land. Communal rights to forest products that are cultivated in situ—such as bamboo, rattan, fruit, honey, and wood (for fuel and construction)—are not recognized.

The relative prosperity of the Pasemah illustrates the difference between development that benefits smallholders and the kind of corporate development sponsored by the government. The prosperity of Pasemah has attracted traders from Lintang and Padang to the north, Chinese-Indonesian merchant families, and Javanese transmigrants from Lampung looking for work. During the New Order, Pagaralam more than quadrupled in size. In 2000 it was officially made an administrative center *(kota madya).* Yet the government did little to facilitate development in Pasemah aside from maintaining the main roads and bringing in electricity. In 2004 there was still no water or garbage systems to meet the needs of this growing market town.

Globalization, Economic Development, and the Struggle for Justice

South Sumatra has a long history of participation in global networks of exchange that brought traders from India, China, Arabia and Europe along with the religious traditions of Buddhism and Islam. In the eighteenth and nineteenth centuries Dutch traders and colonial administrators, and later the Japanese military, used force to expropriate the labor of local peoples and the resources of South Sumatra for their own use. The new Indonesian republic founded after the Second World War adopted a centralized model of government and in a similar way expropriated local resources. The New Order of Suharto that came to power in 1966 claimed legitimacy on the basis of promoting economic development. However, corporate development projects sponsored by the state and international development institutions aimed at increasing the export of cash crops to world markets impoverished the peoples of the lowland forests of South Sumatra, damaged the environment, fostered corruption, and increased the gap between the rich and the poor.

Chapter 2, *"Reformasi* in South Sumatra," tells the stories of student activists in South Sumatra who joined with farmers and workers in their struggle against the injustice of New Order "development." The student-led pro-democracy movement known as *reformasi* raised hopes that democratic reforms would lead to a more just economic system. Four student-leaders of the *reformasi* movement, whom I came to know well, are the focus of this chapter.

Chapter 3, "Who Owns the Land?" addresses the issue of land rights. Following a legal principle formulated by the colonial regime of the Netherlands, all the forest lands of Indonesia (74 percent of its area) are the property of the state. The principle that indigenous people have no property rights to the lands they inhabit and cultivate was widely adopted by colonizing powers. In *King Leopold's Ghost: A Story of Greed, Terror, and Heroism in Colonial Africa,* Adam Hochchild shows how this principle was viciously applied to the peoples of the Congo under the "rubber tyranny." I describe how the New Order applied this principle to the lowland forests of South Sumatra and destroyed the sustainable livelihood of the peoples who lived there. I go on to chronicle how, despite intimidation by private security forces and the Indonesian military, pro-democracy students worked with farmers resisting the loss of their land.

Chapter 4, "No Forests, No Future," follows three campaigns in which activists in the South Sumatra branch of the Indonesian Environmental Forum (WALHI) worked with villagers fighting against companies responsible for damage to the environment. In these campaigns, protests against environmental pollution combined with other grievances, such as conflict over land and the company's failure to hire local people. In cases where companies were financed by international development loans, these projects meant cheaper products for people in the West and an enormous profit for foreign investors and Indonesian corporate moguls at the cost of a sustainable livelihood for villagers in South Sumatra.

Chapter 5, "Struggling for Workers' Rights," tells the story of contract shrimp farmers protesting against exploitation by PT Wachyuni Mandira, a subsidiary of the conglomerate of Suharto crony Syamsul Nursalim. The chapter includes the story of workers protesting against Indonesian subcontractors of the state-owned coal-mining company PT Bukit Asam. These cases show how workers were criminalized for protesting against exploitation and violation of their rights, while *reformasi* activists were accused of promoting violence and disorder and labeled "dangerous anarchists." Through the criminalization of protests, governments and companies were able to avoid dealing with the issues causing the conflicts. The chapter ends with a study of the ways in which people in the burgeoning informal sector of the economy were also criminalized. The most marginal people—street vendors and cycle rickshaw *(becak)* drivers—became victims of local government "law and order" policies that made it difficult for them to provide even the most minimal living for their families.

Chapter 6, "'Where's My Cut?' The State and Corruption," shows how the systemic corruption that developed under the New Order spread to the lowest levels of government and to civil society organizations. Ties between political elites and criminal gangs known as "backing" *(beking)* protect criminal activity and provide "muscle" that political figures and corporations can use against protests. The corrupt are also protected by a corrupt court system. Despite democratic reforms, new networks linking local entrepreneurs and political figures to elites in Jakarta have been established in the post-Suharto era.

In Chapter 7, "Local Autonomy," I explore the way in which "local autonomy" legislation passed in 1999 was implemented in two districts. Decentralization was supposed to make government more democratic and accountable. With no effective reform of a corrupt judicial system, "local autonomy" often simply decentralized the corruption that was endemic in the New Order. Yet, two ambitious and successful district heads *(bupati)* in South Sumatra launched populist programs with an eye to direct election in the next election cycle. While these politicians have continued New Order policies of corporate development, a free press has forced them to be more aware of the effects of their policies on the poor.

Chapter 8, "Islam and the Quest for Justice," describes how Islamic organizations in South Sumatra have responded to new opportunities for political engagement in the post-Suharto era. As the largest predominantly Muslim country in the world today, Indonesia has been regarded as a test case for the compatibility of Islam and democracy. This study suggests that there is no inherent contradiction between Islam and democratic politics. My observation of the grassroots politics of Islamic organizations in South Sumatra suggests that these organizations are providing important lessons in what Alexis de Tocqueville described as the "habits of democracy."

In the concluding chapter, "Indonesia in Global Context: Development, Free Market Capitalism, and Democracy," I argue that for real change to occur, neoliberal capitalism, or "Free Market" economics, must be recognized as a utopian ideology, and that democracy, imperfect as it is, offers the best hope for development that is sustainable and narrows the gap between the rich and the poor. More accountable government is necessary at all levels: international, national, and local. The struggle for justice requires reform in the governance of the international financial institutions that constitute an emergent global government. International financial markets must be regulated and the environment protected for the common good.

Poor countries must be relieved of debt so that national governments can be accountable to their citizens. Farmers and workers must mobilize to pressure their governments to promote more equitable and sustainable forms of development.

Methodology

I first learned about the conflicts and issues I describe in this book at the office of LBH in Palembang. I then visited the site of the conflict with an LBH or WALHI staff member to talk with villagers firsthand about what had happened and their understanding of the actions of the company and government officials involved. After reading through LBH reports and press releases on the conflict and the volume of newspaper clippings on the issue collected by LBH and WALHI volunteers, I constructed a narrative chronology of the conflict.[27] My reading of the newspaper reports always led to further questions, which took me back to LBH and WALHI staff who had worked with villagers. I followed many of these disputes over several years, returning to South Sumatra every year from 1994 through 2005. I spent most of my sabbatical year (1998–1999) in South Sumatra, and in 2002–2003 a Fulbright award allowed me to divide my time between Jakarta and South Sumatra.

When I was not in Indonesia, I followed issues in South Sumatra through newspaper sources and e-mail postings by organizations of farmers or workers that LBH and WALHI helped to set up. A special word needs to be said about reports made by Taufiq Wijaya, which were distributed by e-mail or published in local newspapers. Many were also posted on the Web by the Institute for the Free Flow of Information (ISAI) and picked up by international NGOs and reposted on their web sites. Taufiq Wijaya's reporting played a crucial role in getting information out about many of the conflicts I describe. I generally received his reports in e-mail from LBH and WALHI staff. These are listed under his name in the bibliography of news sources at the end of the book.

Whenever possible I returned to villages for follow-up interviews or spoke with representatives of a village at the LBH office. When I was not able to follow an issue personally I employed LBH and WALHI staff and volunteers and activists from other NGOs as research assistants. I tried to interview company officials for their view of a conflict, and in the account I have given, I explain when I was denied an interview. I also interviewed government officials whenever possible, including Syahrial Oesman, *bupati* of Ogan Komering Ulu, Alex Noerdin, *bupati* of Musi Banyu Asin, and Rosihan Arsyad, governor of South Sumatra (1999–2004).

I selected case studies for this book on the grounds that they (1) illustrated factors that made a protest fail or succeed; (2) shaped the attitudes of people involved, for example, about the possibility of change or the effectiveness of different strategies such as taking company property hostage to force a company to negotiate; and (3) because I had collected relatively complete data and was satisfied I could provide an account that reflected the different perspectives of villagers, company representatives, and government officials. Jamila Nuh (director of WALHI, 1996–1997), Nur Kholis (director of WALHI Sumsel, 1998–2001; director of LBH-Palembang, 2001–2005), Abdul Situmorang (director of WALHI Sumsel, 1999–2001), Yeni Rosliani (director of the Women's Crisis Center, 1998–2005), and other LBH and WALHI staff who could read English or were trying to improve their English skills read and discussed a draft of each of the case studies I present, providing me with further insights. In addition, two faculty members at Sriwijaya University, Amzulian Rifai and Zainab Bakir, and one faculty member from the State Islamic University Raden Fateh in Palembang, Muhammad Sirozi—all of whom had studied in either the United States or Australia—read and commented on an early draft of this book. While I benefited enormously from the comments of these readers, I take full responsibility for the account of the cases I present in this book.

Chapter 2

Reformasi in South Sumatra

Oppression and abuses of power
Are too numerous to mention. . . .
Stop, stop, don't go on.
We're fed up with greed and uncertainty.
　　—Iwan Fals, "Demolish," a hit song of 1990

THE FIRST STUDENT-LED PROTESTS against New Order development policies took place on January 16, 1974, when Prime Minister Kakuei
Tanaka of Japan visited Indonesia. A crowd estimated variously at twenty
to a hundred thousand joined students protesting that "development" primarily benefited foreign investors, political elites, and Chinese-Indonesian
businessmen. This demonstration turned into a riot, and a mob began looting the commercial center of Jakarta. This riot, which came to be known
as the Malari Affair, an acronym for "the January 16th disaster," may have
been instigated by thugs hired by Ali Murtopo, head of Special Operations
for Intelligence and Subversion. It is said that he wanted to discredit the
student protest movement and bring down his rival, General Sumitro, head
of the Operational Command for the Restoration of Order and Security.
Officially, Malari was treated as a plot by radical socialist activists to over-
throw the government. Student leaders were imprisoned and the government clamped down on the press.[1]

Before the election of 1978, students in Jakarta, Bandung, Yogyakarta,
and Surabaya again organized antigovernment protests, this time targeting
vote rigging, coercion of voters, and the reelection of President Suharto to
a third term.[2] Leaders of the protests were arrested and put on trial, and
the government passed the "Campus Normalization Act," which abolished
student councils and placed student activities under strict control by university rectors. With the suppression of political activity on university campuses, student activism split into two streams. Some students began to estab-

lish nongovernmental organizations (NGOs); others moved into campus mosques and joined a *dakwah* movement of Islamic proselytizing with the slogan "Islam Is the Solution." This movement is described in Chapter 8.

The NGO Movement

The NGO movement started in 1971 with the establishment of the Legal Aid Institute (Lembaga Bantuan Hukum, or LBH) as a legal service for the poor. In the early seventies LBH took cases such as the Simprug Case, in which slum dwellers were evicted from an area to be developed with luxury housing in South Jakarta, and the Lubang Buaya Case, in which poor people were evicted to build Taman Mini, a government-sponsored national culture park. After the 1978 election, LBH activists became increasingly critical of government policy. Working with students, they took the lead in organizing a campaign for the "rule of law" *(negara hukum)*. In 1980 LBH established the Legal Aid Foundation of Indonesia (YLBHI) to develop a critique of the social and political structures that gave rise to injustice. Four focus areas were identified: civil and political rights, land and environmental rights, workers' rights, and women's rights. Over the next decade, activist lawyers such as Todung Mulya Lubis, Abdul Hakim G. Nusantara, Fauzi Abdullah, and Mulyana W. Kusumah transformed LBH from a professional charity for individual cases into a political force for democratic change.

LBH lawyers worked with NGOs, known in Indonesian as *lembaga swadaya masyarakat* (LSM), established by student activists. In *Non-Government Organizations and Democratic Participation in Indonesia* (1995), Philip Eldridge has described the extraordinary number of NGOs that were created in the 1970s and 1980s. Eldridge distinguishes two kinds of NGOs: those that worked to empower the poor economically but avoided confrontation with the government, and advocacy NGOs that took a critical stance toward the government. The New Order accused advocacy NGOs of being antigovernment and sowing conflict in society. The New Order also attempted to restrict NGO funding from external sources.

In the 1980s, advocacy NGOs began to organize peaceful mass protest actions against development projects that marginalized and impoverished farmers. The most famous protest was against the Kedung Ombo dam, a World Bank project that displaced farmers in Central Java, who were given little or no compensation for the loss of their livelihood.[3] In 1994 the Indonesian Supreme Court awarded compensation to the people of Kedung Ombo. Although the government quickly appointed a new judge who annulled this decision, the legal victory suggested that some government functionaries recognized the injustice of New Order policies. The reversal of the Supreme Court ruling also showed that the battle for democratic reforms and civil rights could not be won in courts controlled by the government. A campaign for "rule of law" would not be enough to reform New Order authoritarianism.

The NGO movement came to South Sumatra in the 1980s. The Bureau to Serve Society, an NGO founded by young lawyers to provide legal counsel to the poor, became LBH-Palembang in 1982. The first development-oriented NGO, the Foundation for Village Social Welfare (KEMASDA), was founded in 1984 by eight activists in Ogan Komering Ilir. In an area where there is widespread poverty because the population is only seasonally employed by a state-owned sugar plantation and factory, KEMASDA administers aid programs sponsored by national and international NGOs. Since the Asian Economic Crisis of 1997, the Indonesian government has also provided funds to KEMASDA, which oversees a microcredit program that operates in fifteen villages and provides scholarships that pay school fees for poor children.[4]

LBH staff and student activists, including Jamila, joined with development-oriented workers in 1986 to found Kuala Merdeka, the first NGO to work with street children in Palembang. In 1987, LBH-Palembang established WALHI-Sumsel as a local branch of the Indonesian Environmental Forum (Wahana Lingkungan Hidup Indonesia).

In Palembang LBH, WALHI and other NGO activists worked closely with young reporters at the *Sriwijaya Post*, South Sumatra's first daily newspaper, which began publishing in 1987. The paper was owned by a group of local businessmen in partnership with Gramedia, publisher of the highly respected national newspaper *Kompas*. When the *Sriwijaya Post* began to publish news about farmers protesting the loss of their land and intimidation of protestors by the regional military command, Soleh Thamrin, the editor and one of the paper's owners, was accused of libeling the governor, Ramli Hasan Basri. Ramli, who was frequently described as a "little Suharto," was known to have become wealthy in the course of approving land concessions. Threatened with arrest and jail, Soleh Thamrin decided he must sell his interest in the paper. Aman Ramli, son of the governor, tried to buy a controlling interest in the paper, which led to a struggle for control that lasted from 1993 until January 1996, when the office of the paper was sacked by hired gangsters who destroyed computers and other equipment. On February 2, 1996, Gramedia stopped publishing the *Sriwijaya Post* and did not resume publication until June 9, 1997.[5]

The *Reformasi* Movement in South Sumatra

In 1990 President Suharto appeared to recognize the contributions of devel-opment- oriented NGOs. In his Independence Day address to the nation he announced a new policy of "openness": "Democracy indeed requires a lot of consultation, discussion, exchanges of view and dialogue. . . . We must view differences of opinion as dynamic. . . . Our common task in the years to come is . . . to develop further the people's iniative, creativity and partici-pation in development."[6] Some restrictions on the press were lifted and the "Campus Life Normalization" regulations, which had criminalized student activism, were revoked.

A small group of young artists, poets, and intellectuals in Palembang began to act as gadflies to provincial officials. Under the leadership of Tarech Rasyid, they founded the Musi Cultural Study Group and started a journal of arts and culture called *Dinamika*. They had read Paulo Friere and Pablo Neruda and dreamed of starting a cultural movement for democ-racy. Anwar Putra Bayu, a young poet and playwright, established Teater Potlot, which produced two of his plays, *Kursi* (Chair) and *Patung* (Statue), both veiled criticisms of the New Order. These young critics provided a venue for others to protest as well. Dr. Hajji Gadjahnata, who preached in the Al Gazahli mosque on the campus of Sriwijaya University, contributed an essay to *Dinamika* in which he described his vision of a civilized and cultured society rooted in Islam. The Musi Cultural Study Group did not succeed in sparking a political awakening through literature and art, but in 1994 the cultural critics joined student demonstrators at Sriwijaya Univer-sity protesting an increase in tuition in what would become the pro-democ-racy *reformasi* movement.

A new campus of the university had been built in Indralaya, about thirty kilometers from Palembang. The project was funded by the Asian Devel-opment Bank, but an increase in tuition was required to pay for comple-tion of the new campus because there had been cost overruns and corrup-tion in the tenders. Only two to three hundred students out of a student body of two thousand were brave enough to join the protest, but even this was astonishing. Furthermore, members of the faculty quietly supported the demonstrating students, as they too were disturbed by the increasingly obvious corruption in government as well as in the construction of the new campus.

Military units from Sriwijaya Corps, the territorial command stationed in Palembang, were summoned to the campus. When the soldiers appeared, the students appealed to them for support, chanting, "ABRI [the Indonesian military] is our friend." Two years later, the army would be viewed as the enemy of the students. On that day, the commander warned the rector that the students might try to burn down his house, and he recommended using high-pressure fire hoses to disperse them. The rector objected, predicting (correctly) that the students would leave of their own accord when the time for evening prayers approached.

Jamila emerged as one of the leaders of the protesting students. When I interviewed her, she invited me to go with her to LBH-Palembang where the students had sought advice about their right to demonstrate. The three small rooms that LBH used for an office were smoke-filled and full of animated discussion. Chairil Syah, the director of LBH-Palembang, was a charismatic figure who had attracted idealistic students looking for intellectual tools to confront New Order authoritarianism. Inspired by the success of student-led protests against the Kedung Ombo Dam, he was recruiting law students from Sriwijaya University to document the protests of villagers in South Sumatra whose land was being taken over by corporations owned by cronies of Suharto. The LBH office had become a place where students, reporters, farmers, and NGO activists met and engaged in discussions that pushed the limits allowed by the New Order. Looking back, Jamila recalled that at first students from Sriwijaya University did not connect their protests over the increase in tuition to abuses of power and corruption in the New Order. It was only gradually, in discussions at LBH, that they began to see themselves as part of a larger protest movement. At LBH they learned to use the language of human rights to frame their emerging struggle for democratic reforms.

Sriwijaya University authorities did not revoke the increase in tuition, but they did respond to the protests by arranging bus service to the new campus, as housing for students had not yet been built. The road to Indralaya was narrow and there was a great deal of traffic, so the bus journey was dangerous. Bus drivers tried to complete the trip as quickly as possible because they could make more money on shorter routes in Palembang. The result was bus accidents, which galvanized a small group of student activists to organize further protests. Jamila recounted:

> When the first accident happened, there were no serious injuries. A few of us organized a boycott of the buses. We stopped attending school for a week, distributed fliers and blockaded the road where the buses picked up students. But campus security guards chased us away. Then a bus went into a ravine, and students were injured. Our protest started to receive support. We tried to meet with the governor, because in those days the governor made all decisions. We were told that we would have to write a letter explaining why we wanted to see the

governor and request an appointment. We finally got a meeting, but nothing changed. Then in December 1994, a bus went off the road causing the death of seven students and the bus conductor. Hundreds of students joined our protests. We marched from the old campus to the governor's office. The police were suddenly friendly. They stopped traffic so we could pass. The entire yard in front of the governor's office was full of people; there were maybe a thousand students and hundreds of soldiers and police. The governor, Ramli Hasan Basri, was angry. The president of the Student Senate told me that he said, "You can just come and talk. It's not necessary to bring thousands of students to yell in front of my office." Ian Iskandar jumped to the podium to announce that the governor agreed to meet with five students in his office. Then the demonstrators started chanting, "Come down; come down!" I saw that students were no longer afraid to protest. The governor agreed to speak. The security guards cleared a space where he could stand. We were very surprised, and everybody started clapping. This was probably the first time that the governor had come out to speak to protesters. He promised in front of national journalists that a rail connection would be built between Palembang and Indralaya so the students could travel safely to the new campus. He said that in the meantime more buses would be put on the route and they would travel in a convoy for safety. Those promises were never kept.

Jamila also described how the government used what was called "the family approach" to deal with protesting students. If a student was identified as organizing a protest, his father would be visited by security forces who warned him to control his offspring. If the father worked for the government, his job was on the line. Jamila's father had died when she was only eight years old, so she was not worried. But when she returned home to the island of Bangka for the school holiday, she learned that police officers had contacted the husband of a cousin, who worked for the government. The police had been surprised to learn that she was the niece of a former military officer and mayor, and they directed her cousin to tell her to be more "careful." When this warning was not sufficient, her cousin was summoned by the *bupati* of Bangka, who said that Jamila must be made to stop organizing further protests. This order made Jamila very uncomfortable: "It was quite embarrassing for my relatives. They said that I was being selfish, only thinking about myself and not considering others, especially my sisters and brother. There was no one with whom I could talk about what was the right thing to do. Friends in Bangka told me I would go to jail. But, in the end I decided I should do what I thought was right. Well, the more people who oppose what I do, somehow, the more determined I am to do it."

From the beginning of 1995 through July 1996 a small group of activist students and cultural critics joined forces to challenge the ideological facade of the New Order. Yeni Roslaini, another organizer of protests after the bus accident in December 1994, was one of the founders of the Forum for Discussion of Freedom of the Press and Activist Education, formed after the New Order banned *Tempo* and two other news magazines in July 1994. The forum organized a small demonstration when the attorney general upheld the ban on *Tempo*. They demanded that Tommy Suharto, the youngest son of the president, be prosecuted when national papers reported that he had received much of the money embezzled by Eddy Tansil from the Indonesian Development Bank. They protested again in 1996 when Eddy Tansil escaped from jail after his conviction.

In 1995, when twenty-one students were arrested for protesting at the National Legislature in Jakarta, Jamila, Yeni, and other activist students organized a demonstration to support them. Jamila recalled: "The crowd looked big, but really there were less than twenty protestors. All the other people were undercover police, who took photographs of the demonstrators." Yeni and student activists at Sriwijaya University began to network with student activists at other universities in Palembang, establishing the Student Forum to Awaken Society. That year both Yeni and Jamila were recruited by Yayasan Bina Desa, a Jakarta NGO for village development, to attend a leadership training workshop for student activists.

Chairil Syah, Tarech Rasyid, and investigative reporters JJ Polong and Taufiq Widjaya, along with Jamila and other activist students, started a new LBH/WALHI newsletter, *Lembing KAYU*.[7] Articles by JJ Polong and Taufiq Widjaya described how farmers protesting the loss of their land faced intimidation by military units. They reported that PT Tanjung Enim Lestari Pulp & Paper was building one of the largest paper and pulp factories in Southeast Asia in Muara Enim, which would pollute the rivers and air.

The South Sumatra government responded to the protests and demonstrations with intimidation. When Tarech Rasyid and his circle of cultural critics tried to revive their journal in 1995, the government banned it after two issues on the grounds that it contradicted the national ideology of Pancasila. Tarech narrowly escaped arrest only because the officer sent to carry out the order had known his father, a military officer who had fought in the revolution; the officer gave Tarech a warning and told him to disappear. Tarech decided to "hide" in plain sight with reporters from national news media so that if he were arrested, it would be reported.

On July 27, 1996, the New Order cracked down on its critics in Jakarta. Paramilitary thugs backed by soldiers moved against students who had occupied the headquarters of the opposition party, the Indonesian Democracy Party (PDI) to protest the ouster of Megawati Sukarnoputri as party leader. The attack on the students was brutal and bloody. It lasted only a few hours, but it launched the largest and most violent antigovernment riots of the New Order. Poor people in Jakarta took to the streets shouting for democracy. They burned buses and cars, set banks and government buildings on fire, and barricaded the streets.

This riot marked a turning point in the emerging *reformasi* movement because it demonstrated that underneath the surface of apparent prosperity there was widespread disaffection with the New Order. Political scientist Arbi Sanit observed, "What this has demonstrated is the very real potential for a people's power movement in Indonesia." Adi Sasono, a critic of the New Order from an Islamic perspective, was more blunt: "The choice now is between a greater say for people in politics or revolution on the streets."[8]

Authorities in South Sumatra cracked down on protest. Yeni reports that the police went to her home and frightened her mother. Her father was no longer living, so the government put pressure on her brother, a civil servant, who tried to convince her to stop participating in the demonstrations. Local reporters were summoned by the commander of Sriwijaya Corps, Susilo Bambang Yudhoyono (who became president of Indonesia in October 2004) and directed to submit all articles for approval before publication.

After the crackdown in July 1996, the small group of activists in Palembang turned away from political protests to focus on social programs. Yeni, JJ Polong, and others established an NGO to work on women's issues. Tarech Rasyid, Jamila, and Yamin started the first program for street children in Palembang. Tarech published a pamphlet entitled "I Accuse the Intellectuals," exhorting academics and government officials to take responsibility for what was happening in society, as well as a collection of essays entitled "Illuminating a People's Economy," which called for economic democracy and social justice. He also became chairman of the Center for Development of Business and Management at a private university in Palembang.

In 1997 Indonesia was seared by the El Niño drought. In South Sumatra the vast acacia tree plantations of Musi Hutan Persada Ltd (MHP) were five to six years old. The plantations provided excellent fuel, as they were littered with dry leaves and dead branches. When fires set to clear land for new oil palm plantations jumped to the acacia, they burned fiercely and spread rapidly, devouring stands of rubber trees owned by local farmers. The result was an environmental and economic disaster. Fires in undisturbed forests are generally ground fires that destroy undergrowth, which recovers relatively quickly, but fires in acacia plantations or logged-over areas are canopy fires, which burn with great intensity and destroy everything.[9]

Environmental concerns drew many students into the *reformasi* movement. From Wigwam, a club at Sriwijaya University that organized hiking and rock climbing for nature lovers, they moved on to WALHI, where they became involved in documenting environmental problems and land conflicts. Nur Kholis (director of WALHI, 1998–1999; director of LBH, 2001–2005) remembers that when he visited farmers in their villages he became aware that there was an enormous gap between what he had learned in his law classes and the world outside. Another volunteer, Syamsul Asinar, explained, "The people living around the big operations like MHP and PT Exspan [an oil company] and the palm oil factories, they were the poorest with the lowest standard of living, and I saw there was no trickle-down effect." At LBH/WALHI the activists learned about human rights and the idea of "empowering people."

Satellite images showed that most of the hot spots in the fires of 1997 in South Sumatra were located in concessions given to eleven corporations for the development of forestry and oil palm plantations. Jamila was director of WALHI in 1997. She recounted, "When the big forest fires happened, the government did not do anything to try to stop them. They just blamed farmers." Abdul Wahib Situmorang (director of WALHI, 1999–2001) recalled, "Officials at the Department of Forestry in Palembang and the Center for Environmental Research at Sriwijaya University said that local people started fires to clear land. But at WALHI we saw that corporations with concessions were responsible." WALHI/LBH filed suit in the Palembang District Court asking for Rp 2 billion (approximately US$200,000) in compensation for farmers and for restoration of the forest. On Earth Day they organized a demonstration calling on the Provincial Legislature to support local farmers who had lost everything. Military and government officials and the rector of Sriwijaya University warned Jamila to stop the protests, and the secretary of the South Sumatra legislature accused her of being a communist. The national leadership of WALHI and LBH protested the assumption that any critic of the government must be a communist and succeeded in obtaining a letter of apology from the chairman of the Provincial Legislature.

Nur Kholis was elected director of WALHI when Jamila left to study in the United States at the end of 1997. He presented the case against MHP in court. The judge ruled that satellite photos were not acceptable as evidence; LBH would have to produce witnesses to the setting of the fires. The court's verdict, rendered in October 1998, was that only two of eleven companies charged were guilty. MHP and one other company were ordered to establish a fire-prevention policy and pay court costs. No fine was levied and no compensation paid to farmers who had lost their livelihood. During the court case Nur Kholis was forced to move three times because of repeated "visits" from intelligence agents, soldiers, and police. He carried three identity cards with different addresses in an effort to keep the police from knowing where he could be found.

MHP appealed the judge's decision, and in November 1999 the conviction was reversed. Nevertheless, activists at LBH and WALHI considered the case a breakthrough because it was the first time that environmental laws had been applied to corporations operating in South Sumatra.

The Asian Economic Crisis

The pro-democracy *reformasi* movement began to win support from the middle class after the Asian Economic Crisis (known as *krismon,* short for *krisis moneter* or financial crisis) hit Indonesia in the summer of 1997. After a precipitous drop in the value of the rupiah in January 1998, prices for basic commodities skyrocketed. Activists in Java organized demonstrations against the increase in prices for basic foods. In Palembang university students were quick to follow their example. The protestors demanded an end to corruption, cronyism, and nepotism (*korupsi, kolusi, nepotism,* popularly referred to as KKN). At Sriwijaya University professors allowed students to miss class in order to protest.

By February 1998, the protests had spread to market towns in South Sumatra, where they turned violent and took on an anti-Chinese cast. When I read in the international press reports of a riot in Pagaralam, where I had lived for two years in the 1970s, I was stunned. The Pasemah who grew coffee high in the mountains were relatively prosperous and seemed unlikely to riot. The reporter for the *Sriwijaya Post* who got news of the Pagaralam riot out to the world was Emil Makmud. He was stationed in Lahat, which is located halfway between Palembang and Pagaralam. Late in 1998, I went looking for Emil to learn what I could about how the riot had started. The owner of the hotel where Emil rented a room sent someone to find him and then hovered anxiously as we talked. I learned later that he was upset because Emil gave me photos taken on the day of the riot. Everyone had learned to be cautious under the New Order, and not much had changed in the five months since Suharto's resignation.

Emil said that he just happened to be in Pagaralam on the morning of February 16, 1998. He heard that high school students had requested permission to mount a demonstration so he stayed around to see what would happen. The idea to organize a protest had come from university students who had returned home in January to celebrate the end of the Islamic fasting month. On the Sunday evening before the demonstration planned for Monday, the students learned that the mayor had denied permission for a protest rally. The next morning they met in the central market where they had planned to conduct their protest to decide what to do. Migrants who had come to the rich coffee-growing area in search of work were also gathered in the market. A crowd formed. Someone called out, demanding that people take action against "Chinese merchants who profit from the high price of basic foods." Someone else went into a shop and began dumping flour and sugar on the ground. A frenzy of looting and destruction followed. Pasemah living near the market told me that looters carted off TVs and air conditioners while the police stood by. One witness claimed that even government employees had been seen carting off stolen goods. The small military unit stationed in Pagaralam withdrew until reinforcements from the army post near Muara Enim arrived three hours later. Emil's photos show shops that had been broken into with the shelves empty and floors littered with goods; streets strewn with debris from the looting; soldiers attacking people with clubs and karate kicks, and young men running away from the soldiers. It appears that the rioters were mostly men looking for work. Unemployment had rapidly increased after the Asian Economic Crisis hit Indonesia. When the police began arresting looters several days after the riot, only one student was arrested, and he was charged with throwing stones.

In the Pagaralam riot it was primarily shops owned by Chinese-Indonesians that were attacked. The targeting of Chinese-Indonesians was apparently provoked by television and newspaper reports of a rally on February 8, 1998, at the Al Azhar Mosque in Jakarta where speakers claimed that Chinese-Indonesians were responsible for the economic crisis. The rally was organized by the Indonesian Committee for World Muslim Solidarity (KISDI). Ahmad Sumargono, chairman of KISDI, charged the Center for Strategic and International Studies, a New Order–era think tank directed by Jusuf Wanandi, brother of a prominent Chinese-Indonesian businessman, with political engineering that harmed Muslims. KH Abdul Qadir Djaelani called upon the government to confiscate the wealth that non-*pribumi* (i.e., nonindigenous) conglomerates had transferred abroad. The chairman of the KISDI youth group called for the formation of a "command post" that would "face traitors of the nation like Sofjan Wanandi [brother of Jusuf Wanandi] or whoever stands behind them." He concluded his speech with the appeal, "Live honorably or die a martyr's death! God is Great!"[10]

KISDI had been founded in 1987 to support Palestinian Muslims during the first Intifada. During the Bosnia war (1992–1995), KISDI called for volunteers to fight against (Christian) Serb aggression. In 1998, Suharto turned to KISDI and other Islamic organizations to mobilize opposition to the *refor-*

masi movement, which was said to represent the forces of "communism" and "secularism." Courted by Suharto's son-in-law, Lieutenant General Prabowo Subianto, KISDI's leaders, who were closely associated with the leaders of the Indonesian Council for Dakweh (Dewan Dakwah Islam Indonesia or DDII), saw a possibility for Islamizing Indonesia through political means. They apparently hoped that an Islamic regime might come to power with support from the Indonesian military. According to H. Ahmad Sumargono: "We know that in order to change things in Indonesia, you have to have the military on your side. That's why we like Prabowo so much." [11] In early 1998 KISDI helped to divert anger about the economic crisis from Suharto to Chinese-Indonesians.

Pasemah friends whom I asked about the Pagaralam riot maintained that the looters were motivated by economic envy and greed rather than racial animosity. Like the coffee-growing Pasemah, Chinese-Indonesian merchants had generally prospered under the New Order. They were the middlemen who bought Pasemah coffee and arranged for it to be exported. The Pasemah said that they could get a better price for their coffee from these merchants than from the government-managed cooperative, because the head of the cooperative took a cut on every transaction. During the riot, some Pasemah helped Chinese-Indonesian merchants by hiding their cars and other valuables. In any case, the Chinese-Indonesian merchants in Pagaralam did not flee after the riot. When the mayor ordered them to open their shops again, they requested police protection and reopened for business.

When I visited Pagaralam five months after the fall of Suharto, there were few signs that much had changed. In the market the passageways between stalls were a slime of mud and rotting vegetables; streets were littered with garbage; roads around the market were deeply rutted or unpaved. When I asked why nothing was done to maintain the market or roads, I was told that the mayor had used his office to acquire land and build a new gas station at the edge of the town. The legacy of the New Order—a political culture that allowed officials to enrich themselves while ignoring the public good—remained strong.

The Final Days of the New Order

As the legitimacy of the New Order eroded in early 1998, intimidation of activists increased. Intelligence officers monitored all activities at LBH. Volunteer activists and LBH staff were summoned by the police for interrogation, accused of subversion for criticizing Pancasila, the five basic principles of the Republic of Indonesia. Word spread that security forces were kidnapping activists throughout Indonesia. Undercover agents went to the house where Nur Kholis and his two younger brothers rented rooms. They told his brothers that if Nur Kholis participated in further demonstrations, he would be "popular" (with the police) or *"disemen"* (encased in cement and dumped in the ocean). Nur Kholis was summoned for questioning as a witness in the "Pancasila Case." Knowing that witnesses were quickly transformed into suspects, Nur Kholis refused the summons on the ground that he had been engaged as a lawyer by LBH activists. The police issued a second summons, and then a third and final one, which meant that Nur Kholis was subject to arrest for failure to respond to it. But he managed to keep moving one step ahead of the police up to the day Suharto resigned.

On May 1, 1998, students from all the major universities in Palembang organized a march to the governor's office. This was the largest *reformasi*

Poster of activists kidnapped and "disappeared" by the military in the final months of the New Order.

demonstration in South Sumatra to date, consisting of several thousand students. Over the following two weeks, *reformasi* demonstrations demanding that Suharto step down took place almost daily. On May 14, 1998, the day after four student demonstrators in Jakarta were shot and killed, thousands of students gathered in front of the Provincial Legislature. The demonstration was peaceful until late in the afternoon. Then police wielding batons charged into the crowd. Some students were injured and had to be taken to the hospital. Others began throwing rocks at the police. Before the melee got out of control, the call for evening prayers rang out, and the students gradually left the scene.

The next day the front page of the *Sumatera Ekspres* featured photos of the demonstration at the Provincial Legislature and of a mass of people marching over the Ampera Bridge across the Musi River to join the demonstration. That morning a small group of students gathered at the Monument to the Heroes of the Revolution next to the Ampera Bridge to conduct a memorial service for the Jakarta student "martyrs." Another group of students demonstrated at the police station, protesting the attack on demonstrators the previous afternoon. The riots that erupted that day did not start at these locations. They began on Jalan Veteran, a major street where several car showrooms are located. According to witnesses interviewed by reporters from the *Sriwijaya Post,* young men who looked like soldiers (short hair, fit, carrying satchels) arrived in trucks. No one knew where they came from. One reporter thought they were recruited from gangs associated with the military because he saw a handgun fall out of the waist pack worn by one of the leaders. The young toughs began to throw rocks at the plateglass windows of the car salesrooms. They set tires on fire to attract a crowd and then urged people to join in the attack. The police and army units in Palembang did not respond to the disorder for several hours.

In the afternoon, incendiary devices were thrown into car showrooms, and rock throwing spread to stores and banks throughout the business district. When schools were let out, students joined in randomly breaking the windows of shops and houses they passed. As dusk approached, fires broke out at Palembang's old market, located at the edge of the Musi River below the Ampera Bridge. This neighborhood is densely populated, and people swarmed about trying to save the goods in their stalls. Smoke from the fire could be seen for miles, and this attracted more people. Major looting began as darkness fell.[12]

The riot on May 14 appears to have caught everyone by surprise. Reporters for the *Sriwijaya Post* who were close to activists and student leaders said that they had had no warning that there would be attacks on businesses. They were convinced that the riot had been instigated by outsiders, most probably gangs associated with the military. Rumors circulated that Lieutenant General Prabowo Subianto, son-in-law of President Suharto, who was later found to be involved in fomenting the riots in Jakarta, had been seen in Palembang. It was said that the riots were intended to be used to justify military repression of the *reformasi* movement.

Newspaper headlines on May 15 proclaimed that Palembang was still in the grip of rioting. Photos showed crowds watching showrooms on Jalan Veteran burn, soldiers confronting a mass of people trying to cross the Ampera Bridge, army units patrolling the main street, Jalan Jendral Sudirman, a burning car near Cikini Market in the center of the city, and another crowd in front of Palembang's main mosque watching the fires in the old market.

By Friday morning, May 17, 1998, wild rumors were circulating in Palembang. When I telephoned from the United States, I was told that the provincial parliament building had been attacked, the major supermarket had been burned down, and everyone was afraid to leave their houses. While middle-class people stayed home and exchanged rumors by telephone, poor people and students were in the streets. A large crowd gathered at Masjid Agung after Friday prayers to watch the fires, which were still burning. But the army began to reestablish control. Ampera Bridge was closed to prevent more people from coming to the city center, and soldiers began patrolling the business district. The front page of the newspaper the next day featured a photo of an army tank on Jendral Sudirman with people waving at it while trash burned in the street. On the editorial page a cartoon showed two little kids carting off a TV set, shouting, "Look, Mom, we got a TV!"

By Saturday the center of Palembang was calm, but looting continued in neighborhoods across the river and at the edges of the city. *Preman,* gangsters who run protection rackets in parking lots and shopping areas, appear to have taken control in these areas. Where merchants had paid protection money, looting did not take place. Elsewhere, *preman* joined in or led the looting. Merchants painted *"Islam"* or *"Pribumi"* (indigenous, i.e., not Chinese) on their shops, but in many areas the looters did not pay attention to who owned the shops they attacked.

Despite the riot, *reformasi* activists in Palembang continued to mount demonstrations demanding Suharto step down. On May 19, 1998, over a thousand students gathered in front of the Provincial Legislature to listen to speeches by Chairil Syah and other local *reformasi* leaders. On May 21, 1998, Yeni and other student activists were at the campus of Sriwijaya University planning for the next demonstration when they heard a microphone announcement: "Attention, attention. Suharto has resigned." At first they could not believe their ears. Some ran off in search of a television or radio to confirm the news. Abdul Situmorang was among the students gathered in the plaza in front of the rector's office when he heard the news. The crowd exploded with excitement; the students cheered and hugged each other. Boys stripped off their shirts. Then the students began to sing the song that everyone knew from school celebrations of Indonesian Independence Day, "Hail, hail, be joyful. Everyone be joyful. Our country is free. *Indonesia Merdeka.*"

In October when I returned to Palembang, signs of the riot were still visible. The damage to the Provincial Legislature had been repaired, but some shops on the main street were still boarded up. On Jalan Veteran, the Toyota salesroom was scorch-marked and the showroom for Tommy Suharto's Timor sedan was closed down. Disco Aries on the third floor of a hotel still had broken windows. Banks in the center of town had been renovated so that no windows faced the street, and one could still see graffiti proclaiming *"Pribumi"* scrawled on the walls of many smaller shops.

On roads entering neighborhoods where Chinese-Indonesians lived, gates had been erected and security guards posted. I was told that some wealthy families bought apartments in Singapore in case of further trouble, but there was no exodus of Chinese-Indonesians from Palembang. Although their businesses had been looted, people had not been attacked. *Reformasi* activists and religious leaders established the Institute for Humanitarian Solidarity. They urged Chinese-Indonesian businessmen not to move away

Palembang five months after the riots of May 1998.

and set up a fact-finding team. One hundred days after the riot, a collective prayer ceremony with Catholic, Protestant, Buddhist, Hindu, and Muslim leaders took place.

While the poor could only hope that things might improve after the fall of Suharto, the riot caused great anxiety in many middle-class residents of Palembang, who feared that violence could erupt again. They argued that the army was required to provide stability. They agreed that change was necessary, but they pointed out that the leaders who came to power after Suharto would have no experience in governing. The new government might well be incompetent and even more corrupt than the New Order.

After the Fall of Suharto

For *reformasi* activists the thrill of success began to dim in the days following Suharto's resignation, as they realized that their struggle was not over. In retrospect, Abdul Situmorang says that this was when differences among pro-democracy and Islamist groups supporting *reformasi* emerged: "Some of the students wanted a civilian coalition to take charge of the government and arrange for elections because they did not want Habibie, Suharto's vice president, to become president. Others agreed with the appointment of Habibie until a general election could be held." Students supporting an Islamic solution to the problems of Indonesia were not yet well organized in South Sumatra, but they contributed to a simmering debate about how to continue the struggle for a more just society. Gradually agreement emerged that the *reformasi* activists would continue to mount demonstrations on substantive issues, such as corruption, bringing Suharto to trial and ending "Dual Function," the policy that justified the political role of the military. Tarech Rasyid's new pamphlet entitled "Return Sovereignty to the People" (Kembalikan Daulat Rakyat), circulated among activists.

In August 1998 a new governor was appointed. Like his predecessor, Governor Rosihan Arsyad was from the Indonesian military (a former naval officer), but he showed an unexpected willingness to listen to protesters, once coming out of his office to talk with farmers evicted from their land. Student activists applauded and waited to see what he would do.

A new commander was assigned to Sriwijaya Corps, the territorial command stationed in Palembang. A group of students from the Muhammadiyah University took this opportunity to protest against the military. They went to the division headquarters, where they unfurled a banner demanding an end to Dual Function. Within minutes, a group of thugs appeared and attacked them under the eyes of soldiers standing guard. One of the leaders of the protesting students appealed to the officer in charge for protection. He was pushed into a car out of harm's way, but the soldiers did nothing to stop the attack. While the officer phoned for reinforcements, the thugs disappeared, leaving two students so badly beaten that they had to be hospitalized. This incident exposed the ties between the military and local *preman* gangs and reflected confusion in the military about its role in the era of reform.

A year later, on October 5, 1999, students from all the major universities in Palembang organized another demonstration at the division headquarters against a draft law on emergency powers that would give military commanders the power to act on their own authority in case of civil unrest. Armed men in civilian clothes emerged from behind the demonstrators and launched an attack on them. A cry went out, "Run, run!" Meyer Ardiansyah, a student from a private university, took off with the other students, but he turned into a side street where four attackers followed him. When he tripped and fell, they kicked and beat him. The attackers were joined by a fifth man. When Meyer struggled to his feet and headed for one of the houses that lined the street, the fifth attacker stabbed him in the stomach and again in the back with his knife. Meyer fell to the ground. A witness emerged to try to help him, but the attacker warned the man not to help. After protesting, he went back inside his house and watched Meyer die.

LBH and a team representing the private university led by Tarech Rasyid pressed the police to investigate the killing. However, it was almost three months before an arrest was made in late December. The fifth attacker was a known *preman* from the Kertapati neighborhood of Palembang; the other four were identified as soldiers from the intelligence branch of the army. Immediately after Meyer's death the commander of Sriwijaya Corps had denied that any military personnel were involved. Now the case of the four soldiers was separated from that of the civilian charged with Meyer's killing. The killer turned out to be a member of the New Order paramilitary organization Pemuda Panca Marga. He claimed that he had heard someone order, "Attack and kill" *(Serbu dan bunuh)*, and because he was close to the soldiers and angered by the students protesting against them, he was carried away by emotion and stabbed Meyer. He also confessed to being a police informer. Nevertheless, military officials denied that the attack on the students had been orchestrated by military intelligence.[13]

Meyer's killer was sentenced to two years in jail. The four soldiers were disciplined by the military: one was sentenced to five months, two to four months, and the last one to two months in prison. Despite the nominal sentences handed down, *reformasi* leaders celebrated, because during the New Order, military and civilian authorities had never been required to admit to responsibility for student casualties in the suppression of protests. On the other hand, the killing of Meyer revealed that the military was using paramilitary *preman* organizations against protestors so that it would not be charged with human rights abuses. Furthermore, the commander of Sri-wijaya Corps had refused to appear before the Provincial Legislature for questioning with regard to the Meyer case on the ground that the legislature had no authority over the military.

Intimidation of reporters also continued. In February 1999, *Lampung Post* reporter Taufik Wijaya was threatened by police because he was inter-viewing farmers in Ogan Komerig Ulu who were protesting the loss of their land. Syamsul Asinar, an LBH activist, was beaten up by police in Palem-bang because he had photographed them when they were harassing people. This led the Alliance of Independent Journalists (AJI), an organization formed after *Tempo, Detik,* and *Monitor* were banned in 1994, to protest because intimidation of the press was still going on in the *reformasi* era.

The *reformasi* struggle had brought down the New Order, but political reforms that would bring genuine democracy in which the rights of ordi-nary farmers and workers were respected and their voices heard were still only a dream. As Nur Kholis put it, "After the fall of Suharto, it turned out that we still faced difficult problems. One by one the elements of the *refor-masi* agenda that we agreed on have been left behind . . . the road is still long . . . the people are still oppressed."

Yeni Roslaini and WCC staff celebrating her birthday at the WCC office.

Jamila Nuh and Abdul Wahib Situmorang in front of the South Sumatra branch of WALHI.

What Made a *Reformasi* Activist?

I asked some of the students at LBH and WALHI if they would write an autobiographical essay for me describing how they had come to be *reformasi* activists. Afterwards I interviewed each of them, filling in details that I didn't understand. The stories of four of the young activists whom I came to know well are very instructive in demonstrating the characteristics of *reformasi* activists.

Jamila M. Nuh, the oldest of four children, was the daughter of a religious teacher who owned a small fertilizer store in Bangka. Jamila's parents had an arranged marriage when her father was thirty-four and her mother only sixteen years old. Jamila was eight when her father died while on the hajj, but her memories of him are a source of her idealism in struggling against the injustices of the New Order. She also learned stubbornly to

Nur Kholis meeting with villagers and government officials.

Jamila and street children at a camping program organized by Yayasan Kuala Merdeka.

resist injustice, in conflict with her mother, who had quickly remarried a man who earned no money and spent the inheritance left to her children. Jamila recalls that there was no money to pay school fees, and she cried with shame when her mother just ignored the letters from her school. After a fight with her stepfather when she was thirteen, Jamila ran away to an uncle's house. She lived there and helped to prepare food for her aunt's tea stall while she completed the last year of middle school. Then she was sent to Jakarta to help care for her cousin's new baby in exchange for having her school fees paid so that she could go to high school. When Jamila graduated in the first rank of her class, her cousin offered to send her to university as well, but Jamila refused the offer: "I didn't want to be dependent on my relatives. I wanted to be free to do what I chose."

Back in Bangka everyone pressured her to marry. "No one except my aunt understood my desire to go to university," she recalls. With help from a prospective suitor, Jamila went back to Jakarta to take the university entrance examination. While she waited for the results, she found a job in a bookstore. She learned that she had been accepted at Sriwijaya University, but she did not have the money to pay tuition. She applied to the Association of Indonesian Muslim Intellectuals (ICMI) for a scholarship, and her friends at the bookstore took up a collection to help her buy a bus ticket to Palembang.

The scholarship from ICMI did not come in time for Jamila to register for school, but the vice rector of Sriwijaya University offered to provide financial assistance. He also invited Jamila to live with his family and help his wife in exchange for room and board. Jamila was also offered a room in a *pesantren* (traditional Islamic boarding school) by Dr. Usman Said, an Islamic leader associated with the conservative Islamic mission organization, Dewan Dakwah Islam Indonesia (DDII). But Jamila was determined not to be dependent on anyone. She found a family with no connection to the university who gave her a place to stay in exchange for helping with laundry and housework.

When students in the law and engineering faculties first began organizing protests against the increase in tuition at Sriwijaya University, Jamila was reluctant to join them. The vice rector who had helped her was now the rector. To criticize or oppose such an influential patron would be an unacceptable breach of propriety. She struggled with the obligation she owed the rector and the sense of being controlled by that obligation. "When I was elected to the student senate, the rector made a speech inaugurating the new officers. He referred to an article in the *Sriwijaya Post* that quoted me, and he said that I had embarrassed the university. This was a difficult moment for mc. I felt that I owed him gratitude, but I also believed that I should be able to say what I thought. I finally decided that I could protest so long as I was not doing it only for myself but for the good of the whole community. The protestors may not have been the best students, and we caused him [the rector] sleepless nights, but we influenced a lot of people and made them see the corruption and abuse of power by the military."

At the end of 1997 Jamila came to the United States for an English course. We agreed that I would pay for her tuition and expenses in exchange for her working as my research assistant during my sabbatical year in Indonesia. Much later, Jamila related that her activist friends had urged her not to go to America. They were certain there must be a hidden reason why someone would provide money to study in America and suggested that I was a CIA agent.

When news came in early 1998 that *reformasi* activists were being kidnapped, Jamila was told that her name was on the list of those to be picked up in South Sumatra. So she stayed in the United States to study instead of going back to Indonesia with me. Jamila received an MS degree in environmental studies from Ohio University in 2003. She now works with a major NGO in Jakarta leading training programs in sustainable development.

Like Jamila, Yeni Roslaini was an unusually independent young woman. She grew up in a family with strong modernist Islamic values. Her grandfather was a well-known religious leader *(kiai)* in Ogan Komering Ulu, a district four to five hours' drive to the southwest of Palembang. Her parents moved to Palembang where they were teachers in a Muhammadiyah (modernist Islamic) school. When Yeni was little the family had to live with relatives—twelve people, three generations in three rooms.

Yeni was especially close to her father. He did not object when she organized her first protest in middle school because the headmaster did not support student activities. He only told her to be certain that she was protesting because it was right, not because it was popular. Yeni asked to go to a government high school so that she would not be known as the daughter of an influential teacher. In high school she organized a protest against extra fees.

In Yeni's final year of high school, her father died of a heart attack. She had to give up her plan to go to university in Medan, North Sumatra, because she needed to stay in Palembang to help her mother. Instead she went to Sriwijaya University. She emerged as the leader of protests against hazing rituals within the first week of enrolling and succeeded in getting the university administration to ban hazing. In 1998 Yeni founded the Women's Crisis Center (WCC), the first NGO in South Sumatra to deal with violence against women. In 2004 a national law on domestic violence was passed. Yeni devotes herself to educating government officials and women's groups about violence against women. More and more women are coming to WCC every week. The staff struggles to handle all the cases.

In Indonesia it is culturally inappropriate for young women to call attention to themselves. Women students dress modestly and tend to be quiet in class. Jamila and Yeni stand out for their fighting spirit. They are also alike in that their fathers died before they became *reformasi* activists. There was no male authority figure who could be pressured by the government to control them.

This was also true in the case of Nur Kholis. His father, who died just before Nur Kholis graduated from high school, was the leader of Javanese migrants who moved to South Sumatra in the early 1950s because there was no more land in East Java. He was one of the revolutionaries who fought against Dutch forces in the bloody Battle of Surabaya in 1945, but he chose not to pursue a military career after Independence. The Javanese settlers moved to a sparsely populated area of tidal marshes in the district of Banyuasin, about a hundred kilometers from Palembang, where they cultivated positive relations with the local people who tended rubber gardens and collected forest products. The Javanese settlers opened swampland for rice cultivation and planted coconut plantations. The early years were hard. Nur Kholis recalls that when he attended the government primary school in his village, he was one of the few students who owned a pair of shoes. He says his father taught him that farming was the most honorable way *(paling halal)* for a Muslim to earn a living because it did not involve charging interest or any other forbidden activity. Even if Nur Kholis never became a farmer, his father said, he must remember that he had been raised by farming.

Nur Kholis was sent to study in a *pesantren* when he was twelve. The school was located two days' journey from his home. In the *pesantren,* he recalls, he learned that a person must live a life that is of some use to people. For high school Nur Kholis and two of his brothers attended a modernist Islamic school *(madrasah)* in Palembang. Nur Kholis hoped to study Islam at the state Islamic Institute, IAIN Raden Fatah, in Palembang while at the same time attending Sriwijaya University to study law. But there was no money for double tuition, so he chose law. At Sriwijaya University, he joined a student organization for hiking and rock climbing. In his third year, he organized an expedition to climb Mount Leuseur in Aceh Province. At the time he did not realize how ambitious an undertaking this was, for the trip would take fifteen days of difficult hiking and climbing, and involve obtaining permission from government authorities and the military to enter an area where the Achenese separatist movement was based. Nevertheless, Nur Kholis and three other students completed the trip. On it, Nur Kholis says, he and his comrades learned to trust one another and realized they could do things that no one expected of them. Nur Kholis became director of WALHI at the beginning of 1998. In 2001 he was elected director of LBH-Palembang. He also serves on the national board of WALHI and on the Election Supervisory Commission for South Sumatra.

Like Nur Kholis, Abdul Situmorang's activism was shaped by values he learned in an Islamic school. He is known affectionately as Ucok, a nickname used by the Batak people of North Sumatra where his parents come from. His father came to Palembang as a young man to seek his fortune. He started a garment business and then brought his wife from North Sumatra. Ucok was born the following year. He was sent to study with his grandfather, a respected leader of the modernist Islamic organization Muhammadiyah, who taught in a *pesantren* in South Tapanuli, North Sumatra. Ucok says that his grandfather taught him to think in a modern way and not just follow tradition. "The difference is that he used Islamic teachings as a knife to examine problems. I don't use Islamic teachings because I see Islam has failed to defend oppressed people and to protect the environment. But that does not mean I do not believe Islam. I use it to communicate with God."

At Sriwijaya University Ucok studied economics. He says that he was already "political" when he became a WALHI activist, but in organizing WALHI campaigns he learned to think scientifically about environmental problems and more systematically about politics. His parents worried that, as an activist, he might be beaten up by security forces or worse, but they did not try to make him stop his work at WALHI. Elected director of WALHI-South Sumatra in 1999, he helped farmers organize when the new PT TEL pulp and paper factory dumped its waste in the Lematang River, causing fish kills, and he mounted campaigns against illegal logging. In 2001 Ucok came to the United States for graduate study. After completing a master's degree in 2003, he returned to Indonesia to work in South Sumatra. He now works for a United Nations program in Jakarta, providing education to members of the National Legislature about population and other issues.

These four young activists were children of middle-class families. Like most of their peers at university, they had close relatives who worked in the government under the New Order, yet they took enormous risks to protest the injustice they saw around them. When these *reformasi* leaders tried to explain how they became activists, each of them spoke of Islam as providing a moral compass, but none of them saw Islam as a simple solution to the problems of poverty and injustice in Indonesia. They have gradually come to understand that they are involved in an ongoing struggle together with poor people in developing countries throughout the world.

Chapter 3

Who Owns the Land?

Whether the colonist needs land as a site for the sake of the wealth buried in it, or whether he merely wishes to constrain the native to produce a surplus of food and raw materials, is often irrelevant; nor does it make much difference whether the native works under the direct supervision of the colonist or only under some form of indirect compulsion, for in every and any case, the social and cultural system of native life must be shattered.
— Karl Polyani, *The Great Transformation*

RIGHTS TO LAND in South Sumatra were traditionally managed according to customary law *(adat)*. *Adat* recognized individual rights to cultivated land *(tanah garapan)* and rights to communally owned and managed land *(tanah adat* or *tanah ulayat)*. Individual land rights included irrigated rice fields *(sawah)* and land planted in rubber, fruit trees, or vegetable crops. Communal rights to forest lands were associated with a *marga*, originally a clan, transformed under Dutch administration into a territorial unit. By consensus a community might grant migrants the right to individually cultivate plots of communal land. Unlike a legal property right, individual usage rights existed only as long as the land was cultivated. If the land was abandoned, rights returned to the community. No land could be sold.[1]

To transform traditional land rights into legal property rights, a farmer must obtain a land title from government authorities. This is a complicated procedure involving expensive bribes to officials. In South Sumatra only 15 percent of the land has been registered. In one district in the lowland forest, 97 percent of the land cultivated by people is not titled.[2]

Besides raising chickens, ducks, goats, and a few cattle, farmers in the lowland forests formerly cultivated rice in *sawah* adjacent to the rivers. They harvested fish in the shallow lagoons *(lebak lebong)* that form in rivers during the rainy season and collected resin, wild honey, rattan, bamboo, and wood for construction from the communal forest. During the colonial era farmers also began to cultivate rubber trees, which provided cash income.

Despite their simple subsistence economy, some villagers were prosperous enough by the beginning of the 1990s to send their children to the university in Palembang.

The Basic Forestry Law of 1967 recognized communal rights of indigenous peoples to forest lands, but following colonial law the state is the legal owner of the forests and retains the authority to grant usage rights to other entities, such as corporations. This chapter describes how the sustainable economy of lowland villagers was transformed after the World Bank recommended that Indonesia develop the plantation sector to increase exports of rubber, sugar, palm oil, tea, coffee, coconut, and chocolate. In the 1980s the New Order granted usage rights to corporations for the development of industrial forestry and oil palm plantations in the forests of the outer islands. Ninety percent of these projects were located in Sumatra and Kalimantan. The large land concessions that expropriated the land and resources of indigenous people for the benefit of a small political-bureaucratic elite and foreign investors were typical New Order "development" projects. They resulted in increasing rural poverty, forcing villagers to move to cities, as they could no longer secure a livelihood, and creating environmental destruction that continues to affect the health and well-being of all Indonesians.

The companies that benefited from these concessions were generally owned by close associates of Suharto. Members of the Suharto family usually received a subsidiary interest. Rights to 91,531 hectares of land in South Sumatra were granted to companies in which the Suharto children had, and still have, a share. Suharto's daughter Siti Hardiyanti Rukmana ("Tutut") is a partner in six palm oil companies, three rubber companies, two industrial timber companies, and an oil company with operations in South Sumatra. In 1999, the South Sumatran Attorney General's Office reported that none of the companies in which Suharto's children held a share had paid any land taxes.[3]

Throughout the 1990s farmers from remote villages all over South Sumatra came to LBH-Palembang looking for help because their land had been taken over by a corporation and they were threatened with arrest if they resisted. The number of land conflicts increased sharply in the second half of the decade, as can be seen in Table 4 prepared by LBH.

I first became aware of these land conflicts in discussions at the LBH office in 1994. As a student volunteer, Jamila went to Kundi village in Bangka in 1995 to help document the land claims of villagers and the repressive actions of security forces. In 1998, as director of WALHI, Nur Kholis worked with villagers fighting the industrial forestry company PT Musi Hutan Persada (MHP). Abdul Situmorang followed Nur Kholis as director

Table 4

LBH-Palembang Cases	1995	1996	1997	1998	1999
Land conflict	12	28	39	85	130
Civil and political rights	4	16	17	15	14
Environmental issues	4	11	4	5	5
Labor issues	11	5*	13	22	35

* The decrease in the number of labor protests and strikes was due to the government crackdown in the aftermath of the attack on pro-democracy supporters of Megawati at the PDI headquarters on July 27, 1996.

Nur Kholis (far right) after a meeting with farmers involved in a land conflict. (Author and colleague Ann Tickamyer stand in the center of the group.)

of WALHI at the beginning of 2000, and he and Nur Kholis worked with villagers who were making renewed efforts to reclaim their land in the post-Suharto period.

A list of land conflicts brought to LBH-Palembang between 1994 and 1999 shows that the majority of 193 conflicts involved palm oil or rubber companies (136), industrial forestry companies (25), or transmigration projects (19). Just six corporations were implicated in 89 land disputes: PT

Musi Hutan Persada (MHP), an industrial forestry corporation owned by Suharto crony Prayogo Pangestu (16) and five palm oil companies—PT London Sumatera (Lonsum; 24), PT Multarada Multi Maju (18), PT Perkebunan Nusantara VII (13), PT Surya Bumi Agro Langgeng (10), and PT Mitra Ogan (8). In this chapter I tell stories illustrating how corporations were able to transform development projects into a profitable form of exploitation and describe the obstacles faced by farmers and NGO activists as they struggled for the rights of smallholders.

Oil Palm Plantations

In the 1990s, the World Bank promoted the development of plantations through a profit-sharing scheme called the Nucleus Estate and Smallholder Scheme (NES). A state-owned enterprise would establish a "nucleus" *(inti)* factory within a larger *"plasma"* area of smallholders. This scheme is commonly referred to as *inti/plasma.* In theory the state-owned corporation makes a contract with local farmers to produce a certain crop and provides technical advice and loans. NES schemes had both economic and social objectives. They were supposed to develop unproductive land, increase export earnings from cash crops, improve farmers' income, integrate agriculture with processing and marketing, speed up the transfer of technology to farmers, create new jobs, and stimulate economic growth in areas outside of Java.[4] The NES schemes were integrated with transmigration programs resettling people from densely populated Java to less populated areas.

In the 1990s, a growing world market for palm oil led the government to extend the NES concept to private corporations. Abuses in NES on the part of private corporations were rampant. According to the law, local government officials had to clarify that land released in concessions was unproductive (with no cultivated crops). Corporations frequently obtained this certification by bribing the appropriate official, and farmers found that land where they had planted rubber trees and other crops was included in a plantation concession. When cultivated land is included in the concession, the corporation is required to negotiate with local farmers to compensate them for their crops. Typically, however, there was no negotiation and no compensation paid. When compensation was paid, the amount was minimal. Villagers who did not want to participate in the scheme were forced to do so through intimidation by military forces hired by companies as security guards.

Villagers in South Sumatra found it difficult to understand their relationship to the company in an *inti/plasma* scheme. The land in the concession was divided into two-hectare plots called *paket*. Farmers who had cultivated land in the concession area were to be given rights to a number of *paket* equivalent to the land they had farmed. However, these rights were encumbered by loans taken out by the company for construction of a factory to process oil palm fruits, so title to the land was held by the bank. In theory, after the loan had been repaid through a deduction from the price paid to *plasma* farmers for the harvest, villagers would be given clear title to their *paket*. However, farmers were not informed about the terms of the loan or the schedule of repayment. To date no villager has received a land title. In some places a village cooperative was set up to represent villagers in an *inti/plasma* scheme. In rare instances, the cooperative was directed by an educated and responsible villager who could successfully negotiate with a company. More typically, there was no oversight of what the company charged villagers for management and maintenance of the plantation, so that after payment on the loan, villagers received almost no income from the harvest of their *paket*.

In short, farmers forced into an NES scheme lost a sustainable livelihood and became dependent on a company to disperse a share of the profits from oil palm grown on land they had formerly cultivated. Farmers who did not receive *paket* because their land claims were not recognized were reduced to becoming unskilled laborers on a plantation. They could no longer collect forest products or start a new garden under the forest canopy because rights to the forest had been granted to the corporation. The minimum wages paid to unskilled laborers reduced them to poverty, and they knew that their employment could be terminated at any time.

Government officials and village heads who assisted a company in obtaining a concession were rewarded with *paket*. Thus, local authorities generally sided with the company in disputes over the size of a farmer's holding or compensation for crops. Some village heads also enriched themselves by selling false land certificates that could be turned in for *paket*. This clouded the legitimate claims of farmers whose land was included in a concession.

Amzulian Rifai conducted research on land disputes involving palm oil companies in South Sumatra for his Ph.D. dissertation at Melbourne University.[5] He reports seventy-eight conflicts between villagers and companies in seventy-five concessions in six districts of South Sumatra. These included claims that:

- Farmers' land was taken illegally by force (34 cases)
- No compensation was paid for crops on land included in a concession (21 cases)

- Rubber trees owned by villagers were destroyed by companies using fire to clear land (10 cases)
- Farmers' land was included in a concession, but they were excluded from the profit-sharing scheme (13) cases.

Under the New Order, companies used military units against protesting villagers. With the end of the New Order, companies employed private security forces, recruiting local village youths and paying them handsomely. At the same time, many farmers renewed their efforts to reclaim land seized by corporations. The conflict between farmers and a company was frequently transformed into an inter- or intravillage conflict between farmers who wanted to reclaim land and those who had become security guards or otherwise benefited from the *inti/plasma* scheme. Some companies were accused of deliberately inciting such conflicts and of portraying protesting villagers as dangerous troublemakers.

People of Kundi versus PT Gunung Sawit Bina Lestari (PT GSBL)

The people of Kundi village on Bangka Island off the coast of South Sumatra could not be classified as poor. They grew rice, vegetables, and fruit for their own needs. They raised chickens and bought fish from fishermen in the neighboring village. Rights to communal forest land allowed them to collect jungle crops and wood for cooking and building. They used forest land to cultivate rubber trees and pepper as cash crops. When the price of pepper on the world market was high, some farmers saved enough money to go on the hajj.

In 1995, PT Gunung Sawit Bina Lestari (GSBL), the company of a local businessman, was given a concession of 10,000 hectares to establish oil palm plantations in three districts. One concession included the land of Kundi village. The farmers who settled in Kundi in the 1950s had been guerilla fighters in the Indonesian revolution. They had been given their land by Indonesia's first president, Sukarno, and they preserved a document signed by him.

On June 1, 1995, GSBL brought in heavy equipment and began to build a road into the area of Kundi. Only after this happened were the headmen of Kundi and two neighboring villages informed by government officials that GSBL had been granted a concession in the area. The headmen were told to explain to the villagers that GSBL would pay the legally stipulated compensation for crops grown on the land and farmers would be employed on the plantation and in the oil palm factory that would be built.

Villagers understood the danger of opposing a government-sponsored "development" project under the New Order. In two of the villages people were divided about whether they should accept the compensation or fight for their land. GSBL was able to pressure resisters into compliance. In contrast, the five thousand people of Kundi united to oppose the expropriation of their land. When the village headman demurred, "I cannot resist, because I'm a government official," they chose Tarto Surah (known as Pak Tarto), a charismatic fifty-three-year-old farmer, to lead the fight. The farmers of Kundi took a collective oath that none of them would "sell" their land to the company.[6]

On June 8, 1995, Pak Tarto sent a letter to GSBL stating that the villagers of Kundi did not want to give up their land. He explained that Kundi was not a poor or backward village, and people could earn more as farmers than they would be paid as laborers on the oil palm plantation. He warned that fertilizers and pesticides used by the company would wash into the ocean where they could affect the shrimp, crab, and fish that local fishermen depended on for their livelihood. There was no reply to the letter. Pak Tarto then went to the GSBL headquarters, but no one would talk to him.

At the end of June, district officials summoned the village headmen of Kundi and other villages whose land was included in the concession to a meeting. The village heads learned that local government authorities had not been consulted before the GSBL concession was granted and that district officials did not support the takeover of village land, but, the officials insisted, nothing could be done to oppose GSBL.

At the beginning of July, GSBL tractors began to clear land. A plot of one-year-old rubber trees planted by a Kundi villager was destroyed. Abang Syarifudin, the son of a Kundi farmer, returned from Jakarta to help his father fight for his land. He and Pak Tarto sent letters of protest to the National Human Rights Commission, government ministries, WALHI in Jakarta, the governor of South Sumatra, and the *bupati* of Bangka. They went to the local offices of the political parties and the teachers' organization to ask for support. But no one could help them.

In August, the people of Kundi decided that they themselves would stop the land clearing by GSBL. About two thousand villagers went to the fields and stood in front of the bulldozers with signs that read: "Please Pak Suharto, Don't condemn our village," "Don't sell our village," and "We know that the Indonesian military protects the people." Although the bulldozers stopped, Pak Tarto was summoned by the police. In response, villagers went to Palembang, a journey by bus and boat that took an entire day, to solicit the help of LBH, which sent Jamila to Kundi to assist the villagers in documenting their land claims and the actions of GSBL and local officials.

Activist reporters from the *Sriwijaya Post* wrote articles about the struggle of the Kundi farmers, and LBH staff helped the villagers organize a branch of the Farmers' Prosperity and Solidarity Union. This provoked the *bupati* of Bangka to issue a statement saying that he would ensure farmers received compensation for their crops, adding that "certain persons" were "dramatizing the villagers' fears."

LBH arranged for Pak Tarto and other village leaders to go to Jakarta in September 1995 to present their case to national political figures. Representatives of the opposition Indonesian Democracy Party (PDI) agreed to take up the Kundi case with the minister of forestry. The director general of the Department of Agriculture agreed to reconsider the location of the GSBL concession. The head of the National Human Rights Commission stated that the Kundi case could be considered a case of human rights abuse. Village leaders were promised that they would be protected from intimidation by local security forces.

But when Pak Tarto returned from Jakarta, he was picked up by the local police again. This time he was not taken to the police station but to a private house, where he was held for several days. Upon his release, Pak Tarto was issued a warning, but he and the villagers of Kundi refused to be intimidated. Instead they escalated their protests. On September 19, 1995, hundreds of villagers, including women, children, and elderly people, demonstrated at the GSBL headquarters. Then they went to the field where a bulldozer was clearing land and asked GSBL employees to leave. They tore out the GSBL boundary markers and uprooted newly planted oil palms.

LBH called upon GSBL to stop clearing land until the conflict was resolved. The *bupati* declared the villagers' actions to be a criminal attack on private property, but he formed a team to investigate their land claims. The team could not determine whether cleared land had been previously cultivated, and it filed a report stating that GSBL had only cleared "unproductive" land. A local military unit was sent to occupy Kundi, and village leaders were summoned by the police. GSBL agreed to stop clearing new land until the dispute was resolved.

At the end of October, Pak Tarto returned to Jakarta to talk to officials who had promised to help the people of Kundi. Once again they told him that they would look into the case. But on his return to Bangka the police intimidation continued. Pak Tarto was picked up again and told he would be charged as a traitor because the Kundi movement was a threat to security. When the protests did not stop, the police went to Pak Tarto's house at night, but he refused to go with them because they did not have a warrant. The next day, he was picked up and held for three days. Thereafter, the police summoned him at regular intervals, and he was required to go to Montok to report to them about Kundi. This went on from the end of 1995 until the fall of Suharto in May 1998. Three months after Suharto stepped down, GSBL signed an agreement stating that it would return the land it had cleared to Kundi villagers and would not extend its plantation any farther.[7]

The success of Kundi village aroused envy and hope in farmers in neighboring villages. At the official ceremony to mark the boundary of Kundi land, the *preman* leader who headed the GSBL security force led an attack on farmers who came to the ceremony from a neighboring village. Their motorcycles were thrown into a river and a car was vandalized. Presumably this was a warning to other farmers hoping to reclaim land from GSBL. Police present at the ceremony took no action to stop the vandalism or arrest the vandals.

The success of Kundi villagers in their struggle to regain their land can be attributed to three unusual factors. First, GSBL was owned by a local entrepreneur rather than a Suharto crony or a foreign company that might have had more leverage in maintaining rights to the concession. Second, Kundi villagers had a document that supported their land claims. Finally, the leadership qualities shown by Pak Tarto were remarkable, as he was able to keep the villagers united while diverting official anger toward himself.

In January 2000, Jamila returned to South Sumatra to conduct research on the conflict between the people of Kundi and GSBL. When I visited her in August, I was taken to see the land that had been returned to villagers for communal use. The villagers did not want to plant oil palm because they would have to sell their harvest to GSBL, and they did not think they would be given a fair price. They had first tried to plant rice, but this turned out not to be a suitable crop. Therefore they were considering allowing the land to return to forest. We visited a forest plot where the villagers demonstrated how productive forest land could be. We were shown rubber trees and pepper plants intercropped under the forest canopy with twenty other cultivated plants, including coconut palms, eleven kinds of fruit trees, and fifteen other edible crops.

People of Wonorejo versus PT Multrada Multi Maju (MMM)

The conflict between the people of Wonorejo village and a foreign-owned company, PT Multrada Multi Maju (MMM), is more typical of what has happened in land conflicts in South Sumatra.[8] Wonorejo was settled in the 1970s by Javanese transmigrants from Lampung in the south. The indigenous people of this sparsely settled area welcomed the Javanese farmers as neighbors, and the *marga* head gave them land to farm. The settlers carved fields out of the jungle for rubber and coffee trees and a few hectares of paddy. They did not become wealthy, but they managed to do a little better each year until 1993 when the subdistrict head *(camat)* was approached by representatives of MMM, which wanted to open a plantation in the area.

The farmers of Wonorejo explained to me how a company would approach a village head and ask him to recommend a concession to the *camat,* who would then forward the recommendation to the *bupati,* who would forward it to the provincial legislature, which would forward it to the governor, who would forward it to the Ministry of Forestry, which granted the concession. At each stage, a bribe was paid to the appropriate official. The local community had no input at all in the process. The farmers of Wonorejo found that their rice fields and rubber tree stands were included in the 15,000 hectare MMM concession.

With about 530 rubber trees to a hectare and a planting of 3 to 4 hectares, the farmers had secured a sustainable living. Now they were told they would be paid US$3 to US$12 per hectare in compensation for crops planted on the land. They could not understand how a company could be granted the right to appropriate their resources and land while offering them little more than positions as laborers on the oil palm plantation.

The people of Wonorejo went to LBH-Palembang for help. LBH lawyers helped 912 families from six villages establish a branch of the Farmers' Prosperity and Solidarity Union (KSKP). The farmers elected Pak Sabowo from Wonorejo as the chairman of their new organization. Pak Sabowo had come from Java at the age of eighteen to work in the oil fields, where he joined a union affiliated with the Indonesian Communist Party (PKI). When the PKI was made illegal after the coup against Sukarno in 1965, Pak Subowo was arrested and held for seven months as a category C prisoner (a designation referring to people who belonged to an organization affiliated with the PKI). After his release he found it difficult to get work. He took a job breaking stones for road construction and worked as a hired laborer in the rice fields. In 1982, he finally obtained a few hectares of land in Wonorejo. Over the next ten years he and his family cleared four and a half hectares of land for a rice field and coffee garden. They believed they had achieved their dream of being self-sufficient farmers.

On behalf of the farmers of Wonorejo, LBH lawyers argued that the MMM concession had violated the law that stipulated only unproductive land could be granted for development of plantations. Furthermore, they argued, threats and intimidation had been used to force farmers to give up their land. Government officials sided with MMM.

The conflict erupted again in 1997, the year of the El Niño drought.

Fires set by MMM to clear land got out of control and burned the remaining coffee, rubber, and durian trees in Wonorejo. MMM refused to take responsibility for the loss on the grounds that it had been a dry season and fires were natural. On August 12, 1997, men from Wonorejo went to the MMM factory to try to force company representatives to meet with them. The manager refused to see them, and the frustrated men set fire to a building used to store fertilizer. The following week twenty-nine men in Wonorejo were arrested for setting the fire.

Pak Subowo met with the governor of South Sumatra, Ramli Hasan Basri, on December 17, 1997. He described how the land that villagers relied on for their livelihood had been taken over by MMM. According to newspaper reports, the governor promised to investigate the claims of Wonorejo villagers and, if confirmed, to obtain compensation and withdraw MMM's concession. Instead, on January 5, 1998, Pak Subowo and fourteen other farmers were arraigned in court for setting fire to the MMM warehouse.[9]

The following week, Nur Kholis accompanied Pak Subowo and the other farmers to Jakarta to present an appeal to the National Human Rights Commission.[10] The *reformasi* movement was emerging, which strengthened the hand of the commission, and the farmers were promised that their case would be investigated. Again nothing happened. Prosecution of Pak Subowo and the Wonorejo farmers began in February 1998. The men say that in the jail they were beaten by *preman* (gangsters). The police looked on and did nothing to stop the violence. By May the New Order was teetering, and the farmers, still in jail, were waiting to hear their sentences. Forty students from universities in Palembang, calling themselves Sumatra Student Solidarity with Farmers, went to Lahat to demonstrate support for them. They unfurled a banner that read "Agrarian Reform for a New and Just Society."[11] Two days later President Suharto resigned. But this did not help Pak Subowo, who was sentenced to one year in jail. The other Wonorejo farmers received a sentence of six months.

When released from jail at the end of July, the farmers and ninety-five families from seven villages around Wonorejo went to the Lahat District Legislature to demand the return of land taken by MMM. Again university students from Palembang joined the demonstration, insisting that the legislature recognize the land rights of farmers. The students sang *reformasi* songs and waved a banner proclaiming, "Give back land seized by PT MMM in 1993." The villagers set up small stoves in the lobby of the legislature and announced that they would stay until the district government acted. The next day the legislature appointed a team to investigate the claims of villagers against MMM.[12] MMM lobbied members of the district legislature, warning that revoking their concession would threaten future foreign investment in Indonesia. The government took no action. On December 4, 1998, Wonorejo villagers blockaded the road to the MMM factory.[13] Finally government authorities declared the disputed land to be in status quo, meaning that both parties to the conflict were barred from using the land until the conflict was settled.

MMM now agreed to negotiations over compensation for crops on land included in the concession, but insisted that it would not return land to local farmers. LBH lawyers estimated that the farmers' land claims amounted to about 1,300 hectares of the 15,000 hectare concession. The Kikim subdistrict government announced that MMM would compensate farmers at a rate of US$30 per hectare and urged the farmers to be patient. People in Wonorejo did not want compensation. They wanted their land. MMM representatives refused to meet with them, and on February 10, 1999, Wonorejo farmers again blockaded the roads to MMM. This caused the *bupati* of Lahat to issue a statement warning that if farmers were not patient, it meant that their protests were no longer "pure." This thinly veiled threat led the farmers to abandon the blockade. On February 13, 1999, MMM representatives met with people from Wonorejo and other villages with land claims. At the end of March, company representatives announced that three villages had agreed to accept payment of US$50 per hectare. The people of Wonorejo and one other village, however, rejected this settlement. They still hoped to have their land returned to them.[14]

While the contested land was still in status quo, the oil palms were not being harvested. The economy of Indonesia was reeling from the Asian Economic Crisis, pushing over one-quarter of the people in South Sumatra into dire poverty. Pak Subowo and other representatives of the KSKP appealed to South Sumatra's new governor, Rosihan Arsyad, saying that they were not able to feed their families because their land had been taken and there were no jobs. With the governor's permission, on April 28, 1999, farmers from Wonorejo began to harvest oil palms on land where their rubber trees had once stood. On May 4, 1999, the police chief in Lahat stated that both villagers and MMM were permitted to harvest on the disputed land.[15]

Despite gaining access to their land, the farmers of Wonorejo found it almost impossible to sell their harvest because factories required a certificate of ownership. Since the fruits must be processed quickly after harvest, much of the harvest spoiled. When a buyer was finally found, the farmers were given a very low price. Although the governor had granted permission for villagers to harvest the oil palms, on November 4, 1999, MMM's security force seized ten farmers who were harvesting and turned them in to the police. People from thirteen villages protested for three days at the police station. LBH lawyers pointed out that the men were harvesting on land for which they had not received compensation. After a week, hundreds of farmers gathered at the police station demanding the men's release. The police then allowed the men to leave but warned them that they would be prosecuted for stealing oil palm fruits.

That evening, the house of the MMM manager, eleven other buildings housing staff members, and a fertilizer warehouse were burned down. Newspapers reported that the crowd returning from the police station "went amok." Governor Rosihan described the attack on MMM as "brutal." Nur Kholis pointed out to the press that the land conflict between villagers in Wonorejo and MMM had been going on for over six years and argued that the Lahat district government was partly to blame for what had happened because the conflict was still not settled.[16] Nevertheless, public opinion turned against the Wonorejo farmers. Wonorejo villagers denied that they had set the fires at MMM and accused MMM of hiring young toughs to attack the factory in order to divert attention from the land conflict. When I talked with farmers in Wonorejo in 2001, they pointed out that no one had been arrested for setting the fires and claimed that MMM later hired the men responsible as security guards.

After the fire, MMM shut down its operations in Kikim district. The local manager announced that the company required guarantees that the police would protect MMM property before the factory would reopen. He repeated that the company was prepared to pay compensation to villagers, but in exchange farmers must accept that MMM had been granted exclusive usage rights to the land. He suggested that protests against MMM were no longer "pure," because when settlement with one village was reached, outsiders claiming to be from Kikim made new claims.

At this point Governor Rosihan decided that land conflicts must be resolved to maintain law and order. In his view, the best solution would be to give farmers a stake in oil palm plantations through the *inti/plasma* system. He urged MMM to accept farmers with land claims as *plasma* and promised farmers that he would see that they and their families had enough food until the problem of land rights was resolved.[17] With the governor's directive that farmers could no longer harvest on contested land, MMM reopened its factory.

As protests by farmers escalated, the police adopted a strategy of criminalizing their actions. In February 2000, Pak Subowo was arrested a second time for "stealing" oil palm fruits. Villagers from Wonorejo went to the office of the chief of police in Palembang to protest. This demonstration led to the arrest of 13 more farmers. By 2001, criminal charges had been brought against 111 farmers involved in conflicts with oil palm companies.[18]

At his trial, Pak Subowo was sentenced to seven months in jail. When

I went to Wonorejo with Jamila in July 2001, his wife was working with her daughter and several other women in a small patch of rented *sawah*. With Pak Subowo in jail, the family had no source of income, so fellow villagers tried to help out. The women told us that families in Wonorejo had lost 309 hectares to MMM. The compensation that MMM finally paid to them amounted to only US$2.25–$3.25 per tree. Now they struggled to feed their children. Some villagers had turned to brick making, which brought in barely enough to keep their families alive. The women complained bitterly that without a few hectares of productive land they would not be able to survive and send their children to school.

The men in Wonorejo said that all the documents they had gathered to support their land claims had been seized by the police when Pak Subowo was arrested a second time. Nothing had changed as a result of *reformasi*, they said. The village headman had been selected by the *camat* in 1997 during the New Order, and he did not support them. The new chairman of the local KSKP who had replaced Pak Subowo was a former village headman, who had used "money politics" (bribes) to win the election. He treated his office like a New Order official, they said, demanding payment whenever anyone needed his signature.

The men said that they wanted to return to *adat*, customary law. They explained that *adat* meant respect for the individual and collective land rights of people who work the land. *Adat* came from the ancestors and it required a man to engage in environmentally sound and sustainable cultivation of the land to preserve a livelihood for his descendants. The farmers pointed out that oil palm and timber corporations had been responsible for major forest fires in 1997. Such disastrous fires had never happened before. They contrasted their sense of responsibility for the community and the land with the refusal of corporations to take responsibility for the social and environmental consequences of their operations.

On the day in April 2001 that Pak Subowo was finally released from jail, he was rearrested on the same charge by police from Lahat and taken to jail, where he was beaten until he was unconscious.[19] Outraged by this parody of justice, LBH lawyers issued a press release. The story of Pak Subowo appeared in local and national newspapers, and he became an icon of the struggle for justice being waged by farmers in South Sumatra.[20] Shortly after Pak Subowo was finally released, he suffered a stroke from which he has yet to recover.

In the last decade the amount of land converted to oil palm plantations has doubled to nearly five million hectares, making Indonesia the second largest palm oil producer in the world. This vast expansion of corporate plantations was supported by the World Bank. After the Asian Economic

Crisis, the International Monetary Fund and the World Bank provided a financial "rescue package" including further measures to promote investment in the palm oil industry, requiring that Indonesia lift the ban on foreign investment and allow plantations to be established on "nonproductive" production forest land. The International Finance Corporation, a private lending branch of the World Bank Group, provided loans and guarantees to the largest edible oil corporations in the world to expand their operations.[21] There has been no similar development program providing support in the form of loans or processing facilities to smallholders.

Industrial Forestry

During the New Order, indigenous people were rarely able to resist the appropriation of their land by companies owned by well-connected elites, such as Prayogo Pangestu, head of the Barito Pacific Group, which holds sixty-eight timber concessions in Indonesia.[22] In South Sumatra alone, Barito subsidiary PT Musi Hutan Persada (MHP) was given a concession in 1991 of almost 400,000 hectares.

After the fall of Suharto, villagers throughout Indonesia mobilized to demand the return of their land. In September 2001 twenty-five disputes between MHP and villagers in South Sumatra were documented by WALHI and LBH. In this part of the chapter I tell the story of three conflicts between villagers and MHP. In the first case villagers succeeded in reclaiming 3,000 hectares of forest land, perhaps because their protests received attention in the press. The remaining two cases illustrate how corporations are able to wield political influence in order to protect their interests.

People of Marga Benakat versus PT Musi Hutan Persada (MHP)

Koim, an old man recognized as an authority on *marga* tradition, recalled that in 1920 the Dutch Controleur Botenburg in Palembang had recognized the right of Marga Benakat to 2,000 hectares of forest. When Dutch authorities made part of the communal forest of the seven villages of Marga Benakat into a government forest reserve, the *marga* was compensated with 1,000 hectares of forest nearby. The agreement was signed by the *pasirah* of Benakat on October 25, 1932. Koim argued, "If the Dutch respected our rights to the forest, how is it that our own government does not respect our rights?"[23]

In 1992 MHP began clear-cutting land in Benakat subdistrict, including 3,000 hectares of communal forest known as Rimbo Sekampung, which was claimed as *marga* land by seven villages. In June 1993, 716 household heads from Marga Benakat signed a letter protesting against MHP harvesting *marga* land, which they sent to the *bupati* of Muara Enim. That letter, followed by others, received no response. By 1994, while the villagers were still appealing, MHP had clear-cut about 1,000 hectares of land in Rimbo Sekampung.[24]

In August 1994, Koim wrote a letter to WALHI in Jakarta requesting help, and LBH-Palembang was asked to investigate. Its report, released on September 17, 1994, revealed that MHP was harvesting protected trees over one meter in diameter and security forces were intimidating protesting villagers from Marga Benakat. In one area angry villagers had resorted to burning down the dormitories of MHP workers. LBH director Chairil Syah argued that although de jure the forest was under the authority of the Ministry of Forestry because the New Order did not recognize *marga* rights, de facto the right to preserve the forest was in the hands of local communities. A small group of student activists joined with LBH, forming a solidarity committee to support the smallholders of Benakat and demanding that military forces be withdrawn from the villages.

The case of Benakat coincided with demonstrations supporting the farmers of Kedung Ombo in Java, which were reported in the international press. Furthermore, in the brief period in the early 1990s when Suharto loosened control of the press, newspaper reports on the conflict pressured local government officials to intervene when companies violated the law and used security forces against protestors.

The governor formed a team consisting of government officials, military officers, village heads, LBH representatives, and leaders from Benakat villages to conduct an investigation of MHP activities in Rimbo Sekampung. The team recommended that the contested land be put in status quo.[25] In 1995 MHP returned 2,000 hectares of undisturbed forest and 1,000 hectares of cleared land to villagers from Marga Benakat. In 1996 the government replaced the two village heads who had supported the protests. This action, coupled with reimposed restrictions on the press, effectively suppressed campaigns to reclaim land waged by farmers in other villages until the fall of Suharto.

People of Desa Pelawe versus MHP

Pelawe is a very old village on the Musi River with several thousand inhabitants. Four *kampung* (settlements) cling to one side of the Musi, and a fifth, located on the other side, is accessible by a footbridge. In Pelawe there are no telephones and no electricity except for what is supplied by a few privately owned gasoline generators. Once people traveled by bamboo raft downstream to Palembang in two or three days. Today the journey can be made in less than a day by motorboat, though nobody in Pelawe owns one. Instead people travel by motorcycle or *oplet* (a taxi-van) over a dirt road (that is almost impassable during the rainy season) to the main road, where they can get a bus to Palembang; altogether the trip takes a full day. Yet Pelawe is only a short distance from the Pertamina installation in Pendopo, only a few hours from Palembang. The government has not maintained the road from Pelawe to Pendopo or extended electricity from there to the village.

In 1991 MHP and PT Kurnia Musi Plywood Industry were granted concessions in the forest around Pelawe.[26] When MHP brought in heavy equipment to clear-cut the forest and prepare land for an acacia plantation, villagers mobilized to stop the harvest of timber and to preserve their rubber trees. The village headman was told that the land was now owned by Tutut, Suharto's daughter. To quash opposition to MHP, the district military command established a camp next to Pelawe. Everyday the troops "exercised" by running through the village. On one occasion, a soldier shot at a villager known to be a leader of protests against MHP.[27]

In 1994, after the people of Marga Benakat were successful in reclaiming Rimbo Sekampung, people in Pelawe made another attempt to reclaim their land. Their protests led the *bupati* of Musi Rawas to issue guidelines for concessionaires: (1) land to be clear-cut by a company must be inspected for plantings by local officials and notice given to local residents; (2) companies must pay compensation for plantings destroyed in an amount to be negotiated with owners of the crops; (3) compensation must be paid directly to the owners and witnessed by the village head and the *camat;* (4) companies must pay a fee to village government for trees harvested on unplanted land; (5) companies must clear *alang-alang* grass (a fire hazard), which takes over when the forest is clear-cut.

In December 1995 Pelawe farmers demonstrated because MHP and PT Kurnia Musi Plywood Industry failed to follow the guidelines set forth by the *bupati.* After agreeing to meet with the protestors, company representatives did not show up at the time and place arranged, so men from Pelawe seized vehicles belonging to MHP and took several employees hostage. Soldiers stationed in the village took no action, claiming that they were outnumbered by the villagers. This brought the *bupati* to Pelawe. He promised to take action against the companies for violating his directives. The police summoned men from Pelawe to be questioned about the "theft" of MHP vehicles, and Governor Ramli Hassan Basri announced that land concessions to corporations would not be revoked. In protest, university students in Palembang organized a demonstration in support of farmers in Pelawe, but after the July 27, 1996, attack on supporters of Megawati in Jakarta, a government crackdown on all protests brought the campaign in Pelawe to an end.

Satellite photos identify Pelawe as one of the hot spots in the 1997 wild-fires. Villagers say that fires set by MHP got out of control and burned down hundreds of hectares of their rubber trees. One family lost eleven hectares of rubber trees in the fires, and their son, Saparuddin, had to give up his university studies in Bandung and return home. He convinced people in Pelawe to seek help at LBH in Palembang.

As the *reformasi* movement emerged in February 1998, six hundred people from Pelawe organized a sit-in at MHP headquarters. The *bupati* came to Pelawe to arrange for negotiations with MHP, and he agreed to establish a team to determine how much village land had been taken over by MHP in 1991. The Pelawe farmers asked for and were given assurances that security forces would not be sent back into the village. The team set up by the *bupati* reported that 1,154.8 hectares of cultivated land had been taken over by MHP, but Governor Ramli Hassan Basri again rejected the possibility that any land concessions in South Sumatra could be revoked.

After the resignation of Suharto in May 1998, six thousand people participated in a demonstration organized by LBH in Palembang in September to demand that land taken over for industrial forestry and oil palm plantations be returned to farmers. The newly appointed Governor Rosihan Arsyad met with farmers and LBH and WALHI staff to discuss the demands of farmers. He promised to resolve land conflicts in the province within three months. In each district a team composed of provincial and district officials, LBH and WALHI staff, and representatives of farmers' organizations was organized to collect information to be forwarded to the Ministry of Forestry and Plantations in Jakarta.

Saparuddin represented the farmers of Pelawe. He spent three months of 1999 in Jakarta trying to present documentation of Pelawe land claims— as recorded on a map made in the 1930s by the Dutch colonial government—to the appropriate Ministry of Forestry officials. He and other village leaders from South Sumatra were referred from one person to another at the ministry. Finally, in desperation, Saparuddin accosted the minister of forestry as he was getting out of his car in a parking lot. His persistence paid off. Just three days before a new minister of forestry was installed, a decision on land conflicts was finally issued: (1) land would be returned to villagers who could provide proof of ownership; (2) the governor of South Sumatra must provide an equivalent amount of land in another location to companies with concessions; (3) land returned to villagers would be owned by the Ministry of Forestry but communally managed by villagers. Unfortunately, Indonesia's new president, B. J. Habibie, signed a new Forestry Act (No. 4/1999), replacing the 1967 Basic Forestry Law. The law described people who live in and depend on the forest as "communities with customary laws" and stated that customary land is included in state forests and can be granted as a concession to private or state-owned companies.

In February 2000, LBH-Palembang arranged for representatives of the KSKP to go to Jakarta to pressure the new administration of President Abdurrahman Wahid to recognize farmers' land rights. However, the president was engaged in a battle for civilian control of the military and was not prepared to take on the issue of land reform.

In July 2000, I went to Pelawe with Abdul Situmorang. The conflict with MHP was still ongoing. Farmers gathered in the house of Saparuddin's father to talk with us. They said that the new village head had been approached by PT London Sumatera (Lonsum), which wanted to open an oil palm plantation in the area. The village head proposed that land returned to Pelawe by MHP be included in a concession to PT Lonsum. As the village head did not own land in Pelawe, the farmers objected that he should not be in a position to decide what happened to the land. They knew, however, that the headman would be rewarded by PT Lonsum for obtaining permission to establish the plantation, and Pelawe was divided between his supporters who had been promised employment by PT Lonsum and farmers who wanted to fight for individual legal title to their land.

The farmers asked: "Where can we go for help? We've been to everyone. It's hopeless!" Before the 1999 election, candidates from Partai Demokrasi Indonesia (PDI) had come to the village and promised to help them in their struggle for land rights, but once elected the politicians forgot their promise. None of the major political parties has since taken up the issue of land conflicts.

People of Rambang Lubai versus MHP

On February 16, 2000, more than three thousand people from eleven villages in the subdistricts of Rambang Lubai and Rambang Danku went to the governor's office in Palembang to demand the return of their land. They erected tents and declared they would stay until their demands were met.[28] This was the high point of the campaign for smallholders' land rights.

The campaign was not led by LBH and WALHI but by Junial Komar, a native son of South Sumatra who lived in Jakarta, where he had developed ties to Vice President B. J. Habibie, who became president in May 1998. In an interview in July 2000, Junial Komar said that as soon as he heard the announcement of Suharto's resignation, he called Rambang Lubai and urged villagers to start collecting information to support their land claims because "big changes were coming." He recalled, "In 1994 when farmers in Rambang Lubai first organized to reclaim land, people were still frightened of confrontation with authorities. In Rambang Lubai one villager was shot by soldiers guarding MHP's operations. But after the fall of Suharto, things were different." [29]

Junial Komar then returned to South Sumatra and became a candidate of the conservative Islamic Crescent Moon and Star Party (PBB) in the district of Muara Enim for the National Legislature in the 1999 election. He appealed to voters by mounting a campaign for land rights. LBH decided to stay aloof from Junial Komar's campaign, because they were suspicious that he was using the issue of land rights to further his own political ambitions.

Junial Komar did not win election to the national legislature, but he decided he would "lead a movement in accord with the people's aspirations." MHP had begun an intensive program of clear-cutting in an area claimed by nine villages in Rambang Lubai. Villagers demanded that MHP return 26,600 hectares and pay compensation for trees cut down on *marga* land. On July 24, 1999, Junial Komar accompanied representatives of the nine villages to the MHP base camp in Suban Jeriji. A MHP spokesman denied that the company had "taken one meter of land or one tree from the people."

A demonstration of Rambang Lubai villagers in the Muara Enim district capital on September 11, 1999, was the largest demonstration ever seen in the district. It was followed by a demonstration on October 7, 1999, in Palembang at the governor's office.[30] The *bupati* of Muara Enim said that he would help Junial Komar so long as villagers did not resort to violence. He appointed a team to investigate the villagers' claims. Junial Komar also went to the National Human Rights Commission, the Provincial Legislature, and the Ministry of Forestry and Plantations.

After the fall of Suharto, his crony Prayogo Pangestu, the owner of the Barito Group, became vulnerable to prosecution for corruption and violation of the law. As long as B. J. Habibie was president, Prayogo managed to avoid prosecution. Rumors circulated that he had bribed Attorney General Andi Ghalib. In October 1999, the National Legislature rejected President Habibie's accountability report and elected Abdurrahman Wahid as the new president.

The director of MHP then agreed to meet with Junial Komar, the *bupati* of Muara Enim, and representatives from the governor's office. An agreement was reached that MHP would not harvest more trees in Rambang

Lubai until the issue of land rights was resolved. Moreover, MHP agreed to return the disputed land and pay compensation for trees cut down if farmers could prove to local officials that they were the legal owners of the land. Three days later this agreement was revoked by MHP on the ground that the land was owned by the state so it could not be returned to villagers.

Governor Rosihan then threatened to put the disputed land in status quo. MHP began organizing counterdemonstrations; 2,500 "workers" protested in Muara Enim on the ground that they would lose their jobs if the contested land were put in status quo. According to Junial Komar, most of the protestors had been hired by MHP, because the number of demonstrating "workers" far exceeded the number of MHP employees. He arranged for an even larger demonstration outside the office of the governor in Palembang.

MHP next proposed a system of dual usage, whereby villagers would cultivate crops in newly planted forest stands, and suggested that a religious leader be chosen as a mediator to work out this arrangement. Junial Komar rejected this idea. The governor then announced that he would set up a team to investigate the land claims of Rambang Lubai. At the end of December, the team issued its report; only 600 hectares of land were declared to be the legal property of Rambang Lubai farmers. Junial Komar objected: this finding was ludicrous because over 5,000 families were involved. On the other hand, he admitted that the figure of 26,000 hectares claimed by villagers included the land of Rambang Dangku, because until the administrative reforms of 1983, Rambang Dangku and Rambang Lubai had been a single *marga*. Rambang Lubai reduced its claim to 12,000 hectares.

On February 16, 2000, more than three thousand people from Rambang Lubai went to Palembang and declared that they would camp out in front of the governor's office until their claims were recognized. Governor Rosihan Arsyad returned from Jakarta the next day to meet with the protestors. That same day the minister of forestry, Nur Mahmudi Isma'il, announced that the attorney general's office was investigating the alleged misuse of reforestation funds by five major figures linked to former president Suharto.[31] The list of those accused included Prayogo Pangestu; Suharto's daughter, Siti Hardiyanti Rukmana (Tutut); and Suharto's half-brother, Probosutedjo. Suripto, the secretary-general of the Ministry of Forestry, accused MHP, Prayogo Pangestu, and Siti Hardijanti Rukmana of manipulating documents regarding the size of MHP's concession in South Sumatra to obtain reforestation loans of US$35 million and of having misused the loans. Suripto said that Prayogo Pangestu had cheated the government of US$13 billion in repayment of reforestation fund levies.[32]

Governor Rosihan asked Junial Komar to send the villagers of Rambang

Lubai back home because he feared an outbreak of violence. Junial Komar refused to do this, so the governor ordered four tanks and security forces to stand by. He also arranged for a kitchen to be organized to feed the villagers camped in front of his office while he tried to set up a meeting with the director of MHP. This meeting did not take place, because the director of MHP failed to show up, but the villagers from Rambang Lubai agreed to return home when the governor promised to go to the Minister of Forestry for help in settling the dispute.[33]

On February 19, 2000, the national newspaper *Republika* published an accusation made by MHP lawyers that Junial Komar was trying to blackmail the company by demanding US$30,000 as a negotiator. Junial Komar admitted having requested that MHP pay the cost of his trips to Jakarta for meetings, but maintained that he had not received any other monies. He issued counteraccusations that MHP had tried to bribe him to drop the campaign. The director of LBH-Palembang issued a statement suggesting that MHP was attacking Junial Komar in order to shift the focus of public attention away from the land conflict. Nevertheless, MHP lawyers had successfully undermined Junial Komar's reputation as an honest broker.

On February 24, 2000, Governor Rosihan declared the disputed land in Rambang Lubai and Rambang Dangku in status quo. However, MHP continued to harvest trees on the ground that the provincial government did not have authority over forestry concessions. On February 29, 2000, angry villagers attacked the MHP base camp and took three MHP vehicles hostage. MHP was forced to evacuate its employees.[34] Six weeks later, Suripto, the secretary-general of the Ministry of Forestry, announced that he would go to Rambang Lubai to settle the conflict. A crowd of more than five thousand suspicious villagers, many carrying machetes, greeted the helicopter that brought Suripto. They told reporters that they would take Suripto hostage if they were not satisfied with his decision. But Suripto emerged from the meeting to declare, "Up until now, corporations have been facilitated in obtaining land; now it is time to give compensation."[35] Compensation would be determined by the provincial government, and 12,050 hectares of land would be returned to villagers in Rambang Lubai.

Unfortunately, the story of Rambang Lubai does not end on a happy note. After months of waiting for MHP to pay compensation and return land, the people of Rambang Lubai learned that the entire tract of 12,000 hectares was to be legally transferred to the government of South Sumatra to be used "for the interest of the local community." They were forced to accept a version of an *inti/plasma* scheme called Community Forest Management. In theory this transformed villagers into stakeholders in MHP, which would contract with them to plant, clear, and weed the plantation forest and to guard trees from fire. The village council would be paid 7 percent of the value of the harvest and a small fee for management of the forest. But this payment would be forfeited if there were any damage to the forest or MHP property due to conflicts.[36]

In the end, many farmers in Rambang Lubai claim that MHP simply paid villagers to add their signatures to the Community Forestry Management agreement. The share of profits paid to villagers for harvest of the forest has amounted to no more than a few dollars per family. No one received compensation for trees harvested on the land taken over by MHP; the money was paid to a foundation established to improve the welfare of villagers, which was headed by Junial Komar. He used the money to build a modern *pesantren* (Islamic religious school) near Rambang Lubai. Villagers say that Junial Komar grew rich from their struggle.

Land Rights for the Poor or Corporate Development?

In an interview in August 2000, Governor Rosihan Arsyad acknowledged that under the New Order there had been collusion between local government officials and corporations wanting land concessions: "Yes, money talks."[37] In 2002 the National Land Agency in South Sumatra distributed 19,095 certificates for small plots of land to poor people. At the ceremony presenting these certificates, Governor Rosihan acknowledged that up to that time government policies on the management of agrarian resources had resulted in a decline in the quality of the environment, a structural imbalance in power relations between users and owners, and land conflict. He urged that in the future natural resources be developed with a concern for both the environment and justice.[38]

In March 2001, the secretary-general of the Ministry of Forestry, Suripto, pressed the attorney general to prosecute Prayogo Pangestu for twelve violations of the law, including tax fraud and corruption in the use of government reforestation funds.[39] But Prayogo escaped prosecution because President Abdurrahman Wahid decided that the businesses of New Order oligarchs were essential to the economy.[40] Under threat of impeachment, the president chose instead to fire the minister of forestry because he had refused to fire Suripto. In May 2001, it was Suripto who was summoned by the police for questioning on the charge of selling state secrets.

In June 2001, Baharuddin Lopa, a new attorney general known for his incorruptibility, made another attempt to prosecute Prayogo Pangestu.

He summoned Prayogo from Singapore where he had fled.[41] But Prayogo escaped prosecution again, because a month later Baharuddin Lopa died unexpectedly in Egypt.

The Indonesian Bank Restructuring Agency (IBRA) declared that the cumulative debts of seventeen Barito Pacific Group companies totaled over US$1.25 billion, making Prayogo Pangestu the second largest debtor in Indonesia. Prayogo was able to make a deal during debt-restructuring negotiations pledging twenty debt-ridden companies to the IBRA in exchange for allowing him to retain control of the Barito Pacific Group. When the PT TEL paper and pulp factory owned by Barito Pacific Group went on line in 2000, the company was the recipient of windfall profits, because most of its costs were calculated in the devalued Indonesia rupiah while its sales were reckoned in US dollars.[42] Prayogo Pangestu, his partners, and foreign investors got the profit while the defaults of Prayogo and the companies in his corporate empire became public debt. In 2003, Ross McLeod, editor of the *Bulletin of Indonesian Economic Studies,* delivered a "postmortem" on the IMF recovery program in Indonesia. He stated that IBRA had failed to retrieve anything like the full value of assets put under its control. This meant that the debt recovery program had resulted in an enormous distribution of wealth away from the general public into the hands of the Suharto family and several conglomerates.[43] The Indonesian people were left to repay Prayogo's foreign debts. In July 2004, the government of Megawati Sukarnoputri granted Prayogo Pangestu a release and discharge decree certifying that he had repaid all his debts and was free from prosecution. Prayogo lives in Singapore, which ensures his safety should there be another effort to prosecute the oligarchs who had remained above the law under the New Order.

Despite the fact that corporate development projects caused conflicts over land and reduced indigenous farmers to poverty, the World Bank and affiliated financial institutions, along with the Indonesian government, have continued to promote such projects since the fall of the New Order. In the next chapter we will see how industrial forestry also destroyed the forests of South Sumatra, thus threatening the future livelihood of all residents.

Chapter 4

No Forests, No Future

No longer do we enjoy life
There is no bright hope for tomorrow
Attacked by garbage, polluted air above
Our land is full of haunted villages.
                    December 1995

Society has begun to feel skeptical
Security forces still wield an iron fist
People's lives are difficult, searching for a mouthful of rice
Because sprouting crops are attacked by pollution.
                    July 2000

    —Tamin Neklikesabe from Muara Niru[1]

INDONESIA HAS THE THIRD most extensive area of tropical forest on earth and is one of the richest centers of biodiversity. In the fifteen years between 1983 and 1998, however, over one-third of Indonesia's forests were handed over to commercial logging companies, and another third were designated for conversion to plantations. In 2001 the World Bank predicted that the forests of South Sumatra would disappear by 2005.[2] This prediction is being realized. According to the South Sumatra Forestry Office, only 3.3 million out of 11.3 million hectares of forest remained in the province in 2001; two million hectares of the remaining forest were degraded.[3] In 2003, WALHI and the Foundation for Environmental Advocacy (YALHI) launched a campaign in South Sumatra with the slogan "No Forests, No Future."[4]

In South Sumatra and elsewhere in Indonesia the development of vast oil palm plantations and industrial forestry for paper and pulp production have irretrievably damaged the forests.[5] Rivers are silting up, fish are disappearing, and landslides and flooding are becoming an annual occurrence. Industrial and mining pollution further endangers the health and well-being of people. In June 2003, the World Bank released a report entitled "Indonesia Environment Monitor" that described illegal and untreated disposal of 90 percent of solid and hazardous waste, uncontrolled urbanization, widespread forest fires, contamination of urban water sources, and air pollution. The authors of the report warned that one in three children—30 million people—faced health problems from pollution. Yet they expressed little hope for change. Former environment minister Sonny Keraf said, "The economy is always prioritized and social problems are sidelined." [6]

Indonesia has laws to protect the environment, but these laws and policies that support good resource management are rarely enforced. Government officials say that they cannot impose sanctions on companies that violate environmental laws because these companies bring in foreign capital that is needed by the government to repay loans to foreign banks and international financial institutions. These companies are also important employers, so prosecuting or sanctioning them would hurt their employees. In the view of government officials, these are convincing reasons for not enforcing environmental legislation. However, the logic does not hold. The "development loans" that must be repaid are for establishing unsustainable industries that exploit the natural resources of Indonesia. The profits end up enriching a small number of oligarchs and foreign investors at the expense of the land and people whose livelihood is destroyed in the process. WALHI studies have found that forests have twenty-three times more economic value if managed by local communities. [7]

In this chapter I present three case studies that illustrate the complicated politics of environmentalism in Indonesia. I describe how NGO activists worked with villagers who suffered the effects of pollution from paper and pulp production and from gold mining. I show why it is so difficult to sanction companies that violate environmental regulations by considering protests against a state-owned fertilizer factory that is responsible for air and water pollution in Palembang. In all these cases environmental issues are only part of the story; the struggle for a safe environment is also a struggle against corruption and for policies that support a sustainable living for poor people.

PT Tanjung Enim Lestari Paper and Pulp Production (PT TEL)

The major road leading out of Palembang connects to the trans-Sumatra highway linking Aceh in the north to Lampung in the south. It is heavily trafficked by trucks hauling wood, oil palm fruit, rice, coffee, and other goods. In the tropics, where overloaded trucks thunder over asphalt melting in the sun, and monsoon rains hammer down on the uneven surfaces, roads deteriorate quickly. Speeding vehicles and poor road conditions make any trip a life-endangering adventure. In July 2000, I set out with caution and anticipation, accompanied by Abdul Situmorang, to see the paper and pulp factory opened that year by PT Tanjung Enim Lestari (PT TEL), a subsidiary of the Barito Pacific Group of Prayogo Pangestu.

In Muara Enim, the capital of the district where the PT TEL factory is located, we suddenly encountered newly paved streets, evidence of the close relationship between the local government and directors of PT TEL. The factory is easily seen from the road since the land around it has been clear-cut and leveled. Against the expanse of packed red earth, the white walls surrounding PT TEL's operations suggest a fortified outpost carved from the jungle. Security guards posted at the gate allowed us to enter after checking with authorities inside. The suspicious attitude of PT TEL staff was understandable, as the company had a long history of confrontation with local farmers and WALHI and LBH activists.

Protests began in 1996, shortly after PT TEL was given a concession of 1,600 hectares of land to build one of the largest pulp and paper factories in Southeast Asia. The concession included protected forest and the land of five villages. Villagers earned a comfortable living tapping their rubber trees, cultivating fruit trees, growing vegetables, fishing, and trading. They could not believe that their land and livelihood would be taken from them. They wrote letters to district and provincial authorities, and they sought help from LBH. Nur Kholis, director of WALHI at the time, objected that the presidential decree regulating the acquisition of land for the public good should not apply to expropriation of land for a private corporation. He pointed out that the amount of compensation offered to villagers did not reflect the true value of their land and rubber trees, nor was it enough to allow them to buy land elsewhere. Despite the protests, the PT TEL project went forward.[8]

After the fall of Suharto in May 1998, the national leadership of WALHI called upon the new president, B. J. Habibie, to reform management of natural resources and enforce environmental laws. In particular, they called for the cancellation of land concessions made to members of Suharto's family and his close associates, including PT TEL. Protests against PT TEL began to focus on the *bupati* of Muara Enim, Hasan Zen, South Sumatra's governor, Ramli Hasan Basri, and local government officials, who appeared to be major beneficiaries of the process through which land was transferred from villagers to PT TEL. One issue was payments from PT TEL to the *bupati* and governor for their approval of the concession; a second was the discrepancy between what PT TEL claimed to have paid in compensation for crops on concession land and what farmers actually received.[9] LBH decided to test the spirit of reform in the post-Suharto era. They went to the police and charged the governor and *bupati* with corruption.

In October 1998, labor protests against PT TEL erupted. Local men employed as construction workers on the factory demanded an increase in wages. These men, many from the roughly one thousand families that had lost their land, understood that when the factory was completed the following year there would be no more work. In January 1999, villagers organized a demonstration, surrounding the construction site to prevent contractors from proceeding with work. In February 1999, LBH and WALHI activists helped the villagers mount a peaceful demonstration pressing PT TEL to deal with the problem of people in the local community who no longer had a sustainable livelihood.[10] In April the villagers sent a delegation to the governor's office demanding fair compensation for their land.

The PT TEL factory was expected to employ one thousand Indonesians and sixty expatriates. Only two hundred local workers would be employed, as most of the Indonesians would be people from other areas with experience in paper and pulp factories. In April 1999 graduates of universities in Palembang mounted a protest, arguing that PT TEL should hire local people rather than recruit outsiders. The *bupati* of Muara Enim also urged PT TEL to hire more local people. LBH and WALHI urged PT TEL to deal with the issues of compensation and corruption; the NGO activists worried that competition for the few jobs available would divide villagers and the problem of the greater majority who had lost their livelihood would be forgotten.

Government officials took no action, so on May 3–4, 1999, farmers blockaded the entrance to the PT TEL factory with barbed wire and vowed to stay until their demands were met. Contractors were forced to shut down the construction site. Military units were sent to the factory. When the protestors refused to abandon the blockade, the soldiers used high-pressure hoses to disperse them. Older villagers told reporters that the soldiers had behaved like Dutch and Japanese colonial troops. Suharyono, director of LBH-Palembang, pointed out that the villagers' demonstration had been peaceful. Nur Kholis, director of WALHI, warned that attacks on peaceful protestors would ignite the anger of villagers.

Two weeks later, the new governor of South Sumatra, Rosihan Arsyad, announced that he would act to resolve claims for compensation as quickly as possible. He was not able to resolve the problem of PT TEL, however, because President B. J. Habibie could not afford to acknowledge challenges to land concessions made to corporations, which would alienate powerful oligarchs. His government was in desperate need of income from export crops to repay a rescue loan of US$43 billion dollars from the IMF and other donors.

In November 1999, the High Court in South Sumatra cleared (former) *bupati* Hasan Zen, (former) governor Ramli Hasan Basri, and Cendana (referring to the family of Suharto) of corruption in the acquisition of land by PT TEL on grounds of insufficient evidence. Only two lower officials in the *bupati*'s office were convicted and sentenced to jail. This verdict ignited protests. Saying that the police had made no effort to collect evidence, villagers took the compensation contracts they had signed with PT TEL and sworn affidavits stating that they had not received the amounts promised to the attorney general in Palembang and sent a delegation to the attorney general in Jakarta. Despite their efforts, the case against Hasan Zen and Ramli Hasan Basri was closed.

At the same time that villagers and activists were protesting corruption by government officials in the granting of the PT TEL concession and the failure to pay villagers fair compensation for their land, environmental issues were raised. Only after construction on the paper and pulp factory had already begun did PT TEL release its Environmental Impact Assessment (EIA). In 1997, Down to Earth, an environmental NGO based in the United Kingdom, produced a report entitled "Pulping the People: Barito Pacific's Paper Pulp Factory and Plantations in South Sumatra (PT Tanjung Enim Lestari & PT Musi Hutan Persada)," pointing out that the EIA provided little information about treatment of waste that would be discharged into the Lematang River, although over a hundred thousand people in thirty-two villages downstream from the factory depended on the river for bathing, fishing, and other water needs. The report noted that there would also be serious air pollution from nitrogen oxides, sulfur dioxide, and hydrogen sulfide, foul-smelling gases that would cause acid rain and damage to crops and property. In addition, the factory would produce vast amounts of solid waste containing toxic materials that threatened drinking water from nearby wells; Down to Earth emphasized the necessity of constructing a landfill site to prevent or minimize the possibility of contamination.[11]

Down to Earth contacted environmental organizations in Japan and Europe where banks and companies involved in the PT TEL project were based, building an alliance of local, national, and international NGOs to fight the project. Friends of the Earth in Scotland exerted pressure on the Bank of Scotland, a leading member of the financial syndicate funding PT TEL. NorWatch targeted Norwegian, Swedish, and Finnish companies and banks. Japanese NGOs urged Marubeni Corporation and Nippon Paper Industries and directors of the Japanese Overseas Economic Cooperation Fund to withdraw from the project. Farmers from Muara Enim were brought to Japan to speak in person about the effects of the PT TEL project on their lives. In March 1999, Down to Earth and NorWatch sent observers to assess the problems at PT TEL.[12] Foreign contractors began to take note of the conflicts surrounding the project. Two companies sold subsidiaries that were contractors in the PT TEL project. NorWatch lamented that this would not solve the problems at PT TEL, as there was little likelihood that new owners would be any more concerned with the environmental and social costs of the project. The NGOs did not succeed in persuading any investors to withdraw.

Based on information from Down to Earth, WALHI released a warning that chlorine waste dumped into the Lematang River would result in serious long-term health problems, including hormonal abnormalities, reproductive problems, and birth and developmental defects.[13] WALHI challenged company managers to take their drinking water supply from below the effluent output if they believed their own environmental impact statement. Residents living downstream from PT TEL joined farmers who had lost their land in protests against the company. This campaign persuaded PT TEL to replace the chlorine processing technology with a more environmentally sound process, demonstrating that local and international NGOs working together can sometimes achieve limited victories.

Lampung Post reporter Taufiq Wijaya kept the PT TEL project in the public eye with a series of articles that exposed ongoing problems with the project: "PT Tanjung Enim Lestari Factory Only Benefits Investors," "Siti Hardiyanti's Paper Factory Disperses Chlorine and the Label of Communist," "PT TEL Demo Broken up by Security Forces," "Alcohol and Prostitution Flare up at PT TEL." The police threatened to arrest him if he did not stop writing about PT TEL.[14]

Public awareness of the environmental problems associated with pulp and paper production and the development of tree plantations gradually increased. The economics faculty at Sriwijaya University organized a workshop on "The Impact of Chlorine on People and the Environment." The agriculture faculty organized a symposium on "The Ecosystem of the Musi River Watershed." A WALHI newsletter pointed out that the conversion of natural forest to tree and oil palm plantations led to erosion causing five million cubic tons of mud per year to be dumped into the Musi River. Dredging operations could remove only some two million tons. Navigation upriver to Palembang would soon present problems for ocean-going vessels. The Musi could no longer effectively transport waste dumped into the river, with the result that pollution of the water supply in villages was increasing. Loss of the forest cover and siltation of rivers would also increase flooding.

At the end of 1999, six lowland villages were flooded, proving that fears about the consequences of clearing forests for plantations were justified.

PT TEL started production trials at the Muara Enim factory in December 1999. Shortly thereafter, villagers began complaining about a foul smell that came from the factory and fish kills in the Lematang River. On December 15, 1999, eight hundred people went to the factory and asked to meet with the management. No one would come out to listen, so the angry crowd threw stones at the factory, set fire to logs piled on the site, and vandalized trucks and other equipment. Military security forces were called in.[15]

To quell further unrest, Governor Rosihan Arsyad pressured PT TEL to give local people a stake in the enterprise. PT TEL finally agreed to recruit two hundred and fifty local residents for their security force, to build a local market, fund a cooperative, and pay school fees for two hundred children from villages whose land had been included in their concession. However, company managers refused to discuss complaints about fish kills or the odor from the factory.

The promise to hire local youth as security guards for PT TEL created new problems. In addition to pitting people from one village against those from another, the hiring of local youths overturned the traditional social structure of villages. The young security guards were paid a good salary by village standards, while farmers and heads of families had lost their land and livelihood. This inversion in power and wealth contributed to the erosion of respect for elders and led to outbreaks of violence and disorder. Youths employed as security guards frequently acted with impunity toward people who opposed PT TEL.

At the end of February 2000, representatives of the Indonesian Center for Environmental Law, the National Environmental Agency, and Ben Boer, a professor of environmental studies from Sydney University in Australia, went to South Sumatra to investigate the environmental impact of the PT TEL factory. Villagers who lived near the factory gathered to express their complaints. They told the environmentalists that their rubber trees had been clear-cut and the land planted in acacia to supply the paper and pulp mill; this was a violation of the law stating that only nonproductive land should be included in a forestry concession. They complained that the smell from the factory sometimes made people ill and that fish from the river had a bad odor and rotted quickly, significantly reducing their value in the marketplace because people were afraid to eat anything from the Lematang River.

Men who earned their living as fishermen soon found that they could no longer support their families. Nur Kholis, the new director of LBH-Palembang, and Abdul Situmorang, who had been elected director of WALHI, helped them to form the Communication Union of Fishermen (IKAN). On Earth Day they launched a media campaign to pressure PT TEL to stop polluting the Lematang River. PT TEL agreed to meet with members of IKAN, but LBH and WALHI representatives and activists from two other local environmental NGOs were barred from the meeting—a tactic often used when a company wanted to buy off protestors. While the representatives of PT TEL listened, no concrete actions were forthcoming.

In May 2000, a week-long workshop organized by Bioforum on "NGO Strategy on Export Credit Agencies" was held using the PT TEL project as a case study. Participants in the forum criticized the PT TEL project on financial grounds, citing the instability of the paper and pulp market; on moral grounds because of the use of military units to intimidate farmers protesting the loss of their land; on environmental grounds due to destruction of natural forests and serious water and air pollution; and on political grounds because the PT TEL project benefited foreign investors and Suharto cronies, not the people of Indonesia.

When I arrived at the PT TEL factory with Abdul Situmorang two months later, Arnold Bakara, technical manager at the factory, challenged me to prove that I was a professor and not a spy from Greenpeace. In the end, he agreed to talk with me, although he would not discuss or show me waste treatment facilities at the factory.[16] He asserted that the PT TEL factory was a development project of great benefit to the Indonesian nation. "Formerly there was only unproductive land here, now there is a factory with jobs." He appeared to be completely unaware that protesting villagers had lost their sustainable way of life. When challenged, he admitted that PT TEL could not supply enough jobs for people living around the factory, but in his view protests were due to unrealistic demands on the part of local residents. He complained, "Now everybody wants something and is ready to demonstrate to get it."[17] In his view, the government had to take a strong stand to protect factories, so that foreign investors would feel secure.

Abdul Situmorang took me to a fishing village on the Niru River downstream from the PT TEL factory where we talked with fishermen from IKAN. The men crowded into the small room that was the home of Tamin Neklikesabe, who composed the traditional verses *(pantun)* introducing this chapter. They complained that PT TEL sometimes dumped untreated waste into the river at night and that foul-smelling air was released by the factory. People could no longer use river water for bathing, and the fish catch had radically declined in number and quality. They also said that when PT TEL had met with IKAN, company officials offered to pay for a well in the village, but the fishermen rejected the proposal, worried that if they accepted, PT TEL would consider the problem solved.

Five months after my visit, IKAN was still appealing to the governor of South Sumatra to take action. But pleas expressing concern about the environment and the effects of pollution on people could not compete with the power and influence of foreign investors and well-connected business moguls. In response to ongoing unrest at the PT TEL factory, the Japanese ambassador came to South Sumatra to meet with the governor and obtain assurances that PT TEL's operations would be protected. Governor Rosihan Arsyad gave him what he wanted.

The development of paper and pulp production as an export industry has been a major factor in the disappearance of Indonesia's forests. Because all types of wood can be used for paper and pulp production, clear-cutting becomes cost effective in the short term. Industrial timber plantations and natural forest concessions do not produce enough fiber to supply the paper and pulp mills, so producers also resort to illegal logging in protected forests. Down to Earth estimates as much as 70 percent of the wood used for paper and pulp production comes from illegal logging.

The destruction of forests has led to serious erosion, causing flooding and siltation of the rivers and a major decrease in the fish that people depend on for food. Degradation of remaining forests causes landslides. Pollution of rivers with waste materials from paper and pulp production and deterioration in air quality have caused health problems of all kinds, particularly skin and respiratory diseases. Yet, the negative impact of pulp and paper production on the environment is still discounted by the government. In 2004, Nabiel Makarim, the minister of the environment, recognized PT TEL as one of eight companies given a green label (one down from the top gold label, which was not awarded) for its environment management policies. The assessment was made on the basis of a questionnaire that the company filled out and "spot checks" by officials.

PT Barisan Tropical Mining (BTM)

To reach the Rawas gold mine from Palembang, Abdul Situmorang, Jamila, and I traveled by car for six hours to Lubuk Lingau and then another hour up into the Barisan Range to Muara Tiku, where the Tiku River joins the Rupit River, a tributary of the Musi. There we rented a small flat-bottomed taxi boat that took us up the Tiku for another hour and a half.[18]

Rawas Mine is operated by PT Barisan Tropical Mining (BTM), a subsidiary of the Australia-based Laverton Gold NL.[19] Setiawan Djodi, a business partner of Tommy Suharto, the youngest son of President Suharto, is a director of Laverton Gold NL. In 1986, BTM was awarded a contract of work with a concession covering 117 square kilometers. Development of the mine began in 1996, and it opened in January 1997. The mine has four open pits, each with its own large waste dump. Near the gold extraction plant is a tailings dam and a settling pond. The mine produces 75,000 to 100,000 ounces of gold a year. The cost of production in mid-1998 was US$257 per ounce of gold, not particularly low. However, from mid-1997 until the end of 1998, production from the mine was hedged at US$406 per ounce, which would have made it very profitable. In 1997 a second concession covering 1,620 square kilometers surrounding the original area was obtained. A third concession covering 410 square kilometers was granted in 1998.

People living in the area of the mine settled there starting in the 1950s. They planted rubber, coffee, and durian trees, and they gathered forest products, such as rattan and wild honey, which were sold in local markets. They also panned for gold. The Tiku River provided fish and people grew the vegetables they needed. They had a simple but sustainable livelihood. The Memorandum of Understanding between the government and the mining company stated that people could not be forced to give up their land to the company, but in 1991 local government officials and the military pressured settlers to "sell" their land. They were told that the land was state-owned and they would be imprisoned for obstructing development if they resisted.

Waste washing down from the mining site has caused the Tiku River to become so muddy that villagers can no longer use river water for cooking and can no longer pan for gold. Women in the settlement we visited must now walk two kilometers to a spring higher on the slopes of Mount Tembang to fill ten-gallon containers with clear drinking water. The villagers also complain that, since the mine opened, they get skin rashes and feel itchy when they bathe in the river. They attributed the death of a child in August 1998 to pollution in the river. They say that the little girl itched all over and her body turned blue before she died. A few months later, on December 16, 1998, the waters of the Tiku River turned dark-brown and dead fish floated to the surface. This incident, the fall of Suharto in May 1998, and the awarding of the third concession to BTM led people living in seven villages along the Tiku River to contact WALHI for help.

WALHI staff arranged to monitor the river water quality for two months. They found that after a heavy rainfall the river was contaminated with cyanide. Again *Lampung Post* reporter Taufiq Wijaya was the person who brought the environmental problems of villagers to public attention. The Institute for the Free Flow of Information (ISAI) and many environmental NGOs–Jaringan Advokasi Tambang (JATAM), Project UnderGround, the Indonesian Nature Conservancy, Down to Earth, CNR Solidarity Network,

Oxfam, the antiglobalization organization EarthWins, and the Mineral Policy Institute–posted his articles on their Web sites.[20]

The negative publicity, WALHI press statements, and protests by villagers finally convinced the management of BTM to meet with villagers on February 8, 1999. The exchange between the two sides was sharp. BTM representatives maintained that poisonous waste materials from mining were filtered out in settling ponds before water was released into the Tiku River. Villagers responded that before BTM opened its operations the waters of the Tiku had been clear but now they were muddy. They asked why there was a sign posted in the BTM camp that read (in English) "BTM employees are forbidden to bathe and wash in the Tiku River." Company representatives maintained that the sign was meant to discourage people from using the river as a toilet and for bathing because this was embarrassing to foreigners. BTM accused villagers of using potassium to poison fish and causing the fish kills, citing the finding of Professor Hilda Zulkifli from Sriwijaya University. The villagers responded that the cost of potassium was too high to make it practical to use as a fish poison. The BTM representative argued that people in the eight villages downstream from the mine had much to gain from the company because BTM was responsible for development in these villages. Villagers asked why they were only learning this after the mine had been in operation for two years.

In the end, little was achieved. The villagers made four demands: (1) BTM must restore the Tiku River to its condition before mining started; (2) BTM must take responsibility for medical problems due to water pollution; (3) BTM must stop using explosives that affected villagers' durian trees; and (4) BTM must negotiate with villagers before extending its operations into the new concession. BTM responded that it would be impossible to fulfill the first and third demands. Mining companies had never been required to restore rivers to their pristine condition. The most BTM could do was to drill a bore well in each village. WALHI issued a press release outlining villagers' protests and urged the Ministry of Mines to revoke the new concession.

In May 1999, BTM began surveying and exploring the new concession. In response, Abdul Situmorang and WALHI activists helped the villagers form the Alliance of Mining Victims. The villagers began to document their complaints. In addition to the discharge of poisonous wastes into the Tiku River, they argued that blasting made their durian trees drop their fruit prematurely, and dust churned up by trucks and lights turned on at night scared away wild bees that provided honey. WALHI pointed out that over fifteen thousand people living in the region of the mine were affected by its operations. In July 1999 forty villagers went to protest at the office of the *bupati* of Musi Rawas District. The *bupati* defended BTM's environmental record. In February 2000, sixty villagers signed a letter to the *bupati* demanding that action be taken about seepage of poisonous materials from mine tailings and requesting that the mine provide jobs to local people. WALHI issued a press statement calling on the Local Environmental Impact Control Agency to take action on pollution of the Tiku River.

In March 2000, BTM began closing down the Rawas mine, which was exhausted, but problems at the mine site continued. In May 2000, another fish kill occurred on the Tiku River. Oxfam Community Aid Abroad in Australia sent Jeff Atkinson, their mining ombudsman, to investigate. He reported:

> During a heavy rainstorm on 6 May, we observed a sudden massive increase in the suspended sediment load in the Lasun River, which flows from the mine-site into the Tiku River. The stream, which had been relatively clear, quickly turned a spectacular yellow-brown. Immediately after the storm, while on the Tiku River in a small boat, we observed that all the streams flowing into the river from the mine side were yellow-brown in color, while those flowing in from the other side were clear. The following day we noted that the Belinau and Pusan Rivers (which also flow into the Tiku River) were also heavily discolored with sediment.

These observations suggest that heavy monsoon rains cause erosion of cleared land at the mining site and breaches in the settlement ponds and tailings dam, which are located on the steep slopes of Tambang Mountain. Jeff Atkinson's confidential interview with a former official of the Ministry of Mines also confirmed villagers' other complaints. The official told him:

> In the case of land compensation, yes, I recall that BTM had a problem with the locals. BTM had badly prepared maps for the compensation of land, crops and buildings. Thus, it is very likely that BTM used the [power of] local authorities to [negotiate] the compensation. At that time this was a common practice. . . . The BTM project has been suffering from a shortage of financing since the beginning. I believe that the site management staff is not too concerned with the local people and with environmental management in general. . . . BTM has been breaking many rules. . . . The Tiku river should not have been polluted by the mine if BTM complied with the AMDAL [environmental management and monitoring plan].[21]

Three weeks later, two officials from the Ministry of Mines visited the Rawas site and assured villagers that there was no pollution!

On my visit to the mine in July 2000, the new director for public relations admitted that in September 1998, while a new tailings dam was being constructed, BTM had discharged mine waste (including cyanide) directly into the river.[22] He claimed that this was no longer being done and took me to see the settling ponds. I was told that BTM was contracting with local villagers to reforest the tailings deposits in compliance with the environmental management plan. Fifteen people were employed each day to stake giant nets that would hold the soil until trees were established. The work was hot, tiring, and poorly paid, yet local people were desperate for any way to earn money. BTM had to rotate the jobs among villages every two weeks to prevent villagers from fighting over the chance to work.

After my visit to the mine, I was contacted by Gavin Lee, the BTM official responsible for "minimizing the impact of the mining operation on the environment and maximizing the benefits to the local community." Lee had been involved in an altercation with a local reporter who claimed to have found more than ten places where the tailings dam was leaking. The reporter had lodged a complaint with the police because Lee had seized his camcorder. Lee accused me of sending the reporter to the Rawas mine. In an exchange of e-mails, he did not deny that there were problems with the tailings dam. Rather, he wrote that he did not believe problems could be solved by using the mass media. He described people who lived near the mine as "very hardheaded" and said that they became "emotional and occasionally resorted to violence as a solution." He called himself a harsh critic of WALHI because he believed the activists incited local people. He particularly objected because Oxfam mining ombudsman Jeff Atkinson had not requested permission from BTM before taking water samples from the Tiku River.

In 1999, Forestry Act No. 41 banning open-pit mining in protected forests was passed by the National Legislature. Environmental activists were hopeful that democratic reforms might lead to more sustainable policies for resource development. At the same time, the owners of BTM had formed a new company, Barisan Sumatra Mining (BSM) and been granted a concession in an area adjacent to the Rawas mine site. Their new concession extended into Kerinci-Sebelat National Park. They lobbied to be exempted from the law banning mining in protected forests. In October 2002, the National Legislature approved a plan reclassifying protected forests as "production forests," which allowed six mining firms to resume open-pit mining operations. BTM/BSM was granted permission to begin mining in Kerinci-Sebelat, the habitat of the Sumatran tiger and other rare species.

In 2004 the Extractive Industries Review (EIR), a report commissioned by the World Bank, was released. The commission that prepared the report was headed by Emil Salim, former minister of the environment for Indonesia. The EIR found that World Bank support for mining projects did not alleviate poverty. The authors of the report called for the World Bank to stop subsidizing oil companies by 2008 and mandate "free, prior, and informed consent" by indigenous people in areas to be mined. Although 82 percent of World Bank–financed oil projects supply consumers in the United States and Europe, the board of directors of the bank rejected the first recommendation on the ground that people in developing countries need energy. The bank modified the second recommendation, changing "consent" to "consultation." [23]

PT Pupuk Sriwijaya (Pusri)

PT Pusri, the biggest fertilizer company in Southeast Asia, opened a factory at the edge of the Musi River just downstream from Palembang in 1963. People living in settlements nearby the Pusri complex of factories say there have been problems with air and water pollution ever since the first factory opened. During the New Order they could do nothing about pollution because protestors would be accused of being communists. At the end of

Life at the edge of the Musi River near the Pusri factory.

1997, as the *reformasi* movement emerged, thirty families were brave enough to protest in a letter addressed to the director of Pusri, the governor of South Sumatra, the mayor of Palembang, and the chairman of the Palembang City Legislature. They asked to be resettled, because the smell of ammonia, the constant sound of factory operations, and water pollution were affecting their health. No action was taken in response to their letter.[24]

After the fall of Suharto, legislation passed establishing a free press made it more difficult for government authorities to ignore complaints from the public. In June 2000, local newspapers reported that people living near the

Open drains in Palembang; garbage is washed into the Musi River by the rain.

Pusri factory downstream from Palembang.

Jamila interviewing residents of the village next to the factory.

Pusri factories had problems breathing and suffered from persistent head-aches and smarting eyes due to ammonia discharged by the factory. Some experienced convulsive vomiting. Local residents also described skin ulcers and rashes and mass fish kills in the Musi River they attributed to pollution from Pusri. One resident told reporters: "It is easy to know when PT Pusri dumps waste in the Musi River. If river fish and shrimp are cheap in the market, there was a fish kill from Pusri waste." In July 2000, the governor of South Sumatra summoned the director of Pusri to discuss the problem of pollution. After this meeting, Pusri announced that they would establish a green belt around their factories to absorb noise and protect people from direct exposure to ammonia. But the company denied that it had violated regulations for liquid waste disposal and blamed pollution of the Musi River on rubber factories that dumped their waste into the river.[25]

On September 29, 2000, twenty-eight people, including three small chil-dren, were hospitalized due to an ammonia leak. This captured the interest of the local press and national media.[26] WALHI and Yayasan IMPALM, another local environmental NGO, demanded that the Environmental Impact Management Agency conduct an environmental audit of Pusri. Resi-dents living near the factories sent letters to Pusri documenting the number of people affected by the leak, asking for compensation for their medical problems and requesting that Pusri resettle them farther from the factory. Pusri representatives dismissed the incident on the grounds that the effects of inhaling ammonia were not fatal and victims had been treated at the Pusri hospital. When the newly empowered provincial legislature called for an investigation of pollution by Pusri, however, the company did agree to resettle some people who lived near the factory.

On October 8, 2000, local newspapers reported that residents again smelled ammonia. Pusri denied that there had been another leak, but a police investigation confirmed the complaints of residents. The next day the governor ordered the Environmental Impact Management Agency to take immediate action.[27] WALHI, LBH, and yet another environmental NGO, Yayasan Advokasi Linkungan Hidup Indonesia (YALHI) charged Pusri with violation of environmental laws and threatened to sue it on behalf of victims of the ammonia leak.[28] Nur Kholis and Abdul Situmorang explained that they knew prosecution of Pusri was not a realistic possibility because judges would be paid off by the company and evidence that it was respon-sible for pollution would be found insufficient. Nevertheless, they hoped the threat of prosecution might lead to reform.

The governor announced that no legal action could be taken until the report of the Environmental Impact Management Agency had been com-pleted, and he urged the agency to act expeditiously. The agency stated that it did not have sufficient manpower for the investigation.[29] Because it did not complete its investigation, the police investigation that had to precede a court case against Pusri could not be carried out. Although local newspapers reported that legal action against Pusri would go forward, disagreement over the standards to be applied to liquid waste discharged into the Musi River led to another impasse. According to Pusri, environmental regulations required the pH of the waste be between five and nine, which meant that waste from Pusri was just within the legal limit. The Commission on the Environment rejected this standard on the ground that people living along the Musi below the factory used river water for bathing.[30] When Pusri finally admitted that it had found an ammonia leak in factory number four and shut down the factory, it still maintained that no environmental laws had been violated.

Residents of Tiga Ilir, the settlement closest to the fertilizer factories, asked Pusri for US$100 per family in compensation for trauma, plus reimbursement for medication and scholarship aid for their children.[31] Pusri then announced that it would hire one hundred and fifty people from settlements near the factory.[32] YALHI organized a demonstration on November 1, 2000, because the company had not yet taken action regarding the victims of the ammonia leak on September 29. Pusri representatives promised to provide scholarships, free medical care, and small loans to the community and urged residents to drop the law case.

At the end of November, Pusri announced that it would pay compensation to the victims of the ammonia leak.[33] Residents of Tiga Ilir agreed to have Benny Setiawan, a lawyer associated with YALHI, act as their agent in the negotiations. LBH and WALHI activists say that Benny Setiawan was paid US$500 by Pusri for arranging a settlement. Companies often dealt with protests by paying off the leaders of the protestors.

Problems at the Pusri factories continued. On December 7, 2000, local newspapers reported an explosion at factory number three in which three employees were injured.[34] LBH and WALHI helped residents in settlements around the Pusri factories establish the Palembang Community Forum on Industrial Environment (FOLSIP) and set up a team to monitor pollution of the Musi River by Pusri. The team reported that between January and August 2001 there were eleven massive fish kills below the Pusri factories. Complaints about pollution were put forth in a series of "Open Letters" to the press under the name of FOLSIP. In March 2001, national newspapers picked up the story of pollution by Pusri.[35] Pusri denied that there had been fish kills. Benny Setiawan set up an organization called the Communication Forum for the Environment (FKPL) to counter FOLSIP. He told residents of Tiga Ilir that they would gain nothing through protests and urged them to seek redress from Pusri. Pusri mounted a public relations campaign explaining their environmental management system.

On Earth Day, June 5, 2001, approximately one thousand residents from settlements around the Pusri factories participated in a demonstration organized by WALHI. This event was reported in the national newspaper *Kompas*, which also reported that victims of the ammonia leak the previous year had still not been compensated.[36] In July 2001, when the provincial legislature took up the issue of pollution by Pusri, the company said they would make improvements if it was proven that Pusri was responsible for pollution of the Musi River or health problems of local residents.

On August 21, 2001, there was another explosion at the Pusri plant. The headline in the local newspaper, "All Chemical Industries Pollute the Environment," signaled that Pusri had changed its strategy.[37] The executive director of Pusri pointed out that Pertamina, the state-owned oil company, discharged waste into the Musi River but did not spend a penny in compensation for the effects of its action. He pointed out that Pusri had spent US$13.4 million on liquid-waste treatment and programs to reduce noise and air pollution. Finally, he claimed that protestors were not truly concerned about waste disposal; rather, demonstrations against Pusri were organized by a provocateur who was trying to take advantage of the situation (to get a pay-off). In another article Benny Setiawan accused protestors of having a "hidden agenda."[38] In 2001 Pusri announced that it had spent US$200,000 for community projects, such as repair of mosques, road improvement, scholarships for students, and health and medical aid. Pusri also established a fund of US$300,000 for small loans to individuals and US$140,000 for group loans.

In 2002 the governor of South Sumatra and the mayor of Palembang issued new regulations on air and water quality and the disposal of liquid waste. Meanwhile Pusri continued to deny that FOLSIP's demands for damages and compensation due to pollution had any foundation.

On July 3, 2003, the *Sriwijaya Post* reported that once again masses of dead fish were floating in the Musi River.[39] According to Sofyan Mahmud from the provincial Environmental Impact Management Agency, the fish kill proved that there were still fish in the river, which meant that scientists who said that pollution from Pusri caused a reduction in the population of fish were wrong.

Government officials understand that Pusri is responsible for both air pollution and pollution of the Musi River, but they believe the company cannot be prosecuted or forced to meet environmental standards. The director of the Palembang City Environmental Impact Management Department told LBH lawyers (off the record) that she could not support the charges against

Pusri because the case was "politically sensitive." The provincial police chief said that Pusri played such an important role in the local and national economy that activists and residents should not make such a "big deal" about pollution. The director of the Provincial Environmental Impact Management Agency pointed out that over four hundred companies discharge waste materials into the Musi River. He cited the case of Sri Melamin Rezeki, a joint venture with PT Pusri, as one example of the constraints under which the Environmental Impact Agency must act. Sri Melamin Rezeki, which started commercial production of melamine in August 1994, was given three warnings for discharging chemical waste into the Musi River. But, he said, because the company has hundreds of employees, it was not possible to close it down or apply sanctions simply because it violated environmental laws. In conclusion, he observed, "At the Ministry of the Environment in Jakarta there are thick files containing information on environmental violations and cases from all over Indonesia that cannot be prosecuted due to a lack of law enforcement. What can you expect local government to do if the national government cannot do anything to polluters?"

Pusri uses various incentives to ensure that government officials do not press the company on environmental issues. For example, government officials are offered the use of company facilities for weddings and other social occasions. Newspaper editors are also pulled into this kind of relationship with Pusri. Like PT TEL and BTM, Pusri has found it cheaper to buy off protestors than to deal with pollution. Interviewed by Jamila, the director of the Environmental Department at Pusri admitted that the company did not have the latest technology for waste treatment and that settling ponds were seldom checked to ensure that waste discharged met environmental standards. But he argued that complaints to the media, protests to the government, and involvement of WALHI or LBH did not contribute to a solution of environmental problems. Rather, as director of Pusri's Environmental Department, he, with his staff, worked directly with the local community when pollution occurred. FOLSIP had been given direct access to their office twenty-four hours a day to report problems.

People living in settlements around the Pusri factories are so poor that they must put the economic needs of their families before concerns about pollution. People complain of chronic respiratory and skin problems, but they do not have a clear understanding of the long-term health problems associated with exposure to chemical pollution. They say, "So far no one has died from smelling ammonia or eating bad fish." Ansori, a resident interviewed by Jamila in 2001, said that Pusri had given him a loan of US$750, which was to be repaid in three years at 6 percent interest. Ansori had spent his loan on a sewing machine, which he uses to make pillowcases and tablecloths to sell in the market. None of the people receiving loans had made any loan payments through 2003, and Pusri had not pressed for payment. Now incidents such as a fish kill or ammonia leak are viewed as opportunities to benefit from another payoff by Pusri.

This solution to protests over pollution carries a high cost to society and hidden costs to Pusri. Managers at Pusri complain that residents threaten to go to journalists whenever they smell ammonia in order to extort more money from them. They complain that members of the provincial legislature pressure them to fund "projects," which allow legislators to take a payoff. The practice of buying off critics has also attracted "gangsters with ties" *(preman dasi)*, who threaten to organize protests if Pusri does not make a "community development project grant" to people whom they claim to represent.

LBH, WALHI, and other environmental organizations confront a system of collusion between company managers and government officials that protects the economic interests of a few at the expense of the many. Villagers who once derived a sustainable livelihood from the land have been forced to migrate to cities in search of work, swelling the numbers of unemployed, so marginalized that they are reduced to pandering for handouts. The poor are forced to adopt a strategy of short-term economic survival rather than seeking long-term change in the enforcement of laws that would ensure a safe environment. Chapter 5 demonstrates why these compromises are necessary through recounting the stories of exploited workers struggling for their rights.

LBH and WALHI activists have been most effective when partnering with international, Japanese, and Western NGOs, which can supply information about the dangers of pollutants and apply pressure on investors. The most important tool of activists has been media campaigns that educate the public and motivate greater awareness of the threat to the environment that comes from unregulated industries.

Chapter 5

Struggling for Workers' Rights

One-third of the world's labor force is either unemployed or under-employed. Of the 150 million unemployed around the world, 75 per-cent lack any unemployment insurance protection, and even the richest countries in Europe and North America reduced the protection pro-vided by unemployment insurance in the 1990s. The vast majority of the population in many developing countries, including informal sector wage-earners and self-employed persons, has no social protection whatsoever.
—*World Employment Report*[1]

WHEN OIL PRICES COLLAPSED in the mid-1980s, the New Order lib-eralized investment regulations in order to attract investors. Foreign corpo-rations were given tax abatements and guaranteed a docile, low-paid labor force. The only legal labor union was the official, government-controlled All-Indonesia Workers' Union (SPSI). SPSI was more committed to provid-ing a cheap and disciplined labor force for international investors than to protecting the rights of workers. Independent labor organizing was a crimi-nal activity, and an informal ban prevented strikes until 1990.[2] Military and police surveillance and harassment of labor organizers did not completely suppress labor strikes, which increased throughout the 1990s until the 1997 Asian Economic Crisis led to bankruptcies, the closing of factories, and a massive increase in the number of unemployed.

According to an International Labor Organization 2004–2005 employ-ment report, the conditions faced by workers throughout Southeast Asia have deteriorated over the last ten years. When the Asian Economic Crisis hit Indonesia, the International Monetary Fund protected investors and banks. Multinational companies transferred their operations to China, Thailand, Vietnam, and Korea, where wages were lower and conditions more stable. In Indonesia the brunt of the crisis fell primarily on the urban poor. In 2004 unemployment in Indonesia was officially declared to be 9.5 million, whereas actual unemployment had risen to 43 million, approxi-mately one-fifth of the population.[3]

In 2000, workers were granted the right to establish their own organizations. *Reformasi* activists hoped that organized labor might become a political force in a more democratic Indonesia. Instead, there has been a proliferation of labor organizations, resulting in a weak labor movement.[4] Furthermore, as Vedi Hadiz points out, the interests of workers are not represented by other political groups. "All the new major political parties arguably represent, though to varying degrees, new alliances among some old New Order elites and therefore inherit the disposition to exclude labor from political processes."[5]

The Campaign for Workers' Rights in South Sumatra

In South Sumatra, the minimum wage is set by the governor, who is advised by a council composed of provincial government officials, SPSI representatives, and various merchants' associations. Workers have no effective voice on this council. In 2000, the minimum monthly wage in South Sumatra was Rp 280,000 ($US35). By 2003 it had been increased to Rp 403,500 (US$50.50) for a family, still far below the poverty level of US$1 a day per person.[6]

Ten different national labor unions established branches in South Sumatra. Yet workers, like farmers involved in land conflicts, generally turned to LBH-Palembang for assistance when their rights were violated or they were involved in a dispute with an employer. In 2001, fifty-four disputes involving almost thirty thousand workers were brought to LBH-Palembang. These cases covered a wide range of issues, including sixteen disputes over wages; twelve over the failure of a company to make the legally required severance payment to terminated workers; and ten over violations of various other workers' rights.

Success in protecting the rights of workers has been limited. LBH has supported the establishment of grassroots organizations as a first step toward building a labor movement able to represent the interests of workers politically. In September 1999, LBH brought five local groups of workers together in the United Workers Communication Forum, which is affiliated with a network of independent labor organizations in North Sumatra, West Sumatra, Lampung, and Jakarta. From a base of one hundred members in 1999, it grew to a membership of five hundred workers in 2000. Further growth has been hampered by the high rate of unemployment and the reluctance of government officials to enforce labor laws against state-owned corporations or corporations owned by powerful elites. This has frequently led workers to take the law into their own hands. They have resorted to attacks on corporate property or threats of violence in order to bring companies to the negotiating table. However, when violence breaks out, protesting workers are criminalized and victimized a second time.

This chapter describes three labor disputes in South Sumatra that show the formidable obstacles faced by workers demanding their rights and the dismal prospects that face unskilled laborers who have migrated to cities in search of work. The first dispute involves workers protesting violations of the labor law by an Indonesian-owned subcontractor of the state-owned coal-mining company PT Bukit Asam. In the second conflict, contract shrimp farmers protested exploitation and illegal actions by PT Wachyuni Mandira, a corporation owned by Suharto crony Syamsul Nursalim. I conclude by describing how the activities of street vendors *(pedagang kaki lima)* and cycle rickshaw *(becak)* drivers, the most marginal groups in society, have been criminalized by new regulations issued by the Palembang city government.

PT Tambang Batu Bara Bukit Asam (Bukit Asam)

In January 2000, over three hundred workers were dismissed by PT Sumber Mitra Jaya (SMJ), a subcontractor of PT Bukit Asam, without notice or severance pay.[7] In February the workers went to LBH-Palembang. They had heard that SMJ was replacing them with workers recruited in Java who would be paid a lower salary. Meanwhile the Javanese employees who had been hired were complaining that SMJ was paying them a lower salary than had been promised.

A demonstration at the office of Bukit Asam on March 7, 2000, by more than three hundred workers led to a meeting between workers, LBH staff, representatives of Bukit Asam and SMJ and local government officials. At this meeting Bukit Asam disclaimed all responsibility for SMJ's failure to pay terminated workers the legally required severance payment, and SMJ rejected the claims of the workers. Security forces told workers waiting outside to return home.

On March 13, 2000, LBH staff and protesting workers returned to the offices of Bukit Asam. A second meeting with SMJ managers was arranged. This time officials from the Department of Manpower and members of the Muara Enim district legislature were present, and SMJ committed to disburse severance pay to the discharged workers by March 31, 2000. LBH staff and a committee of workers would work with SMJ staff to determine the amount of severance pay given to workers (which depended on the length of employment). New obstacles arose. SMJ now claimed that the

Department of Manpower had authorized the dismissal of a certain number of workers so that not all workers should be given severance pay. This led the workers to appeal again to the *bupati* of Muara Enim, who had been instrumental in brokering the first deal. The *bupati* agreed that SMJ appeared to be breaking the agreement that had been reached and said that he would do what he could.

On April 1, 2000, SMJ announced that, as a "goodwill gesture," the company would provide severance pay to 174 terminated workers by the middle of April. This "gesture" excluded almost half the terminated workers, who then turned on their representatives in the negotiations, accusing them of betrayal. They threatened to burn down company property or take hostages if nothing was done.[8] However, SMJ failed to deliver on the promised severance payments in the middle of April, so the emerging division among protesting workers was forgotten. SMJ workers who had not been terminated now joined in the protests, launching a three-day strike. SMJ blamed the strike on intimidation exerted by terminated workers.

On April 26, 2000, the governor intervened, pressing SMJ to make the required severance payments. SMJ announced that severance payments would be distributed within three days. This did not happen. On May 3, 2000, workers seized twelve SMJ vehicles after arranging for media coverage by the local Palembang television station. Local police and SMJ security forces stood by while the wives and children of workers encircled the vehicles. The women told television reporters that their families were going hungry because their husbands had no jobs and no severance pay. The workers announced that they would hold the vehicles until severance payments were made. They sent representatives to Palembang to seek a meeting with the governor. Nothing happened for two days, so workers seized two more vehicles on May 5, 2000, and the women threatened to occupy the offices of Bukit Asam.[9] Two more vehicles were seized on May 6, 2000, and another one the following day. On May 10, 2000, the women broke through the line of security guards and police and occupied the office of Bukit Asam.

That same day the governor invited the protestors and representatives of Bukit Asam and SMJ to meet with him, but the workers now refused to attend further meetings. The police issued an ultimatum that the vehicles held hostage must be returned to SMJ within twenty-four hours or force would be used. Two platoons of the Mobile Police Brigade were brought in to reinforce security guards at SMJ. On May 11, 2000, at 9:00 p.m., the police broke into Bukit Asam headquarters firing shots and setting off a melee. According to the demonstrators, one worker was shot and nineteen others, including several women and a security guard, were injured.[10]

The following day SMJ released funds to a local bank to pay all 341 terminated workers, who were promised that the money would be distributed within a week. That afternoon the vehicles held hostage were returned to SMJ, and a week later the money was finally distributed.

Police Violence and the Criminalization of Protest

The police attack on women and children at Bukit Asam provoked LBH to organize a protest of farmers and workers against police violence.[11] In the name of the South Sumatra Farmers and Workers Resistance Movement, hundreds of farmers and workers gathered at Police Headquarters in Palembang on June 12, 2000. The police chief refused to meet with the demonstrators. Some in the crowd began to push against the barbed-wire barricades, and a few threw stones. At that provocation the police were given an order to disperse the crowd. They attacked with rattan whips and batons; a reporter and a woman were badly beaten.

Most of the protestors fled in the direction of the LBH office in a neighborhood at the edge of Palembang. On the way to LBH, three of the farmers assaulted two policemen. When this information reached police headquarters, a battalion of police was sent to surround the LBH office. The police searched all the neighboring houses for demonstrators who might be hiding. The standoff between the police and LBH staff in the office lasted into the night until the arrival of Chairil Syah, former director of LBH-Palembang, who had been sent by LBH-Jakarta to negotiate with the police.

The next day local newspapers accused LBH-Palembang of supporting the use of violence by protestors. Ten protestors—four farmers, one worker, three students, one LBH staff member, and one WALHI volunteer—had been picked up by the police. They were charged with insulting an officer, and each was sentenced to four months in jail. LBH was forced to move its office because people living nearby were frightened by the police action.

This incident led the governor to convene a hearing on police violence. According to the police report, the underlying cause of the violence was the workers' refusal to engage in further negotiations and the occupation of Bukit Asam offices by women and children. The police argued that they were obligated to act in the name of the supremacy of law because the standoff between workers and security forces at Bukit Asam had gone on for seven days. The report described the outbreak of violence at the Bukit Asam complex as having been instigated by "unknown individuals who wanted to create anarchy and chaos," which led to the mob becoming "brutal and lawless." The police claimed that they fired rubber bullets into the crowd only after Molotov cocktails were thrown at them. In conclusion, the police report notes that on May 12, 2000, when SMJ finally turned over the money for severance payments to a local bank, protesting workers returned the vehicles they had seized to SMJ.[12]

Government officials intervened to pressure SMJ to comply with the law only after mass actions on the part of workers. After the June 12, 2000, protest against police violence, however, LBH staff decided to give up the strategy of mass demonstrations, because farmers and workers were victimized a second time when they were jailed and their families lost the limited support they could provide.

Industrial Shrimp Farming

In the 1970s, the World Bank made loans financing industrial shrimp farming in Indonesia. Shrimp exports to Japan and Western markets were expected to bring high earnings. Between 1986 and 1991, the dollar price of prawn exports doubled, and prawns became Indonesia's second largest agricultural export after rubber.[13] Industrial shrimp farming was supposed to improve the standard of living of shrimp farmers, but as with other industrial agriculture projects, shrimp farmers were left poorer than ever.

The Gajah Tunggal Group, Indonesia's seventh largest conglomerate, established the world's largest industrial shrimp farm in the province of Lampung on the southern tip of Sumatra.[14] Industrial shrimp farming by Gajah Tunggal was funded by loans from the World Bank, the Export-Import Bank of Japan, and Nursalim's Bank Dagang Nasional Indonesia. To ensure the success of his operation, Nursalim cultivated ties with military officers in the Suharto government. Two retired generals and one naval commander were put on the board of Wachyuni Mandira.

Industrial shrimp farming was managed by local subsidiaries of Gajah Tunggal, PT Dipasena Citra Darmaja (Dipasena) in Lampung and PT Wachyuni Mandira in South Sumatra, and organized on a variation of the *inti/plasma* system. Traditional shrimp farmers who lived in the concession area were to be incorporated in the *plasma* scheme as contract farmers. Outsiders could purchase rights to become contract shrimp farmers for approximately US$1,000. Contract farmers were given two shrimp ponds to manage, equipment for aerating and harvesting the ponds, and a simple house. The contract farmer was required to repay the company for these out of profits from the shrimp harvest. The farmer was also provided with a modest allowance and a small monthly stipend of food and other essentials—35 kg rice, 3 kg sugar, 2 kg cooking oil, 2 cans of powdered milk, ¼ kg coffee, ¼ kg washing soap, and 20 liters of kerosene—until he could conduct his first harvest. The stipend and subsidy were also deducted from profits. Contract farmers were required to sell their harvest to Gajah Tunggal at a price set by the company. In short, these farmers were in the position of indentured servants or sharecroppers. Even worse, if the harvest failed due to disease or some other cause, the farmers found themselves deeply in debt to the company.[15] The *plasma* scheme also allowed Gajah Tunggal to transfer debt incurred for construction of processing, refrigeration, and shipping facilities on to the contract farmers, whose ponds were used as surety for the loans. When shrimp farmers signed their contracts, they were told that in eight years they would be debt-free. However, they were given no accounting of what they owed or of how the price for the shrimp they raised was to be determined.

In 1995, the Gajah Tunggal Group was given a further concession of 170,000 hectares of coastal wetlands in South Sumatra, which included a conservation area and land already under cultivation by 2,200 farmers. Although these claims totaled less than 2,000 hectares of the 170,000-hectare concession, rather than negotiate with the villagers as required by law, Wachyuni Mandira relied on security forces to deal with villagers who did not want to become contract farmers.

With the emergence of the *reformasi* movement in late 1997, the contract farmers began to protest.[16] They said that the monthly food supply was less than adequate; they were not allowed to leave the premises of Wachyuni Mandira without permission and were treated like slaves. Furthermore, the equipment provided by the company did not meet what had been described in their contracts. In January 1998, Wachyuni Mandira increased the food supply and the monthly stipend to US$23 a month. The farmers still regarded this concession as insufficient.

In September 1998, three months after the fall of Suharto, six representatives of the shrimp farmers went to LBH. They charged the company with cheating contract farmers in the price paid for the shrimp harvest and a continuing vagueness in credit agreements. In addition, the representatives pointed to the strictures that six levels of permission were required before a farmer could leave the site and that friends could not visit without permission from company officials. Furthermore, contract farmers were frequently expelled by Wachyuni Mandira without reason or compensation. The shrimp farmers wanted information about their debts and terms of repayment, and they wanted to renegotiate their contracts and rules that restricted their freedom. The farmers who came to LBH said that over a thousand shrimp farmers had mounted a demonstration at Wachyuni Mandira headquarters in Desa Bumi Pratama Mandira, the company town in the center of the ponds, but the company had taken no action on their demands.

Student activists who talked with the shrimp farmers at LBH volunteered to support them in an appeal to the governor and the South Sumatra legislature. When approached by the protesting farmers, the vice governor arranged for a meeting between the farmers' representative and Wachyuni Mandira managers. He also revealed that no environmental impact report had been filed by Wachyuni Mandira, so the company was technically operating illegally.[17] Members of the legislature promised to pressure Wachyuni Mandira to provide information on debts and negotiate with shrimp farmers on other issues.

The first meeting between contract farmers, LBH staff, officials from the governor's office, and managers from Wachyuni Mandira took place on September 22, 1998. While hundreds waited outside, participants in the meeting agreed that a team should be formed to investigate the issues raised by the contract farmers. At the insistence of LBH staff, five representatives of contract farmers were included as part of the Temporary Contract Shrimp Farmers Negotiating Team. Although contract farmers objected to the inclusion of police and security forces on the team, as this would frighten farmers who were questioned, they were overruled.

Reports in the national press brought public attention to the situation of contract shrimp farmers in South Sumatra. Clementino Dos Amaral of the National Human Rights Commission visited Wachyuni Mandira, giving the farmers hope that their situation would improve. The investigating team found the protests of contract farmers justified, and Wachyuni Mandira managers agreed to meet and discuss further concessions. For three weeks, the Temporary Contract Shrimp Farmers Negotiating Team and Wachyuni Mandira managers talked. The monthly stipend was increased to US$45, and in October increased again to US$65. But Wachyuni Mandira refused to renegotiate the terms of farmers' contracts or change the oppressive rules imposed on them. Company officials also declined to provide information about the status of debts and terms of repayment.

In October, Wachyuni Mandira managers and the Temporary Contract Shrimp Farmers Negotiating Team were summoned to Palembang to stand before a lands-rights commission recently established by South Sumatra's new governor, Rosihan Arsyad. As director of WALHI, Nur Kholis and other LBH staff accompanied representatives of the contract farmers to this meeting. The commission directed Wachyuni Mandira to provide a copy of the farmers' loan contract within one week and to complete negotiations over other issues raised by the shrimp farmers within two weeks.

This deadline passed without any action being taken by Wachyuni Mandira. The company stated that it would wait until after the meetings of the Special Session of the People's Consultative Assembly, which was tasked with reforming electoral laws before the 1999 presidential election. The new laws would signal where power would be located after implementation of political reforms, and this might allow Wachyuni Mandira to seek support for its position at the highest level of government.

On November 12, 1998, contract farmers gathered to consider what to do in the face of Wachyuni Mandira's maneuvering to block and delay negotiations. They decided to mount a demonstration the following day. On November 13, 1998, over twenty-five hundred shrimp farmers gathered in front of the manager's office with banners reading: "Before contract farming, we were free to sell shrimp" and "We are not the enemies of workers [at Wachyuni Mandira]." Wachyuni Mandira managers made no response. The following day, the shrimp farmers gathered again and conducted a sit-in demonstration until dusk. That night the electricity at Wachyuni Mandira was shut down, and the front office of "Department Bravo" at the shrimp ponds was smashed up. On the third day, the contract farmers gathered on the sports field to conduct a free speech forum. One group split off and tore down the kiosk where people bought tickets to the ferry that carried them out of Wachyuni Mandira. As the situation spiraled out of control, the manager's office, security posts, the executive mess, and other buildings were set on fire. Wachyuni Mandira called in police and army units to quell the riot. When the marines arrived, they surrounded the complex and mounted an armed attack on farmers leaving the site. Four farmers were shot and many more were beaten up.[18]

The governor announced that he was frustrated that shrimp farmers had taken the law into their own hands. He issued an order to the police to find out who was responsible for the riot and accused LBH of supporting violent actions by the shrimp farmers. Munarman, director of LBH-Palembang at the time, denied that LBH would support protestors breaking the law; the job of LBH was only to help them to secure their rights. He reminded the public of the issues that had provoked the shrimp farmers: the refusal of Wachyuni Mandira to provide information about repayment of loans taken out on farmers' shrimp ponds, rules restricting the freedom of contract farmers, and the use of security forces to intimidate protestors. As director of WALHI, Nur Kholis pointed out that Wachyuni Mandira was operating illegally because it had not filed an environmental impact statement.

In the weeks following the riot, three battalions from the marines, army, and police were stationed at Wachyuni Mandira. The besieged shrimp farmers and their families found that the electricity was shut off and no one was allowed to leave the site. Company managers circulated a notice stating that the riot had been the action of "anarchist" farmers; contract farmers were given one week to sign a statement saying that they had not been involved in the violence. Otherwise they would be presumed guilty, and their contracts would be terminated. Fifty-one shrimp farmers were picked up by security forces, threatened with arrest, and beaten until they agreed to sign a document voiding their contracts with Wachyuni Mandira. They and their families were then expelled with severance pay of US$40 per family or US$20 per individual.[19] When these farmers protested to the governor, Wachyuni Mandira's lawyer maintained that the farmers had withdrawn from their contracts voluntarily under no threat of force.

The security forces tried to keep reporters away from Wachyuni Mandira's operations in OKI, but Taufiq Wijaya, the reporter for the *Lampung Post* who had reported on conflicts with MHP described in Chapter 4, managed to gather eyewitness testimony from shrimp farmers who walked eight hours through the wetlands in order to escape the siege at Wachyuni Mandira. They identified individuals who had been responsible for the fires and had later been hired by Wachyuni Mandira's security force.

One of the farmers interviewed compared being a contract farmer at Wachyuni Mandira to living in a concentration camp.[20] If security guards thought they smelled shrimp cooking, a farmer would be accused of stealing shrimp for his family and expelled without any compensation. If equipment malfunctioned or a farmer protested about the way he was treated, he might be expelled. Endang Suparmono, a member of Contract Shrimp Farmers Negotiating Team who fled from Wachyuni Mandira to bring his wife and child to the hospital in Palembang, said that the farmers and their families at Wachyuni Mandira were going hungry because their monthly food supply was not distributed. People could not get medical care or medicines because they were not allowed to leave the site. Taufiq Wijaya's reports were published on the Internet by the Institute for the Free Flow of Information (ISAI) and in local newspapers.

Reports of conditions at Wachyuni Mandira led student activists in Palembang to undertake a hunger strike. Nationally known human rights activist Munir, head of the Commission on the Disappeared and Victims of Violence (KONTRAS), called for the troops to be pulled out from Wachyuni Mandira and negotiations to be resumed. The National Commission on Human Rights sent a representative to South Sumatra to investigate. On February 8, 1999, Sidney Jones of Human Rights Watch Asia went to Palembang to investigate possible human rights abuses. She met with Endang Suparmono at the LBH office. Reporters later quoted her as saying that conditions at Wachyuni Mandira under the New Order were a form of "modern slavery." She pointed out that after the Asian Economic Crisis, Syamsul Nursalim had passed on to the shrimp farmers all the foreign debt of Gajah Tunggal, which was in dollars, thereby tripling the farmers' debt so that each farmer owed US$70,000 for his two ponds.

As Endang Suparmono was leaving the interview with Sidney Jones, he was arrested by the police and accused of stealing shrimp and involvement in the November riot.[21] In jail he joined thirty-eight other previously arrested farmers. Sixteen of the farmers were sentenced to eight months in jail, but as members of the Contract Shrimp Farmers Negotiating Team, Mulyadi and Endang Suparmono were sentenced to up to five years. The jailed shrimp farmers went on a hunger strike in May 1999; they declared that they had not been involved in the violence at Wachyuni Mandira and appealed to the governor and the courts to uphold the law by protecting farmers rather than corporations.[22] Nothing came of this appeal. Instead, as in the case of PT TEL, the Japanese ambassador received assurances from Governor Rosihan Arsyad that the property of foreign investors would be protected. The governor went on to state that the operation of Wachyuni Mandira was "essential to the government and society," because in addition to providing foreign export earnings, the company provided jobs to thousands of people.

When I interviewed the governor in August 2000, he reiterated his view that the riot at Wachyuni Mandira in November 1998 had been unwarranted. He acknowledged that complaints of contract farmers about their contracts, the need for a doctor at the location, the number of levels of permission required to leave the site, the low basic-maintenance allowance, and transparency in the price paid for the shrimp harvest were justified, but he believed that Wachyuni Mandira had dealt with all but the last of these problems. In his view, Wachyuni Mandira was an important development project in what had formerly been a useless, mosquito-infested swamp.

Interviewed by a reporter for the *Far Eastern Economic Review* in 2000, Syamsul Nursalim claimed that Dipasena, the Gajah Tunggal subsidiary in Lampung that was the prototype for Wachyuni Mandira, was to be a model development project: "I wanted Dipasena to be a showcase, to bring people into the middle class." He blamed the failure of his dream on bad luck and lawlessness in post-Suharto Indonesia. He explained, the first shrimp harvests in 1995 had been disappointing, forcing farmers to take on more debt. By 1996 yields had improved, but the El Niño drought in 1997 and the devaluation of the rupiah after the Asian Economic Crisis forced Dipasena to cut the price at which shrimp were purchased from contract farmers to 70 percent of the price on the open market. At the same time, the devaluation of the rupiah meant that the debt of shrimp farmers more than tripled. The reporter added his own assessment, "[S]ince the company was the sole provider of feed, fry, power and other basics to the farmers, it took a huge bite out of their income—so large that the [contract farmers] constantly had to borrow more to stay afloat."[23]

In 1998 the Indonesian Bank Restructuring Agency (IBRA) identified Syamsul Nursalim (along with Prayogo Pangestu) as one of the top three debtors in Indonesia, owing US$3.35 billion. Nursalim pledged to turn over PT Dipasena Citra Darmala to IBRA in order to cover the debts of the Nursalim Bank. Title to the company was not transferred to IBRA, however, and members of the Nursalim family continued to direct operations at Dipasena. In 2000, IBRA officials alleged that Nursalim had withheld critical information about the enormous debts of contract shrimp farmers. Kwik Kian Gie, a former economics minister, called the Gadjah Tunggal group of Nursalim and Prayogo Pangestu's Barito Pacific group "black" conglomerates and accused them of paying analysts to conduct "a disinformation campaign suggesting that if the [owners] were jailed, the companies they founded and built would go bankrupt and many employees would lose their jobs." He concluded, "So the robber barons are being hailed as the saviors of labor."[24] The assessment of the banker appointed by IBRA to oversee Nursalim's companies was that the terms of the farmers' loans and the prices they were paid for shrimp set them up to fail.[25] Attorney General Marzuki Darusman pressed for prosecution of Nursalim for fraud and misrepresentation, but Indonesia's new president, Abdurrahman Wahid, blocked prosecution, citing the importance of the conglomerate's foreign earnings and the jobs it provided.

When shrimp farmers at Dipasena learned that their collective debts to IBRA totaled US$400 million, they bitterly protested the company's accounting. In the words of one, "We've worked for ten years generating valuable dollar exports, and we've got nothing to show—nothing."[26] In October 1999, Dipasena shrimp farmers organized a sit-in at the office of the governor of Lampung. When no action was taken, many farmers drained their ponds and sold the shrimp. Others claimed the ponds as their own property. The dispute turned into a conflict between groups of contract farmers and employees of Dipasena who processed the shrimp for market. In March 2000, when Nursalim visited Dipasena to urge contract farmers to go back to work, he had to be rescued by helicopter from an enraged mob while two of his bodyguards and one shrimp farmer were hacked to death with machetes.[27]

While the revolt at Dipasena in Lampung escalated, Nursalim's Gajah Tunggal group focused on making Wachyuni Mandira profitable.[28] In September 2000, villagers in Gajah Mati learned that Wachyuni Mandira was going to expand its operations into an area that included 640 hectares of land farmed by 320 families.[29] They protested to the vice governor, but they were unable to stop Wachyuni Mandira from converting yet more mangrove wetlands into industrial shrimp farms.

I was denied permission to visit Wachyuni Mandira in the summer of 2000. Friends at LBH warned against going there without a letter of permission, because I might find myself in a dangerous situation that could be blamed on the shrimp farmers. I spoke on the phone to Wachyuni Mandira managers in Jakarta, who told me that all the contract farmers who had left Wachyuni Mandira had done so voluntarily.

When title to Dipasena was finally turned over to IBRA, the Indonesian government was left to deal with thousands of angry contract farmers, employees worried about losing their jobs, and an environmental crisis. The infrastructure of the shrimp ponds had not been maintained, and white spot disease had cut the harvest to one-tenth of previous levels.[30] In August 2000, the police occupied the shrimp ponds at Dipasena to provide security and protect property that now belonged to the Indonesian government. In October 2000, violence broke out between employees pushing for a government loan to restart operations at Dipasena and contract farmers demanding they be allowed to take control of their own ponds.[31] They pointed out that when President Abdurrahman Wahid had visited Dipasena in July 2000, he had told the shrimp farmers to sell their shrimp on the open market if the conflict with Dipasena was not resolved.

While the leaders of protests at Wachyuni Mandira were criminalized, Nursalim managed to evade criminal prosecution. In April 2001, he was arrested and accused of causing the state to suffer losses of US$1.68 billion through the misuse of loans to his Bank Dagang Nasional Indonesia. However, he was released after one day in detention and allowed to fly to Japan to receive medical treatment. He settled in Singapore, which does not have an extradition treaty with Indonesia. When Megawati Sukarnoputri became president in 2001, her husband, Taufik Kiemas, who had ties to individuals on the board of Gajah Tunggal, became the advocate of Syamsul Nuraslim. Despite strong protests from the IBRA Oversight Committee, in October 2002 Nursalim received a further dispensation from IBRA and was allowed to cover a major part of his debt with assets and extend the repayment period for the remainder. (The latter condition violated a cabinet decision of March 7, 2002.) Investigators estimate that Nursalim repaid about 10 percent of the debt owed to IBRA. Although IBRA had classified Nursalim as an "uncooperative debtor," he was granted a release and discharge decree certifying he had repaid all his debts in July 2004, before President Megawati left office. This also freed Nursalim from the threat of prosecution for corruption in the handling of funds at Bank Dagang Nasional Indonesia.[32] As Nursalim maneuvered to retain control of profitable assets and escape prosecution in Indonesia, the Gajah Tunggal group began investing its Indonesian profits in China.[33]

As this case study of the world's largest industrial shrimp farm illustrates, neoliberal economic policies that promote cash export crops do not alleviate poverty. Industrial shrimp farming is capital-intensive, and profits go to investors. A small number of technical experts, often foreigners, have well-paid jobs; but the high rate of unemployment means that local workers get very low-paid jobs. Contract farmers in the Gajah Tunggal concessions who formerly harvested shrimp using traditional methods ended up poorer than before the company took over their land; they were left with Gajah Tunggal's debts and polluted ponds.[34]

By 2001, it was becoming apparent that industrial shrimp farming was not sustainable.[35] Up to 70 percent of the shrimp farms established with support from the World Bank on the north coast of Java in the late 1970s had already been abandoned due to pollution from the high levels of chemicals and antibiotics used. By 2003, overexpansion of industrial shrimp farming worldwide had caused a surplus, and prices collapsed by 50 percent.[36] As early as 2000, the Network of Indonesian Non-Governmental Organizations for Forest Conservation (SKEPHI) warned that industrial shrimp farming was destroying mangrove forests that protect the coasts. Half of Indonesia's mangrove forests had already been destroyed, mostly for shrimp farms.[37] The enormous destruction wrought by the tsunami that ravaged the west coast of Aceh and North Sumatra in December 2004 was due in part to the loss of mangrove forests on the coast. In March 2005, the government of Indonesia announced that it would spend US$5 billion to build sea walls and regreen the mangrove forests on Aceh's coast to reduce the impact of possible future tsunamis.[38]

Street Vendors (*Pedagang Kaki Lima* or PK5) and Trishaw *(Becak)* Drivers

After the Asian Economic Crisis hit Indonesia in 1997, many companies were forced to terminate employees and others shut down their operations or went into bankruptcy. Unemployment skyrocketed. Like villagers who had moved to cities and market towns in search of work, the newly unemployed sought to provide for themselves and their families in the "informal economy" as street vendors *(pedagang kaki lima)* or household help, driving a cycle rickshaw *(becak)* or working in construction. The South Sumatra Department of Labor reported in January 2003 that 100 thousand people were registered as unemployed. The number of those who were underemployed and did not earn a sustainable living was much higher. Out of a population of 7.2 million in the province, over 1.8 million lived below the poverty line. In Palembang city alone, 30 percent of the population lived in poverty.[39] As the unemployed sought work elsewhere, South Sumatra found itself exporting workers to sixteen countries.

In 1997 Yeni became a coordinator for the Community Recovery Program. Headed at the national level by Emil Salim, this effort to support the poor provided small grants to organized groups of people. Yeni was in charge of assessing groups in South Sumatra that applied for grants and supporting them in their endeavors. She traveled throughout South Sumatra working with farmers and villagers who had moved to market towns in search of a way to make a living. One group that was funded was the Advocacy Network for the Urban Poor (JAMUR), an organization of *becak* drivers in Palembang that was affiliated with the Urban Poor Consortium, a well-known NGO founded in Jakarta by Wardah Hafidz.[40] JAMUR was given a grant of US$9,000 to buy cycle rickshaws so that drivers would not have to pay rent for their vehicles. The wives of *becak* drivers and groups of women were given small grants so they could buy equipment to make food to sell or stock a small stall with fruits, vegetables, or other commodities.

In February 2000, the Palembang city government began to try to deal with the burgeoning informal sector by banning street vendors and *becak* from main streets.[41] Citing a 1981 law on the maintenance of "cleanliness, security, order, and beauty" in the city, the mayor issued an order that street vendors who refused to move would be fined the equivalent of US$3 or sentenced to three months in jail.[42] The street vendors responded with a circular calling for resistance.[43] Their slogan was "Better disorder than starvation." The Palembang city government claimed that *becak* drivers caused traffic jams and were a safety hazard; *becak* were banned from the main streets of the city. JAMUR organized a protest against the new regulations. A long cavalcade of *becak* pedaled down the main street to the mayor's office, where the drivers demanded to meet with him and members of the city council. They said that if they were banned from the main shopping areas, they would not be able to earn enough to feed their families. Their slogan was "Main streets are not only for the rich. Poor people also have rights."

The *becak* drivers formed a new organization, the Palembang Becak Union, and day after day they demonstrated.[44] They also protested police brutality when *becak* drivers were beaten up because they waited outside markets on the main streets. After more than two weeks of daily demonstrations, the regulation banning *becak* from the main streets was withdrawn.[45]

This solution turned out to be short-lived, however. In December 2002 the Palembang city government announced that all *becak* drivers would be required to have a license. In order to obtain one, a man had to be between the ages of seventeen and fifty and have an identification card proving that he lived in Palembang. The Palembang Becak Union organized a demonstration against this regulation on the grounds that many drivers who could not meet the requirements for a license had no other way to earn a living. They asked the government not to limit the number of *becak* until some other form of employment was available to unskilled laborers.

Street vendors were also subjected to harassment and intimidation by police enforcing new laws against vending on the main streets.[46] In February 2001, police tore down the stalls of vendors in a location that was to be developed for the 2004 National Games (PON). LBH issued a press release pointing out that laws against street vendors were a legacy of the New Order and were not reasonable in the economic conditions created by the Asian Economic Crisis.[47] LBH argued that these laws also violated international covenants recognizing the economic, social, and cultural rights of all people.

In 2002 Palembang officials again attempted to clear vendors from the main streets.[48] According to police estimates, in just two main streets of Palembang six hundred vendors had established stalls. Street vendors were told they should relocate to traditional markets or to a street near the old market along the edge of the Musi River. NGOs helped the street vendors form neighborhood organizations and brought these organizations together as the Street Vendors Solidarity Union (PSPKL). The vendors stated that they were willing to move to a new location that was clean and orderly, but they pointed out that the order to move ignored major problems.[49] Wherever the vendors relocated, there would be conflicts with vendors already established in the area, not to speak of conflicts with shopowners. The vendors would also have to make "wild" payments *(pungutan liar* or *pungli)* to police and gangs *(preman)* operating in the area.

As predicted, when street vendors moved to the areas specified by the government, conflicts erupted.[50] There were not enough stalls for all the vendors trying to make a living in the city. Vendors who did not have a regular location seized the opportunity to move into the new stalls constructed by the city. Vendors being relocated found that most of the new stalls were already taken, so many returned to their former locations. Those who relocated protested that there was not enough business in the new locations.

Furthermore, some new vendors moved back on to the main streets, saying they were willing to risk arrest in order to be able to provide whatever income they could for their families. They developed a warning system whereby they could disappear when a police raid took place. When they were caught, they bribed the police or paid a fine.

In September 2002, a police raid ended in violence. Several of the street vendors were attacked and beaten up by a group of men in civilian clothes who accompanied the police. The street vendors accused the police of using gangsters *(preman)* in the raid. The police acknowledged that they had requested support from a "volunteer security force" in a tough neighborhood and from "others concerned about order" in Palembang.[51]

The use of *preman* to enforce the new city regulations against street vendors proved to be an omen of things to come. Raids on vendors and *becak* drivers escalated in the lead up to the National Games, which were celebrated in South Sumatra in 2004.[52] By the summer of 2005 there were no more vendors or *becak* on the main streets. *Preman* gangs working with police had "solved" the problem. A new campaign was under way to "relocate" street vendors who plied their wares on other streets in the center of town. A representative of PSPKL told newspaper reporters, "Everyone [the city government] uses for security and cleanliness is a *preman;* Palembang is becoming a city of *preman,* controlled by *preman.*"[53]

The Army of the Poor

The major response of government officials in Palembang and other market towns in South Sumatra to the problems of a growing population of unskilled migrants from rural villages and massive unemployment has been to harass the poor. Officials seem to see their duty as responding to the concerns of a middle class that feels threatened by the poor who try to earn a living as street vendors or *becak* drivers. This translates into making the problems of massive unemployment and poverty less visible. Nothing has been done to try to provide the poor with a way to earn a living.

Of course, local officials do not have the capacity to deal effectively with the problem of urban unemployment, which is rooted in the destruction of rural communities. The first steps must be taken at the international level with debt relief. Instead of transferring money to Western banks and institutions to repay loans of the Suharto regime and private corporations that defaulted on their debt, the government could spend more on education, health, and other forms of support for the poor in Indonesia. After the

Asian Economic Crisis, money was made available to the poor in the program of miniloans that Yeni helped to administer. But such funding does not provide a sufficient basis for moving people out of poverty.

Workers in South Sumatra may be marginally better off today than under the New Order because at least their protests are reported in the local press. But corporations and the elites that own them still stand above the law. As the case studies in this chapter show, what LBH and other progressive NGOs can achieve in promoting the rights of workers is very limited. In the next chapter we shall see how corruption, collusion, and nepotism so corroded government at all levels that workers and farmers had little hope that officials would uphold their rights.

Chapter 6

"Where's My Cut?"

The State and Corruption

The New Order did not rest exclusively upon repressive and political institutions. Within its structures it encompassed a vast and complex alliance of state officials, politico-business families and business interests that extended from Jakarta down to the regions and villages of Indonesia. A system of predatory power relations provided the cement of such an alliance focusing around a corps of power holders within the state apparatus itself who stood as gatekeepers to the allocation of the monopolies and contracts that constituted the currency of economic life in Indonesia.

—Richard Robison, *Indonesia: The Rise of Capital*[1]

THE CENTRAL DEMAND of the *reformasi* movement that brought down Suharto was an end to corruption, collusion, and nepotism *(korupsi, kolusi, nepotisme)*, or KKN. The practice of bribery *(sogok)* is so rife that it has infected the language itself. Among the more colorful expressions are *uang suap*, literally a mouthful of money, which refers to the way a mother handfeeds a child; *uang pelicin*, slippery money that smoothes the way; *uang rokok*, or cigarette money; *amplop*, an "envelope" of money; *titipan*, which refers to money given in trust that a promise will be fulfilled; *uang terima kasih*, thank-you money; *jatah*, a "share" or one's cut of a lucrative (illegal) activity; and *proyek*, which derives from the English "project" and refers to government funding that provides an opportunity for taking a "cut."[2] Popular slang for special forms of bribery use acronyms. KUHP refers to the criminal code *(Kitab Undang-Undang Hukum Pidana)* and "Pay money, case finished" *(Kasih uang habis perkara)*. AMPI, which stands for *anak, menantu, pejabat, istri* (children, in-laws, subordinates, and wife), is used for nepotism. In South Sumatra, where speech is more direct, one simply asks, "Where's my cut?" *(Lokak saya mana?)*

In 1978 economist Richard Robison coined the expression "bureaucratic capitalism" for the political and economic system that the New Order established. He describes it as a modern form of appanage, the provisions made for the maintenance of younger children of kings. In such a system, the demarcation between public service and private interest is blurred. Under the New Order, bureaucratic capitalism became "the means for sustaining a military state and for providing officeholders with patronage for themselves, their families, and the political factions to which they owe their authority."[3] By the end of the 1980s, the political economists Hal Hill and Andrew MacIntyre described the New Order as "a self-perpetuating patronage system from top to bottom, rewarding those who have a place in it and penalizing all who are excluded." They argued that it would be "extremely difficult for any reformist movement or coalition to bring about major changes from within the system or open it up in more democratic or pluralist directions."[4]

Corruption and abuse of power permeate every level of government in South Sumatra. In this chapter, I describe how subdistrict governments followed the example set by the New Order in "harvesting" profits from local resources and show how villagers tried to reclaim their rights to these resources after the fall of Suharto. After the passage of "local autonomy" laws in 1999, corruption spread to district elections where legislators were charged with electing the district head *(bupati)*. Some *reformasi* activists organized protests against "money politics." Others changed sides and sold their services to candidates who set up "success teams," which set about buying votes. I also describe campaigns targeting misappropriation of funds by the Provincial Legislature and corruption in funding for the National Sports Week (PON). These cases illustrate the obstacles faced by *reformasi* activists working to end KKN. Finally, I describe how corruption in the judicial system led to Yeni's prosecution for libel.

Corruption extends beyond the government to civil society organizations. When major funding was redirected to NGOs after 1997, relatives and cronies of high government officials set up new NGOs to take advantage of funding opportunities. Corruption also involves relations that police and political elites forge with gangster organizations *(preman)* known as "backing" *(beking)*. The web of connections that allows government officials and well-positioned entrepreneurs to profit from public resources links local government officials, businessmen, and *preman* to elites in Jakarta. Although these shadowy connections are difficult to nail down, one well-known example of such a network, the "Palembang Mafia," is traced out.

Harvesting Local Resources

In the final years of the New Order, local governments followed the example set by the New Order in expropriating natural resources for the benefit of government officials. According to customary law *(adat)*, rights to local resources belong collectively to the people of a *marga* who live in nearby villages, and decisions or disputes relating to resources were mediated by village elders. In the mid-1990s, local governments in South Sumatra began to claim the right to control the harvest of these resources. The result was overexploitation, a decrease in productivity, and an increase in rural poverty.

Lebak Lebung

During the rainy season in South Sumatra rivers in the lowlands overflow their banks, forming shallow lagoons *(lebak lebung)* where fish accumulate. Once a year villagers would collectively harvest the lagoon and distribute the catch among all inhabitants of villages with rights to the *lebak lebung*. In 1996, the district governments of Ogan Komering Ilir (OKI) and Musi Banyuasin (MUBA) took over rights to the *lebak lebung* on the grounds that (1) they were being overfished; (2) conflicts among villagers over the division of the harvest were frequent; and (3) villagers did not have the means to develop the resources economically.[5] The district government planned to auction the rights to harvest the *lebak lebung*. The regulations for the auction required that bidders must have resided in the district for six months, but villagers did not have the capital to win the auction. A Chinese-Indonesian businessman in Palembang who had the financial resources simply used a villager as a front to bid in the auction. The contractor who won the auction needed to maximize the catch in the year he had rights to harvest, so the new system quickly led to overexploitation of the *lebak lebung*. Between 2001 and 2002 in most subdistricts in OKI, the size of the harvest, and therefore income from the auction of rights to the harvest, declined steeply from Rp 3.5 billion to Rp 2.5 billion.

The new system also escalated conflicts over the harvest of the *lebak lebung*. If the middleman contracted with outsiders to harvest the *lebak lebung*, villagers protested and on occasion attacked them. If the middleman hired local people, those who were not hired protested, and the villagers who were hired sometimes objected that they were paid too little considering the value of the harvest. There were also conflicts between contractors who wanted the *lebak lebung* to be as large as possible and farmers who planted rice on the surrounding *sawah*.[6]

In November 2000, residents of six villages in OKI organized a demonstration against the auction system as an abuse left over from the New Order.[7] Responding to increasing yearly protests, the government revised the auction system in 2003.[8] New regulations stipulated that 55 percent of the proceeds from an auction would be used for village development. This has not satisfied people, as the money is not given to the village that had traditional rights to a *lebak lebung* but to a fund for village development controlled by the district government, which still receives 23 percent of the auction proceeds. Villagers still complain about the auction, but they have little hope of regaining their rights.

"Golden Saliva" (Swallows' Nests)

Wild swallows' nests, long recognized as a valuable commodity, are called "golden saliva" *(liur emas)*. Traditionally, three villages—Lubuk Mabar, Sukajadi, and Tanjung Raya—in Lahat District shared rights to harvest nearby caves where wild swallows nested. Harvesting began with a ritual requesting permission of the swallows to take their empty nests. Harvesting took place once in three months, and nests with fledglings were not touched.

In 1997, the Lahat district government took over the right to harvest nests in the caves and set up an auction.[9] Leaders of the three villages wrote letters of protest to the *bupati* of Lahat, the governor, the minister of forestry and plantations, the National Legislature, and the president of Indonesia, but they received no response to their appeals. In November 1997, the headman of one of the three villages who was a leader of the protests was attacked and severely beaten by unknown persons. Villagers say that thugs hired by the contractor who had won the auction were behind the attack.

With the fall of Suharto in May 1998, the Lahat government showed a new willingness to reconsider the villagers' claim to the swallow-nest harvest. In August, the Lahat legislature conducted hearings at which representatives from the three villages spoke. In October, the *bupati* agreed to return the right to harvest swallows' nests to the villages if a share of the profit (US$9,000) was paid to the district government. The villagers celebrated this small victory, but in December the offer was withdrawn.

With support from WALHI, the villagers formed an organization, the Forum of Three Villages, to press their claims. In February 1999 they began a series of demonstrations at the district government offices in Lahat. In April they took their protests to the Provincial Legislature, where they succeeded in negotiating the right to oversee the harvest and receive one-third of the profits. In August, however, the contractor who had won the auction harvested the caves without informing villagers. He also broke the agreement to pay one-third of profit to the villages, claiming that he could only afford to pay half that amount.

The villagers organized another demonstration at the Provincial Legislature, followed by further demonstrations in Lahat throughout September

and October. They demanded that government officials and village representatives be present at the next harvest. Without notifying the villagers or
the Lahat government, the contractor conducted an early harvest. When
villagers learned of this, they demanded that the contractor's right to harvest be revoked.

The Lahat legislature set up a special commission to investigate the problem and recommended that the contract be revoked. This action, however,
required approval from the Minister of Forestry and Plantations. By February 2000, the contract still had not been revoked. Representatives from the
Forum of Three Villages joined the Farmers' Prosperity and Welfare Union
(KSKP) and went to Jakarta to participate in a demonstration organized by
LBH demanding resolution of land conflicts in South Sumatra. The farmers
were promised that the Ministry of Forestry and Agriculture would investigate their complaints.

In May 2000, the villagers issued an open letter announcing their intention to take control of the caves. When they found that there were almost
no swallows there, they were enraged and set fire to the abandoned kiosk
of the contractor. A few days later, two villagers were arrested for setting
the fire, leading to new protests but no change in the situation with regard
to the caves.

"Money Politics" *(Politik Uang)* at the Local Level

In 1999 the National Legislature passed Laws No. 22 and 25 to undo cen-
tralization of power under the New Order. To avoid encouraging separatist movements in prosperous provinces, districts were selected as the level
to implement local autonomy. Members of a district legislature were to
be directly elected on a party slate. The district head was to be elected by
the district legislature. The elections provided an opportunity for political
entrepreneurs to win control of local resources and lucrative government
contracts.

The district of Musi Rawas (MURA) was one of the first in South Sumatra to elect a district head *(bupati)*.[10] Although Law 22 was not yet in effect,
the MURA legislature took advantage of the spirit of reform to set its own
rules for the election.[11] In the first round of voting five pairs of candidates
for *bupati* and vice *bupati* were selected to proceed to a final vote from a list
of thirty-six candidates who had submitted their names for nomination.

Three pairs of candidates were from the Indonesian Democratic Party
of Struggle (PDI-P), which held the largest number of seats in the legisla-

ture. Each candidate formed a "success team" *(tim sukses)* to lobby legislators for their vote. Supriyono, the official PDI-P candidate, hired Waisun, a student activist who had recently returned home to South Sumatra from Jakarta, to head his success team. Waisun explained: "I need a political investment here. I was in Jakarta for years. I need to become known here. When I was an activist, the government considered me a rebel. Here I can clear my name and build a network for my future political career." Waisun set up the Union of Sekanti People, an organization purportedly representing the Musi ethnic group, to support Supriyono.

His rivals also organized support groups based on ethnic identity, capitalizing on the traditional rivalry between people of the *rawas* area of marshland and those who live along the Musi River. Prana Sohe, a local businessman, who was the nephew of one candidate and the son-in-law of another, formed an organization of Rawas people to support both their campaigns. He hired another former activist to organize demonstrations in support of his candidates. As Prana Sohe explained: "Three people are enough to establish an NGO or forum. Then you make your voice as loud as possible. You protest here and there. Then the candidates and legislature will pay attention to you, either as a potential enemy or ally. It is as simple as that."

Behind a facade of demonstration and counterdemonstration, the candidates' success teams set about trying to buy the votes of the legislators. Prana Sohe explained that he met with members of the MURA legislature "to urge them to base their choice on the quality of the candidate." However, at the end of a meeting, he acknowledged that he usually offered money (starting at US$500). This was not a bribe, he said, but a way "to help the legislators conduct a very important election for MURA society."

Joesep Supriyono, the official candidate of PDI-P, won the election by a plurality of five votes. Many *reformasi* activists opposed his candidacy on the ground that he was a retired military officer and not a native son *(putra daerah)* of Musi Rawas. They alleged that he had conducted "money politics," pointing out that his success team was observed meeting with members of the legislature in a luxury hotel in the district capital. Their protests led to a police investigation, which provoked the Minister of Regional Autonomy to announce that if the police could prove there had been bribery, the election would have to be nullified.

To no one's surprise, the bribery investigation turned into a farce.[12] A losing candidate revealed his own efforts to bribe legislators in an effort to have the election invalidated. Prana Sohe said he wanted to expose the bribery of legislators because they were too greedy. "They take money from candidate A, then again from candidates B, C, and so on. After scooping up money here and there, they choose whomever they please."[13] In the end, the police determined that Supriyono's election was valid because only his opponents could be proven to have engaged in bribery.

"Hot Money" (Uang Panas)

Despite efforts to reform the system, government officials in the post-Suharto period continued to act as if they were entitled to appropriate public funds for their own use. A corrupt judicial system insulated corrupt officials from prosecution. The most successful campaigns against corruption relied on reports in the press that aroused public outrage, which could then be channeled to challenge the government directly.

In one illustrative case in 2000, the Provincial Legislature appropriated US$260,000 for Yayasan Kesejahteraan DPRD, a foundation established for the welfare of legislators and their families. Each legislator received US$3,600 to cover transportation and other costs. The legislation appropriating public funds for Yayasan Kesejahteraan DPRD was passed as the governor was preparing his annual accountability report to the legislature, which may explain why he made no objection, given that he was politically vulnerable. When the scandal broke, he was accused of collusion. In response LBH organized a group of lawyers, the Team of Advocates to Save the People's Money (TEMPUR), which took the case to the criminal court in Palembang and to the State Administrative Court. Before a date was set for trial, the governor convinced the lead lawyer in TEMPUR to join his defense team, and the case was dropped.[14]

Not to be deterred, reformasi activists set up a new NGO to combat corruption in government, the Indonesian Forum for Budgetary Transparency (FITRA). Headed by Aziz Kamis, known as a rather opportunistic activist, FITRA targeted the governor, asserting that between 1998 and 2000 Rosihan Arsyad's documented assets increased from approximately US$16,000 to more than US$300,000. Indeed, FITRA charged that the real amount of the governor's wealth was more than US$700,000.[15] The governor maintained that his new wealth was due to "gifts" from relatives. His supporters charged that FITRA's campaign was an act of revenge because the governor had not granted Aziz Kamis funding for various proposals he had put forth.

In 2002 the Provincial Legislature proposed to more than double legislators' monthly salary to US$2,400, substantially more than the annual income of most people in South Sumatra. FITRA launched a campaign charging legislators with acting in their own interests rather than the public good.[16] While almost 2.5 million people in South Sumatra were living below the poverty line, 75 percent of the provincial budget was going to operating costs (salaries and facilities for legislators) and only 25 percent to public services. By this time public outrage at the legislature was so great that the legislators backed down and gave up their salary increase.

In 2003, once again legislators tried to siphon off a major chunk of public funds by appropriating US$900,000 as an allowance for housing and transportation.[17] Only the representative from the Islamic *reformasi* party, Partai Keadilan, refused to take his allotment of US$12,000. Public outcry over the legislators' action led some political parties, particularly the Islamic ones—Partai Kebangkitan Bangsa (PKB), Partai Bulan Bintang (PBB) and Amien Rais' *reformasi* party, Partai Amanat Nasional (PAN)—to direct their representatives to return the money.

This time, Nur Kholis, who was director of LBH-Palembang, was chosen as the new head of TEMPUR. He pressed the South Sumatra High Court to take up the case of misappropriation of funds by the legislature.[18] The case required a police investigation, but the police claimed they could not investigate public officials without permission from the Minister of Home Affairs. At the end of April, local newspapers reported that the home affairs minister had not yet acted because he had not received an official request from the High Court to authorize a police investigation. Meanwhile, the publicity given to the case led the legislature to retract its action, directing on February 26, 2003, that disbursements to legislators be returned within two months. By April 26, 2003, only thirty-three out of seventy-five legislators had complied, so the time limit was extended.[19] The case was eventually resolved at the end of May when all the legislators had finally returned the money.

Proyek: Pekan Olahraga Nasional (PON)

The selection of South Sumatra to host the National Sports Games (Pekan Olahraga Nasional, or PON XVI) in 2004 provided contractors with lucrative opportunities for a "cut" of funding for contracts constructing facilities for the games. At the same time, contractors who won bids for these *proyek* contributed to the welfare of government officials; for example, the contractor who built the housing complex for athletes made a present of a new house to the governor.

Inspired by Teten Masduki's Indonesia Corruption Watch, a respected national NGO, *reformasi* activists in South Sumatra had established South Sumatra Corruption Watch (SSCW) to monitor corruption in project funding. In 2000, SSCW launched a campaign targeting corruption in tenders related to PON XV.[20] SSCW pointed out that the contract for athletes' equipment had gone to a firm in Bandung, West Java, owned by a brother of Governor Rosihan Arsyad, and also charged that another brother of the governor, who was the contractor for housing the athletes, had inflated his costs.

These charges led to an investigation by the public prosecutor, but he reported that there were no grounds for prosecution. SSCW challenged the prosecutor's findings, forcing him to revise his report. He then stated that the markup in costs by the contractors was not as large as that alleged by SSCW. No further action was taken in the case, although over the course of seven months to May 2001, over sixty articles on corruption in PON tenders appeared in four local newspapers.[21] Activists said that the governor had persuaded the head of SSCW to stop pressing the case.

In 2001 Governor Rosihan Arsyad began fund-raising to build facilities for PON XVI in South Sumatra. SSCW activists charged that illegal gambling interests were funding PON in return for protection. They also argued that the governor was using "contributions" from prospective contractors to build up a war chest for the 2004 gubernatorial election. They thought that a campaign against illegal gambling would bring together Islamic organizations focusing on moral issues and pro-democracy groups concerned about money politics. Activist reporters were invited to a strategy meeting to plan the campaign. Shortly thereafter the office of the Islamic Students Association (HMI), where the meeting was held, and the offices of the *Sriwijaya Post* were attacked by gangsters *(preman)*. Telephone calls to the police failed to bring help until after the vandals had left. The activists understood that they had been warned off their campaign.

The following year SSCW was enveloped in scandal. An audit by Indonesia Corruption Watch (ICW), a funder of SSCW, found irregularities, and further support was terminated. When the chairman of SSCW celebrated his marriage with an expensive reception a few months later, activists passed along rumors that the festivities had been paid for by Governor Rosihan Arsyad. This was the end of SSCW as an effective organization.

Red Plate NGOs (LSM *Plat Merah*)

As shown in the cases examined above, some *reformasi* activists quickly found a place in the webs of patronage associated with government office. This undermined the reputation of NGOs as genuine *reformasi* organizations. Suspicion of NGOs as the vehicles of self-interested individuals began after the 1997 Asian Economic Crisis, when international aid organizations decided to channel money meant to alleviate the impact of the crisis on the poor through local NGOs rather than the Indonesian government, which was known for widespread corruption. The new NGO funding generated a feeding frenzy, as people formerly dependent on government *proyek* positioned themselves to obtain NGO funding. Many new NGOs were established, chaired by wives or other relatives of government employees. In South Sumatra these were known as "red plate" *(plat merah)* NGOs, because the directors drove cars with the red license plates of government officials. The public soon developed a cynical attitude. In a play on the Indo-nesian name for NGO, *lembaga swadaya masyarakat* or LSM, people asked: "What does LSM stand for? *Lokak saya mana?* or 'Where's my cut?'"

For example, when funding was made available for street children pro-grams in 2000, on the basis of a survey conducted by the Department of Social Science at Atmajaya University in Jakarta estimating that there were between 2,500 and 4,000 street children in South Sumatra, the province was allotted twenty-five "packets" of US$50,000, each packet to serve 160 children.[22] At the time, Kuala Merdeka and three other small local NGOs had programs for street children in Palembang.[23] The new funding, how-ever, was divided among three of these NGO and seventeen new NGOs established by teachers, wives of government officials, or other individuals. The result was that most of the money was used for "administrative costs" associated with setting up an office and salaries. None of the NGOs pro-vided shelter for the street children. When funding for the programs ended in 2001, all the new NGOs established in 2000 disappeared—though the street children had not.

A Corrupt Judicial System

Rather than providing a channel for redress of grievances and justice, the courts and the law in Indonesia are widely used to criminalize protest and protect the guilty. Cynicism about the judicial system is expressed in a bit of wordplay that equates the "basic law" *(undang undang dasar)* or UUD of Indonesia with *ujung ujungnya duit* ("in the end it's all about money"). The story of Yeni Roslaini's prosecution for libel *(pencemaran nama baik)* illustrates how bribery influences judges' decisions and the bizarre way in which the law can be manipulated.

In 1999, Yeni and several colleagues founded the Women's Crisis Cen-ter (WCC) to counsel and provide support to victims of rape and domestic violence. One of the first cases brought before WCC involved a fifteen-year-old girl who had been raped by the son of her father's employer. After the girl's father reported the rape to the police, he was fired from his job.

Before the case went to trial, the girl's family went to WCC for help. At the trial, the defense produced a doctor's report that differed from the initial medical report on the rape, which WCC had seen. According to the new medical report, there was no evidence of rape, so the accused was not convicted. Witnesses had testified that the defendant had taken the girl to a hotel, so instead he was sentenced to seven months in jail for abducting an underage girl. This decision was appealed, and the sentence changed to one year's probation.

During the trial, WCC staff conducted a public awareness campaign, distributing pamphlets explaining that rape was a crime. Interviewed by a newspaper reporter, Yeni said, "What the perpetrator did is barbaric and inhuman." The defendant sued her for libel.[24] Although LBH mounted a vigorous legal defense, Yeni was convicted and sentenced to two months in jail. By this time, the case was receiving attention in the national media, and women activists across Indonesia mobilized to protest if Yeni was sent to jail. The case was appealed all the way up to the Indonesian Supreme Court, which has an enormous backlog of such cases. As of 2005 Yeni was still awaiting a final decision.

The *Preman* Connection: *Beking*

Preman, from the Dutch *vrij man* (free man), is generally translated as gangster or thug, but in South Sumatra where men are expected to cultivate a macho attitude, *preman* live on the edge of respectability. Honor *(harga diri)* is a central value, and men are expected to respond to an insult with violence. Traditionally, men carried a knife, either a machete when going to the fields or forest or a *keris* (ceremonial dagger) when making a formal visit. There are many local expressions for a macho attitude, especially in a young man: *juaro* means like a fighting cock; *petakoan* refers to a youth who is always testing his prowess against others; *gilo renang* means "crazy/not crazy," someone with an "attitude." A young tough from a "good home" is described as *budak nakal,* that is, a youth who makes trouble but is not a criminal.

South Sumatra has the reputation of being a violent and dangerous place, and I was told that Interpol has a special section called Kayu Agung after the capital of Ogan Komering Ilir (OKI) district in lowland South Sumatra. Young men in OKI traditionally leave home to make their fortunes in the world. They go to Malaysia or another Southeast Asian country, where they link up with a network of other fortune seekers from OKI and seize any opportunity, legal or illegal, to get rich quick. When a young man returns home with his new wealth, no one asks how he got the money. He is welcomed back and becomes a respected member of the community.

Many different kinds of *preman* are distinguished in South Sumatra. Young men who hang out in the *pasar* (market) and drink and get into fights are called *preman kampungan*. A gang involved in illegal activities, often smuggling, who may also work as security guards for warehouses are known as *preman sindikat*. Policemen with ties to such gangs are called *polisi preman*. *Preman berdasi* are *preman* who wear a tie. *Preman intelek* are educated *preman*. These *preman* serve as front men for their followers, who are thugs for hire. *Preman intelek* are the connection between the thugs and the government officials and businessmen who hire them to rough up student protestors, intimidate villagers, or act as provocateurs in peaceful demonstrations.

Preman gangs in Palembang like to think of themselves as providing a service *(jasa)* to the community. They "protect" neighborhoods where thievery is common. For example, the Kertapati *preman* guard the train station; the Boombaru *preman* guard ships docked in the harbor below Palembang; and Bugis *preman* guard Sungai Batang, where Bugis sailing vessels dock. Ideally, *preman* do not steal from people in their own territory. Some of the older or well-established *preman* have even become respected members of the community, making the transition from protection rackets to being legitimate contractors for large companies such as Pertamina. *Preman* from Plaju, where the Pusri plant is located, and *preman* from Hoktong, where rubber-processing plants line the edge of the river, also often become legitimate contractors.

The relationship between *preman* and police and security forces in South Sumatra goes back to the 1950s, when the sons of soldiers, known as *anak kolong* (army kids), formed a *preman* gang. As is illustrated by the following cases, many *preman* gangs have close connections to local police and security forces.

In Pendopo and Talang Ubi, remote districts in the lowland forests between Palembang and Lahat, the oil wells of PT Expan Nusantara (Expan) are guarded by security forces. Villagers in Pendopo and Talang Ubi call these security guards "Kopassus," because some were formerly soldiers in Kopassus, the much-feared Special Forces "red berets" of the Indonesian army. The villagers understand that the guards are protecting Expan from protests. They tell of the time that a valve on the oil pipeline exploded, causing a fire that burned for three kilometers along the pipeline and killed five people. When villagers organized a demonstration protesting negligence on the part of Expan, the security forces burned down one villager's house and killed a protestor.

According to villagers, the security guards also work closely with a local gang of thieves who steal pipe from Expan.[25] In March 2002, a farmer named Jamal found a pile of pipe cut into two-meter lengths hidden in his grove of rubber trees. Later, Jamal observed two men moving the pipes to the road where it could be transported out of the area. He reported this to a security guard, who in turn reported to the chief of Expan's Security Force and to the police. Talang Ubi villagers knew the identity of the two men who had moved the pipe to the road. They say that the men told them that they had been paid by *preman* and the pipes had been stolen with the knowledge of a police officer. One villager reported that he heard a policeman offer to sell pipe to a man from another village. Another villager added that he had seen a police officer in a coffee stall in Pendopo talking with local *preman* who were known to steal pipe. The villagers agreed that a red car had been used to transport the stolen pipe, and they said that only two people in the district owned such a car: a rubber merchant and the local police chief.

Jamal, who reported the stolen pipe that he saw on his land, was chairman of the Talang Ubi branch of the Farmers' Prosperity and Welfare Union (KSKP). Shortly thereafter, on the pretext of his involvement in a protest against MHP the previous year in which villagers held a vehicle owned by MHP hostage for a short time, he was arrested and charged with theft. Talang Ubi villagers went to the district government to protest Jamal's arrest. They believed MHP had paid the police to arrest him and charged that the prosecutor was rewarded with the gift of a cell phone. LBH staff defended Jamal at his trial, where he was found not guilty.

A syndicate of police and gangsters engaged in stealing pipe appears to have been in existence for a long time. In 1992 the police chief of Talang Ubi was removed after only one year because he was caught "backing" *(beking)* a pipe-stealing syndicate. The officers involved in the syndicate were transferred but not charged. People say that this case was "put in the icebox" (*dipetieskan,* or "P tiga S"), a play on words that refers to an official order to stop an investigation (*Surat Perintah Penghentian Perkara*—SP3). They report that the police chief who was behind the syndicate is now a member of the district legislature.

Villagers in Pendopo have a wealth of stories about unsolved crimes that they believe involved the police. Once, they say, they saw an out-of-uniform police officer driving a truck transporting cattle. He said that he had bought the cattle in Tanjung Baru, but the next day the villagers heard that cattle had been stolen from a nearby village. Villagers do not report such crimes because they are afraid that they will be accused of the theft.

Another lucrative racket involving *preman* gangs and police is motorcycle theft. When someone reports a vehicle stolen, the police "find" it for a price. They explain that there must be "compensation" to a middleman. If the owner is willing to pay US$100–200, the vehicle can be retrieved. Alternatively, the thieves buy a new title for the vehicle from the police for about US$250 so they can resell it.

The police are said to be involved in *beking* gangs that deal in drugs as well. A small-time drug dealer explained that he paid the police about US$12 for a "site" where he could sell drugs. Otherwise, he would be arrested and required to pay "settlement" money of US$50–100. After local newspapers reported that two police officers were caught with Ecstasy in a drug raid at a café in Pendopo, the café was closed down, but the officers were never charged.

Illegal logging provides another lucrative opportunity for payoffs. Owners of "wild" (illegal) sawmills must pay off police, and drivers of trucks that transport the wood must pay a "tax" at police roadblocks. Alternatively, the police may take lumber as payment in kind or offer to buy the wood for less than its market value.

Preman and Politics

During the New Order, "youth" organizations such as Pancasila Youth, Pemuda Panca Marga, and the Communication Forum of the Sons and Daughters of the Indonesian Military were gradually transformed into paramilitary groups that provided "muscle" against critics of the regime. The New Order regime also forged connections with *preman* gangs, particularly after 1983–1984, when President Suharto commissioned street executions of thousands of thugs by government security forces.[26] This operation, known as Petrus, which stands for "mysterious killings" *(pembunuhan misterius),* provided an opportunity for police and security forces to "control" criminal gangs in exchange for a "cut." In this system, known as "backing" *(beking),* criminal activities were protected by government officials in exchange for a share of the profits, and *preman* acted as enforcers when official security forces were under scrutiny for human rights abuses.

After the fall of Suharto, *preman* became involved in local politics in South Sumatra. The younger brother of Governor Rosihan Arsyad became the head of the South Sumatra Youth Front (BPS), an organization established by a local labor organizer in 1999. BPS shared its office with the Patriot Party, a political party established by Yapto Suryosumarmo, the leader of Pancasila Youth, the paramilitary wing of Golkar. The head of BPS was said to have boasted that it was able to "convince" protestors to accept the governor's choice of an interim *bupati* for the new district of

Banyuasin. Soon people began to say that BPS stood for the Preman Front of South Sumatra *(Badan Preman Sumsel)*. In an interview, the head of BPS admitted that it had some *preman* leaders, but he added, "We don't accept that label as true, because there are those who do not accept the name of *preman*."[27] He described BPS as a "moral force" because *preman* represented important values, such as protection of the community. Therefore it was "proper for them to sell" *(layak jual)* their services. For example, he said, *preman* leaders use their power in the neighborhoods they control to settle conflicts over land or business, and BPS worked with the provincial Department of Transportation to provide security on buses.

The link between government officials and *preman* is generally represented by a figure like Azis Kamis. As a student in 1985, he was an activist in Islamic-oriented development organizations.[28] When Suharto began to court Muslim leaders to counter the emerging *reformasi* movement in the early 1990s, Azis Kamis joined the Golkar youth organization (KNPI) and set up a number of government-linked NGOs in South Sumatra. In the aftermath of the 1997 economic crisis, one of his NGOs was funded by the Urban Poor Consortium in Jakarta to set up cooperatives for cycle rickshaw *(becak)* and river-taxi drivers. In 2000, Azis Kamis played an important role in organizing *becak* drivers to resist regulations imposed by the Palembang city government, thus solidifying his status as a political broker. When Azis Kamis set up FITRA after the demise of South Sumatra Corruption Watch in 2001, he was given funding to provide financial training to village councils.

When FITRA targeted Governor Rosihan Arsyad for corruption, some people said that this was Azis Kamis' revenge for the governor's not giving him project funding. In the 2003 gubernatorial election, when Rosihan Arsyad was in a closely fought battle with Syahrial Oesman, Azis Kamis mobilized two local *preman*-linked groups—the United Palembang Social Community and the Sumsel Youth Front—and large numbers of rickshaw drivers and street vendors for a demonstration supporting Syahrial Oesman, who was eventually declared the winner (see next chapter).

The Palembang Mafia

Formal and informal networks link powerful political figures at the center of government in Jakarta to provincial, district, and subdistrict officials, military commanders, business moguls, local entrepreneurs, and *preman*. In South Sumatra, the network of ties that connect Taufik Kiemas, the husband of former president Megawati Sukarnoputri, with political and business elites in South Sumatra is known as the Palembang Mafia. TK, as he is known, grew up in Palembang and attended Sriwijaya University during the 1960s. In his youth he is said to have been a "cross boy," slang for youths who careened around on motorcycles and hung out with a semicriminal gang known as Bala 12 (Troop 12). At the same time, TK was a member of the Indonesian Nationalist Students Movement (GMNI), the youth wing of Sukarno's political party. After the fall of Sukarno in 1965, TK was imprisoned for eighteen months. In jail he solidified a relationship with Adjis Saip, also a member of GMNI, that was to last a lifetime.

In 1973, Taufik Kiemas married Sukarno's daughter, Megawati, after the death of her first husband in a plane crash and the annulment of a second marriage to an Egyptian diplomat.[29] In 1979 the state-owned oil and gas company Pertamina gave Megawati and TK licenses (in the names of their children) to open gas stations in Jakarta. This provided them with a prosperous income, and TK was able to help old friends such as Adjis Saip, who was given a construction project in Palembang in the early 1980s.

Rumor has it that Taufik Kiemas convinced his wife to enter politics, joining the Indonesian Democracy Party (PDI), an offshoot of Sukarno's Nationalist Party. In 1993 the New Order decided that PDI chairman Surjadi must be replaced when he began calling for an end to corruption and a limit on the number of terms a president could serve. TK may also have pushed for Megawati to take over leadership of the party. Fearing that she might gain significant support in elections scheduled for 1998, the New Order arranged for a special party congress to oust her as party chairman. This transformed Megawati into a symbol of the *reformasi* movement.

In the 1999 election that took place after the fall of Suharto, Megawati's new party, PDI Struggle (PDI-P), won a plurality of the votes. Although Megawati did not win election to the presidency in the People's Consultative Assembly, Taufik Kiemas and two of his brothers were elected to the National Legislature. As PDI-P held the most seats in the legislature, TK emerged as an influential political broker, using his power to place his own people on the central committee of the party. Adjis Saip became head of PDI-P in South Sumatra. TK also expanded his network of contacts among business tycoons, such as Prayogo Pangestu, and investors, offering to facilitate deals through using his political connections.

During Megawati's presidency (2000–2004), TK further consolidated his power by assuring the appointment of three cabinet ministers from South Sumatra, as well as other influential officials, such as Attorney General Muhammad Abdul Rachman and Basrief Arief, another Palembang native. In response to an interviewer's question about the number of people from South Sumatra appointed to top positions in state banks and security positions, TK responded, "It's just a coincidence, but yes, our sense of brotherhood is very strong. [US President] Bush is like that, too, with people from Texas, right? Do people call it the Texas mafia?"[30]

Taufik Kiemas is known for brokering lucrative government projects, such as the US$2.3 billion Jakarta Outer Ring Road, a US$2.4 billion railway stretching the length of Java, and a US$1.7 billion trans-Papua highway.[31] Indonesia's three biggest debtors—Marimutu Sinivasan, Prayogo Pangestu, and Syamsul Nursalim—sought TK's help in brokering deals that allowed them to renegotiate the terms of repayment on their debts and escape prosecution.[32] Two of Taufik Kiemas' brothers are commissioners of companies owned by Nursalim. TK admits to "sometimes helping as a mediator" but denies that he makes any money from the deals he arranges.

The Palembang Mafia is known to connect such well-known figures as Taufik's brother, Nazaruddin Kiemas, who represents Muara Enim District in the National Legislature (DPR) and in 2004 replaced Adjis Saip as chairman of PDI-P in South Sumatra, with Dudy Makmun Murod, the son of an army commander on the Gajah Tunggal board of directors; Lieutenant General Ryamizard Ryacudu, a "hard-line" officer from South Sumatra, who was appointed commander of the Strategic Reserve (Kostrad) in June 2002; Yapto Suryosumarmo, former chairman of Pancasila Youth, a New Order paramilitary youth organization; and Habib Husein Al-Habsyi, a blind Muslim cleric jailed for twelve years for a 1985 bombing at Borobudur.[33]

Even some former *reformasi* activists have joined TK's network, including M. S. Zulkarnain, a national director of WALHI, and Muhamad Yamin, who helped defend victims of the Kedungombo dam project in Central Java. LBH staff say that Yamin, a member of the 1994–1995 Team to Defend Democracy and a founder of Yayasan Kuala Merdeka, is now known as "Komisi 10 Ribu" (Ten Thousand Rupiah Commission) because he expects to be tipped when he helps to arrange a meeting with TK. In 2002 he was featured in a *Tempo* article on the nouveau riche of the post-Suharto era.[34]

Perhaps the strangest of all is TK's link to Pius Lustrilanang, a young *reformasi* activist whose father was a professor at Sriwijaya University. In early 1998, Pius was kidnapped and tortured by the Indonesian military special forces, Kopassus. After he was released, he went to Geneva to testify before the Human Rights Commission, despite having been warned by the military not to talk. Ironically, Pius was recruited as the commander of an elite PDI-P paramilitary group, Brigade Siaga Satu (Brigass), which is trained by former members of the same Kopassus unit that kidnapped him in 1998. Pius Lustrilanang has now established Brigass Lustrilanang Security as a freelance paramilitary "security force" that sells its services to the highest bidder.

In the post-Suharto period, Megawati and Taufik Kiemas grew rich; in 2001 Taufik Kiemas was identified as the third richest member of the National Legislature. He filed an official report on the value of their assets, which listed US$6 million, numerous gas stations, fourteen houses, substantial landholdings, eighteen cars, and four motorcycles. However, *Fortune* magazine estimated the true figure for Megawati and TK's wealth as US$10 million.[35]

The exorbitant corruption in South Sumatra is fueled by Indonesia's natural wealth, which government officials have been able to exploit in partnership with local cronies or sell to foreign corporations. In 2005 South Sumatra was listed as one of the five most corrupt provinces in Indonesia, along with other rich provinces—Jakarta, South Sulawesi, North Sumatra, and Riau.[36] Profits from rents on resources support a web of patronage that extends down to the lowest level of government and into civil society.

This system of patronage and bribery has been described as a "culture of corruption." Yet no one I know in South Sumatra approves of the bribery of government officials or collusion in arranging contracts. People feel trapped in a system that they do not know how to dismantle. In the next chapter we examine to what extent "local autonomy" laws passed in 1999 in order to make government more democratic and accountable have succeeded.

Chapter 7

Local Autonomy

Democracy in Name Only?

> In theory, decentralization can provide the impetus for poverty reduc-
> tion and good governance because with decentralization, elements of
> civil society have the opportunity to monitor the way the government
> behaves more closely and also to bring the concerns and suggestions
> of the poor closer to the government.
> —Sudarno Sumarta, Asep Suryahadi, and Alex Arifianto,
> "Governance and Poverty Reduction"[1]

IN 1999, AFTER THE FALL of the New Order government, Indonesia
passed "local autonomy" legislation. Decentralization was a primary com-
ponent of the effort to democratize government in Indonesia. In the early
stages, the districts of Musi Banyuasin (MUBA) and Ogan Komering Ulu
(OKU) in South Sumatra elected new *bupati*. The winning candidates, Alex
Noerdin and Syahrial Oesman, have emerged as two of the most dynamic
politicians in South Sumatra in the post-Suharto period. Both men promised to bring development to their districts and announced populist programs promoting local welfare. Alex Noerdin was awarded the Manggala
Karya Kencana Prize in 2002 and the Satya Lencana Wirakarya Award in
2003. In 2002, Syahrial Oesman was given three national awards for his
promotion of village cooperatives, for his success in maintaining OKU's
record as a "rice barn" of the nation, and for his achievement in implement-
ing the national family planning program.

Both men are former New Order bureaucrats. They built new political networks linking national elites and local businessmen seeking access
to natural resources and lucrative government projects *(proyek)*. They
employed former student activists as campaign organizers in order to maintain a facade of popular support, but both were accused of using "money
politics" to win elections. The stories of their political fortunes illustrate
the complex interplay between the politics of project funding *(proyek)* and
democratization through decentralization.

Alex Noerdin: *Bupati* of Musi Banyuasin (MUBA)

MUBA was a rich prize for the *bupati* who won the election scheduled for June 2001. The district has oil and natural gas reserves as well as South Sumatra's remaining forest lands. In 2001 MUBA contributed US$82.7 million in royalties on natural resources to the central government.[2] Politicking over election procedures that might favor one candidate over another was intense, and the MUBA legislature twice agreed to postpone the election.[3] This benefited Alex Noerdin, who had been appointed interim *bupati* by the governor.

In the MUBA legislature elected in 1999 there were five factions: PDI-P (16 seats); Golkar (10); a coalition of Islam-oriented parties (9); the Renewal Faction (5); and the military/police faction (5). This meant that the successful candidate would have to woo legislators from more than one party, a situation that generally led to vote buying or "money politics."[4] But as director of LBH Nur Kholis pointed out to the press, vote buying was almost impossible to prove unless the financial records of legislators and their families and close associates were made public.

Alex Noerdin was nominated by the faction of Islamic-oriented parties. The election took the form of a three-way race between the PDI-P candidate, the Golkar candidate, and Alex Noerdin, all of whom could claim to be "native son" *(putra daerah)* candidates.[5] PDI-P tried to block Alex Noerdin's nomination on the ground that not all members of the Islamic-oriented parties were present when he was nominated, but their objection failed and the election proceeded. When Alex Noerdin won the election with twenty-five votes, his victory was attributed to "money politics." The MUBA election was said to be the most expensive *bupati* election in South Sumatra.

Alex Noerdin forged a diverse network of support for his campaign. Some members of his "success team" came from Golkar-affiliated organizations, such as the head of the Indonesian National Youth Committee (KNPI), and Nopianto, a leader of the Pancasila Youth. Nopianto argued that the idealism of *reformasi* had to be combined with practical politics. He explained that money is the most important thing in *bupati* elections: "Experience and other qualifications are secondary. Participation of people either in supporting or protesting candidates requires money. Demonstrations are a way of developing a democratic society and an important strategy to support a candidate. The easiest way to get the people to a demonstration is by giving them money. The more money you have, the more people you can bring to join the demonstration."[6] Although Nopianto is not from MUBA, he maintains that his work in organizing support for Alex Noerdin was "objectively right" because all of the other campaign organizers for *bupati* candidates were from outside the region. For Nopianto, who has a car and an office equipped with computer, telephone, fax machine, and air conditioner (rare luxuries in South Sumatra), "The best result is that you get money and facilities, and your candidate wins the election."

Other members of Alex Noerdin's success team were *reformasi* activists like Hendri Zainuddin, an NGO activist who organized a long list of "people's organizations" supporting Alex Noerdin. Hendri says that he arranged meetings with members of the MUBA legislature on behalf of Alex Noerdin and alleges that PDI-P legislators were offered a Mitsubishi car in exchange for their vote. The twenty-five legislators who voted for Alex Noerdin spent three days in a fancy hotel in Jakarta just before the election, returning to Sekayu, the capital of MUBA, only three hours before voting began. This strategy of isolating legislators from lobbying by other candidates was regarded as very clever.

Alex Noerdin was installed as *bupati* of MUBA on the last day of 2001. He launched a five-year plan, "Prosperous MUBA in 2006."[7] Despite its abundance of natural resources, MUBA had the highest rate of poverty of any district in South Sumatra, with just over 50 percent of the population living below the poverty line.[8] Villagers said that so much land had been incorporated into concessions for oil palm and timber production that in some areas up to one-third of young men had no land to cultivate and no job. Due to poverty and the poor condition of the roads, the district was famous for "road pirates" *(bajing loncat)*, who stopped cars at night to ask for a "donation to fix the road." MUBA also had the highest rate of illiteracy of any district in South Sumatra, with only 56 percent of students completing nine years of school.[9]

Alex Noerdin promised to provide electricity and clean water to villages, establish more village health clinics and clinics for workers, and provide health and life insurance (US$2,500 benefit) for all people in MUBA. He launched "Nine Years of Compulsory Education," promising to eliminate school fees for elementary and middle school students. In 2003 the program would be extended to "Twelve Years of Compulsory Education." New schools would be built, and part-time teachers without degrees would receive a modest increase in salary.

"Prosperous MUBA in 2006" was to be financed by development of the rich natural resources of the district, which had been identified as one of nine districts in Indonesia with the highest potential for investors. Alex Noerdin maintained that the resources of MUBA should be developed locally rather than simply exploited by multinational corporations like Conoco-Philips, which holds a large concession in MUBA. At his initiative, the MUBA government formed a partnership with the Bandung Institute of Technology to take advantage of a law passed in early 2001 ending state-owned Pertamina's exclusive rights to oil and gas production.[10] Instead, a jointly owned company, PT Petro MUBA, would develop so-called wild wells, oil wells from the colonial period managed (illegally) by local residents.[11] Villagers with wild wells would be organized into cooperatives to sell their oil to PT Gada Kilang, a partnership with the MUBA government, which would build a new refinery.

In July 2002, I went to MUBA to see how Alex Noerdin's ambitious plans to improve education and welfare were being implemented. LBH staff member Syamsul Asinar, who had worked with farmers in MUBA involved in a conflict with the Conoco-Philips Oil Company, arranged for me to talk with villagers living along the main road to Sekayu, the district capital.[12] People said that schools still levied "special" fees and there was a shortage of teachers, but they were pleased that the cost of education had been reduced and hopeful that new schools would allow their children to complete more education. They said that they had heard reports that medical treatment was free at the hospital in Sekayu, but more accessible village clinics built during the New Order still had not been staffed.

While the salaries of village officials in MUBA had been more than doubled to US$30 a month for the village head and US$23 for members of the village council, people said that corruption was still rampant. Farmers pointed to the village head's new car and claimed that he took a cut of up to 40 percent from village development projects. He also benefited from the government program distributing rice to the poor at a special low price (this program was in place in 2000/2001). Men who worked on buses and trucks transporting the rice, and government officials, all took a cut of the rice, with the consequence that the poorest villagers who received it had to pay a higher price than had been announced to make up the difference. People said that protests would be useless, because the head of the village council was in league with the village headman.

A visit to Sekayu, the capital of MUBA, in 2005 showed where most of the expenditure on development had gone. The road from Palembang to Sekayu was newly paved, cutting the time of the journey from four hours to less than two. Broad, newly paved roads led to venues built for the 2004 National Games. There were a horse pavilion and an Olympic swimming pool and new hotels. But villagers living only fifteen kilometers from Sekayu said that there had been very little improvement in their lives. A few people had been fortunate to get a low-cost electrical connection, but everyone else had to do without, as they would have to pay for one of the expensive connections that were still available. People still had to send their children to Sekayu if they were to go to high school. According to a report in a local newspaper, almost half the elementary schools in the district were in desperate need of repair or rebuilding.[13] Finally, nothing had been done about the problem of water, and the village wells were going dry.

Several attempts to visit villages with wild oil wells were stymied by the condition of the roads, which were unpaved and impassable after a rain.[14] In 2005 the road to Suban Burung, a district with wells, was completely blocked by an oil tanker that was sunk in the mud and a heavy truck that had become lodged in a ditch when it tried to go around the tanker. In the village of Sungai Angit, the wild oil wells had still not been developed, and the ground around the villagers' jerry-built wells was soaked in dirty crude oil.[15] Villagers had yet to see any profit from the promised partnership with the MUBA government. A visit to the office of Petro MUBA revealed a brand-new office building and associated structures, all of which were empty.

In July 2004, I asked a member of the MUBA legislature to provide his assessment of "Prosperous MUBA in 2006."[16] He explained that, because of the focus on foreign investment, remote villages had yet to see any benefit from the new development programs. Clean water was still a serious problem. The wells, rivers, and irrigation ditches where people get water for bathing and other uses are often black with oil seeps or oil spills. Remote villages still did not have electricity. Furthermore, Alex Noerdin's development programs attracted contractors looking for projects, and this put government officials in a position to ask for bribes. Corruption was so pervasive that the following year ten MUBA district officials made an official complaint to the national Commission to Eradicate Corruption.[17] No action had been taken at the time I left South Sumatra.

Interviewed in 2004 and again in 2005, Alex Noerdin explained that he had difficulty funding all the programs he had proposed because 85 percent of royalties on oil, gas, and coal extracted from MUBA still went to the central government, while another 3 percent went to the provincial government and 6 percent more was divided among the neighboring districts, leaving only 6 percent for the MUBA government.[18] Furthermore, he complained, the provincial and national governments did not use income received from MUBA to maintain the infrastructure of national and provincial roads and bridges in the district. Therefore, district government funds had to be used, and the MUBA government was forced to borrow for infrastructure development that would attract foreign investment.

Pointing to his accomplishments as *bupati*, Alex Noerdin emphasized improvements in health and education. He claimed that 44 percent of villages now had electricity and 47 percent had clean water. He believed that the sports facilities built for the National Games in 2004 would make MUBA the sports capital of Indonesia. In terms of efforts to attract foreign investment, he was particularly proud that in MUBA the number of phone lines per capita was the highest in Indonesia. And he pointed to the small airport built outside Sekayu for the National Games, which would have multiple uses, serving foreign investors and planes belonging to the Forestry Department to spot forest fires. When I went to see the airport, however, there were neither planes nor staff there.

According to reports in local newspapers, there has been a decline in poverty rates in MUBA. An April 2002 article in the *Sumatera Ekspres* put the poverty rate at 49 percent; a July 2003 article reported a poverty rate of 32 percent.[19] And in an interview in February 2004, Alex Noerdin claimed that the poverty rate in MUBA had been reduced to 24 percent. Even if these figures exaggerate the decrease in poverty, there is reason to believe that Indonesia's slow recovery from the Asian Economic Crisis, accompanied by democratic reforms, are making a difference. Alex Noerdin is managing to combine New Order type corporate development projects with some attention to the public welfare.

Alex Noerdin is already being talked about as a potential candidate for governor of South Sumatra. First, however, he faces the challenge of a direct *bupati* election in 2006, if he chooses to run for a second term. Since the kind of vote buying that determined the 2000 election will no longer be possible, Alex Noerdin appears to be shaping a new strategy. The election of representatives to the district legislature in 2004 demonstrated that voters are not loyal party followers. PDI-P lost eight of its sixteen seats, and Golkar added only one seat to the ten it held; the remaining twenty-one seats went to small parties, such as the new Islamic Justice and Prosperity Party (PKS), which ran an anticorruption campaign and won two seats. Recognizing the decline of parties as power brokers, Alex Noerdin distributes favors equally across the parties, rather than building a base of support in one party. When attacked by critics, he uses former activists to organize counterdemonstrations by "people's organizations." In this way, he is distributing patronage to a network of organizers that he hopes will help bring in votes. Alex Noerdin has also been cultivating local religious leaders *(ulama)* by visiting Islamic schools *(pesantren)*. In his vision for "Prosperous MUBA," he points to the development of a society based on religious values as a goal. In addition, he provides funding for the projects of the *ulama,* and at election time he will call on them for their support.[20]

In MUBA, as elsewhere in lowland South Sumatra, poverty is linked to the problem of land rights. In 2001, LBH documented twenty land conflicts there.[21] In the past, land was not a scarce resource. When Nur Kholis' father led a group of Javanese settlers to MUBA in the 1950s, they were given land by the indigenous Musi Banyuasin people. Local people grew rubber and fruit trees in the forest, farmed highlands with dry rice, and collected rattan and wood from the forest. Rivers supplied abundant fish. The Javanese settlers transformed marshland into irrigated fields *(sawah)* and planted groves of coconut palms. The lives of the Javanese settlers were difficult at first, but the migrants became quite prosperous by the early 1980s, when MUBA became known as the "rice barn" of South Sumatra. As production grew, new enterprises transporting goods to and from Palembang sprang up. By this time Musi Banyuasin people and Javanese farmers were intermarrying, and no distinction was made any longer between Javanese settlers and local people.

In contrast, Javanese who came later on transmigration projects implemented by the New Order during the 1970s are sometimes still resented as intruders. In the transmigration projects, each family was given a plot of 2.4 hectares. Often the land was not suitable to cultivate familiar crops, and the government provided little support for innovation or experimentation. Some families gave up and returned home to Java or moved to another transmigration project where they hoped the land would be better.

When corporations were given land concessions for the development of oil palm plantations in the 1980s, they were required to include the established Javanese transmigrants as *plasma* in their projects. The Javanese farmers were given title to *paket* (a share in the plantation equal to the profit from a plot of two hectares) in exchange for their land and paid a minimum wage to clear land and plant oil palm. MUBA people could see no advantage to joining such schemes. But after the Asian Economic Crisis of 1997, cash export crops, such as palm oil, became very profitable. Life improved for the Javanese who were *plasma*, while the indigenous people of MUBA were slipping into dire poverty. Their land rights were not recognized by the government. The forest was being cut down by palm oil companies, logging companies, or illegal loggers; the rivers were silting up from erosion, and the fish catch had decreased dramatically.

I learned about the struggles of landless people in MUBA from Pak Jafar, whom I met at the LBH office in Palembang.[22] From 1969 to 1972, Pak Jafar was a village head in Sungai Lilin subdistrict; then he worked for many years as a medical assistant in a government health clinic at a transmigration project. Upon retirement, he was given a plot in the transmigration site that was later included in a land concession to an oil palm corporation. In 2000, he emerged as the leader of a group of landless farmers, both MUBA people and Javanese, who wanted to farm their own land rather than join a *plasma* scheme. With support from LBH, Pak Jafar negotiated with MUBA government officials for permission to farm conservation forest land that had been clear-cut by illegal loggers. The farmers were given "usage rights" *(tanah ulayat)*—rights to use the land as a group, not individual ownership rights—and they were warned not to set fires that could spread to the forest. The settlers were hopeful for the future; it was their understanding that a person could get clear title to land if they had farmed *tanah ulayat* for twenty-five years.

The 587 families, led by Pak Jafar, built a village called Dusun Belido, which was divided into four settlements in which MUBA and Javanese farmers lived together. They set up their own government, Forum Tiga Dusun; every Friday night all the farmers met to organize collective work and settle disputes. When I went to Dusun Belido in 2003, I saw the one-room school that the settlers had built and met the teacher they had hired from their own resources. A small mosque was under construction.

Life in Dusun Belido was hard. From 8:00 a.m. to 3:00 p.m., the men worked as day laborers on the London Sumatra (Lonsum) oil palm plantation. They knew that once the plantation land was cleared and planted, heavy equipment would be used for maintenance and only a few day laborers would be hired. After a long day's work, they returned to clear the

The author (seated middle) and her colleague Professor Ann Tickamyer with farmers in Belido (and journalist Andrew Steele).

imperator grass from their own plot of land, where they planted vegetables and dry-farmed rice for their own use and corn and peppers as cash crops. They also planted rubber trees and oil palms, which would become productive in several years.

In 2002 the Ministry of Conservation put up a sign on the road into Dusun Belido marking the area as a conservation forest. Pak Jafar was summoned to the Conservation Department in Palembang and told that Dusun Belido was an illegal settlement. He went back to LBH for help. They managed to get a document from the MUBA district government stating that they had been granted permission to cultivate deforested land, but this was not the end to their problems.

The settlers of Dusun Belido were caught in a turf war between the Department of Forestry and the MUBA district government. In September 2003, forestry and conservation officials met with MUBA district officials and agreed that, for the time being, the settlers could stay in Dusun Belido. However, they were told that at a later date their land would be included in a concession for an oil palm plantation even though the area was designated as a conservation forest.

The people of Dusun Belido point out that there are many concessions in Sungai Lilin subdistrict—the American company Cargill, known in Indonesia as PT Hindoli, has 600,000 hectares, PT Santosa has 12,000 hectares, Lonsum and a Malaysian company also have large concessions. They ask why the government gives vast tracts of land to corporations, while farmers' rights to a 2.4 hectare plot are not secure. They are angry because MUBA forestry officials have asked them to pay a tax on the land they cultivate even though the government does not recognize their land rights. One farmer protested, " 'Prosperous MUBA in 2006' means prosperity for people who already have something, not prosperity for the poor." Another expressed the anguish of people in Dusun Belido: "If the government helps us, thank God. All we really need is an opportunity because we will work hard. People here could be prosperous if the government would help with seeds and fertilizer, cattle and training. Why does the government give land to Lonsum but give nothing to us?"

In 2005 I learned that Pak Jafar and five other farmers in Dusun Belido had been arrested. When President Susilo Bambang Yudhoyono announced a government crackdown on illegal logging, ambitious police officers charged the leaders of Dusun Belido with logging in a conservation forest. Since illegal logging is very lucrative, the cases of Dusun Belido farmers were assigned to six different judges, in the expectation that each of the accused would pay a bribe for a reduced fine and jail sentence. When it became apparent that the accused were poor farmers with no money, the cases were consolidated and the charge of illegal logging dropped; instead, the men were charged with squatting in a conservation forest. I spoke with one member of the three-judge panel that tried their case shortly before the verdict was released. He understood that there had been a miscarriage of justice in the original arrest, but explained that the law had to be upheld.[23] The farmers were given a minimal fine and reduced jail time, and told that they must leave the farms they had planted in the conservation forest. The people of Dusun Belido are supposed to be "relocated" to another area in MUBA, but they do not know where or when, or if they will be forced to become *plasma* on an oil palm plantation.

Alex Noerdin's proclamation of "Prosperous MUBA in 2006" and his efforts to provide land for the settlers of Dusun Belido suggest that democratic reforms lead elected officials to pay somewhat more attention to the needs of the poor than under Suharto's New Order. But Alex Noerdin continues to follow New Order policy makers in seeing development as primarily a matter of foreign investment and government–private partnerships in corporate projects.[24] This means that development funding goes for corporate infrastructure, and the needs and rights of poor farmers, like the settlers of Dusun Belido and those who live in other remote villages, take a distant second place to the interests of investors.

Syahrial Oesman

The election of a new district head for Ogan Komering Ulu (OKU) was scheduled for January 2000. Legislation outlining procedures for the election of *bupati* had not yet been enacted, but the OKU legislature elected in 1999 was determined to proceed regardless.[25] The eighty candidates who put their names forward for district head included many political figures from the New Order, such as a former *bupati* of OKU, two former *bupatis* from other districts in South Sumatra, the son of former governor Ramli Hasan Basri, the son-in-law of the mayor of Palembang, and five candidates with a military background.

The New Order party, Golkar, exhibited its sophistication in the political maneuvering that set the rules for the *bupati* election. Although PDI-P was the strongest party in the legislature, legislators agreed that a committee consisting of the chairman of the legislature, three vice chairmen, and two representatives from each of the factions would decide on six pairs of candidates to proceed to the final stage of the election. Therefore only three out of sixteen members of the selection committee were from PDI-P. As a result, Golkar-connected candidates from the New Order were the top three vote getters.

When *reformasi* activists launched protests against this selection process, the successful candidates organized counterdemonstrations by groups claiming to support a "native son" *(putra daerah)*—Danau Ranau people in support of the son of Ramli Hasan Basri, Belitang people in support of the son-in-law of the Palembang mayor, and Komering people in support of Syahrial Oesman. Ignoring protests, the OKU legislature moved to the final vote. As the voting took place, some two thousand people gathered outside the district legislature, some demanding postponement of the election, others supporting it. Security forces stood by to make sure that violence did not break out. With a plurality of only thirteen out of forty-five votes, Syahrial Oesman, a bureaucrat who had headed the Public Works Department in OKU, was declared the winner. Syahrial Oesman's victory over candidates with greater financial resources surprised almost everyone.

Bribery of legislators in the OKU *bupati* election was openly acknowledged. In an interview in the *Sriwijaya Post,* Ramli Hasan Basri said he would not be surprised to hear that his son had won, given that money politics was common in all elections.[26] Abu Daud Busrom, dean of the law school at Sriwijaya University, commented that the OKU legislature had "played a good game, collecting money from candidates, but using better judgment in the final vote."[27]

Syahrial Oesman had forged a network of support that linked local entrepreneurs with political elites in Palembang and Jakarta. While working in the OKU Public Works Department, he developed ties with local businessmen such as Yahya Mas, the director of PT Moyo Segaro Agung, a conglomerate with subsidiaries in construction, publishing, and catering. As a member of the board of the South Sumatran University Alumni Organization, Syahrial Oesman was also connected to a wider network of contractors and well-placed officials throughout South Sumatra, such as Adjis Saip, chairman of the provincial legislature; Taufik Kiemas, the husband of Indonesia's President Megawati; the director of PT Bukit Asam, the state-owned coal company; and (retired) General Makmun Murod, an associate of Syamsul Nursalim, owner of the Gajah Tunggal Group.

Despite official protests, the Ministry of Home Affairs ratified the OKU election results, and Syahrial Oesman was installed as *bupati* on February 25, 2000. He immediately initiated reforms increasing the powers of village-level officials and authorized the establishment of village-level security forces. The number of subdistricts *(kecamatan)* was doubled, increasing the number of paid subdistrict and village leaders and extending Syahrial Oesman's political network.

When Syahrial Oesman took office in 2000, almost 31 percent of the population in OKU was living below the poverty line.[28] As elsewhere in lowland South Sumatra, poverty was largely due to the loss of land and forest resources when concessions were made to companies for the development of oil palm plantations. LBH documented nineteen ongoing land conflicts in OKU.[29] One conflict came to national attention in 1999 when a national news magazine reported that the Indonesian army had evicted families in eighteen villages from 12,000 hectares of land for a military base, but the army then leased the land for the establishment of an oil palm plantation.[30]

In an interview in January 2003, Syahrial Oesman told me that he had resolved all land conflicts in OKU by returning authority to the village heads to negotiate directly with the corporations involved.[31] At his invitation, I went to OKU to talk to villagers. I chose Desa Bindu, Desa Durian, and Desa Kedondong where Untung Saputra, an LBH staff member, had worked with villagers in a dispute with plantation owner PT Mitra Ogan. The villagers told me that under pressure from Syahrial Oesman to resolve land conflicts, PT Mitra Ogan had instituted the *inti/plasma* system. I was shown letters from Mitra Ogan explaining that farmers would be given title to a number of *paket* (or *kapling,* a plot of two hectares) depending on the amount of land they had farmed before the plantation was established. In exchange, they had to agree to follow all rules and policies of the village cooperative, which would act as partner with Mitra Ogan.[32] The company would retain the right to manage the plantation; deed to the land would be retained by the bank until loans for construction of a factory to process palm oil had been repaid. Villagers would receive a portion of the profit from harvests after loan payments and the expenses of management and maintenance of the plantation had been deducted from the price paid for the harvest.

Villagers said that Syahrial Oesman told them that they must accept the company's offer or face the consequences. They found it difficult to understand the nature of their relationship to Mitra Ogan. They wanted to plant whatever crops they chose on their land. Instead, they were given titles (which were actually held by the bank) to numbered plots in an unidentified location. They observed that the number of *paket* distributed did not always match the amount of land people had formerly farmed. Village officials received a large number of *paket.* No one liked this solution to the conflict with Mitra Ogan, but the villagers were exhausted by their long struggle and had little hope of achieving a better resolution of the conflict.

Monthly receipts showed that a villager's share of profit from harvesting averaged about US$12 per *paket* a month, far less than farmers could earn by cultivating the land themselves with crops of their own choosing. Mitra Ogan determined the charges for management and maintenance, so the company could ensure its profit at the expense of villagers. Villagers complained that they were being cheated, but they did not know what they could do about it. The head of the village cooperative could not demand transparent financial reporting from Mitra Ogan, nor could he negotiate a fairer division of profits.

While forced to institute profit sharing, Mitra Ogan did not appear to have changed its predatory policies. The company announced in 2001 that it would build a new oil palm processing factory next to Desa Bindu. On November 5, 2001, the villagers sent a letter to Syahrial Oesman and to the chairman of the OKU legislature protesting that Mitra Ogan was going ahead with construction without the agreement of the Bindu village council. The villagers pointed out that waste material from palm oil production, which is poisonous, would be discharged into the Komering River. During the previous rainy season, water from settling ponds from the existing factory had overflowed into the river causing a massive fish kill in the *lebak lebung*. Although Mitra Ogan had admitted responsibility for this incident and promised to compensate the village, the village council had yet to receive any payment. The villagers asked that unresolved land conflicts be settled before more land was taken over by Mitra Ogan. They proposed that the company pay a fee to the village council for the use of village land, and they wanted it to give preference to villagers when hiring employees for the new factory. They also wanted assurances that the new factory would not cause further pollution.

The chairman of the OKU legislature went to Bindu to talk with villagers, and he wrote to Syahrial Oesman on November 26, 2001, requesting that a team be set up to investigate their complaints. A month later, Syahrial Oesman issued an order directing the subdistrict head of Bindu to investigate and report back to him. Nothing came of this investigation. At the time of my visit in February 2003, construction of the new factory was proceeding, and villagers were still protesting. A villager whose garden plot had been taken for the factory found that there was no effective channel for him to resist appropriation of his land.

Syahrial Oesman's reputation for dynamic leadership was due to his Village Empowerment and Development Program, which implemented a requirement of the Indonesian constitution that has rarely been acknowledged elsewhere in Indonesia.[33] Village councils in OKU would be allotted

10 percent of the OKU budget for development projects. In 2001 and 2002, the Desa Durian village council received US$3,500 for development. The village council had no experience in planning or carrying out development, so they decided to invest the money and use the earnings for village administration.[34] They bought two *paket* from Mitra Ogan. Villagers said that the Village Empowerment and Development Program made no difference in their lives. They were not consulted in the decision to buy *paket*, and they feared that income from the *paket* would simply flow to village elites who sat on the village council.

Villagers expressed frustration because direct election of the village headman and the village council had yet to bring about a more accountable government. In Desa Kedondong, there were two candidates for village headman in the election that took place on May 20, 2003.[35] One was the incumbent, a man in his sixties with a large extended family in the village; the other was a younger man who was chairman of the village council. The challenger resigned from his position and conducted a vigorous campaign, going door-to-door to talk about village development. Nevertheless, the incumbent won the election by a narrow margin, primarily because his family supported him. Villagers said that now all the benefits of office went to the headman and his family.

Farmers in OKU do not feel that their interests have been served by Syahrial Oesman. As in New Order development programs, corporate interests have had highest priority. However Syahrial Oesman can claim to have done more for farmers than the New Order, which simply refused to recognize the land rights of indigenous people. Oil palm companies were pressured to deal with land disputes by including local farmers in *inti/plasma* schemes and giving them some share of the profits. In 2002, on National Farmers' Day, Syahrial Oesman distributed almost three hundred land titles to OKU farmers, but these are still merely "gestures" rather than actual structural reform.[36]

From *Bupati* of OKU to Governor of South Sumatra

Syahrial Oesman took the next step in his political ascendancy by becoming a candidate in the gubernatorial election of 2004, where he once again managed to pull off an upset victory.[37] The incumbent governor, Rosihan Arsyad, was the PDI-P majority party candidate, with twenty-six seats in the South Sumatra legislature, which was to elect the next governor. Added to that, Rosihan was promised support by Golkar with its fifteen seats. As a former naval officer, he expected the military faction, with eight seats, to support him as well. This should have easily given him enough votes to win.

Syahrial Oesman chose Mahyudin, a vice rector at Sriwijaya University, as his running mate, supposedly on the advice of Fuad Bawazier, finance minister under Suharto. Mahyudin and Fuad Bawazier were linked through the Association of Islamic Students (HMI), whose national alumni organization is chaired by Fuad Bawazier. After the fall of Suharto, Fuad Bawazier aligned himself with PAN, the Islamic-oriented reform party of presidential candidate Amien Rais. This gave Syahrial Oesman a link to the Reform Faction led by PAN in the South Sumatra legislature. Syahrial Oesman also exploited the rivalry between the army and the navy to pick up five votes from the military faction. Rumors credit Lieutenant General Ryamizard Ryacudu, a powerful general from Ogan Komering Ilir (OKI), with successfully urging army officers to vote for Syahrial Oesman.

An alliance with Eddy Santana Putra helped Syahrial Oesman split the vote of Golkar legislators. Syahrial Oesman had worked with Santana in FKPPI and KNPI, important Golkar support groups. The Golkar-linked NGO organizer Azis Kamis was another supporter of Syahrial Oesman. These men were able to call on Golkar-affiliated groups used for demonstrations. On election day, five thousand demonstrators rallied in front of the legislature in support of Syahrial Oesman. A few months later, the same network helped Eddy Santana win the mayoral election in Palembang.

A split in PDI-P also gave Syahrial Oesman more votes. One faction of PDI-P supported Rosihan Arsyad, the official party candidate, while another threw its votes to Syahrial Oesman. The gubernatorial election was said to have become a battleground between President Megawati, who supported the official PDI-P candidate, Governor Rosihan, and her husband, Taufik Kiemas, who supported Syarial Oesman. Megawati later disciplined the legislators who voted for Syahrial Oesman, expelling them from the party.[38] Taufik Kiemas had the last word, though. The election of a new PDI-P chairman for South Sumatra was won by his brother, Nazaruddin Kiemas.

Syahrial Oesman defeated Rosihan Arsyad by only one vote. People said that the decisive vote was cast by a legislator who was brought from the hospital by Syahrial Oesman's success team so he could vote. This legislator had previously resigned from the legislature due to illness, but Syahrial Oesman's success team argued that he still had a right to vote, as his replacement had not yet been installed. In return Syahrial Oesman is said to have paid the man's medical bills.[39]

Syahrial Oesman's victory demonstrated that candidates could not rely on party discipline alone to win an election. Personalized networks of influence trumped party affiliation. Rumors abounded about the cost of legislators' votes in the election and where the money came from. Legislators who voted for Syahrial Oesman were said to have received up to US$15,000, while those who voted for Rosihan Arsyad were said to have received only US$5,000–$7,000. Syahrial Oesman also provided money to organizations that mounted demonstrations supporting his candidacy, including Golkar organizations and such local groups as the SumSel Youth Front, the Union of Muhammadiyah Students, and the United Palembang Social Community. In total, people said that up to one million dollars had been spent. But I was advised not to write about this, because "money politics" could not be proved.

I had to sort through rumors from more and less informed sources to see where the money might have come from. Ponco Sutowo, the son of General Ibnu Sutowo, who made his fortune as director of Pertamina in the early years of the New Order, is said to have been a major funder of Syahrial Oesman's campaign. Syahrial Oesman had cultivated a relationship with the Sutowo family as *bupati* of OKU, renaming the government hospital in the district capital in honor of Ibnu Sutowo. Dudy Makmun Murod, son of (former) General Makmun Murod and a director of Wachyuni Mandira (see Chapter 4) is also said to have provided funds. Rumor identifies former Governor Ramli Hasan Basri as another source of funds. He was said to have been angry that Governor Rosihan had not helped his son obtain the position of *bupati* of Banyuasin.

Reformasi activists said that bosses of gambling and prostitution rings in Palembang also supported Syahrial, because Governor Rosihan had clamped down on their activities and closed the official prostitution complex. They also identified Haji Halim, the "timber baron," who acquired this epithet as a major player in the laundering of wood from "wild" (illegal) sawmills, as a contributor to Syahrial Oesman's campaign. Haji Halim, who descends from an old Palembang family, has timber concessions in Banyu Asin, OKI, and MUBA districts. His company was accused of setting forest fires in 1997 to destroy evidence that they had engaged in illegal logging outside the concessions and to burn fields they claimed to have reforested. Haji Halim also maintains close ties with Alex Noerdin, and as a founding member in South Sumatra of the Democrat Party, which nominated Susilo Bambang Yudhoyono as President in 2004, he has powerful national-level allies as well.

Although the South Sumatra legislature certified the gubernatorial election as clean and free of "money politics" on August 8, 2003, controversy simmered on as the Home Affairs Ministry and the president still had to certify the election. A demonstration demanding that the Home Affairs Minister forward election results to the president was said to have been sponsored by Lieutenant General Ryamizard Ryacudu. As the time for the inauguration of a new governor approached, President Megawati Sukarnoputri had still not authorized Syahrial Oesman's appointment. The installation ceremony was postponed indefinitely, and rumors circulated that a new election might be held. But on November 6, 2003, three months after the election, Syahrial Oesman was finally given an official appointment and installed as governor.[40]

Syahrial Oesman has launched an ambitious new program of corporate development. On my 2005 trip to South Sumatra, I attended a seminar where the governor announced an agreement with the China Development Bank and China Exim Bank and the state-owned mining company PT Bukit Asam to build a coal-fired power plant in South Sumatra. A Chinese company and an Indonesian consortium will build the plant. Another agreement provides Chinese financing for a new railway and transportation system for coal from the Bukit Asam mines.[41] These projects are expected to yield trickle-down benefits for people in South Sumatra. The governor agreed to arrange an interview with me, but he left with the president of Indonesia on a trip to China before the interview could take place.

Local autonomy laws decentralizing power from the central government to district-level government have opened up opportunities for ambitious local politicians and entrepreneurs to build new networks of power and capture control of local resources and government funds. Often rising figures were New Order bureaucrats from the Public Works Department, where negotiations with local businessmen took place. This pattern has been observed by several political scientists.[42] As Mike Malley points out, "Rather than encouraging the creation of publicly accountable regional governments, decentralization has facilitated their capture by local elites."[43] Vedi Hadiz elaborates:

> [Decentralization] involves the entrenchment of a form of democracy that is run by the logic of money politics and violence and which is primarily dominated by old New Order elites who have reinvented themselves within new political vehicles.... Decentralization has merely helped to consolidate and entrench their position.... The essential leitmotif of Indonesian political economy over the last four decades—the instrumental appropriation of public resources for the purposes of private capital accumulation—has not been altered.[44]

This critique is echoed in the Indonesian press, and elites in Jakarta use evidence of corruption in provincial and district government to argue for a reconsolidation of power at the center.[45] However, the rise of Alex Noerdin and Syahrial Oesman requires a more nuanced analysis of the effects of decentralization. Although Alex Noerdin and Syahrial Oesman continue the New Order pattern of corporate development, their semipopulist policies support the argument that democratization can produce marginal gains in welfare for the poor as compared with the centralized authoritarianism of the New Order. Direct election of *bupati* and governors, to be introduced after 2005, may further empower poor and marginal groups. But in order for real change to take place, the model of corporate development that widens the gap between rich and poor must be challenged.

The fortunes of Alex Noerdin and Syahrial Oesman also show that politicians cannot rely on political parties as effective instruments of mobilization. In the *bupati* and gubernatorial elections, many legislators appear to have sold their votes to the highest bidder. As a result of this kind of corruption and the failure of government to meet the needs of the poor, many voters in the 2004 elections abandoned the major political parties in favor of smaller new parties. Both Alex Noerdin and Syahrial Oesman have so far resisted identifying with one particular political party. They have also begun to cultivate ties to influential Islamic leaders at both the local and the national levels. This suggests that Islamic organizations will play an important role in determining whether further reform takes place in Indonesia. In the next chapter we shall look at how Islamic organizations in South Sumatra have responded to new opportunities for political engagement.

Chapter 8

Islam and the Quest for Justice

Democratization will not proceed in Indonesia until it is actively supported by the Islamic community and until the values of democracy
are explicitly articulated as compatible with Islamic doctrine.
—Conference on "Islam in Modern Indonesia"[1]

SOUTH SUMATRA HAS A STRONG Islamic heritage. In the late nineteenth century, Palembang was known as a center of the "Hadrami Awakening," a movement that brought new currents of Islam from the Middle
East to Southeast Asia. The Hadrami are descendants of traders from
Yemen, and many use the name Said (Sayid), which sometimes denotes a
descendant of the Prophet. In 1848 Kemas Haji Abd Allah established an
Islamic press in Palembang, where the journal *al-Bashir* (The Harbinger)
was published. By 1885 the Hadrami community of Palembang consisted
of two thousand people and was the second-largest Hadrami community in
Indonesia after Aceh. By 1890 there were 230 institutions of Islamic education in Palembang.[2]

In the early twentieth century, South Sumatra became a stronghold of
Sarekat Islam, an organization of Muslim batik traders. In the 1920s Sarekat
Islam had eighteen thousand members, over one-third of whom lived in
South Sumatra.[3] Youths who returned home from their studies in Java
or outside Indonesia in the 1920s and 1930s brought with them the idea
of "modern Islam." They established branches of the progressive Islamic
organization Muhammadiyah in market towns like Pagar Alam and Kota
Batu Ranau. Many people in South Sumatra received their first education
in schools established by Muhammadiyah volunteer teachers.[4] Nahdlatul
Ulama (NU), the traditionalist Islamic organization established in 1926
by Islamic teachers *(ulama),* opened branches in Lahat and Bukit Tinggi
in 1936–1938.[5] In Indonesia's first national election in 1955, the Muslim
party Masyumi received 20.9 percent of the national vote. In South Sumatra, however, Masyumi won 45 percent of the vote, and the Islamic parties
together won almost 65 percent.

In South Sumatra, Islam and the moral values it represents are viewed as essential elements of a just society. Recent statistics demonstrate the extent of Islamic influence. According to the provincial Bureau of Statistics, in 2002 South Sumatra had 5,525 mosques, 1,015 *musholla* (a small building or room set aside in a public place for daily prayer), and 4,209 *langgar* (a neighborhood prayer house).[6] In 2003 President Megawati Sukarnoputri came to Palembang to reopen Masjid Agung, a mosque built by Sultan Mahmud Badaruddin in the first part of the eighteenth century that has been beautifully renovated over the last five years with donations from worshippers. More and more middle-class parents are sending their children to Islamic schools. A new Islamic elementary school, Azahara, serves the middle-class suburb of Polygon, and the most prestigious (and expensive) school in Palembang is an Islamic elementary school with a conservative Wahabi orientation.

Islam and the New Order

The New Order attempted to use the politics of patronage to coopt the support of Islamic organizations. If this failed, Islamic leaders were given a clear warning not to meddle in politics.[7] Despite the regime's attempts to control every aspect of civil life, during the New Order Islamic organizations remained the most resilient and independent elements of civil society. Leaders of the major ones—Muhammadiyah, Nahdlatul Ulama (NU), and the Association of Muslim Students (HMI)—sought the most strategic way to deal with New Order policies that aimed at eliminating Islam as a political force. Other Muslim activists founded NGOs focusing on forms of economic development that would benefit the poor, such as the Association for Pesantren and Community Development (P3M) and the Social and Economic Research, Education, and Information Institute (LP3ES).[8] Many students joined a movement of *dakwah* (Islamic proselytizing, primarily directed at nominal Muslims), which maintained that society would become more just only when Muslims committed themselves to live by the teachings of Islam.

By the mid-1980s, an Islamic revival was well under way in Indonesia. For the middle class, Islam provided a unifying set of values in a rapidly modernizing world where traditional ethnic-based forms of identity were being undermined. For the working class, the mosque provided community in the new and often alien urban environment. For students, Islam provided a safe way to criticize the authoritarianism of the New Order. When the preacher Kiai Haji Zainuddin M.Z. came to Palembang in the late 1980s, he drew record crowds. He used the popular image of Islam as a compass that helps to direct people in the right direction and emphasized the importance of unity in the Islamic community. His sermons, full of parables and jokes that drew on Islamic values, suggested that New Order elites were egotistical and individualist. People in South Sumatra called him "bold" *(berani)* for his subtle criticism of powerful officials.

By the 1990s, the signs of *dakwah* were everywhere on university campuses. *Musholla* had been built so that students could perform the daily prayers. Women students were adopting Islamic dress—long skirts or pants, a loose blouse with a high collar, and the head-covering known as a *jilbab.* Students formed Qur'an study groups. University and high school students tended to see the *dakwah* movement and the emerging democracy movement as two sides of the same coin; both shared the goal of establishing a more just society. But most students preferred *dakwah* to NGO activism; it was less dangerous, and they were reassured that their objections to the New Order were morally justified.

The *dakwah* movement has many strands. One, known as Renewal (Pembaruan), originated in 1970 when Nurcholish Madjid, as president of the Islamic Students Association (HMI), provoked heated controversy by calling for Islam to be separated from politics with the slogan "Islam Yes, Islamic Party No."[9] In *Civil Islam: Muslims and Democratization in Indonesia* (1999), Robert Hefner describes how this call led a generation of Muslim leaders to develop a vision of tolerant and liberal Islam that is compatible with democracy. There are also *dakwah* organizations that can be described as fundamentalist or antidemocratic. For example, Eggi Sudjana, a founder of the militant Indonesian Committee for World Muslim Solidarity (KISDI) and supporter of the Indonesian Council for Dakwah (DDII), has maintained: "The mechanisms of Islam are comprehensive. Therefore, with regard to Islam, there is no need for democracy. Islam promotes mutual consensus through deliberation. In relation to the laws of God, there is no need for deliberation and consensus, it's simply a matter of implementation of the laws or compliance or obedience."[10] In post-Suharto Indonesia, yet more radical and militant Islamic organizations emerged onto the political stage advocating the adoption of Islamic law *(sharia)* as a first step toward establishing an Islamic government in Indonesia. As Anders Uhlin has pointed out: "Islam, like any major religion, is complex enough to lend itself to support all forms of political systems, from the most authoritarian to the most democratic. The question is which interpretations are the most influential and powerful in a certain context."[11]

As the largest predominantly Muslim country in the world today, Indonesia has been regarded as a test case for the compatibility of Islam and democracy. In this chapter I describe how the debate over the political expression of Islamic values evolved in South Sumatra as the New Order came to an end.

"Islam Is the Solution"

The Indonesian Council for Dakwah (DDII) was founded in the 1970s by Muhammad Natsir and other leaders of the Islamic political party Masyumi. President Sukarno had banned Masyumi in 1960, accusing party leaders of involvement in the regional rebellions of the late 1950s. At the beginning of the New Order in 1966, Masyumi leaders were released from prison but banned from further participation in politics. As a result, Natsir founded DDII with the goal of Islamizing Indonesian society from the ground up through *dakwah*. DDII promulgated a literalist Islam, urging a return to the Qur'an and Hadith and emphasizing the outward signs of Islamic commitment, such as Islamic dress, separation of the sexes, Arabic forms of address, and the five daily prayers.[12]

Beginning in the late 1970s, under the charismatic leadership of Imaduddin Abdulrahim (known as Bang Imad) in Salman Mosque on the campus of the Bandung Institute of Technology (ITB), the *dakwah* movement spread to university campuses throughout Indonesia. Inspired by the teachings of the Muslim Brotherhood in Egypt, Imaduddin wrote in *Kuliah Tauhid* (Lectures on the Unity of God) that *tauhid* means all aspects of life and society should be imbued with Islamic values and modeled on the life of the Prophet and his followers. The *dakwah* movement interpreted jihad as a holy struggle waged against "Western" ways of life—secularism, liberalism, capitalism, communism, and materialism. *Panduan Usroh* (The Usroh Guide), published by Imaduddin and his colleagues, provided instructions for building a movement for a society based on Islamic values.[13] The slogan of the movement was "Islam is the solution."

Indonesian economist Rizal Ramli has recalled: "When I was at ITB in the late 1970s all the student political activity revolved around the student centre. But ever since the government imposed restrictions on campus politics [1978], the student centre has been dead. All the activity is now funneled to the mosque. Young people need an outlet for their political aspirations and they will find it where they can."[14] Jalalluddin Rachmat explains that Salman Mosque became "a sanctuary for the expression of political dissatisfaction and frustration. . . . When they look around them, young Muslims begin to see that development is not the panacea it's made out to be, so they embrace Islam and hope their religion can solve all their problems."[15]

The 1979 Iranian revolution demonstrated the power of Islam as a political force and inspired Islamist students in Indonesia. After 1979, however, the New Order regarded Islam with increasing suspicion. Imaduddin was jailed in 1979 but then allowed to leave Indonesia for the United States, where he entered a Ph.D. program. In 1984, the congregation of a mosque in Tanjung Priok, a poor area in the port of Jakarta, demonstrated against military personnel who tore down posters advocating that women wear the Muslim head covering. The armed forces responded with murderous force, killing an estimated two hundred people. The massacre served as a warning to all groups that saw Islam as a way to mount political resistance to the New Order.[16]

In 1985 the New Order passed legislation requiring every legal mass organization to adopt Pancasila as a fundamental ideology. Islamic organizations were presented with a choice of giving up Islam as their fundamental principle or going underground. The Islamic Students Association (HMI) split over the issue, and those who were determined to resist New Order control formed the Council to Safeguard HMI and went underground. In Palembang, Pelajar Islam Indonesia (PII), a youth affiliate of Masyumi, also went underground.[17]

The *dakwah* movement kept a low profile throughout the 1980s, but *dakwah* leaders gradually built a network of Islamic study circles, known as *usroh* (nuclear family or cell), and later as *halaqah* (Arabic for a circle of students and their teacher) or *tarbiyah* (the Arabic word for education under a teacher who provides moral guidance). Hermawan Dipoyono, an early activist at Salman Mosque, recalled: "I myself started the first *usroh* in Salman Mosque, maybe the first *usroh* in Indonesia. I was sent to Malaysia by Imaduddin, where I found books by the Muslim Brothers. I brought them back and started translating them into Indonesian. This was in 1976–1977. It was a dangerous time to do *dakwah*. I would translate a few pages, and they would be copied and passed around. We studied these in our *usroh*."[18] In this way students encountered works written by Sayyid Qutb, Hassan Al Banna, Mustafa Masyhur, and Sa'id Hawwa. A translation of Sayyid Qutb's *Ma'alim fit Thariq, Petunjuk Jalan* (Pointing the Way) published by DDII was particularly influential. On some university campuses, students were also introduced to left-leaning Islamic intellectuals such as Ali Shari'ati (1933–1977), an Iranian influenced during his studies in Paris by the writings of Jean-Paul Sartre, Che Guevara, and Frantz Fanon. Shari'ati transposed the Marxist language of class struggle into an Islamic vocabulary, highlighting the roles played by the arrogant *(mostakbirine)* in relation to the disinherited or oppressed *(mostadafine)*.

In South Sumatra, the *dakwah* movement first took root in Al Ghazali Mosque on the campus of Sriwijaya University. After the Friday sermon, Dr. Gajah Nata responded to anonymous questions from students with guidance based on Islamic principles. In the small library attached to the mosque, students had access to DDII publications. The new currents of liberal Islamic thought represented by the Renewal movement were discussed at IAIN Raden Fatah in Palembang, but students in the *dakwah* movement at Sriwijaya University maintained that, as Nurcholish Madjid had been educated in the West at the University of Chicago rather than in the Middle East, his teachings did not represent "true" Islam.

The New Order Turns to Islam

New Order policy toward Islam changed at the end of the 1980s as Suharto sought to win the support of Islamic organizations in the face of growing criticism from both the military and student activists.[19] In 1989 the New Order gave Islamic courts jurisdiction over marriage, inheritance, and donations. The following year, Suharto went on the hajj and approved the formation of the Association of Muslim Intellectuals (ICMI). This organization, which was led by Suharto's protégé, B. J. Habibie, promised Muslims a more prominent role in government. Imaduddin was given a position in ICMI. But other prominent Muslim leaders rejected the new organization. Most notably Abdurrahman Wahid, leader of Nahdlatul Ulama and a founder of the Democracy Forum, argued that Suharto was trying to coopt Muslim support in order to retain his power: "The competition between power centers in our country in the 1990s reflects the need on the president's part for the widest possible support from society, which means from Islamic movements as well. To get that support, identification of national politics with Islam is necessary."[20]

Through his private foundations, such as Yayasan Dharmais, Suharto channeled funds to Islamic organizations for approved projects. In Palembang, such a private foundation established in 1989 was given funding for an Islamic academy providing training programs in entrepreneurial skills for rural youth. At the national level the Ministry of Religion established the Union of Mosque Youth (IRM), an organization designed to direct Islamic activism among students. As one leader of IRM in Palembang explained, "Youth have a tendency to political involvement, but this tendency can be minimized through the involvement of Islamic-oriented youth."[21] Six areas of activity were authorized for mosque youth groups, which were known as Remaja Masjid: Qur'an study groups, Islamic preschools, Islamic scouts, human resource development programs, entrepreneurial development programs, and family welfare programs.

A Remaja Masjid group organized the first mosque-based *dakwah* programs for high school students in Palembang in 1992. By 2003 Remaja Masjid groups claimed that over seventeen thousand children in South Sumatra had graduated from their Qur'an reading classes. Support from the New Order, however, also tainted the reputation of Remaja Masjid. According to a former Remaja Masjid chairman in Palembang, when funding (*gula*, literally sugar) was provided by the New Order, the solidarity and dedication that had characterized *dakwah* in the 1980s was lost.

As opposed to Remaja Masjid groups, Islamic study circles on university campuses resisted cooptation by the New Order. They organized nationally as the Institute for Campus Dakwah (LDK) with the aim of training leaders for the struggle to establish an Islamic society. Emphasizing social service and political education, LDK leaders maintained, however, that *dakwah* was a moral movement as distinguished from a political movement.

Organizations that viewed Islam as a political force also reemerged on university campuses in the 1990s. Students in Java launched demonstrations in 1991 protesting a state-sponsored lottery on the ground that Islam forbids gambling; two years later the government dropped the lottery. Anies Rasyid Baswedan, one of the leaders of the lottery protests in Yogyakarta, announced: "We don't want it to stop here. . . . We're thinking about democracy. We have been cool for fifteen to twenty years and we see the [lottery] as a starting point to gather student power. . . . We would like to push the government into giving the people better access to political and economic resources."[22]

In the Palembang branch of the Islamic Students Association (HMI), a vigorous debate emerged over the role of Islam in the political reform of Indonesia. HMI was the largest and most important organization of Muslim students in South Sumatra, with seventeen sub-branches in faculties of Sriwijaya University, the IAIN Raden Fatah, the Muhammadiyah University, and private universities. During the New Order HMI had provided leadership training for students later recruited by the three legal political parties—Golkar, the Indonesian Democratic Party (PDI), and the United Development Party (PPP). As a Palembang HMI leader explained, "HMI is an important organization for establishing networks. Your university no longer matters—you are all HMI."[23] The HMI alumni network (KAHMI) was a cross-party network that was a major force for political stability and support for the New Order. Now, with the emergence of protests at Sriwijaya University as described in Chapter 2, some HMI members began to question their ties to KAHMI and the New Order.

In 1994 the limits of tolerance for Islamic "extremism" were tested by Al Arqam, a quietist messianic Islamic movement founded by Asaari Muhammad in Malaysia in 1967. The Al Arqam community in Palembang, led by the charismatic preacher Musta'in Zamhari from the district of Ogan Komering Ilir (OKI), was established in a neighborhood of closely packed houses in the heart of the city. Members worked to establish an economically self-sufficient community, setting up small businesses to produce *halal* foods and Islamic clothing, books, cassettes, and pamphlets. Many members were students or lecturers at Sriwijaya University. When I attended a wedding and the fortieth day head-shaving celebration for a baby in the community, I learned that weddings were frequent, because Al Arqam leaders arranged marriages and promoted polygamy and large families. The community observed strict separation of men and women, and they adopted distinctive forms of dress from the Middle East—men wore long white robes and turbans; women, a black *cadar* that completely covered the body. They were often described as *"fanatik"* because of their unusual dress.

In July 1994, Prime Minister Mahathir Mohammad of Malaysia banned Al Arqam as heretical, alleging that Asaari Muhammad claimed to be a new prophet. At the urging of the government, the Indonesian Council of Ulama (MUI) followed suit and issued a ruling banning Al Arqam. The community in Palembang disappeared. Al Arqam followers adopted Indonesian dress and regrouped in Lampung Province, where they hoped not to attract the attention of authorities.

Many members of HMI in Palembang objected to the banning of Al Arqam, and they expressed their views in editorials to local newspapers.[24] The danger of criticizing the New Order was again made clear, however, by the government-organized attack in July 1996 on *reformasi* student activists who had occupied the headquarters of the Indonesian Democratic Party (PDI) in Jakarta.

Islam and Reformasi

After the attack on *reformasi* activists at the PDI headquarters in July 1996, HMI in Palembang split into two factions, one supporting the New Order and the other hoping to move HMI to a position more critical of the government.[25] The latter faction called itself HMI-*progresif*. They argued that the HMI leadership training course was merely an indoctrination into the New Order and decided to revise the training given to new members. On the final day of the new training, the conflict between the two factions came to a head. Leaders from the conservative faction declared the training invalid. After much debate, a compromise was reached: the new trainees of HMI-*progresif* would be accepted as HMI members, but they would not be given certificates stating that they had completed HMI training.

The following year, when the time came to train the next cohort of recruits, the split in HMI deepened. The conservative faction reported the *progresif* faction to the regional military command in Palembang, and HMI-*progresif* was put under military surveillance. The election of a new HMI chairman resolved this crisis with an agreement to once again accept new members trained by HMI-*progresif*. The *progresif* faction would also be allowed to organize discussions of political and economic issues. In early 1998, as the effects of the Asian Economic Crisis of 1997 began to be felt and *reformasi* activists escalated calls for Suharto to step down, the leaders of the HMI-*progresif* won support for a motion to withdraw from the National Committee of Indonesian Youth (KNPI), the government-sponsored umbrella organization for youth groups. This action brought HMI into the *reformasi* movement.

Shortly thereafter, in March 1998, leaders of Campus Dakwah Organizations (LDK) throughout Indonesia formed the Action Committee of Indonesian Muslim Students (KAMMI) and joined the call for Suharto to step down.[26] In Palembang, this sparked a further consolidation of the *reformasi* movement. LDK leaders from Sriwijaya University and IAIN Raden Fatah established a South Sumatra branch of KAMMI. Then KAMMI and HMI formed the Young Islamic Generation (Gemuis), bringing in the Muslim high school student organization (PII), the Muhammadiyah Youth Group, the Student Forum for Civil Society (FORMAD) and the Plaju Islamic Youth Union to coordinate demonstrations by Muslim students in support of political reform.

In the final months before Suharto resigned on May 20, 1998, KAMMI demonstrations in support of *reformasi* were a favorite subject of photographers; the photos showing orderly columns of students dressed in white with green scarves marching in step countered the establishment view that student protests were a disruptive force that would only bring conflict and chaos. Disciplined solidarity was viewed as an important virtue by KAMMI leaders. Andi Rahmat, a Jakarta-based KAMMI activist, explained that this solidarity came from the Islamic concept of *wala'* (rendering one's loyalty and willingness to be led).[27] Fahri Hamzah, KAMMI's first national chairman, explained: "We have a moral stance. If there is a group that desires to cause a disturbance, please, they are welcome to leave our ranks. . . . We are able to guard the coordination of mass action of thousands of people. . . . even in areas that are sensitive to conflict."[28]

Unfortunately, the alliance between *reformasi* activists and the *dakwah* movement at the national level fractured almost as soon as Suharto resigned. *Reformasi* leaders rejected Suharto's appointment of his vice president B. J. Habibie as the new president and demanded prosecution of Suharto for corruption. They organized demonstrations against the policy of Dual Function *(dwi fungsi)*, which gave the military a central role in political institutions. On the other hand, leaders of the *dakwah* movement had no objection to B. J. Habibie, who had been the head of ICMI. They argued that democracy means majority rule, which should lead to the establishment of an Islamic government in Indonesia. In South Sumatra, in contrast, the differences between leaders of Islamic organizations and *reformasi* activists from NGOs were muted, as students began to think about their role in a post-Suharto Indonesia.

Islam and Politics

In the open politics of the post-Suharto period, Islamic student organizations were confronted with the problem of defining the political role of Islam. Leaders of HMI in Palembang expressed the belief that Islamic values should be joined with democratic reforms. Some HMI members joined NGOs to work with *reformasi* activists on the issues of corruption and the environment. Unlike the decentralized decision making of HMI at this time, KAMMI had a more centralized power structure and was less interested in the principles of democracy. Nationally elected leaders determined the KAMMI stand on issues. Provincial branches of KAMMI were required to follow national policies. Both HMI and KAMMI faced a dilemma in claiming to act purely on the moral principles of Islam while engaging in political issues where the interests of powerful individuals were in play.

As New Order elites looked for ways to retain their power and wealth, control of the national HMI organization with its network of branches on university campuses throughout the country became an important political prize. In November–December 1999, HMI held a national congress at which a new chairman was elected. The winning candidate was backed by prominent leaders of the national HMI Alumni Association (KAHMI).

Robby Puruhita, a leader of the HMI-*progresif* faction, who had been elected chairman of HMI Palembang, protested the election. He argued that HMI was being coopted by Jakarta elites who "polluted" the moral basis of the student movement and turned it into a "political" movement aimed at supporting their own interests.[29]

At the National Congress, Robby Puruhita also argued that the statement of HMI values formulated in 1985 under the New Order did not provide guidance on how to implement Islamic values in Indonesia. He proposed that HMI return to Islam as a fundamental principle. This proposal was passed, and a new statement known as the Principles of Islamic Struggle *(Nilai Jihad Kader)* was adopted. Back in Palembang, HMI began to take a stand on political issues. In January 2000, it passed a resolution denouncing the "oppression" and "slaughter" of Muslims in Ambon and demanding that President Abdurrahman Wahid take action. HMI also demanded that the Indonesian army stop attacks on Muslims in Aceh. HMI-*progresif* leaders maintained that they were attempting to "clarify" national issues, not engaging in politics.

HMI Palembang also took up local issues, winning support from student senates in Sriwijaya University, Muhammadiyah University, and IAIN Raden Fatah for a new organization, the Alliance of Environmental Concern, to take up environmental issues. The first campaign called for the creation of a green belt on the coast of South Sumatra. Unfortunately this campaign plunged HMI into complicated issues of land rights and resource control, precipitating the ouster of *progresif* leadership. The local HMI alumni association established a Council to Rescue the Palembang HMI Branch and demanded that the *progresif* chairman stand down, charging that he was allowing HMI to be manipulated by political interests. They claimed that the idea for the environmental campaign had come from Wachyuni Mandira, which was using HMI to mount a campaign against independent "wild" shrimp farmers clearing mangroves for new ponds, because mud from illegal ponds washed inland, damaging Wachyuni Mandira operations.

The Council to Rescue the Palembang HMI Branch pointed out that Robby had not received the training mandated by the national HMI constitution. They accused him of being "not Islamic" and turning HMI-Palembang into an NGO that could become the tool of individual interests. They pointed out that Robby had joined South Sumatra Corruption Watch (SSCW) and argued that this meant his commitment to HMI was uncertain because his loyalties were divided. The takeover of HMI by a conservative group of HMI alumni in Palembang signaled the end of HMI as the most important Muslim student organization in South Sumatra. It was replaced by the *dakwah*-based KAMMI.

The national leadership of KAMMI focused on the Christian-Muslim violence that erupted in Ambon at the beginning of 1999. In March 1999, in a mass jihad rally in Yogyakarta in central Java, KAMMI members marched under the flag of a new Islamic political party, Partai Keadilan, demanding that the government protect Muslims in eastern Indonesia. KAMMI leaders maintained that they were committed to nonviolent protest in support of democracy, but where Muslims were threatened, violence might be required in defense of Islam. KAMMI also organized demonstrations demanding that President Abdurrahman Wahid step down or be impeached for "Bruneigate," a scandal involving funds given to the president by the sultan of Brunei. KAMMI described these protests as "actions" *(aksi)* rather than demonstrations and said they were meant to "call attention to" national issues, like the plight of Muslims in Maluku and corruption. In South Sumatra, KAMMI also organized demonstrations against gambling, drugs, prostitution, and pornography.[30] These demonstrations were very popular. The orderly KAMMI demonstrations over "social issues" were met with approval by government officials, in sharp contrast to demonstrations in support of the rights of workers and farmers organized by LBH and WALHI.

The KAMMI demonstrations against President Abdurrahman Wahid led *reformasi* activists to criticize KAMMI, rejecting its claim that it was a "moral movement" that stood above politics. They reported rumors that Fuad Bawazier, former minister of finance under Suharto and a leader of the national HMI alumni organization (KAHMI), had disbursed US$30,000 to bring students to Jakarta for a mass demonstration against President Abdurrahaman Wahid on January 29, 2001. They argued that KAMMI was being manipulated by political elites.[31] They further objected that KAMMI required the absolute loyalty of members and refused to engage in dialogue with student groups with different views. KAMMI activists, in turn, charged HMI with being "exclusive" because only a small number of students were accepted for the training that led to connections with political elites. Many students found the accusations and counteraccusations of HMI and KAMMI confusing.

Gemuis, the alliance of Muslim student organizations, did not survive escalating accusations that Muslim student organizations were becoming the tools of political elites. In early 2000, when Gemuis organized a demonstration against the national electricity company to protest frequent blackouts in Palembang, KAMMI withdrew its support, saying that Gemuis was being manipulated by political figures. As a result Gemuis disappeared.

Islam in Post-Suharto Indonesia

The more open and democratic politics of the post-Suharto era proved to be a challenge for all Islamic organizations in South Sumatra, including *dakwah* groups and the radical Islamist organizations that emerged after the fall of Suharto. Islamic values emphasize harmony, rule by consensus *(mufakat),* and the unity of the community of Muslims *(umat).*[32] Politics is associated with conflict and egotism, putting individual interests above those of the community.

Dakwah groups emphasized the need for Muslims to unite in the face of attacks from the West. The Dakwah School Forum (FORDS), established in 1998, aimed to bridge the gap between Muhammadiyah and NU. In the words of a FORDS leader, "Don't magnify the differences; why not join together? There must be solidarity."[33] According to FORDS leaders, "politics and religion are one and the same." They organized demonstrations against Israel and the United States, pointing with particular pride to a demonstration in 1999 formed with support from KAMMI and the Anti-Communist and Anti-Israel Islamic Forum. They noted that members of the South Sumatra legislature had come out to speak to the protestors, while demonstrations organized by *reformasi* activists were confronted by police or security forces.

In the more open political environment of Indonesia's first free presidential election in almost fifty years, FORDS leaders found, however, that the apolitical stance that had served so well during the New Order was no longer so effective. They acknowledged that interest in *dakwah* was declining. They said that their membership was now too busy for *dakwah,* and they complained that school administrators, no longer under pressure to support *dakwah* programs, preferred to promote sports activities and scouting.

Remaja Masjid had also embarked on an ambitious program of new *dakwah* activities in 2000.[34] But leaders of the mosque youth group found that their success in producing and marketing Islamic clothes, cosmetics, devotional tapes, and books led to internal conflicts. Authorities of the mosque where the Remaja Masjid office was housed decided that Remaja Masjid should contribute financially to support the mosque. The Remaja Masjid chairman then proposed that the office be moved to his home, which made some members suspicious that he might be diverting profits to his own pocket. They were afraid to challenge him and, instead, quietly dropped out. Some *dakwah* activists joined a political party; others turned to the more radical Islamic organizations that emerged after the fall of Suharto.

In 2000, Dr. Usman Said, a *dakwah* preacher at Al Ghazali Mosque, established a Palembang branch of the Islamic Defenders Front (FPI), an organization founded by Al-Habib Muhammad Rizieq Syihab in the Hadrami community in Jakarta. FPI was founded in response to a Christian-Muslim riot that broke out in Jakarta in December 1998. FPI, which supports the adoption of Islamic law *(sharia)*, is best known for its attacks on Jakarta nightclubs and bars that "promote vice." In September 1999, however, FPI was mobilized to support the new president B. J. Habibie and to confront *reformasi* students protesting the passage of new security laws that would give emergency powers to the armed forces.[35]

In Palembang the establishment of FPI was supported by KAMMI, leaders of two NU *pesantren,* and a Muhammadiyah youth group.[36] FPI joined KAMMI and other Islamic student groups in organizing a demonstration against the United States' attack on Afghanistan after September 11, 2001. FPI also joined with KAMMI, HMI, and SSCW in the campaign against gambling, targeting the governor of South Sumatra (described in Chapter 6). Despite its reputation for violent actions to uproot vice, FPI dropped out of this campaign shortly after a meeting with the governor. This angered KAMMI and HMI leaders, who protested to FPI leadership in Jakarta. FPI in Jakarta refused to become involved. In private, the students voiced their suspicions that the head of FPI was cultivating a relationship with the governor as protection for underground activities. After this, Muslim student organizations withdrew their support from FPI.

In 2001, ninety Islamic leaders, including such radicals as KH Muhammad Bardan Kindarto, arrested in the 1980s for involvement in Komando Jihad, founded a Palembang branch of the Council of Indonesian Mujahidin (MMI).[37] Like FPI, MMI supports the establishment of Islamic law *(sharia).* MMI leaders see the struggle for a more just social order as a struggle against a Western, Christian-Jewish conspiracy to oppress Muslims and weaken Muslim societies. They hope to establish a caliphate based in Indonesia that will unify all Muslims and make Islam a strong force in the world.

Arfan M. Alwy, an alumnus of both HMI and IAIN Raden Fatah, was elected head of MMI in Palembang. MMI embarked on a program of recruitment utilizing radio and study groups in the Mujahidin Mosque. In January 2002, MMI leaders organized a three-day congress in Palembang, inviting Indonesia's vice president Hamzah Haz to be the opening speaker. They predicted that over a thousand people would attend. Alarmed at the emergence of radical Islam in South Sumatra, the governor consulted with prominent Muslim leaders in Palembang. They advised him not to worry. Only a few hundred people attended the congress, suggesting that radical Islam had little appeal in South Sumatra.

While support for *dakwah* and Islamic radicalism appears to have declined, the two major Islamic organizations in Indonesia, Muhammadiyah and Nahdlatul Ulama (NU), seem to have met the challenge of managing political differences in the more open political atmosphere. Despite internal conflicts and stronger competition in recruiting new members, both organizations continue to play a central role in society.

In South Sumatra, Muhammadiyah is strong in Palembang and the market towns chosen as district capitals. It has 60 branches, 160 sub-branches and 15,000 to 20,000 card-carrying members.[38] As elsewhere, Muhammadiyah has a remarkable reputation for civic activism.[39] It has built and manages 7 orphanages, a maternity hospital, 5 clinics, 5 health posts for mothers and children, 4 professional academies, 169 schools, a Muhammadiyah hospital, and the Muhammadiyah University in Palembang. In 2002, Muhammadiyah opened a new Teacher Training Institute in Pagar Alam.

According to Drs. Romli AS, chairman of the Palembang branch of Muhammadiyah, there should be no "politics" in Muhammadiyah. He emphasizes that Partai Amanat Nasional (PAN), the political party established by former Muhammadiyah chairman Amien Rais, is not structurally tied to Muhammadiyah. Members are free to join any political party, Romli says, "but they should not bring their political differences into Muhammadiyah. Politics is a vehicle for individuals to pursue their particular interests and views, whereas the mission of Muhammadiyah is to create a more just Islamic society. An Islamic society is grounded in an Islamic family, and an Islamic family will be realized by Islamic individuals."[40] In Romli's view, the term "Islamic state" *(negara Islam)*, which some people understand as referring to a country governed by Islamic law, simply refers to a nation where the majority of people are Muslims: "In that sense Indonesia is already an Islamic state." Romli points out that there is a great variety of cultural forms of Islamic civilization. He concludes that Islam supports democracy because Islam is an "open teaching" that anyone can understand.

Romli acknowledges that there has been a decrease in Muhammadiyah activities because members are involved in political parties or serve on local election boards.[41] In his view, Muhammadiyah should focus on Islamic education as the best way to create a more moral and just society. He has promoted a plan to add Arabic and moral education to the Muhammadiyah curriculum, because he fears that people no longer consider Muhammadiyah schools superior to other schools.

NU, the organization of more traditional Muslims, is stronger in villages in South Sumatra. NU has a very relaxed bureaucratic structure. There are no membership lists or "card-carrying" members.[42] Under the New Order, NU tended to cooperate with the government and in return received modest government funding for its programs. The election of national NU leader Abdurrahman Wahid as president of Indonesia in 1999 galvanized NU leaders in Palembang. In January 2000, religious teachers *(ulama)* attending a provincial NU congress set forth three goals for the succeeding five years: clarify the duties of officers, strengthen existing programs (many of which were inactive), and establish an NU university in Palembang. A committee of eleven people was selected to oversee these projects (with five members new to the NU board of directors), and a foundation was established to take on the task of raising funds for the new university. Before plans for the university were well under way, internal conflict emerged over who would appoint the rector of the university. The dispute simmered without resolution until after the fall of President Abdurrahman Wahid in August 2001, when the university project was abandoned.

The presidency of Abdurrahman Wahid, popularly known as Gus Dur, could be said to illustrate the dilemma of relying on a charismatic and traditional leader to establish democratic governance. Gus Dur was known as a strong supporter of *reformasi* and democracy. His rhetorical commitment to democracy, however, did not match his actions in office. Gus Dur was known for the arbitrary exercise of power against his critics and the practice of patron–client politics. His minister of religious affairs, who was from NU, appointed NU members to influential positions throughout the ministry, provincial religious affairs departments, and the state-funded IAIN system. In Palembang, the appointment of an NU member as rector of IAIN Raden Fatah in 2003 strengthened those who viewed politics in terms of patron–client ties rather than as a democratic process in which all groups should be represented.

Yet, as leader of NU during the New Order, Gus Dur nurtured a generation of younger NU activists who worked in NGOs to promote development, democracy, and pluralism. In the post-Suharto era, a split emerged between these younger NU members seeking political and social change, and senior leaders who argued that tradition and the authority of religious teachers were the roots of a stable and moral society. This split also appeared in NU in South Sumatra. The younger faction stressed the challenge of globalization and the need to establish a more rational bureaucratic organizational structure for NU. On the other side, senior *ulama* acknowledged that management of NU was not "modern" but argued that change must be approached cautiously. In the election of a new NU chairman for South Sumatra in 1999, the head of a *pesantren* who could be said to represent traditional leadership ran against a candidate from the IAIN who represented a generation of Islamic intellectuals trained in Western-style academic institutions. The winner of the election was the more progressive IAIN candidate. Despite differences, the two leaders have managed to work together in promoting a more active role for NU in South Sumatra.

The relationship between the new political party established by Gus Dur, Partai Kebangkitan Bangsa (PKB), and NU was another source of conflict. As criticism of the president mounted, some NU leaders called for loyalty to the president, emphasizing the problems faced by the new government and the power of entrenched interests associated with Suharto. Others sought to distance NU from the president and PKB. This tension was only resolved by the ouster of Abdurrahman Wahid from the presidency.

By 2004, NU leaders in Palembang were committed to the principle that NU members could belong to any political party. NU chairman in South Sumatra, Drs. Malan Abdullahi, viewed the depolitization of NU as a positive change.[43] He claimed that NU members had learned to work together on projects despite having different political views and pointed with pride to the new NU headquarters as well as to new development projects and youth activities in villages where people are "culturally NU."

Islam and *Reformasi*

Leaders of Islamic student organizations in South Sumatra have continued to network with LBH and WALHI, other NGO activists, and journalists. Some, like Robby Puruhita, joined NGOs; others, like Azimi Asnawi, joined political parties. The strongest connection is between LBH and WALHI activists and leaders of the Justice and Prosperity Party (PKS), successor to the Justice Party (Partai Keadilan) that grew out of KAMMI in 1998.

The Justice Party was established by leaders of KAMMI and other *dakwah* organizations to participate in elections scheduled for 1999.[44] Although based on university campuses, the Justice Party managed to win 1.4 percent of the national vote in the election. To compete in the 2004 election, the party had to change its name to the Justice and Prosperity Party (PKS), as it had not met the required 2 percent threshold in 1999. In 2004 PKS increased its share of the national vote to over 7 percent. In South Sumatra, PKS won four seats in the provincial legislature, an increase of three. The success of PKS in increasing its share of the vote is widely attributed to the party's clean image and strong campaign statements against corruption.

In 2004, people living on the outskirts of Palembang were told that they were to be evicted from their homes so that a new bus station could be built. As government officials pointed out, they did not have title to the land, although many had lived there for decades. They went to LBH for help. Nur Kholis and LBH staff helped them to form an organization so they could negotiate collectively with the government. The government maintained that a new bus station was needed to relieve traffic congestion in Palembang and that a green belt should be preserved around the city. Officials refused to negotiate with villagers to develop a more acceptable plan. Nur Kholis asked PKS for support. PKS took up the issue and was able to delay eviction of the villagers and arrange for a meeting between village leaders and the governor. When I left Palembang in 2005, the issue had not yet been resolved.

People are increasingly alienated from the major political parties due to continuing corruption and the difficulty of legislating reforms that threaten political elites. Politicians who face direct election in the coming years are courting Muslim leaders at all levels. While there is anxiety that politics will corrupt Muslim leaders and Islamic parties, too, if there is no reform of the corrupt justice system, and if the politics of patronage prevails over the spirit of *reformasi*, the argument of radical Islamic groups that reject democracy and favor the adoption of Islamic law may win more support.

Nur Kholis (third from right), PKS representatives, and government officials meeting with residents who are about to be forced to move from their settlement at the edge of Palembang.

In South Sumatra, Islamic organizations are the most significant voluntary associations in which, as Alexis de Tocqueville described in his study of America, people can cultivate the "habits of democracy." NU has sheltered liberal Islamic currents of thought and sponsored development-oriented NGOs. Muhammadiyah's success in civic engagement demonstrates the capacity of Indonesian Muslims to forge bonds of trust and engage in collective activities for the common good. HMI leaders have joined political parties and NGOs to work for reform. KAMMI and PKS have become known for organizing efficient and effective emergency help for victims of conflicts and natural disasters where the government has failed to respond effectively. Thus far in the post-Suharto era, the appeal of *dakwah* and radical Islamic organizations has diminished, but the view they promote–that moral reform and Islamic consciousness offer the best hope for a better future–still has strong appeal.

Indonesia's new democracy could fail in many different ways: leaders of major political parties linked to New Order oligarchs may succeed in blocking democratic reforms and recentralizing power in Jakarta; the Indonesian military may destabilize areas where there are separatist movements and reassert its power in the name of preserving the nation; corruption may continue to siphon off much needed financial resources and undermine trust in government; or international financial organizations may continue to pressure the Indonesian government to implement neoliberal economic policies that benefit elites without seriously addressing the needs of the poor. If these things happen, the argument that only Islam can establish a more just social order will become more appealing. We turn in the final chapter to consider the larger framework of the "development project," or "globalization," in which democracy and religious movements advocating change emerged in Indonesia, Thailand, and the Philippines.

Chapter 9

Indonesia in Global Context

Development, Free-Market Capitalism, and Democracy

Democracy has never come from above, because a true democracy is one that emerges from below.
  —Nurcholish Madjid

Human rights are born not because they fall from the sky, or come from a textbook from a Western university, but because people make complaints and search for freedom from a sense of profound exploitation.
  —Goenawan Mohamad, *Sidelines: Thought Pieces from Tempo Magazine*

IN ANCIENT ROME JUSTICE *(iustitia)* was personified by the goddess Justice, represented as a woman carrying a sword and scales. Her image is still found in courthouses throughout much of the world. The image of Lady Justice symbolizes the ideal of the good society based on equity and fairness, moral principles encoded in law. In contrast to arbitrary rule by the strongest or a resort to violence, justice requires the rule of law. The law must be applied equally to the rich and powerful and to the poor, and the government has only the power given to it by law. There must be judicial institutions with procedures to decide on the appropriate principles for judgment in a particular dispute as well as established channels of appeal.

Laws, however, are not always just. As Todung Mulya Lubis, a founder of LBH, pointed out: "Law is not neutral. Law has never been neutral. Politically, law has always been a product of political struggles in which the law may be used as a tool of repression, legitimacy or distributive justice. This means that law must be fought and its substantive meaning must be directed towards the idea of justice."[1] Political scientists have described justice as an "essentially contested concept" that provides the basis for ethical appeals in contrast to the claim "Might makes right" or political expediency. Viewed through the eyes of an anthropologist, justice is culturally relative, consisting of principles reflected in customs and institutions that

171

people in a particular place and time accept as just. For Islamic reformers in Indonesia, the struggle for justice may be understood as a struggle for rule according to Islamic law *(sharia)*, or as a struggle for laws reflecting the moral principles of Islam that can be realized by the establishment of democratically accountable government. For pro-democracy activists, the struggle for just laws requires a public forum where citizens participate in contestation and negotiation over the fundamental moral principles that legitimate their government and the laws that reflect those principles. From this perspective, justice is not a given, but an ideal that society moves toward through repeated acts of judgment, revising previous views on the basis of new insights and new information.

Like justice, democracy is a concept much abused by authoritarian rulers. The New Order of Suharto, with its depoliticized "floating masses," managed opposition parties, and tightly controlled elections, claimed to be a democracy. But democracy means more than elections in which there are no meaningful alternatives from which to choose. Democracy, as I use the term, requires freedom of speech and association, toleration of differing opinions, protection of minority rights, and channels for the negotiation of legitimate political differences. Military forces must be subjected to civilian governmental control, and government must be limited in its exercise of power to the authority granted to it by its citizens. At its best, democracy allows a widespread conception of the common good to emerge that legitimizes a government; at a minimum, democracy requires channels, including regular free elections, for withdrawing support from leaders who abuse their power.

Given these broad and necessarily vague conceptions of justice and democracy, in this final chapter I turn my attention to considering what struggling for justice means in the context of the world today. I begin by placing the stories of activists, farmers, and workers who struggled against New Order development policies into a broader perspective. I examine how "development" has been used to justify policies allowing political power holders allied to corporate interests to enhance their power and wealth, while pushing people off the land and into cities where they now barely survive. Although the "miracle economies" of East and Southeast Asia were heralded as the success stories of development, in Thailand and the Philippines, as in Indonesia, an NGO movement—consisting of voluntary organizations established to effect social change nonviolently—emerged to combat development projects that victimized the poor. In Thailand, the Philippines, and Indonesia, NGOs laid the foundation for democracy movements that brought down authoritarian regimes, but they have not yet succeeded in challenging the dominance of free-market economics or the neoliberal model of development that has widened the gap between rich and poor throughout the world. I argue that change requires that we recognize neoliberal capitalism, or "free-market" economics, promoted under the rubric of "globalization," is a utopian ideology.

What Happened to Development?

On January 20, 1949, President Harry S Truman called on the former colonial powers to build a new world order based on humanitarian and egalitarian principles: "We must embark on a bold new program for making the benefits of our scientific advances and industrial progress available for the improvement and growth of underdeveloped areas. The old imperialism—exploitation for foreign profit—has no place in our plans. What we envisage is a program of development based on the concepts of democratic fair dealing." [2]

Unfortunately, these idealistic goals were soon compromised by the emerging Cold War competition between the United States and the Soviet Union. While claiming to promote democracy with economic development, the United States provided aid to support authoritarian regimes that claimed to be anticommunist; much economic aid was applied, either directly or indirectly, to pay for military equipment.[3] Southeast Asian nations were major beneficiaries of the American effort to contain the spread of communism. In *Blowback: The Costs and Consequences of American Empire* (2000), Chalmers Johnson describes how America created a ring of satellite states on the Asian side of the Pacific Ocean. In striking ways this mirrored the Eastern European satellites of the Soviet Union. In addition to stationing troops in Okinawa, Taiwan, South Korea, Thailand, and the Philippines, the United States supported authoritarian regimes in South Korea, South Vietnam, Indonesia, Thailand, and the Philippines. American financial support of these governments played a central role in creating the "tiger" and "mini-dragon" economies of East and Southeast Asia.[4]

The World Bank, created by the United Nations in 1945, played a central role in the effort to develop the "underdeveloped" countries of the world. The Bank model of development stressed investment in capital-intensive industrialization and large-scale agriculture. Under Robert McNamara, president of the World Bank (1968–1981), less than 10 percent of US$77 billion-worth of loans went into projects that would directly benefit the poor, such as improved water supply, health, family planning, and education.

McNamara's right-hand man, Muhbub ul Haq, acknowledged, "The bottom 20 percent of the population . . . remained largely outside the scope of [Bank] projects."[5] Regional development banks, aid agencies, and officials from developing countries trained in World Bank programs all adopted this model of development.

In countries where the state took the lead in creating new industrial state enterprises, industries run by government bureaucrats proved to be inefficient and uncompetitive in the world market. As we have seen in the case of Pertamina in Indonesia, they offered sinecures to government bureaucrats or opportunities for well-connected elites to enrich themselves. Where loans from the Bank funded infrastructure that benefited foreign corporations or local elites, as we have seen in the cases of PT TEL and Wachyuni Mandira, they contributed to the profits of large corporations and further widened the gap between rich and poor.

Western aid programs were not meant simply to benefit underdeveloped countries; they were intended to benefit the home economy as well. A good example of this is American food aid. In the 1950s, industrial agriculture in the United States entered an era of overproduction, so the government set up aid programs that channeled food surpluses to developing countries. As US Senator George McGovern explained in 1964: "The great food markets of the future are the very areas where vast numbers of people are learning through Food for Peace to eat American produce. The people we assist today will become our customers tomorrow."[6] Today subsidized agricultural produce is one of America's most lucrative exports.[7]

Recipient countries of American food aid in Southeast Asia and elsewhere found it easier and cheaper to feed growing urban populations with American wheat than to invest in improvements in production, transportation, and distribution of food produced by local farmers.[8] American food aid and subsidized food exports had two interconnected effects: (1) local agriculture could not compete with imports of subsidized food, so farmers migrated to cities in search of jobs; (2) urban migrants formed a labor force that could be tapped for low-wage manufacturing.

American food aid thus contributed to restructuring the world economy. By 1980, subsistence agriculture had declined everywhere except in China, North Korea, and Vietnam. Between 1950 and 1997, the world's rural population decreased by approximately 25 percent.[9] Today, half the world's population lives in or on the margins of cities. As the economist Hernando de Soto observes, former peasant farmers are marginalized in the informal economy in the urban slums of megacities where survival is precarious:

In the last forty years, some four billion people, who had been living in the hinterlands of developing countries and former Soviet nations, have abandoned their traditional way of life. They are moving away from small, isolated communities toward a larger and more global division of labor in the expanding markets that both Adam Smith and Karl Marx had seen emerging in the West two hundred years ago. . . . It is this tide that has transformed Jakarta, Mexico City, São Paolo, Nairobi, Bombay, Shanghai, and Manila into megacities of 10, 20, 30 million and overwhelmed their political and legal institutions.[10]

Meanwhile, between 1950 and 1980 growth in manufacturing in developing countries contributed to economic growth rates higher than those of rich countries in the West.[11] Not surprisingly, among the most successful countries were the dragon and tiger economies of East and Southeast Asia—Hong Kong, Taiwan, South Korea, Singapore, Thailand, Malaysia, and Indonesia—where Cold War expenditures had subsidized growth. These countries came to be called newly industrializing countries (NICs).

The American model of industrialized agriculture also played a role in the transformation of peasant societies. In Southeast Asia agriculture was transformed by new high-yielding varieties of rice developed by the Ford Foundation in the Philippines, which were promoted as a "Green Revolution."[12] Since hybrid seeds are heavily dependent on pesticides, herbicides, and fertilizers, only wealthy farmers were able to afford the necessary inputs. As the major beneficiaries of the Green Revolution, these farmers gradually increased their landholdings at the expense of poorer farmers with small plots. Mechanized agriculture allowed landowners to replace tenant farmers with hired labor. The Green Revolution increased rice production, but the cost to society was significant. As concentration of landholding increased, rural poverty grew and food security was undermined. New industrial agriculture in the form of oil palm plantations, industrial shrimp farming, and acacia farms for paper and pulp production also displaced smallholders and reduced biodiversity.

The increased wealth of the emerging world economic system was primarily going to people in the rich countries and the wealthiest citizens of developing countries. In 1974 the World Bank reported, "It is now clear that more than a decade of rapid growth in underdeveloped countries has been of little or no benefit to perhaps a third of their population."[13] According to the World Bank's *Human Development Report* of 1999, the income gap between the fifth of the world's people living in the richest countries and the fifth in the poorest increased from 30 to 1 in 1960, to 60 to 1 in 1990, and 74 to 1 in 1997.[14] Meanwhile the number of people subsisting below the international poverty line increased between 1987 and 2000 from 1.2 billion to 1.5 billion. In 2000, one-quarter of the world's population lived on less than US$140 per year.[15]

The Debt Trap and Structural Adjustment Programs (SAPs)

A series of economic crises in the 1970s caused a worldwide recession in the 1980s that plunged many developing countries deeply into debt. The cost of the Vietnam War led the United States in 1971 to abandon the gold standard unilaterally, terminating the Bretton Woods Agreement (1944) that established a set of institutions and rules, including a fixed currency exchange rate, to regulate the international economy. In the aftermath of the Arab–Israeli War of 1973, the Organization of Petroleum Exporting Countries (OPEC) decreased production and imposed an oil embargo on countries supporting Israel. This led to an increase in oil prices of 400 percent, forcing developing countries to borrow money to cushion the effects of the price increase. The petrodollar profits of oil-rich countries in the Middle East were invested in Western banks, which in turn quickly set about selling loans to developing countries. Then, in 1979, the Iranian Revolution caused another hike in the price of oil, triggering an increase in the price of consumer goods and a cycle of inflation. To curb inflation, the United States raised interest rates, setting off a global recession. Developing countries dependent on exports suffered as imports by the wealthy countries declined. Their governments soon found that they could no longer pay back the petrodollars they had borrowed, thus producing a debt crisis.

Mexico was the first country to default on its debt in 1982, followed by Brazil. Fearing a collapse of the international banking system, the United States granted Mexico an emergency loan.[16] In the 1980s the International Monetary Fund (IMF) and the World Bank devoted millions of dollars to "rescue packages" and "bridge funding." In the decade ending in 1993, the debt burden of developing countries increased from US$785 billion to nearly $1.5 trillion.[17] Developing countries fell under the control of international financial institutions, such as the World Bank and the International Monetary Fund (IMF), which imposed neoliberal economic policies on debtor nations in the form of required structural adjustment programs (SAPs).

The neoliberal economic principles promoted by Prime Minister Margaret Thatcher and President Ronald Reagan that have come to be known as the "Washington consensus" required poor countries to export their way out of debt and poverty. This was to be achieved by expanding export-oriented extraction of natural resources, development of monoculture industrial agriculture for export, and investment in labor-intensive production for export, which entailed cutting expenditures for health, education, and welfare, privatization of state enterprises, and elimination of restrictions on foreign investment and capital flows. These policies were coordinated by an SAP that the IMF imposed on countries as a requirement for limited debt relief and further loans. The World Bank shifted the focus of its development loans to producing export-oriented economic growth in order that developing countries could repay their debts.

SAPs did not resolve the problem of debt. Rather, they produced what the international NGO Oxfam has called "export-led collapse." Export-oriented policies intensified competition among developing countries, leading to reduced prices for the commodities they produced, particularly timber products, fish, and plantation products such as cocoa. Between 1977 and 2000, real dollar prices fell for forty-one out of forty-six leading commodities produced by developing countries.[18] For example, overproduction of coffee between 1990 and 2000 brought the price of beans to a thirty-year low, so while the world coffee industry doubled in value, the profits did not go to growers but to corporations such as Nestle, Philip Morris, and Proctor & Gamble.[19] Similarly, overproduction of shrimp led to a plunge of shrimp prices, with consequences that were described in Chapter 4.[20] Furthermore, the "conditionalities" for SAP loans fell the hardest on the poor and led to what have been called "IMF food riots." Between 1976 and 1992, 146 riots occurred in thirty-nine of eighty debtor countries attempting to fulfill the conditions of a SAP loan.[21]

Beginning in 1984, debt repayment by developing countries to lending institutions in rich countries began to exceed the amount of loans and investment that went into developing countries. Between 1984 and 1990 net transfers of money for debt repayment to commercial banks in the West amounted to US$178 billion. This "reverse flow" of wealth from poor nations to rich ones is evident in Table 5, which is based on data in UN Human Development reports.

In Southeast Asian countries the financial shocks of the 1970s and the debt crisis of the 1980s were cushioned by increased development aid from Japan and investment from the "tiger economies" of South Korea and Taiwan. By 1989, Japan was supplying more development aid than the United States, and it was focused on Southeast Asia.[22] As increasing wages in Taiwan and South Korea made exports less competitive, companies in these countries shifted production to low-wage countries in Southeast Asia. Indonesia, however, was a special case, as it benefited from the high price of oil in the 1970s, allowing Suharto to reward supporters and support expansion of a middle class dependent on the state for jobs. When the price of oil

Table 5

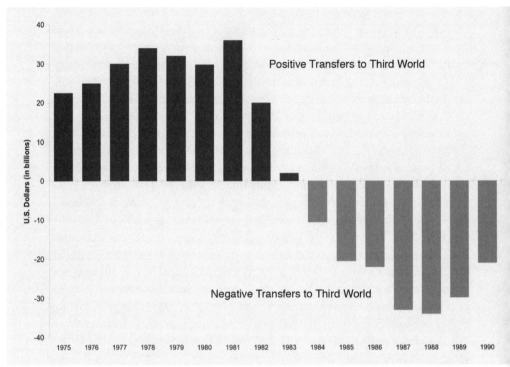

Capital inflows to the poor nations of the Southern hemisphere became positive in the 1990s because there was more foreign investment in fire sales of public assets and resources.

Source: United Nations Human Development Report (1994), p. 64.

Note: The chart as I reproduce it here appears in McMichael, p. 140 (Figure 4.2). Information about capital inflows into poor nations in the Southern hemisphere comes from Philip McMichael (personal communication).

dropped precipitously in 1982, as we have seen, the government began to intensively exploit Indonesia's forest resources.

The 1990s: "Trade Not Aid"

With the fall of the Soviet Union in 1989, neoliberal economics, rechristened as "globalization," became the dominant ideology: "Trade Not Aid" was the new slogan. Western corporations needed the new markets in developing countries to continue to provide rising profits and dividends. A US Department of the Treasury report entitled "The Multilateral Development

Banks: Increasing U.S. Exports and Creating U.S. Jobs" (1994) explains how development aid (predominantly in the form of loans) enriches the rich countries:

> U.S. participation in the development banks provides essential financial support for the work of U.S. export promotion agencies. . . . Since the founding of the World Bank in 1945, we have been their largest and most influential contributing member. We have also been their largest beneficiary in terms of contracts awarded to U.S. firms to help borrowing countries carry out projects financed through the banks. The U.S. procurement record in the development banks reflects the enormous economic stake we . . . have in promoting continued growth in the international economy. . . . To do well at home we must be engaged abroad.[23]

In the 1990s, export credit agencies (ECAs) became an increasingly important source of "development" loans, averaging US$80–100 billion or more per annum, roughly twice the level of the world's total official development assistance.[24] ECAs are government agencies in Western countries and Japan that provide loans and guarantees for projects carried out in developing countries by home-country corporations. Thus the ECA of the UK states that its goal is to "help exporters of UK goods and services to win business and UK firms to invest overseas by providing guarantees, insurance and reinsurance against loss."[25] AT&T, Bechtel, Boeing, General Electric, and McDonnell Douglas are the five biggest beneficiaries of the Export Import Bank (Ex-Im), the American ECA. Just ten American corporations received 90 percent of Ex-Im financing.[26]

ECAs provide insurance that guarantees payment to domestic banks and corporations if there is a default on payment by a foreign government. This means the evaluation of risk does not play an important role in loan decisions. Furthermore, the amount paid out by an ECA to domestic banks and corporations when there is a default on a loan or contract is added to the country's foreign debt. ECA loans now account for up to 25 percent of the bilateral debt of developing countries.

ECA funding played a central role in funding development projects described in this book. Funding for PT TEL (Chapter 3) came from the ECAs of Japan, Germany, Sweden, Finland, and Canada; ECAs also guaranteed loans from an international syndicate of banks based in Austria, Sweden, Finland, the United Kingdom, the United States, Japan, and Korea. Contractors for the project came from Austria, Germany, Sweden, Finland, Canada, the Netherlands, the United States, Australia, and Japan. PT TEL was a high-risk project due to the highly cyclical pulp and paper market, the strong likelihood of overproduction given the capacity of factories already on-line, and the uncertainty of the supply of raw materials.[27] The project went forward because the Indonesian government provided subsidies in the form of discounted financing and access to natural forests. Profits go to Prayogo Pangestu, to Suharto's daughter Siti Hardiyanti Rukmana, with a 16 percent interest through PT Tridan Satriaputri of Citro Group, and to Sumatra Pulp, a Japanese firm owned by the Marubeni Corporation and Nippon Paper Industries, with a 33 percent interest. Seventy percent of the pulp produced is exported to Japan and 30 percent to Europe. The project benefited corporate owners and consumers in Japan and Europe, not the people of South Sumatra. Gajah Tunggal industrial shrimp-farming operations were funded by loans from the World Bank and the Japanese ECA. Similarly, the International Finance Corporation provided loans and guarantees for the development of oil palm plantations in South Sumatra and elsewhere in Indonesia.

Projects funded by World Bank and ECA loans have been responsible for further marginalizing vulnerable groups, who are excluded from participation in development planning.[28] In Indonesia, World Bank loans of more than US$650 million funded transmigration projects resettling 3.5 million people from Java and Bali to the outer islands. These projects resulted in the loss of 3.3 million hectares of rainforest where indigenous people had lived. Much of this land was used for environmentally inappropriate wet-rice cultivation that failed. Sponsored migration that excluded local people from planning and destroyed their way of life laid the ground for violent conflicts after the New Order fell. Similarly, in Thailand the World Bank required the government to set up a semiautonomous body, the Electrical Generating Authority of Thailand (EGAT), as a condition for loans to fund a series of large-scale dams to generate hydroelectric power. EGAT projects displaced thousands of farmers, resettling them—generally on poorer lands and without compensation. As an autonomous agency, EGAT was immune from protests.[29] The *Extractive Industries Review,* a 2004 report on Indonesian projects commissioned by the World Bank, pointed out that Bank funding of industries such as mining and oil did not ameliorate poverty. The report recommended that the Bank require "free, prior, and informed consent" by indigenous people in areas to be mined. But this recommendation was modified by the Bank, changing "consent" to "consultation."[30]

In addition, World Bank and ECA financing fueled corruption in authoritarian regimes that could use their power to suppress protests. A 1997 World Bank report estimated that 20 to 30 percent of Indonesia's development budget was embezzled during the New Order.[31] In 2004, Transparency International named the ten most corrupt leaders in the world. Three were dictators in Southeast Asia who claimed to be promoting development. First on the list was Suharto, president of Indonesia (US$15–35 billion); second was Ferdinand Marcos, president of the Philippines (US$5–10 billion); while Joseph Estrada, as president of the Philippines for only three years, was said to have accumulated US$78–80 million.[32]

ECA loans and other forms of "development aid" also funded the militarization of regimes throughout the world. The British ECA provided loans to Indonesia to buy jets that were used to attack villages in East Timor and to deliver "shock therapy" to the separatist movement in Aceh. Most of Iraq's foreign debt of US$26 billion-plus was used by Saddam Hussein to purchase weapons and military equipment.[33]

ECA funding has also gone to projects that do not meet environmental standards established by development agencies. During the 1990s, ECA-backed investment in the pulp and paper industry in Indonesia amounting to more than US$15 billion led to deforestation of two million hectares per year and the loss of a sustainable living for an unknown number of farmers.[34] The American ECA provided over US$2 billion in loans for the Bataan Nuclear Power Plant in the Philippines, which was built on an earthquake fault at the foot of a volcano. Fortunately, the plant never became operational. In the words of the treasurer of the Philippines, "Filipinos have not benefited from a single watt of electricity," yet they will be repaying the loans for this project until 2018.[35]

The Asian Economic Crisis of 1997

The economic crisis that began in Thailand in the mid-1990s exposed the multiple problems that come with unregulated financial markets and neo-liberal economic policies. From the mid-1980s, foreign investment in low-wage manufacturing for export led to rapid economic growth in Thailand. As wages in Thailand began to rise in the nineties, investors began shifting operations to China, Vietnam, India, and Indonesia where wages were lower. In 1992 Thailand followed the advice of the IMF and the World Bank, opening up its financial market to foreign investors. This led to a large increase in incoming capital as Western banks competed to extend their loan portfolios in Thailand. Thai companies had no trouble obtaining loans, and economic growth appeared to be phenomenal. This spurred a real-estate boom and obscured the downturn in Thailand's manufacturing sector. In 1995 the World Bank declared that Thailand was the world's fastest growing economy in the past decade. Everyone wanted to climb on board. Politicians and cronies colluded in property deals and graft. Fearing that a fall in the value of its currency, the baht, would alarm investors, Thailand clung to a fixed exchange rate. The day of reckoning came when the Bangkok Bank of Commerce failed. As investors pulled their money out of Thailand, it became clear that much of the foreign investment had been based on the hope of quick profits rather than increasing productivity.[36]

Investors began to doubt the economic stability of other Southeast Asian countries, and the crisis quickly spread, impacting the economies of Indonesia, South Korea, Malaysia, and the Philippines. The IMF took advantage of the crisis to impose SAPs in return for rescue loans. In Indonesia, cuts in government spending deepened the recession and increased the suffering of the poorest. In the end, the citizens of Indonesia were left to repay debts incurred by a corrupt dictator and the private debts of Prayogo Pangestu's Barito Group and Syamsul Nursalim's Gajah Tunggal Group.

The NGO Movement

In the 1990s, the international financial institutions (IFIs)—the IMF, the World Bank, the World Trade Organization (WTO), and regional development banks—along with the governments of Western and Southeast Asian countries, began to take note of NGOs that had emerged as strong critics of neoliberal development. This NGO movement consisted of international, national, and local nonprofit and nongovernmental organizations active in the areas of rural development, poverty alleviation, nutrition and health, reproductive rights and birth control, education, refugees, human rights, and the environment. Heralding these NGOs as part of a civil society revolution that could prove "as significant to the latter twentieth century as the rise of the nation-state was to the latter nineteenth," IFIs and governments began to look for ways to coopt, incorporate, and control NGOs in a new model of development called "Good Governance."[37]

In Thailand and the Philippines, as in Indonesia, when students were banned from political mobilizing on university campuses, activists began to establish NGOs to work for democratic reforms and a more just form of development that focused on the poor. As Todung Mulya Lubis explains, "The rapid development of NGOs in the 1970s was . . . a logical result of a government campaign directed at the students. The campaign urged students to go back to the campuses, and not become involved in practical politics. . . . By setting up NGOs, the students renewed their activism."[38] The New Order sought to control NGO activism through laws requiring NGOs to register and restricting them from engaging in politics. The government also sought to coopt NGOs by providing financial support to chosen groups. Nevertheless, organizations like LBH and WALHI constantly challenged the distinction between political and nonpolitical activities and promoted the idea of participatory government.

The NGO movement in the Philippines emerged in the early 1950s when the National Movement for Free Elections (NAMFREL) was founded to prevent and report electoral fraud and violence. The Philippine Rural Reconstruction Movement (PRRM), another NGO founded in the 1950s, focused on development. At the same time, NGO activists began working with squatter communities in urban areas, especially Metro Manila. After declaring martial law in 1972, Marcos suppressed NGO activism, but his authoritarian rule only further politicized NGO activists and the poor. Two human rights NGOs—Task Force Detainees of the Philippines and the Free Legal Assistance Group—were founded in 1974. In 1983, after the assassination of Marcos critic Benigno Aquino, the NGO movement took off again. NAMFREL was revived in 1986 to document vote buying, intimidation, and fraud in the snap election called by Marcos. When democratic government was restored in 1987, nine national networks of development-oriented NGOs formed the Caucus of Development NGO Networks, with close to 3,000 NGO members.[39] In 1991 the First National NGO Congress ratified a Covenant on Philippine Development.

In Thailand, where the name for NGO, *ongkan patthana ekachon,* can be translated literally as "private development organization," the NGO movement began under royal patronage with the establishment of the Rural Reconstruction Movement (TRRM) in 1967.[40] University student volunteers who worked with TRRM gradually became critical of government development programs, which extended the power of the state at the expense of local institutions and did little to improve the lot of poor farmers. After the student-led democracy movement of 1973 led to establishment of a democratic government, activists founded new NGOs, including the Union for Civil Liberty (UCL), the first NGO focused on human rights and democratic reforms. Many NGOs were suppressed when right-wing political forces and the military crushed the democracy in October 1976. But in 1979 the UCL was revived, and it organized the "Campaign for Popular Democracy." NGOs established in the 1980s focused primarily on alternative development strategies that emphasized participatory development and income generating projects. In 1985 the NGO-Coordinating Committee on Rural Development was formed, with 106 member organizations. In 1997, Thailand's largest NGO coalition, the NGO Coordinating Committee on Development, listed 465 NGOs.

As in Indonesia, in Thailand and the Philippines religious traditions provided an alternative vision of development focused on the needs of the poor. In the Philippines, the Liberation Theology movement within the Catholic Church began organizing basic Christian communities among the rural poor, where the colonial legacy of deeply rooted poverty provided fertile ground for rebellion and recruitment by the Communist Party of the Philippines. In Thailand, development-oriented monks were inspired by a Buddhist reform movement led by Buddhadasa Bhikku. They began independent development projects. One of the earliest Buddhist NGOs, founded in 1974, was the Foundation for Education and Development of Rural Areas. In the 1980s, as forests were logged and watersheds destroyed, environmental monks began to ordain trees in an attempt to save the remaining forests. This movement came to be known as Engaged Buddhism.[41]

Grassroots and national NGOs in Southeast Asia formed alliances with international NGOs to expose problems in the planning and implementation of development projects funded by the World Bank and other IFIs. For example, in 1986 participants at an international conference in Malaysia founded the World Rainforest Movement (WRM) in response to a joint proposal of the World Bank and agencies of the United Nations and the World Resources Institute to set up a loan fund of US$7 billion earmarked for the development of commercial forestry that was supposed to manage forests sustainably. Over the last twenty years WRM bulletins have tracked commercial forestry projects and issued warnings about their effect on the environment.

Coalitions of grassroots, national, and international NGOs have an impressive record as advocates of indigenous peoples whose rights were violated by World Bank development projects. One of the earliest protests responded to World Bank funding for a series of hydroelectric dams on the Chico River in the Philippines. This project, initiated by President Ferdinand Marcos shortly after he declared martial law, would have flooded villages and rice terraces of the Kalinga and Bontoc people. The New People's Army, the armed wing of the Communist Party, supported local protests and helped to train militia. As violent clashes between the armed forces and opponents of the dam escalated, NGO critics finally convinced Bank officials to cancel funding for the project. In the 1980s a coalition of Philippine and American NGOs, including the Friends of the Earth and the Philippine Development Forum, convinced the World Bank, the Asian Development Bank, and ECAs in Japan and the United States to reject a proposal to fund the development of geothermal power on Mount Apo on the grounds that the environmental impact assessment was inadequate and the rights of indigenous people were being violated.[42]

In Thailand, NGOs worked with protestors against the Pak Mun Dam, which was to be funded by the Bank. As a result, the dam was redesigned to mitigate the effects on local people. In Indonesia, NGOs pressured the World Bank to end funding for transmigration projects in Sulawesi and Kalimantan that led to conflict with indigenous peoples. In East Timor and West Papua, transmigration projects funded by the Bank fueled local resentments that eventually led to movements of armed resistance.[43]

The international civil society community of NGOs supporting human rights, women's rights, and protection of the environment that emerged over the last fifty years is an important base for the struggle for a more just world order. Organizations like Amnesty International and Human Rights Watch have tried to hold governments accountable to principles enunciated in the UN Declaration of Human Rights (1948). NGOs in Thailand, the Philippines, and Indonesia laid the foundations for democracy movements, popularizing concepts such as human rights and "empowerment of the people." International NGOs continue to press for reforms democratizing governance of the IFIs and debt relief for developing countries that will encourage governments to be accountable to their citizens.[44]

Nevertheless, there are limits to what NGOs can do. At the international level, where the World Bank, the IMF, and the WTO constitute an emergent world government, the asymmetry in power between corporate interests, generally represented by Western governments, and coalitions of NGOs makes change unlikely. In an assessment of the impact of NGO advocacy on the World Bank, Jonathan Fox and David Brown point out that advocacy was most effective when it could be used by internal Bank staff critical of a project; indeed, they believe that advocacy campaigns were often based on an insider tip-off. More important, they conclude that "transnational advocacy coalitions have had more impact on policies than on projects." Fox and Brown argue that Bank projects "would be much less controversial" if policies actually worked as written.[45] They point out that the World Bank itself has acknowledged that compliance with its policies on the rights of indigenous peoples and sustainable development has been limited. The Bank's assessment reports are rarely based on independent, field-based observation.

Furthermore, NGOs in developing countries are dependent on funding from foreign sources, including Western governments. This means that funding reflects the interests of those governments. For example, the United States Aid agency (USAID) withdrew funding for NGOs in Indonesia that advocated an end to mining. Funding for local NGOs is so limited that, as we have seen in the cases of MHP (Chapter 3) and PT Pusri (Chapter 4), local NGO activists can often be bought off or corrupted by corporations or politicians. Finally, NGOs tend to be reactive to failures of planning rather than proactive.[46] Change in national-level development policies requires the creation of broad coalitions, while NGOs are issue-oriented.

The NGO movement demonstrates that the ideal of justice—a fair distribution of the world's resources and wealth—can bring citizens from different cultures together. The demand for a more just form of development gives NGOs moral authority, but moral authority does not change the structural relations of power that subordinate developing countries to powerful international financial institutions and the rich countries that control them. While the democracy movements in the Philippines (1986), Thailand (1992), and Indonesia (1998) led to recognition of civil and political rights and a major reduction in the level of state-sponsored violence, neoliberal economic policies supporting corporate development remain unchanged.

A More Just and Equitable Form of Development?

The World Bank has embraced the NGO movement and now calls for the development of civil society as a check on corruption and the abuse of power by governments. This new approach to development, promoted under the slogan of Good Governance, implicitly blames the failure of development to help the poor on the governments of developing countries.[47] Good Governance calls on governments and institutions funding development to listen to the people but ignores neoliberal policies that lead to a widening gap between rich and poor, political instability, and ethnic and religious conflict. In fact, neoliberal economic policies are promoted as the way to free society from bad government.

Authoritarian rule in Indonesia, Thailand, and the Philippines clearly contributed to development projects that benefited elites and corporate interests and to the abuse of power by government officials. Good Governance reforms focus on ending corruption, representation for middle-class interests, and the rule of law, but they do not change asymmetries of power that determine who benefits from government policies. In an assessment of post–New Order reforms in Indonesia, the World Bank concluded, "Progress on governance had been left largely to a few reformers . . . [who were] floundering under resistance from well-entrenched interests."[48] As seen in Chapter 7, direct elections and decentralization of government promoted as part of Good Governance may make elected officials somewhat more aware of the effects of government policies on the poor, but money still plays a major role in determining who wins elections, and government policies still favor local and national elites.[49]

Corporate interests have a far wider range of resources for shaping policy than do NGOs. Neoliberal policies create wealth, but most of it goes to corporations or ends up in the hands of political cronies. Fifty percent of world trade takes place inside Transnational Corporations (TNCs) between a parent corporation and its subsidiaries.[50] In 2000 the annual revenues of the world's two hundred largest corporations exceeded those of 182 countries with 80 percent of the world's population. Fifty of the largest two hundred economies in the world today are run by TNCs. General Motors is larger than Thailand, Norway, or Saudi Arabia, and Mitsubishi is larger than Poland, South Africa, or Greece. As Richard Robison and Vedi Hadiz emphasize in *Reorganising Power in Indonesia: The Politics of Oligarchy in an Age of Markets* (2004), "the neo-liberal agenda . . . cannot be understood as an abstraction driven by a collection of technopols acting above vested interests, but as an agenda backed by shifting and fluid coalitions with a concrete interest in the configuration of power and the institutions that allocate it."[51] From the heights of power, insiders like the financier George Soros and Joseph Stiglitz, chief economist at the World Bank (1997–2000), are voicing grave doubts about a world order based on free market neoliberal economics.[52]

After fifty years of development projects, the gap between the rich and the poor has grown wider. In 2005 the United Nations reported that one billion people in Asia and Africa live on a dollar a day or less, and 1.8 billion more live on just two dollars a day.[53] In 2000 the United Nations Millennium Declaration identified eight development goals to be achieved by 2015: (1) ending extreme poverty and hunger; (2) universal primary education; (3) gender equality; (4) reducing child mortality; (5) improving maternal health; (6) combating HIV/AIDS, malaria, and other diseases; (7) environmental sustainability; and (8) a global partnership for development.

Longtime critics of the neoliberal ideology that dominates development planning and funding have envisioned a more sustainable form of development in works such as Amartya Sen, *Development as Freedom* (1999), Hernando de Soto, *The Mystery of Capital: Why Capitalism Triumphs in the West and Fails Everywhere Else* (2000), Susan George, *Another World Is Possible If...*(2004), Noreena Hertz, *The Debt Threat: How Debt Is Destroying the Developing World* (2004), and John Cavanagh and Jerry Mander, eds., *Alternatives to Economic Globalization* (2004). International development NGOs, such as Oxfam and Action Aid, have implemented aid programs that target development for the poor. The problem of development is that the influence of powerful corporate lobbies on national governments and the leaders of IFIs outweighs the needs of the poor. Jeffrey Sachs, an economic adviser who formerly advocated neoliberal "shock therapy" in

Bolivia, Poland, and Russia, is now the director of the UN Millennium Project. In *The End of Poverty: Economic Possibilities for Our Time* (2005), he shows the costs of poverty to all societies and argues that it is possible to end extreme poverty, but he warns that the greatest challenge is to ensure that the leaders of rich nations and IFIs honor that commitment.[54]

Free-Market Utopianism

In Europe, the establishment of a market economy in the sixteenth century gradually transformed social relations into economic relations between the owners of capital and those who must sell their labor for a wage. The enclosure movement that abolished traditional and communal rights to land set the stage for the mobilization of people and the products of labor in free trade. With colonialism, the market economy was extended to the farthest reaches of the world, and the sustainable livelihood and traditional way of life of farmers throughout the world was gradually disrupted.

In *The Great Transformation: The Political and Economic Origins of Our Time* (1944), Karl Polyani has described the emergence of free-market economics. First, Polyani demonstrates that free-market or "neoliberal" economics is a utopian ideology based on the premise that unregulated or "free" markets in land, labor, and capital will produce prosperity for all. He shows that free markets are not "natural," but rather "the road to the free market was opened and kept open by an enormous increase in continuous, centrally organized and controlled [government] interventionism."[55] Governments intervene in markets, either to accommodate the interests of the powerful and wealthy or for the common good—for example, by laws restricting child labor, limiting the number of hours in a workday, setting minimum wages, limiting pollution by industry, and setting up central banks to regulate money and credit. On the other hand, over the last half-century IFIs and the Western governments that control them have used neoliberal free-market economics to promote policies that benefit corporate interests through the transfer of rights to land, tax breaks, suppression of protests, and a failure to enforce labor and environmental laws. As part of SAPs, the IFIs have also required governments to cut funding for education and health programs. "Free trade" and free markets are not natural phenomena; they are political constructs.

Second, Polyani shows that there are fundamental flaws in free-market ideology. Neoliberal economics treats labor, money, land, and other natural resources as if they were commodities produced for sale where supply and demand determines a fair price. When labor is treated as a commodity to be exchanged at the lowest possible price, it means that human beings can be paid starvation wages. Population growth and the displacement of subsistence-level farmers throughout the world have led to a labor glut on the world market. To attract foreign investment and create jobs, the world's poorest countries compete in offering the most profitable conditions for corporations—tax breaks, low wages, and a stable workforce. They engage in a "race to the bottom" in which the interests of workers are sacrificed to corporate profits. Jobs that are outsourced to developing countries lead to falling wages, decreased benefits, and subsequent unemployment in developed countries.

The treatment of money as a commodity in an unregulated market precipitates economic crises, like the Asian Economic Crisis of 1997. Economic crises lead to capital flight, bankruptcies, loss of jobs, and political instability. Genuine good governance requires the regulation of financial markets for the common good. Developed countries have established regulatory bodies, but international finance remains unregulated in accord with free-market economic principles.

When natural resources are treated like economic goods produced for sale, there is a lack of concern about the possible exhaustion of those resources and damage to the environment. Unregulated markets allow powerful economic and political groups to put individual profit and short-term interests ahead of long-term concerns for sustainable social and natural environments. In Indonesia, mining companies like BTM (Chapter 6), Freeport-McMoRan, and Newmont extract minerals and oil as cheaply and quickly as possible with minimum concern about the effects of their operations on the surrounding society.[56] Similarly, as we have seen with corporate oil palm plantations and industrial forestry in South Sumatra, when land is considered only as a productive input, there is little consideration of long-term sustainability or damage to the environment.

Neoliberal policies creating a world market for all products have led to intensifying competition for control over natural resources and land. In *World on Fire: How Exporting Free Market Democracy Breeds Ethnic Hatred and Global Instability* (2002), Amy Chua describes how "market dominant minorities," such as the Chinese in Indonesia who are positioned to benefit from neoliberal policies, have been targeted in violent protests by the poor who bear the brunt of the economic and social costs of those policies. Economic competition also fueled violent conflicts that erupted at the end of the 1990s between Muslims and Christians and between different ethnic groups in Indonesia, as well as the emergence of armed separatist movements in Aceh and West Papua. A report of the American Central Intelligence Agency (CIA) entitled "Global Trends 2015" acknowledges the social and political costs of free-market economic policies:

> The rising tide of the global economy will create many economic winners, but it will not lift all boats. [It will] spawn conflicts at home and abroad ensuring an ever-wider gap between regional winners and losers than exists today. [Globalization's] evolution will be rocky, marked by chronic financial volatility and a widening economic divide. Regions, countries and groups feeling left behind will face deepening economic stagnation, political instability and cultural alienation. They will foster political, ethnic, ideological and religious extremism, along with the violence that often accompanies it.[57]

As Polyani prophesized, "With free trade the new and tremendous hazards of planetary interdependence sprang into being."[58] The destruction of forests throughout the world and increased use of fossil fuels in industrializing societies create global warming and threaten the future livelihood of all peoples. Free-market utopianism must be abandoned. Truly democratic and accountable government involves participation by farmers and workers in planning for a future that puts human development and welfare first.

1848 to 1998: The Struggle for Justice

Like the revolutions of 1848, the wave of democracy movements that swept through Southeast Asia in the last three decades of the twentieth century—in Thailand (1973, 1992), the Philippines (1986), Burma (1988), and Indonesia (1998)—were inspired by the ideals of freedom of speech and association, universal human rights, and equality. As in France, the revolutions were led by representatives of the middle class, but they were supported by members of the working class and landless farmers. As Daniel Lev has pointed out, "While royalty and aristocracy naturally claim restrictive rights, justified by birth, and religious hierarchies are blessed by heaven, middle-class groups, lacking innate legitimacy, have no choice but to generalize their appeals— for example, to all who own property or all citizens or even all humanity."[59] While the demands of workers and farmers—the right to work and the right to land—were not the same as the demands of the middle class, the ideal of equality and the concept of universal rights provided the basis for a revolutionary coalition.

As in France, movements demanding social and economic justice were crushed by the military in Indonesia (1965), the Philippines (1972), Thailand (1976), and Burma (1988). Liberties central to democracy were abrogated by dictators supported by the middle class. The demands of the poor were branded as communist and viewed as a threat to society. As Marx predicted, the bourgeoisie have tended to view democracy as a vehicle of middle-class rule, and when the middle classes appear to be threatened by movements of the poor, they have turned to authoritarian rulers.[60] Like Marx, Tocqueville recognized the danger of a society polarized into two great classes, the rich and the poor, but for Tocqueville the greatest danger to the liberty of citizens in a republic was centralized government and the love of power that it breeds. He writes of the February revolution in 1848:

> It was an extraordinary and terrible thing to see in the sole hands of those who possessed nothing, all this immense town so full of riches, or rather this great nation: for, thanks to centralization, he who reigns in Paris governs France. Hence the terror of all the other classes was extreme; I doubt whether at any period of the revolution it had been so great, and I should say that it was only to be compared to that which the civilized cities of the Roman Empire must have experienced when they suddenly found themselves in the power of the Goths and Vandals.[61]

For over a hundred and fifty years repression of working-class and rural protest has been justified on the grounds that the masses are ignorant and prone to violence. As William Callahan writes of the democracy demonstrations in Thailand in 1992, "Even though the mass movement in Bangkok and the provinces was characterized by five disciplined weeks of non-violent mass rallies and hunger strikes, the demonstrators were still labeled a 'mob,' a chaotic and violent group of people who by definition need to be dispersed."[62]

One of the central aims of this book has been to challenge the myth of the dangerous masses that has so often served to justify a return to authoritarian rule. Over the ten years that I conducted research in South Sumatra, I witnessed the capacity of people with little education to engage in participatory democracy, what they would call *musyawarah*.[63] People unjustly deprived of their livelihood and rights showed extraordinary respect for the law. This is not to ignore the fact that violent protests took place, but to emphasize that there is a context for such violence that must be acknowledged. Sometimes violence was provoked because it served the interests of corporations or authorities who could then claim that protestors were violating the law. Elite and state sponsorship of paramilitary "security" forces also played a role in legitimating the use of violence. Finally, when society comes to be polarized into the rich against the poor, and political and legal institutions provide no means for the redress of grievances, violence may seem the only way to press legitimate demands.

The struggle for a more just social order requires governments that are accountable to all citizens. Under the discipline of foreign debt and the pressures of entrenched elites and rising entrepreneurs, governments of developing countries have continued to implement policies that place corporate development first and thus polarize society. Forgiveness of debts and the reform of international financial institutions are essential first steps toward making governments accountable. Equally important are democratic reforms that politically empower the poor. NGOs are middle-class organizations; they do not directly represent the poor. "Good governance" will not be enough to make governments prioritize the needs of the poor and deal with environmental degradation. Political organization of farmers and workers is essential.

Development policies must support smallholder agriculture as opposed to corporate agriculture. Governments in Japan and Europe have taken measures to protect traditional agriculture for cultural, social, and economic reasons. According to the Organization for Economic Cooperation and Development, in 2005 subsidies to agriculture in the European Union, the United States, and Japan totaled US$300 billion.[64] Developing countries do not have enough resources to subsidize their agriculture. Under the domination of neoliberal economic policies, they are also forbidden to protect local agriculture with tariffs. Yet the World Bank acknowledges that multicropped, owner-operated smallholder farms are the most productive form of agriculture.[65] A prosperous rural society of smallholders produces multiple sites of economic exchange and growth that reduce migration to urban areas and the dependence of squatters on government services. Diverse smallholder agriculture provides a greater degree of food security, prevents soil erosion, and preserves some biodiversity through multicropping.[66] It reduces the volume of migration to megacities and the social problems associated with urban slums. It provides a base for local democratic institutions of government.

Activists in local, national, and international NGOs all play important roles in the struggle for a more just world. As they confront the power wielded by international financial institutions, multinational corporations, and national and local political and business elites, it is crucial that they work with farmers and workers to fulfill the promise of universal human rights, reshaping the economic order through democratic movements.

Chronology

The New Order and Post-Suharto Era, 1965–2004

1965   • "G30S" coup, followed by the massacre of between five hundred thousand and one million people said to be associated with the Communist Party (PKI)

1966   • President Sukarno hands over power to General Suharto, beginning the New Order

1971   • First New Order election: Suharto becomes president
        • The Legal Aid Institute (LBH) is established
        • The Indonesian Council for Dakwah (DDII) focuses proselytizing on university campuses

1974   • "Malari" riot targeting Prime Minister Tanaka, the first major protest against corporate development

1975   • Pertamina defaults on loans of US$40 million

1977   • Second New Order election; student protests lead to the Campus Normalization Law, which criminalizes political activities on the part of students
        • NGO and *dakwah* movements emerge

1979   • The Iranian Revolution deepens New Order suspicions of Islamic organizations

1982   • Third New Order election
        • Oil prices collapse; the New Order begins to exploit Indonesia's forest resources

1983   • Petrus mysterious killings of thugs in Jakarta

1984   • Tanjung Priok protest by Muslims and massacre by the military

1985   • Law on mass organizations forces Islamic organizations to take Pancasila as their fundamental principle

1987   • Fourth New Order election

1989   • Policy of "Openness" announced
        • New Order seeks Muslim support; ICMI established

1991   • Muslim students protest the establishment of a national lottery
        • The Institute for Campus Dakwah (LDK) is formed

1992   • Fifth New Order election

1994   • Supreme Court awards compensation to Kedung Ombo farmers

- *Tempo* and two other major news magazines banned
- "Openness" ends

1996
- New Order attack on *reformasi* supporters of Megawati Sukarnoputri at the headquarters of the Indonesian Democracy Party (PDI) ends in the largest riot of the New Order

1997
- El Niño drought and massive forest fires in Sumatra and Kalimantan
- Asian financial crisis strikes
- In the lead-up to the sixth New Order election, *reformasi* protests begin on university campuses

1998
- Leading *reformasi* activists are kidnapped by the military
- March: The Action Committee of Indonesian Muslim Students (KAMMI) joins the call for Suharto to step down
- May 13: Four students are shot on the campus of Trisakti University in Jakarta, setting off protests and riots in Jakarta, Solo, Palembang, and elsewhere
- May 21: Suharto resigns. B. J. Habibie becomes president

1999
- Local autonomy legislation passed
- Proposed law giving emergency powers to the military leads to renewed *reformasi* protests
- First free election for national, provincial, and district legislatures
- Abdurrahman Wahid (Gus Dur) becomes president

2001
- Abdurrahman Wahid resigns
- Megawati Sukarnoputri becomes president

2004
- First direct election of a president
- Susilo Bambang Yudhoyono (SBY) becomes president

Notes

Prologue

1. History of Parlement iii, 555, quoted in E. L. Woodward, *Three Studies in European Conservatism: Metternich; Guizot; The Catholic Church in the Nineteenth Century* (1963 [1929]), 220–221.

2. Quoted in T. J. Clark, *The Absolute Bourgeois: Artists and Politics in France 1848–1851* (1973), 11.

3. *L'Artisan,* September 22, 1830, quoted in William Sewell, *Work and Revolution in France: The Language of Labor from the Old Regime to 1848* (1980), 198.

4. Priscilla Robertson, *Revolutions of 1848: A Social History* (1952), 18; Mark Traugott, *Armies of the Poor: Determinants of Working-Class Participation in the Parisian Insurrection of June 1848* (1985), 11.

5. Letter to Nassau William Senior, April 10, 1848. Alexis de Tocqueville, *Selected Letters on Politics and Society,* ed. Robert Boesche (1986), 207.

6. Robertson, *Revolutions of 1848,* 55.

7. Ibid., 65.

8. Peter Amman, *Revolution and Mass Democracy: The Paris Club Movement in 1848* (1975). Also see Traugott, *Armies of the Poor* (1985).

9. Quoted in Roger Price, ed., *1848 in France* (1975), 102.

10. Ibid., 87.

11. Ibid., 107.

12. Karl Marx, *The 18th Brumaire of Louis Bonaparte* (1852), 25.

Chapter 1: Land of the Nine Rivers

1. Translation by Harry Aveling.

2. Elizabeth Collins, "(Re)negotiating Gender Hierarchy in the New Order: A South Sumatran Field Study," *Asia Pacific Viewpoint* 37:2 (1996), and Elizabeth Collins and Ernaldi Bahar, M.D., "To Know Shame in Malay Societies," *Crossroads* 14 (2000).

3. "Democratic Practice: South Sumatran Field Studies," was funded by the Ford Foundation in Jakarta and conducted by Laurel Heydir and Yayasan Masyarakat Madani.

4. Geoff Forrester and R. J. May, eds., *The Fall of Soeharto* (1999), and Arief Budiman, Barbara Hatley, and Damien Kingsbury, eds, *Reformasi: Crisis and Change in Indonesia* (1999), were immediate attempts to assess the fall of Suharto.

5. For an accessible introduction to the Dong Song cultural heritage in Southeast Asia, see "The Haunting Legacy of Buried Drums," in Robert Brown, ed., *Southeast Asia: A Past Regained* (1995).

6. Barbara Watson Andaya, *To Live as Brothers: Southeast Sumatra in the Seventeenth and Eighteenth Centuries* (1993), xv.

7. Robert Cribb, *Historical Atlas of Indonesia* (2000), 140–148. See Jousairi Hasbullah, *Mamang dan Belanda: Goresan-goresan Wajah Sosial-Ekonomi dan Kependudukan Sumatera Selatan Zaman Kolonial dan Refleksinya pada Hari Ini* (1996), for a local account of South Sumatra under colonial rule in the early twentieth century.

8. On events in South Sumatra during the Revolution, see Abi Hasan Said, *Bumi Sriwijaya Bersimbah Darah: Perjuangan Rakyat Semesta Menegakkan Republik Indonesia di ujung Selatan Sumatera* (1992).

9. Ibid., 158.

10. The New Order and the Indonesian military maintain that the coup was plotted and carried out by the Communist Party. In the "Cornell Paper," Ruth McVey and Benedict Anderson argued that the coup was primarily the result of internal army divisions. Adam Schwarz concludes, "Although not without its flaws—in particular its view that the Communist Party was not involved at all in the coup—on balance the Cornell Paper seems to offer a more credible interpretation of events than the army's contention that the communists were solely responsible." *A Nation in Waiting: Indonesia in the 1990s* (1994), 20.

11. The New Order applied colonial era laws against "insulting the government" and "libeling the president" supplemented by laws passed during the Sukarno era, such as the Anti-Subversion Law of 1963, making it a crime to engage in acts that "distort, undermine or deviate from" the state ideology or that could disseminate feelings of hostility, disturbances, or anxiety among the population."

12. The five principles of Pancasila are: belief in God, the unity of Indonesia, democracy, social justice, and humanism.

13. Richard Robison, *Power and Economy in Suharto's Indonesia* (1990), 23. For an overview of the Indonesian economy in historical perspective, see Howard Dick, Vincent J. H. Houben, J. Thomas Lindblad, and Thee Kian Wie, *The Emergence of a National Economy: An Economic History of Indonesia, 1800–2000* (2002).

14. For an account of the marketing of loans for development projects to Indonesia, see John Perkins, *Confessions of an Economic Hit Man* (2004).

15. Jean Bush Aden, "Oil and Politics in Indonesia, 1945 to 1980," and "Entrepreneurship and Protection in the Indonesian Oil Industry Service," in *Southeast Asian Capitalists*, ed. Ruth McVey (1992); Richard Tanter, "Oil, IGGI and US Hegemony: The Global Pre-conditions for Indonesian Rentier-Militarization," in *State and Civil Society in Indonesia*, ed. Arief Budiman (1990); John Bresnan, *Managing Indonesia: The Modern Political Economy* (1993), 55, 168–171; "Soeharto Family Members Implicated in Pertamina Corruption Cases," *Jakarta Post*, March 8, 2003.

16. Richard Robison, "Neoliberalism and the Future World: Markets and the End of Politics" (2004), 409.

17. Dedi Supriadi Adhuri, "Between Village and Marga, a Choice of Structure: The Local Elites' Behaviors in Lahat Regency, South Sumatra," *Antropologi Indonesia* 26 (Special Volume, 2002).

18. Vedi R. Hadiz, "Capitalism, Oligarchic Power and the State in Indonesia," *Historical Materialism: Research in Critical Marxist Theory,* no. 8 (Summer 2001): 120. Edward Aspinall writes: "[Suharto] used timber concessions, easy lines of credit, contracts in the petroleum industry, and similar perquisites to tie prominent officials to him personally. This pattern was reproduced at all levels of the state, and distribution of patronage became the chief means for securing the cohesion and loyalty of the bureaucracy. Similar methods were used to buy the compliance of retired bureaucrats, party chiefs, and community leaders who might otherwise have been inclined to oppose Suharto." *Opposing Suharto: Compromise, Resistance, and Regime Change in Indonesia* (2005), 27.

19. Aspinall, *Opposing Suharto,* 162 (original source, *Jakarta Post,* June 2, 1998). Also see "Kwik Vows to Continue Fight against 'Black' Conglomerates," *Jakarta Post,* August 29, 2000.

20. "Plundering politicians and bribing multinationals undermine economic development, says TI," Transparency International, London (March 25, 2004), www.transparency.org.

21. The World Bank, *Indonesia: Environment and Natural Resource Management in a Time of Transition* (2001), 9, Table 2.1.

22. Richard Robison and Vedi R. Hadiz, *Reorganizing Power in Indonesia: The Politics of Oligarchy in an Age of Markets* (2004), 80.

23. Amzulian Rifai, "Socio-legal Aspects of Land Disputes in Relation to Oil Palm Plantation Activities: The Case of South Sumatra" (2004). On the oil palm boom, see Anne Casson, "The Hesitant Boom: Indonesia's Oil Palm Sub-Sector in an Era of Economic Crisis and Political Change," *CIFOR Occasional Paper No. 29* (June 2000).

24. Cribb, *Historical Atlas of Indonesia,* 173, 174, and 178.

25. Richard Robison, "What Sort of Democracy? Predatory and Neo-liberal Agendas in Indonesia," in *Globalization and Democratization in Asia,* ed. Catarina Kinnvall and Kristina Jonsson (2002), 97.

26. "Kwik Vows to Continue Fight against 'Black' Conglomerates," *Jakarta Post,* August 29, 2000.

27. Documents that LBH staff copied for me have been placed in the Southeast Asia Library at Ohio University. Because LBH-Palembang has moved its offices several times, I fear that there is no complete archive of LBH documents in Palembang.

Chapter 2: *Reformasi* in South Sumatra

1. On Malari, see David Bouchier, "Crime, Law, and State Authority in Indonesia," in *State and Civil Society in Indonesia,* ed. Arief Budiman (1990); John Bresnan, *Managing Indonesia: The Modern Political Economy* (1993), 137.

2. "White Book of the 1978 Students' Struggle," *Indonesia* 25 (April 1978).

3. Augustinus Rumansara, "Indonesia: The Struggle of the People of Kedung Ombo," in *The Struggle for Accountability: The World Bank, NGOs, and Grassroots Movements,* ed. Jonathan A. Fox and L. David Brown (1998); Bob S. Hadiwinata, *The Politics of NGOs in Indonesia: Developing Democracy and Managing a Movement* (2003), 215-217.

4. Interview with Helmi Nawawi, executive director of KEMASDA (August 2000).

5. In addition to discussions with Ahmad Humaidi and other reporters for the *Sriwijaya Post,* I have consulted the following sources: Ahmad Humaidi, *Kebangkitan Pers Daerah: Sepuluh Tahun Perjalanan Sriwijaya Post 1987-1997* [The Rise of a Regional Press: Ten Years of the Daily Newspaper *Sriwijaya Post* 1987-1997] (1997); *Sriwijaya Post,* February 1, 1996 (1), (2); *Sumatera Ekspres,* January 29, February 2, 1996; *Kompas,* February 1 and 2, 1996.

6. Quoted in Adam Schwarz, *A Nation in Waiting: Indonesia's Search for Stability,* 2nd ed., 1999, 231.

7. Lembing stands for Lembar Informasi Gerakan Lingkungan [Newsletter of the Environmental Movement; *kayu* is Indonesian for "wood"]. My copies of *Lembing KAYU* have been placed in the Southeast Asia Library at Ohio University.

8. Quoted in "Action Dashes Hope for Change," *Herald Tribune,* July 29, 1996.

9. Paul Gellert, "A Brief History and Analysis of Indonesia's Forest Fire Crisis," *Indonesia* 65 (1998); Ivan Anderson, Ifran Imanda, and Muhnandar, "Vegetation Fires in Sumatra, Indonesia: The Presentation and Distribution of NOAA-Derived Data," European Union Ministry of Forestry and Estate Crops (Forest Fire Prevention and Control Project); "Two Firms Guilty of Forest Fires," *Jakarta Post,* October 20, 1998.

10. *Kompas Online,* February 9, 1998.

11. Quoted in Margaret Scott, "Indonesia Reborn?" *New York Review of Books,* August 13, 1998.

12. *Sriwijaya Post,* May 16 and 19, 1998.

13. In addition to interviews with Abdul Wahid Situmorang and other activists present at the demonstration, I have consulted the following sources: *Sriwijaya Post,* December 22, 1999 (1), (2), December 23 and 26, 1999; *Sumatera Ekspres,* December 22, 1999, December 23, 1999 (1), (2), December 26, 1999; *Palembang Pos,* December 22 and 23, 1999.

Chapter 3: Who Owns the Land?

1. Timothy Lindsey, "Square Pegs and Round Holes: Fitting Modern Title into Traditional Societies in Indonesia," *Pacific Rim Law and Policy Journal* (1998).

2. *Sriwijaya Post,* October 5, 2002, April 14, 2003.

3. *Suara Pembaruan,* January 2, January 4, and August 7, 1999. Also see Richard Robison and Vedi Hadiz, *Reorganizing Power in Indonesia: The Politics of Oligarchy in an Age of Markets* (2004); William Ascher, "From Oil to Timber: The Political Economy of Off-Budget Development Financing in Indonesia," *Indonesia* 65 (April 1998).

4. Christopher Barr, "Bob Hasan, the Rise of Apkindo, and the Shifting Dynamics of Control in Indonesia's Timber Sector," *Indonesia* 65 (1998).

5. Amzulian Rifai, "Socio-legal Aspects of Land Disputes in Relation to Oil Palm Plantation Activities: The Case of South Sumatra" (2004).

6. My account of the conflict between Kundi villagers and PT GSBL is based on research by Jamila Nuh, my own interviews with Pak Tarto and Kundi villagers, and the following news sources: *Sriwijaya Post,* September 11, 14, and 20, 1995, March 5, 1998. See Jamila M. Nuh and Elizabeth Collins, "Land Conflict and Grassroots Democracy in South Sumatra," *Antropologi Indonesia* 25, no. 64 (January–April 2001), for an earlier publication on this conflict.

7. *Lembing KAYU,* January 2000.

8. My account of the Wonorejo villagers' campaign to win back their land is based on research by Jamila, my interviews with Wonorejo villagers and Pak Tarto's wife, and news sources listed in the bibliography, p. 234.

9. *Sriwijaya Post,* February 7 and 14, 1998.

10. *Sumatera Ekspres,* January 14, 1998.

11. Ibid., May 26, 1998.

12. Ibid., July 29, 1998, September 24 and 25, 1998; *Sriwijaya Post,* September 24, 1998.

13. *Sumatera Ekspres,* December 5, 1998; *Sriwijaya Post,* December 8, 1998.

14. *Sumatera Ekspres,* March 29, 1999 (1), (2).

15. Ibid., May 4, 1999.

16. *Sriwijaya Post,* November 13, 1999; *Sumatra Ekspres,* November 13, 15, and 25, 1999, December 2, 1999; *Republika,* November 19, 1999.

17. *Sumatera Ekspres,* May 25, 2000.

18. LBH-Palembang, 2001; *Sriwijaya Post,* April 14, 2000; *Sumatera Ekspres,* June 16 and 21, 2000, February 13, 2001, March 13 and 23, 2001; *Palembang Pos,* February 13 and 20, 2001.

19. *Sumatera Ekspres,* April 6, 2001; *Palembang Pos,* April 11, 14, 15, and 20, 2001; *Kompas,* April 18, 2001.

20. *Forum Cyber News,* August 27, 2001.

21. *World Rainforest Movement,* April 2005.

22. David W. Brown, "Addicted to Rent: Corporate and Spatial Distribution of Forest Resources in Indonesia, Implications for Forest Sustainability and Government Policy" (September 7, 1999).

23. Koim's testimony was recorded by an LBH researcher. My account of the conflict between Benakat and MHP is based on discussions with LBH staff.

24. *Sriwijaya Post,* July 19, 21, 25, and 26, 1994.

25. *Sriwijaya Post,* September 22, 1994.

26. My account of the conflict between villagers in Pelawe and MHP is based on an LBH chronology of the conflict, interviews with Saparuddin, LBH, and WALHI staff, and discussions with villagers (July 2000).

27. Ayu Utami paints an evocative picture of the struggle of villagers against the

hired thugs of a corporation operating in the lowland forest of South Sumatra in her novel *Saman* (1998).

28. *Kompas*, February 17, 2000; *Republika*, February 19, 2000; Down to Earth, May 1999, June 2002.

29. My account of the conflict between MHP and the villagers of Rambang Lubai and Rambang Dangku is based on interviews with Junial Komar in Prabamulih (July 23, 2000) and Palembang (August 7, 2000), discussions with LBH staff, and news sources cited in notes. Also see Minako Sakai, "Land Dispute Resolution in the Political Reform at the Time of Decentralization in Indonesia," *Anthropologi Indonesia* (Special Volume, 2002).

30. *Media Indonesia*, September 3, 1999.

31. *Jakarta Post*, February 17, 2000.

32. Ibid., April 19, 2001; *Tempo*, May 22–28, 2001.

33. *Republika*, February 24, 2000.

34. *Sriwijaya Post*, February 29, 2000.

35. Ibid., April 28, 2000.

36. Ibid., June 6, 10, and 29, 2000, September 26, 2002 (1), (2), (3).

37. Interview with Governor Rosihan Arsyad, August 7, 2000.

38. *Sriwijaya Post*, September 25, 2002.

39. *Jakarta Post*, January 8, April 19, 2001; *Indonesian Observer*, April 19, May 14, 2001.

40. *Kompas*, October 20, 2000.

41. *Tempo Interactive*, June 18 and 29, 2001.

42. *Tempo*, May 22–28 and June 17, 2001, September 1, 2003; *Jakarta Post*, August 22, 2003.

43. *USINDO Brief*, June 25, 2003.

Chapter 4. No Forests, No Future

1. A *pantun* is a traditional form of oral verse in four lines.

> *Kami tidak lagi gembira*
> *Karena hari depan tidak ada harapan cerah*
> *Sekarang diserang limbah, polusi udara diatas*
> *Menjadikan daerah kami kota-kota hantu.*

> *Masyarakat sudah merasa sangsi*
> *Aparat masih bertangan besi*
> *Rakyat hidup susah mencari sesuap nasi*
> *Karena tanam tumbuh sudah diserang polusi.*

2. World Bank, *Indonesia: Environment and Natural Resource Management in a Time of Transition* (2001); David W. Brown, "The State of the Forest: Indonesia 2002."

3. *Jakarta Post*, April 6, 2001.

4. *Sriwijaya Post*, January 21, 2003; *Lembing KAYU*, January 2000 (1), (2), (3).

5. Ricardo Carrere amd Larru Lohmann. *Pulping the South: Industrial Tree*

Plantations and the World Paper Economy (1996); Christine Padoch and Nancy Lee Peluso, eds., *Borneo in Transition: People, Forests, Conservation, and Development* (1996); Down to Earth, February 1998; David W. Brown, "Why Governments Fail to Capture Economic Rent: The Unofficial Appropriation of Rain Forest Rent by Rulers in Insular Southeast Asia between 1970 and 1999" (2001), and "Addicted to Rent: Corporate and Spatial Distribution of Forest Resources in Indonesia, Implications for Forest Sustainability and Government Policy" (September 7, 1999); Christopher Barr, "Profits on Paper: The Political-Economy of Fiber and Finance in Indonesia's Pulp and Paper Industries," in C. Barr, *Banking on Sustainability: Structural Adjustment and Forestry Reform in Post-Suharto Indonesia* (2001); Peter Dauvergne, *Loggers and Degradation in the Asia-Pacific: Corporations and Environmental Management* (2001); Michael Ross, *Timber Booms and Institutional Breakdown in Southeast Asia* (2001); World Wildlife Fund, *Oil Palm Plantations and Deforestation in Indonesia* (2002); Anna Lowenhaupt Tsing, *Friction: An Ethnography of Global Connection* (2005).

6. *Guardian Unlimited,* June 25, 2003.

7. *Jakarta Post,* July 29, 1999.

8. Down to Earth, June 1997, 1998; Taufik Wijaya, December 15, 1998 (1), (2).

9. PT TEL reported providing compensation of Rp 6.3 billion, but local farmers reported receiving only Rp 3.7 billion. Down to Earth, August 1999.

10. Ibid., January 1999, March 1999.

11. Ibid., December 1998.

12. Ibid., August 1999, October 1999, February 2000, May 2000, February 2001, May 2001; NorWatch, April 1999.

13. WALHI, June 20, 1997.

14. Taufik Wijaya: January 13, 1999, February 16, 1999, March 17, 1999, April 4, 1999, April 29, 1999, May 5, 1999, December 19, 1999, December 20, 1999; Alliance of Independent Journalists, February 4, 1999.

15. Eleven local farmers were arrested for attempting to burn down the PT TEL factory but were later released without being charged. *Lembing KAYU,* January 2000 (3).

16. Three months after my visit, Abe Ryu Ichiro, a researcher from Tokyo University, visited the PT TEL factory accompanied by WALHI staff. He was treated with similar suspicion and refused permission to see the waste treatment facilities (personal communication).

17. Interview with Arnold Bakara, technical manager of PT TEL in Muara Enim (July 24, 2000).

18. My account of the conflict between villagers living along the Tiku River and BTM is constructed from interviews with villagers, a visit to the mine site, and an interview with Dedi Kurniawan, BTM public relations representative, discussions with WALHI staff, postings on NGO Web sites listed in notes, and correspondence with Gavin Lee of BTM.

19. Laverton Gold NL, the parent company of BTM, is a wholly owned subsidiary of Consolidated African Mines Australia Pty Ltd, a South African/Australian

company with gold-mining interests in Australia, Indonesia, South Africa, Namibia, and West Africa. In 1996, 40 percent of BTM was sold to PT Rawas Limited Singapura and 40 percent to PT Jamtiku Ltd. Hong Kong.

20. Taufiq Wijaya, December 31, 1998; WALHI, January 22, 2000; *Sriwijaya Post,* August 31, 2000; *Jakarta Post,* October 7, 2002; Down to Earth, November 2002.

21. Oxfam Community Aid Abroad Website, March 8, 2000. Jeff Atkinson's report was reposted in part or in full on the following Web sites:

www.jatam.org/indonesia; www.earthwins.com;
www.moles.org/ProjectUnderground; http://domino.ips.org;
www.oxfam.org.au; www.orangutan.com; www.minesandcommunities.org;
http://dte.gn.apc.org; www.mpi.org.au.

22. Interview with Dedi Kurniawan, BTM public relations representative, at the mine site (July 27, 2000).

23. *Economic Justice News,* September 2004.

24. Anton Lucas and Arief Djati's study of the politics of water pollution in East Java, *The Dog Is Dead so Throw It in the River: Environmental Politics and Water Pollution in Indonesia* (2000), inspired Jamila Nuh to do a study of PT Pusri. I draw on her report, "Environmental Politics in Indonesia: Water Pollution along the Musi River in South Sumatra" (ESMS Program, Ohio University, June 2004).

25. *Sriwijaya Post,* June 29, July 14, and July 28, 2000; *Palembang Pos,* July 9, 2000; *Sumatera Ekspres,* June 28, 2000; *Kompas,* October 4 and 8, 2000.

26. *Sriwijaya Post,* September 29, October 6, 2000; *Sumatera Ekspres,* October 3 and 6, 2000; *Palembang Pos,* October 5, 6, and 7, 2000; *Transparan,* October 2, 2000.

27. *Sriwijaya Post,* October 9, 10, and 13, 2000; *Palembang Pos,* October 13, 2000; *Transparan,* October 9, 2000; *Kompas,* October 10, 2000.

28. *Sriwijaya Post,* October 17 and October 19, 2000 (1), (2); *Palembang Pos,* October 15, 16, 19, and 23, 2000; *Kompas,* October 13, 2000; *Forum Keadilan,* October 29, 2000.

29. *Palembang Pos,* November 6 (1), (2).

30. *Sriwijaya Post,* November 10, 2000; *Sumatera Ekspres,* October 17 and 20, 2000; *Kompas,* November 3, 2000,

31. *Transparan,* March 6, 2001.

32. *Sriwijaya Post,* October 21, 2000 (1), (2); *Sumatera Ekspres,* October 20, 2000; *Transparan,* October 16, 2000.

33. *Sriwijaya Post,* November 13, 2000; *Transparan,* November 11 and 24, 2000.

34. *Sumatera Ekspres,* December 7, 2000; *Transparan,* December 8, 2000.

35. *Jakarta Post,* March 29, 2001; *Republika,* March 27, 2001.

36. *Kompas,* June 10, 2001, August 24, 2001.

37. *Transparan,* September 13, 2001.

38. *Sumatera Ekspres,* December 27, 2001; *Transparan,* December 12, 2001.

39. *Sriwijaya Post,* July 3, 2003. For other articles reporting on Pusri's failure to observe environmental regulations, see *Sriwijaya Post,* February 5, 2003; *Sumatera Ekspres,* December 27, 2001.

Chapter 5: Struggling for Workers' Rights

1. From the *World Employment Report (2000)* of the International Labor Organization, available at www.ilo.org'public/english/bureau/inf/pkits/index.htm.

2. A legal strike required that employees apply for permission to the Manpower Ministry. See Adam Schwarz, *A Nation in Waiting* (1994; 1999), 257–261.

3. *Jakarta Post,* December 8, 2004.

4. Labor unions with branches in South Sumatra include the official New Order labor union Serikat Pekerja Seluruh Indonesia (SPSI), a reform-oriented faction of this union, SPSI Reformasi; Serikat Buruh Sejahtera Indonesia (SBSI), a union founded by Mochtar Pakpahan that was banned during the New Order; two Muslim labor unions—Sarbumusi Serikat Buruh Muslim Indonesia and Persatuan Pekerja Muslim Indonesia (PPMI), Front Nasional Buruh Indonesia (FNPBI), an offshoot of the radical pro-democracy organization Partai Rakyat Demokrasi, which is basically run by students (not workers); Serikat Pekerja Nasional Indonesia (SPNI); Serikat Penegak Keadilan Kesejahteraan & Persatuan (SPKP); Kesatuan Pekerja Nasional Indonesia; Gabungan Serikat Buruh Industri Indonesia; and Forum Komunikasi Buruh Bersatu (FKBB).

5. Vedi Hadiz, "Capitalism, Oligarchic Power and the State in Indonesia," *Historical Materialism,* no. 8 (Summer 2001): 142.

6. Data from the South Sumatra Provincial Government reported by the LBH-Palembang Division of Labor.

7. For my account of the conflict between workers and SMJ/Bukit Asam I draw on discussions with LBH staff, LBH-Palembang, 2000 (2), and postings from activists on the Web and news reports cited in my notes.

8. *Sriwijaya Post,* April 1 and 2, 2000.

9. LBH-Palembang, May 5, 2000; *Sriwijaya Post,* May 5, 2000; petani@e-groups .com, May 4 and 5, 2000.

10. *Sriwijaya Post,* May 10 and 13, 2000 (1), (2); petani@e-groups.com, May 16, 2000.

11. Jaringan Advokasi Tambang (JATAM), May 17, 2000.

12. South Sumatra Provincial Police (POLDA), "Pokok-pokok Penjelasan Tentang Bentrokan di PT SMJ M. Enim, Penangkapan/Penahanan Sdr. Subowo dan Bentrok di MAPOLDA Sumsel" [Main Points Explaining the Outbreak of Violence at PT SMJ in Muara Enim, the Arrest of Sdr. Subowo and the Outbreak of Violence at the South Sumatra Police Headquarters], June 16, 2000.

13. Hal Hill, *The Indonesian Economy since 1966* (1996), 147.

14. On the Gajah Tunggal Group, see Yuri Sato, "Corporate Governance in Indonesia: A Study on Governance of Business Groups," in *The Role of Governance in Asia,* ed. Yasutami Shimomura (2004); WALHI National Executive, April 26, 2000.

15. *Far Eastern Economic Review,* June 1, 2000.

16. My account of the conflict between contract shrimp farmers and PT Wachyuni Mandira draws on discussions with LBH and WALHI staff, Web postings and news reports cited in my notes.

17. Taufiq Wijaya, retrieved December 7, 1998 (2).

18. LBH-Palembang, November 19, 1998; Taufiq Wijaya, retrieved December 7, 1998 (1).

19. Taufiq Wijaya, retrieved December 7, 1998 (3), (4), December 17, 1998, January 25, 26, and 27, 1999, February 8, 1999.

20. Taufiq Wijaya, retrieved December 7, 1998 (5).

21. LBH-Palembang, February 8, 1999; Taufiq Wijaya, February 8 and 10, 1999; *Human Rights Watch,* February 12, 1999; *World Rainforest Movement,* March 1999.

22. WALHI Sumsel, May 25, 1999; Lembaga Pemasyarakatan Tanjung Raja OKI, May 25, 1999; *Sumatera Ekspres,* May 25, 1999.

23. *Far Eastern Economic Review,* June 1, 2000.

24. *Jakarta Post,* August 29, 2000.

25. *Far Eastern Economic Review,* June 1, 2000.

26. Ibid.

27. *Sriwijaya Post,* March 3 and 4, 2000.

28. *Sriwijaya Post,* July 10, 2000, October 31, 2002, February 10, 2003.

29. *Asian Times Online,* February 23, 1999; *Indonesian Observer,* October 22, 1999; Jaringan Gerakan Petani Indonesia & Reform Agraria, May 24, 2000; WALHI Sumsel, September 30, 2000.

30. *Tempo,* August 4, 2003.

31. *Tempo Interactive,* October 20, 2000, October 26, 2000 (1), (2), November 4 and 10, 2000; Taufiq Wijaya, September 30, 2000.

32. *Indonesian Business on the Web,* October 21, 2000; *Tempo,* October 21, 2002, December 23, 2002, April 7, 2003, August 4, 2003; *Jakarta Post,* December 19, 2002, July 23, 2004; *Laksamana.net,* July 23, 2004.

33. *Business Intelligence Online,* March 12, 2004.

34. *Jakarta Post,* September 10, 2002.

35. Environmental Justice Foundation, *Smash and Grab: Conflict, Corruption and Human Rights Abuses in the Shrimp Farming Industry* (2003); Down to Earth, May 2000, November 2001.

36. *International Herald Tribune,* May 8, 2003.

37. *Jakarta Post,* April 25 and 26, 2000; *Inter Press Service,* March 17, 2001.

38. *Jakarta Post,* March 17, 2005.

39. *Sriwijaya Post,* January 6, 2003, March 6 and 21, 2003.

40. The Urban Poor Consortium is linked to the Asian Coalition for Housing Rights, an Asia-wide network of NGOs.

41. *Sriwijaya Post,* February 9. 2000.

42. Executive order (SK Walikota No. 17/2002) is referred to as "Palembang BARI" for *bersih, aman, rapi dan indah* (clean, safe, tidy, and beautiful).

43. Jaringan Advokasi Masyarakat Urban (JAMUR), February 15 and 22, 2000; *Sriwijaya Post,* February 15 and 23, 2000; Serikat Pedagang Radial, February 12, 2002.

44. LBH staff member Syamsul Asinar Radjam collected data on organizations of street vendors and cycle rickshaw drivers and their resistance to new regulations issued by the Palembang city government. *Sriwijaya Post,* February 15, 17, 22, 24, and 28, 2000; *Palembang Pos,* February 16, and March 30, 2000.

45. *Sriwijaya Post,* February 29, 2000; *Sumatera Ekspres,* February 29, 2000.

46. Roseka conducted interviews with street vendors (April 2003).

47. LBH-Palembang, 2001.

48. LBH-Palembang, February 9 and 13, 2002; Serikat Pedagang Radial, February 12, 2002; *Transparan,* February 29, 2002.

49. *Sumatera Ekspres,* March 2, 2002.

50. *Sriwijaya Post,* February 29, 2002, March 28, 2002.

51. Ibid., September 11, 2002; *Transparan,* September 11, 2002.

52. *Sriwijaya Post,* November 2 and 5, 2002, December 13, 2002, July 9, 2003; *Sumatera Ekspres,* April 23, 2003.

53. *Berita Pagi,* July 25, 2005.

Chapter 6: "Where's My Cut?"

1. Richard Robison, "What Sort of Democracy? Predatory and Neo-liberal Agendas in Indonesia," in *Globalization and Democratization in Asia: The Construction of Identity,* ed. Catarina Kinnvall and Kristina Jonsson, eds. (2002), 97, citing Richard Robison, *Indonesia: The Rise of Capital* (1986).

2. Expressions for corruption were gathered from informants. M. A. Jaspan, "Tolerance and the Rejection of Cultural Impediments to Economic Growth: The South Sumatran Case," *Bulletin of Indonesian Economic Studies* (June 1967), lists expressions for corruption that were used in South Sumatra in the 1960s.

3. Richard Robison, "Toward a Class Analysis of the Indonesian Military Bureaucratic State," *Indonesian* 25 (1978): 24–25, 37.

4. Hal Hill and Andrew MacIntyre, *Indonesia's New Order: The Dynamics of Socio-Economic Transformation* (1994), 45.

5. District laws Peraturan Daerah Kabupaten Daerah Tingkat II Ogan Komering Ilir, No. 3 (1996), No. 17 (1999), and No. 30 (2002).

6. Aidil Fitri, who became director of WALHI in 2002, collected background information about the auction of Lebak Lebung in OKI. My account is also based on interviews with villagers in OKI, a monograph (n.p., n.d.) by A. Ya'kub and Dadan Afrdian entitled *Kembalikan Lebak Lebung Kepada Rakyat* [Give the Lebak Lebung Back to the People], press releases of Serikat Petani Sumatera Selatan (SPSS), the organization of farmers that opposed the auction, posted on *Jaringan Gerakan Petani Indonesia dan Reforma Agraria,* and news articles cited in my notes.

7. *Jaringan Gerakan Petani Indonesia dan Reforma Agraria,* February 11, 2000, September 19, 2000, November 7, 2000, November 12, 2000.

8. *Sriwijaya Post,* November 23, 2002.

9. Aidil Fitri collected background information on the conflict over harvesting the nests of wild swallows in Lahat. My account is also based on the chronology of the conflict, LBH-Palembang, March 2002.

10. My account of the MURA district *bupati* election is based on interviews conducted by Djayadi Hanan with organizers of campaign support organizations, Waisun, Herman Sawiran, Eka Rahman, Prana Sohe, Juarsyah, Aji Misbach, and Hendri (August 11–15, 2002), a monograph by Amzulian Rifai entitled *Pola Politik Uang Dalam Pemilihan Kepala Daerah* [Pattern of Money Politics in District Elections] (2002), and news reports cited in notes.

11. *Sriwijaya Post,* January 26, 2000.

12. Ibid., March 18, 20, and 24, 2000, April 3, 2000, May 2, 2000 (1), (2).

13. Quoted in Rifai, *Pola Politik Uang Dalam Pemilihan Kepala Daerah,* 20–21.

14. My account of the misappropriation of funds by the South Sumatra legislature in 2000 is based on conversations with LBH staff and a chronology put together by Erwirta.

15. Laksamana.net, October 2, 2001.

16. Abdul Aziz Kamis, 2002; *Sriwijaya Post,* February 28, 2002; Republika online, February 12, 2002 (1), (2).

17. *Sriwijaya Post,* January 11, 2003, February 7, 11, 13, 14, 18, 19, 20, 2003 (1), (2), 24, and 27, 2003, March 7, 8, 10, 12, and 25, 2003; *Jakarta Post,* March 1, 2003.

18. *Sriwijaya Post,* March 13 and 25, April 15, 23, and 24, 2003 (2); *Tempo,* May 5, 2003, 31; Abdul Aziz Kamis (2003).

19. *Sriwijaya Post,* April 24, 3003.

20. Robby Puruhita, a program coordinator for SSCW, provided information on SSCW campaigns and the internal politics of the organization. The PON scandal made it all the way to national media. A selection of articles from different publications is cited in the notes.

21. *Sriwijaya Post,* October 17, 2000, November 30, 2001; *Palembang Pos,* October 23, 2000; *Sumatera Ekspres,* May 8, 2001; *Media Indonesia,* November 13, 2001.

22. Information on street-children projects in Palembang was collected from 1998 through 2004, primarily by observation of Yayasan Kuala Merdeka and conversations with the director, Tarech Rasyid.

23. These NGOs were Yayasan Putra Desa (founded in 1990), Bina Vitalis (founded in 1995), Yayasan Kuala Merdeka (founded in 1997), and Yayasan PUSPA (founded in 1999).

24. *Gatra,* June 23, 2001.

25. Aidil Fitri interviewed villagers in Pendopo and Talang Ubi about the case of Jamal and the *preman* syndicate stealing pipes (2003).

26. See J. Barker, "Controlling the criminal contagion in Suharto's New Order," *Indonesia,* 66 (October 1998); B. R. O. G Anderson, ed., *Violence and the State in Suharto's Indonesia* (2001); Timothy Lindsey, "The Criminal State: *Premanisme* and the New Indonesia," in *Indonesia Today: Challenges of History,* ed. G. Lloyd and S. Smith (2001); Ian Douglas Wilson, "The Changing Contours of Organised Violence in Post New Order Indonesia" (April 2005).

27. Yudhie Syahropi interviewed the head of BPS, May 2003.

28. Yeni Rosliani interviewed Azis Kamis, March 2003.

29. *Sydney Morning Herald,* July 25, 2001; *Fortune Magazine,* September 3, 2001; Laksamana.net, November 2, 2001.

30. "I Have Become the Target," interview with Taufik Kiemas, *Time Asia* (July 15, 2002).

31. *Asia Week,* July 20, 2001; *Asia Times Online,* August 16, 2002; Laksamana. net, August 11, 2002, September 10, 2003.

32. Laksamana.net, June 27, 2003.

33. *Time Asia,* July 15, 2002. Taufik Kiemas' brother Nazaruddin was a founder of PDI-P's paramilitary youth group, Banteng Muda Indonesia (Wild Ox Youth), headed by Eurico Gutierrez, the notorious leader of a militia in East Timor who was indicted for human rights abuses. In 1996 Ryamizard Ryacudu pushed to have a military candidate selected as *bupati* for MUBA, which led to an early *reformasi* demonstration against military involvement in politics. Husein Al-Habsyi called for jihad against Christians in Maluku in January 2000 and sent his militia, Pasukan Mujahideen, to demonstrate against President Abdurrahman Wahid.

34. *Tempo,* May 7–13, 2002. Yamin lost his seat in the 2004 legislative election.

35. Articles on the wealth of Taufik Kiemas and Megawati and accusations of corruption in the Indonesian press include Laksamana.net, November 2, 2001, February 9, 2003, April 7, 2003, May 2, 2003, January 3, 2004; *Tempo,* August 21–27, 2001; *Jakarta Post,* January 16, 2002, January 2, 2003; *Koran Tempo,* January 10, 2003; and *Sriwijaya Post,* January 17, 2003, April 28, 2003. Articles in the international press include *Kyodo News Service,* April 18, 2001; *Far Eastern Economic Review,* August 7, 1999; *Wall Street Journal,* March 19, 2002; and *The Straits Times,* February 24, 2004.

36. *Kompas,* March 23, 2005.

Chapter 7: Local Autonomy

1. Sudarno Sumarto, Asep Suryahadi, and Alex Arifianto, "Governance and Poverty Reduction: Evidence from Newly Decentralized Indonesia" (2004).

2. Data from the National Statistics Bureau (Badan Pusat Statistik) as reported by the United Nations Support Facility for Indonesian Recovery (http://www .unsfir.or.id/).

3. Articles in the *Sriwijaya Post* describing political maneuvering around the election rules include March 1, 13, and 21, 2001, May 10, 2001, June 15, 2001, July 17, 2001, August 1, 2001, and December 20, 2001.

4. Articles alleging "money politics" include *Sriwijaya Post,* May 12 and 21, 2001.

5. In my account of the MUBA *bupati* election I draw on interviews with Subardin, an actvist in Ikatan Keluarga Musi Banyuasin, and on interviews conducted by Djayadi Hanan with Nopianto, chairman of Pancasila Students (Palembang, August 4, 2002, April 3, 2003); Askolani SH, chairman of the Reform Committee of MUBA Students (Sekayu, August 7, 2002, April 4, 2003); Heryati, member of the PDI-P fac-

tion in the MUBA legislature (Sekayu, August 7, 2002); Hasbullah A. Gani (August 7, 2002); Dr. Abbas Mahdin (Sekayu, August 7, 2002); and Hendri Zainuddin, a member of Alex Noerdin's *sukses tim* (April 3, 2003). Protests over the MUBA election are described in the following articles in the *Sriwijaya Post:* January 24, 2001, July 6 and 14, 2001, August 30, 2001, November 29, 2001.

6. Interview conducted by Djayadi Hanan (August 4, 2002).

7. Pemerintah Kabupaten Musi Banyuasin (2001); presentation by Alex Noerdin entitled "Visi Muba Sejahtera 2005"; *Muba Randik: Majalah Informasi Kabupaten Musi Banyuasin* [Beautiful MUBA: Magazine with Information about Musi Banyuasin], April 2003.

8. *Sriwijaya Post*, April 16, 2003. Also see the United Nations Support Facility for Indonesian Recovery Web site (http://www.unsfir.or.id/), which reports data from the 2002 census conducted by the National Statistics Bureau of Indonesia.

9. Information collected by WALHI staff member Imelda.

10. Law No. 2/2001 ended Pertamina's exclusive rights to oil and gas production.

11. *Sumatera Ekspres*, March 30, 2002; *Palembang Pos*, March 30, 2002. A survey by a research center at the Bandung Institute of Technology found 400 wells in Babat Toman, Keluang, Batanghari Leko, and Sungai Lilin subdistricts, of which 170 were being managed by villagers. Generally, several families shared management of a well, which might produce two to three barrels of oil a day.

12. Interview with residents of Dusun Teluk (June 11, 2003).

13. *Sumatera Ekspres*, June 1, 2005.

14. Aidil Fitri, director of WALHI, interviewed villagers who managed "wild oil wells" in MUBA (April/May 2003).

15. Yeni Roslaini visited the village of Sungai Angit and interviewed villagers with wild wells in July 2005.

16. Interview conducted in Palembang (July 8, 2004).

17. I was shown a document prepared by ten MUBA officials entitled "Kronologi Indikasi Pelanggaran Merugikan Negara Pada PEMDA Musi Banyuasin" [Chronology Indicating Losses to the State Due to Corruption by the Musi Banyuasin District Government], dated July 2005. Also see *Kompas*, July 15, 2005.

18. Interview with Alex Noerdin in Palembang (July 24, 2005). Ann Tickamyer interviewed Alex Noerdin in Sekayu (February 19, 2004).

19. *Sumatera Ekspres*, April 22, 2002; *Sriwijaya Post*, July 21, 2003. Also see *Sriwijaya Post*, March 18, 2003, April 16, 2003.

20. *Sriwijaya Post*, June 4, 2003.

21. LBH-Palembang, 2000; *Gatra*, March 16, 1996; *Sriwijaya Post*, November 1, 2002, January 4 and 21, 2003.

22. Interview with Pak Jafar at LBH-Palembang, July 6, 2004; I went to Dusun Belido in July 2004. For another account of the visit to Dusun Belido by journalist Andrew Steele, see *Inside Indonesia* (October–December 2004).

23. I attended the presentation of the defense at the trial of Pak Jafar and other Dusun Belido farmers in Sekayu in July 2005.

24. *Sriwijaya Post,* January 29, 2002.

25. My account of the OKU *bupati* election draws on Ganda Upaya, "Two Bupati Elections in South Sumatra"; interviews conducted by Djayadi Hanan with Herman Syahri, president of Dewan Mahasiswa; Ali Indra Hanafiah, vice *bupati* candidate; Jony Animan, *satgas* of PDIP; and Danial from Syahrial's success team (2000 and 2002); my own interviews with Syahrial Oesman in Prabamulih, January 9, 2003, and Batu Raja, February 10, 2003; and newspaper sources cited in my notes.

26. *Sriwijaya Post,* January 28, 2000.

27. Quoted in Ganda Upaya, "Two Bupati Elections in South Sumatra," 34.

28. Data from the National Statistics Bureau as reported by the United Nations Support Facility for Indonesian Recovery (http://www.unsfir.or.id/).

29. LBH-Palembang, 2000. Also see *Sriwijaya Post,* October 3, 2002, January 20, 2003.

30. *Panji Masyarakat,* July 28 1999.

31. Interviews with Syahrial Oesman in Prabamulih, January 9, 2003, and in Batu Raja, February 10, 2003.

32. Surat Penyerahan Kebun Sawit KKPA, No. DIR/X/296/2000, PT. Perkebunan Mitra Ogan sets forth the relationship between PT Mitra Ogan and *plasma* in the villages of Bindu, Durian, and Kedongdong.

33. *Transparan,* April 24, 2003. Law No. 34/2000 mandated that 10 percent of the district budget should go to village-level governments. The amount of funds to be received by each village in OKU was determined by a research team from Sriwijaya University in cooperation with the OKU government.

34. Untung Saputra interviewed villagers in Desa Durian about the Village Development and Empowerment Program.

35. Untung Saputra collected information on the Desa Kedongdong village headman election.

36. *Sriwijaya Post,* September 25, 2002.

37. In reconstructing what happened in the 2003 South Sumatra gubernatorial election, I found conversations with Taufik Wijaya, Mohamad Sirozi, and Abdul Wahib Situmorang especially helpful, as well as the following news articles: Taufik Wijaya, August 11, 2004; Detik.com, August 5, 2003; Laksamana.net, August 6, 2003.

38. *Sriwijaya Post,* October 7, 2003; Laksamana.net, October 8, 2003; *Koran Tempo,* November 5, 2003 (2).

39. Another story that I heard related to two legislators who asked Rosihan's running mate to guarantee their sons a place in university in exchange for their vote. He rejected the request. When they went to Syahrial Oesman, he said this was a "small matter."

40. November 5, 2003 (1).

41. *Berita Pagi,* July 23, 2005; *Jakarta Post,* July 30, 2005.

42. Vedi R. Hadiz, "Indonesian Local Party Politics: A Site of Resistance to Neoliberal Reform," *Critical Asian Studies* 36:4 (2004); Sudarno Sumarto, Asep Suryahadi, and Alex Arifianto, "Governance and Poverty Reduction: Evidence from

Newly Decentralized Indonesia" (2004); Edward Aspinall and Greg Fealy, eds., *Local Power and Politics in Indonesia: Decentralisation and Democratisation* (2003); Richard Robison, "What Sort of Democracy? Predatory and Neo-liberal Agendas in Indonesia," in *Globalization and Democratization in Asia: The Construction of Identity*, ed. Katarina Kinnvall and Kristina Jonsson (2002).

43. Michael Malley, "New Rules, Old Structures and the Limits of Democratic Decentralization," in *Local Power and Politics in Indonesia: Decentralisation and Democratisation*, ed. Edward Aspinall and Greg Fealy (2003), 115.

44. Vedi R. Hadiz, "Capitalism, Oligarchic Power and the State in Indonesia," *Historical Materialism: Research in Critical Marxist Theory*, no. 8 (Summer 2001): 119.

45. *Jakarta Post*, January 28, 2004, August 29, 2002.

Chapter 8: Islam and the Quest for Justice

1. No author, "Islam in Modern Indonesia," conference sponsored by the United States-Indonesia Society and Asia Foundation, February 7, 2002.

2. On the Hadrami in Palembang, see Natalie Mobini-Kesheh, *The Hadrami Awakening: Community and Identity in the Netherlands East Indies, 1900–1942* (1999); Azyumardi Azra, *Jaringan Ulama Timur Tengah dan Kepulauan Nusantara Abad XVII dan XVIII: Melacak Akar-akar Pembaruan Pemikiran Islam di Indonesia* [Networks of *Ulama* in the Middle East and the Islands of the East Indies in the 17th and 18th Centuries: Tracing the Roots of the Islamic Renewal Movement in Indonesia] (1994); Michael Laffan, *Islamic Nationhood and Colonial Indonesia: The Umma below the Winds* (2003).

3. Jeroen Peeters, *Kaum Tuo–Kaum Mudo: Perubahan Religius Di Palembang 1925–1935* (1997), and "Space, Religion, and Conflict: The Urban Ecology of Islamic Institutions in Palembang," in *Issues in Urban Development: Case Studies from Indonesia*, ed. Peter J. M. Nas (1995).

4. Interview with Amran Halim, rector of Sriwijaya University (1986–1994), in Palembang, November 1, 2002.

5. Interview with H. A. Ibrahim Yusun, head of the Provincial Board of PKB-South Sumatra, conducted by Adang Yuliansyah in Palembang (1999).

6. *BPS 2002 Sumsel Dalam Angka* [South Sumatra in Statistics], Publication of Badan Pusat Statistik Sumsel, Palembang, South Sumatra (2002).

7. See Adam Schwarz, *A Nation in Waiting: Indonesia's Search for Stability* (1994; 1999), 162–163.

8. Philip J. Eldridge, *Non-Government Organizations and Democratic Participation in Indonesia* (1995), 86–97, 177–183; Bob S. Hadiwinata, *The Politics of NGOs in Indonesia: Developing Democracy and Managing a Movement* (2003), 91.

9. Nurcholish Madjid's speech was entitled "Keharusan Pembaruan Pemikiran Islam dan Masalah Integrasi Umat" [The Necessity of Renewing Islamic Thought and the Problem of the Integration of the Islamic Community]. An English translation can be found in Charles Kurzman, ed., *Liberal Islam: A Sourcebook* (1998), 284–289.

10. Van Zorge Report, December 1998; also see Margaret Scott, "Indonesia Reborn?" (1998).

11. Anders Uhlin, *Indonesia and the "Third Wave of Democratization": The Indonesian Pro-Democracy Movement in a Changing World* (1997), 83.

12. William Liddle, "*Media Dakwah* Scripturalism: One Form of Islamic Political Thought and Action in New Order Indonesia," in Mark Woodward, ed., *Toward a New Paradigm: Recent Developments in Indonesian Thought* (1996), 323–356.

13. Imaduddin taught in Malaysia in the early 1970s, where he worked with the Muslim student movement Angkatan Belia Islam Malaysia (ABIM), led by Anwar Ibrahim. *Panduan Usroh* was an ABIM manual. On the Salman movement, see Abdul Aziz, Imam Tholkhah, and Soetarman, "Gerakan Kaum Muda Islam Mesjid Salman" [The Islamic Youth Movement in Salman Mosque], in *Gerakan Islam Kontemporer di Indonesia* [Contemporary Islamic Movements in Indonesia] (1989); Amien Rais, "International Islamic Movements and Their Influence upon the Islamic Movement in Indonesia" (1985); V. S. Naipul *Among the Believers: An Islamic Journey* (1982); John Malcolm Brownlee, "Scripturalism and Religious Liberalism on Yogyakarta Campuses" (1997); Richard Kraince, "The Role of Islamic Student Activists in Divergent Movements for Reform during Indonesia's Transition from Authoritarian Rule, 1998–2001" (2002); Elizabeth Collins, "Islam Is the Solution: Dakwah and Democracy in Indonesia" (2003).

14. Quoted in Schwarz, *A Nation in Waiting* (1999), 174.

15. Quoted in Michael Vatikiotis, *Indonesian Politics under Suharto: The Rise and Fall of the New Order* (1998), 128–129.

16. Overt suppression of Islam was accompanied by covert intrigue. There is evidence that in the 1980s organizations advocating an Islamic state, such as Komando Jihad and Negara Islam Indonesia, were manipulated by Indonesian military intelligence in order to discredit all Islamic political forces. In *Indonesian Politics under Suharto*, Vatikiotis writes: "It is believed, for example, that Ali Murtopo [the head of Military Intelligence] brought together former leaders of the West Java-based Darul Islam revolt, which had been crushed by the army in the 1960s, and actually asked them to reactivate the movement. He is said to have told them they would be helping to stamp out Communism. The real reason is thought to be Murtopo's desire to discredit Islamic political forces before the elections. In the next two years, hundreds of people were arrested and accused of belonging to . . . Komando Jihad. Implausible as this sounds—audacious even—the habit of some New Order followers to believe the best way to shore up their power is to 'engineer' political threats is well attested." (127–129).

17. Interview with Djayadi Hanan in Palembang (July 1994).

18. Interview with Hermawan Dipoyono, chairman of the Salman Mosque Committee, at ITB (February 18, 2003).

19. François Raillon, "The New Order and Islam, or the Imbroglio of Faith and Politics" (1993).

20. Quoted in V. S. Naipaul, *Beyond Belief: Islamic Excursions among the Converted Peoples* (1998), 32–33.

21. Interviews with leaders of Remaja Masjid conducted by Widyawati in Palembang, 1999.

22. *Far Eastern Economic Review,* December 9, 1993.

23. Interview with Azimi Asnawi in Palembang, July 1994.

24. Interview with Azimi Asnawi, chairman of HMI in Palembang, July 1994.

25. My account of conflict in HMI is constructed from interviews with Robby Puruhita, chairman of HMI Palembang (1999) from 2001 to 2003, and with Reza, chairman of HMI at IAIN Raden Fatah, August 1, 2004. Dian Novita also assisted in collecting information about HMI.

26. On KAMMI, see Robin Madrid, "Islamic Students in the Indonesian Student Movement, 1998–1999," *Bulletin of Concerned Asian Scholars* 31 (July–September 1999); Richard Kraince, "The Role of Islamic Student Groups in the *Reformasi* Struggle: KAMMI (Kesatuan Aksi Mahasiswa Muslim Indonesia)," *Studi Islamika* 7 (2000): 3–50.

27. *Jakarta Post,* February 20, 2001.

28. *Gatra,* May 16, 1998.

29. Interview with Robby Puruhita, leader of the *progresif* faction (June 2001). Golkar chairman Akbar Tanjung and Fuad Bawazier, chairman of the HMI Alumni Association, are said to have funded candidates for HMI chairman.

30. My account of KAMMI in South Sumatra is based on interviews with Robby Puruhita, Aswendi, and Djayadi Hanan (2002–2003).

31. *Tempo Interactif,* February 25, 2001.

32. Andrée Feillard quotes Kiai Machrus Ali of NU as saying that the Sunni tradition warns: "Keep away from actions or words that can provoke anger among other people. According to Islamic law, any action that can disturb the society's order is a major sin that will be judged by God." "Traditionalist Islam and the Army in Indonesia's New Order: The Awkward Relationship," in *Nahdlatul Ulama, Traditional Islam and Modernity in Indonesia,* ed. Greg Fealy and Greg Barton (1996), 58.

33. Ahmad Fali Okilas interviewed FORDS leaders Vivin Desfina, Amril, Saudara Zahruddin, Zahruddin Hodsay, and Indra Jaya (1999).

34. Widyawati and Ahmad Fali Okilas assisted in collecting data on Remaja Masjid and FORDS.

35. *Suara Merdeka,* October 4, 1999.

36. Umar Abdullah and Arief Nurhayat assisted in collecting information on FPI in Palembang.

37. Arief Nurhayat assisted in collecting information on MMI in South Sumatra.

38. Umar Abdullah assisted in collecting background data on Muhammadiyah in South Sumatra.

39. See Muhammad Fuad, "Civil Society in Indonesia: The Potential and Limits of Muhammadiyah," *Sojourn* 17.2 (2002): 133–163.

40. *Sriwijaya Post,* December 12, 2001.

41. Interview with Drs. Romli, AS, chairman of Muhammadiyah in South Sumatra, in Palembang, August 1, 2004.

42. Adang Yuliansyah assisted in collecting background data on NU.

43. Interview with Drs. Malan Abdullahi, chairman of NU in South Sumatra, in Palembang, August 2, 2004.

44. Ali Said Damanik, *Fenomena Partai Keadilan: Transformasi 20 Tahun Gerakan Tarbiyah di Indonesia* [The Justice Party Phenomenon: Transformation of the Tarbiyah Movement in Indonesia over 20 Years] (2002).

Chapter 9: Indonesia in Global Context

Epigraph. Goenawan Mohamad, *Sidelines: Thought Pieces from Tempo Magazine* (2005), p. 78.

1. Todung Mulya Lubis, *In Search of Human Rights: Legal-Political Dilemmas of Indonesia's New Order 1966–1990* (1993), vii.

2. Quoted in Philip McMichael, *Development and Social Change: A Global Perspective* (2004), 22.

3. Ibid., 226.

4. Alasdair Bowie and Danny Unger, *The Politics of Open Economies: Indonesia, Malaysia, the Philippines, and Thailand* (1997), 29–30.

5. Quoted in Noreena Hertz, *The Debt Threat* (2004), 97.

6. Quoted in McMichael, *Development and Social Change*, 56.

7. See "Food Aid or Hidden Dumping: Separating Wheat from Chaff," Oxfam Briefing Paper, March 2005.

8. See McMichael, *Development and Social Change*, 56.

9. Ibid., 51, 89.

10. Hernando De Soto, *The Other Path: The Economic Answer to Terrorism* (1989), xxxiii–xxxiv.

11. McMichael, *Development and Social Change*, 75.

12. See Nick Cullather, "Parable of Seeds: The Green Revolution in the Modernizing Imagination," in Marc Frey, Ronald W. Pruessen, and Tan Tai Yong, eds., *The Transformation of Southeast Asia: International Perspectives on Decolonization* (2003), 257–267.

13. Quoted in McMichael, *Development and Social Change*, 120.

14. United Nations Development Program, *Human Development Report* (1999), 3.

15. World Bank, *World Development Report 1999/2000*, 25; United Nations Development Program, *Human Development Report* (1999), 230–231. In 2000 the World Bank and the United Nations Development Program redefined the international poverty line in terms of a daily income with the purchasing power of one dollar in the United States in 1993 (HDR 2000, 4170f). Since the dollar had lost more than a quarter of its value between 1985 and 1993, this statistically lowered the measure of poverty and the number of global poor.

16. Hertz, *The Debt Threat*, 67–69.

17. Walden Bello and Shea Cunningham, "North South View: The World Bank and the IMF" (1994).

18. See "The Rural Poverty Trap: Why Agricultural Trade Rules Need to Change and What UNCTAD XI Could Do about It," Oxfam briefing paper, June 2004.

19. McMichael, *Development and Social Change*, 162.

20. *International Herald Tribune*, May 8, 2003.

21. McMichael, *Development and Social Change*, 137.

22. Bowie and Unger, *Politics of Open Economies* (1997), 40–43.

23. Quoted in "International Financial Institutions: The 'Development' Business," *World Rainforest Movement Bulletin* 95 (June 2005).

24. *World Rainforest Movement Bulletin* 95 (June 2005); Hertz, *The Debt Threat*, 44–50.

25. Quoted in Hertz, *The Debt Threat*, 45.

26. Ibid., 47. The five biggest American corporate beneficiaries of ECA loans and credit collectively cut more than 300,000 jobs, shifting production outside the United States.

27. Christopher Barr, "Profits on Paper: The Political Economy of Fiber, Finance and Debt in Indonesia's Pulp and Paper Industries" (2000).

28. See McMichael, *Development and Social Change*, 46, 129; Andrew Gray, "Development Policy, Development Protest: The World Bank, Indigenous Peoples, and NGOs," in *The Struggle for Accountability: The World Bank, NGOs, and Grassroots Movements*, ed. Jonathan A. Fox and L. David Brown (1998), 281.

29. McMichael, *Development and Social Change*, 46.

30. *Economic Justice News*, September 2004.

31. *Asia Week*, August 15, 1997; *Wall Street Journal*, August 19, 1998.

32. *Guardian Unlimited*, March 26, 2004. See McMichael, *Development and Social Change*, 129. For an informed discussion of Suharto's wealth and corruption in the New Order, see Kees van Dijk, *A Country in Despair: Indonesia between 1997 and 2000* (2001), chaps. 10 and 11.

33. Hertz, *The Debt Threat*, 30–31, 43.

34. *World Rainforest Movement Bulletin* 95 (June 2005). Also see Tove Selin, Aaron Goldzimer, and Roy Jones, "The Shadowy World of Export Credits," Asian Labour Update, at http://www.amrc.org.hk/4301.htm, and Chantyal Marijnissen, "Export Credits: Fuelling Illegal Logging," FERN at http://www.illegal-logging.info/papers/illegal.pdf.

35. Quoted in Hertz, *The Debt Threat*, 50.

36. Pasuk Phongpaichit and Chris Baker, *Thailand's Boom and Bust* (1998), 94–126.

37. Quoted in *Emerging Civil Society in the Asia Pacific Community*, ed. Tadashi Yamamoto (1995), 4.

38. Lubis, *In Search of Human Rights* (1993), 209. On the NGO movement, see Chapter 6, "The Right to Organize: Nongovernmental Organizations."

39. For a comprehensive study of the NGO movement in the Philippines, see *Organizing for Democracy: NGOs, Civil Society, and the Philippine State*, ed. Sidney

Silliman and Lela Garner Noble (1998). Also see Jorge V. Tigno, "People Empowerment: Looking into NGOs, POs and Selected Organizations," in *Democratization: Philippine Perspectives*, ed. Felipe B. Miranda (1997), 83–113, and Eva-Lotta E. Hedman, *In the Name of Civil Society: From Free Election Movements to People Power in the Philippines* (2006).

40. See Shinichi Shigetomi, "Thailand: A Crossing of Parallel Relationships," in *The State and NGOs: Perspective from Asia*, ed. Shinichi Shigetomi (2002), 125–144; William A. Callahan, *Imagining Democracy: Reading "The Events of May" in Thailand* (1998), 95–110; Prudhisan Jumbala and Maneerat Mitprasat, "Non-governmental Development Organizations: Empowerment and Environment," in *Political Change in Thailand: Democracy and Participation*, ed. Kevin Hewison (1997), 195–216.

41. Susan M. Darlington, "Buddhism and Development: The Ecology Monks of Thailand," in *Action Dharma: New Studies in Engaged Buddhism*, ed. Christopher Queen, Charles Prebish, and Damien Keown (2003), 96–109.

42. See Antoinette G. Royo, "The Philippines: Against the People's Wishes, the Mt. Apo Story," in *The Struggle for Accountability: The World Bank, NGOs, and Grassroots Movements*, ed. Johnathan A. Fox and L. David Brown (1998), 151–179.

43. Andrew Gray, "Development Policy, Development Protest: The World Bank, Indigenous Peoples, and NGOs," in *The Struggle for Accountability*, ed. Jonathan A. Fox and L. David Brown (1998), 267–301.

44. On terms for debt forgiveness, see Hertz, *The Debt Threat*, 177–204.

45. Jonathan A. Fox and L. David Brown, "Assessing the Impact of NGO Advocacy Campaigns on World Bank Projects and Policies," in *The Struggle for Accountability*, ed. Fox and Brown (1998), 267–301.

46. On the considerable challenges faced by *reformasi* NGOs in Indonesia, see Bob S. Hadiwinata, *The Politics of NGOs in Indonesia: Developing Democracy and Managing a Movement* (2004), 241–255,

47. The concept of "good governance" first appeared in a World Bank report entitled "Sub-Saharan Africa: From Crisis to Sustainable Growth" (1989).

48. World Bank, *Indonesia: Accelerating Recovery in Uncertain Times* (2000), 43. See Richard Robison, "Neoliberalism and the Future World: Markets and the End of Politics" (2004).

49. Also see Vedi Hadiz, "Decentralisation and Democracy in Indonesia: A Critique of Neo-Institutionalist Perspectives" (2003). On local elites in the Philippines, see John T. Sidel, *Capital, Coercion, and Crime: Bossism in the Philippines* (1999); on Thailand, see Ruth McVey, ed., *Money and Power in Provincial Thailand* (2000); Daniel Arghiros, *Democracy, Development and Decentralization in Provincial Thailand* (2001).

50. McMichael, *Development and Social Change*, 101.

51. Richard Robison and Vedi Hadiz, *Reorganising Power in Indonesia: The Politics of Oligarchy in an Age of Markets* (2004), 5.

52. George Soros, *The Crisis of Global Capitalism: Open Society Endangered* (1998); Joseph Stiglitz, *Globalization and Its Discontents* (2002); "Don't Trust Technocrats," *Guardian Unlimited*, July 16, 2003.

53. *Guardian Unlimited*, January 17, 2005.

54. Sachs writes, "The IMF and World Bank reveal split personalities championing the Millennium Development Goals in public speeches, approving the programs that will not achieve them, and privately acknowledging with business as usual, that they cannot be met." *The End of Poverty: Economic Possibilities for Our Time* (2005), 271.

55. Karl Polyani, *The Great Transformation: The Political and Economic Origins of Our Time* (1944), 146.

56. Down to Earth, November 2003; *Guardian Unlimited*, August 6, 2003.

57. Quoted in Hertz, *The Debt Threat*, 156.

58. Polyani, *The Great Transformation*, 190.

59. Daniel Lev, "Social Movements, Constitutionalism, and Human Rights," in his *Legal Evolution and Political Authority in Indonesia: Selected Essays* (2000), 323.

60. On the ambivalence of the middle class toward democracy, see John Girling, *Interpreting Development: Capitalism, Democracy, and the Middle Class in Thailand* (1996); James Ockey, *Making Democracy: Leadership, Class, Gender, and Political Participation in Thailand* (2004).

61. Alexis de Tocqueville, *The Recollections of Alexis de Tocqueville* (1850; 1949), 75.

62. William Callahan, *Imagining Democracy: Reading "The Events of May" in Thailand* (1998), 36.

63. See Hans Antlov, "*Demokrasi Pancasila* and the Future of Ideology in Indonesia," in *Elections in Indonesia: The New Order and Beyond*, ed. Hans Antlov and Sven Cederroth (2004), on *jasa* (service-mindedness) as a value among the ordinary people of Indonesia. For examples of decentralization leading to more democratic and responsive government in the Philippines, see Alex B. Brillantes, "Local Governments in a Democratizing Polity: Trends and Prospects," in *Democratization*, ed. Miranda (1997), 83–113.

64. Cameron Chapman, "Agriculture and the WTO" (1999).

65. Klaus Keininger and Hans Binswanger, "The Evolution of the World Bank's Land Policy," in *Access to Land, Rural Poverty, and Public Action*, ed. Alain De Janvry et al. (2001), 406–440.

66. Kejiro Otsuka and Agnes R. Quisumbing, "Land Rights and Natural Resource Management in the Transition to Individual Ownership: Case Studies from Ghana and Indonesia" (2001), 97–128. Also see John Laird, *Money Politics, Globalisation, and Crisis: The Case of Thailand: Exploring New Paths towards Sustainable Development* (2000), 351–371, and Saturinino M. Borras Jr. and Jennifer C. Franco, "Struggles for Land and Livelihood: Redistributive Reform in Agribusiness Plantations in the Philippines," *Critical Asian Studies* 37.3 (2005): 331–361.

Glossary

adat	Customary law
bupati	District *(kabupaten)* head
camat	Subdistrict *(kecamatan)* head
dakwah	Islamic proselytizing (primarily among nominal Muslims)
Dwifungsi	The Indonesian Military's "dual sociopolitical and defense function"
inti/plasma	Nucleus Estate and Smallholder Scheme (NES) used to develop industrial agriculture by state-owned and private corporations
kabupaten	District or regency, the regional administrative unit below the level of a province
kecamatan	Subdistrict
keterbukaan	Openness
lebak lebong	Shallow lagoons that form in the rivers during the rainy season
marga	Originally a clan, transformed into an territorial unit during the colonial period
ormas	Social organization *(organisasi kemasyarakatan)*
Pak	A respectful form of address for a man
paket	Rights to a two-hectare plot of land on an oil palm plantation
Pancasila	The five fundamental principles of the Indonesian state: belief in God, the unity of Indonesia, democracy, social justice, and humanism
pesantren	Islamic boarding school
plasma	Contract farmer in a nucleus estate and smallholder scheme (NES)
putra daerah	"Native Son," an expression used to identify local candidates in post-Suharto elections
reformasi	"Reformation" identifying democracy activists demanding Suharto step down

status quo   Both parties to a land conflict are restricted from further use of the land

suku   Ethnic groups that speak a distinctive dialect, generally named for the area where they lived

tanah ulayat   Customary land rights granted to a group collectively to use (but not sell or let) the land

tarbiyah   Arabic for education under a teacher who provides moral guidance

umat   Members of a religious community, generally used to refer to the community of all Muslims

Bibliography

Aden, Jean Bush
  1988. "Oil and Politics in Indonesia, 1945 to 1980." Ph.D. diss., Cornell University.
Adhuri, Dedi Supriadi
  2002. "Between Village and Marga, a Choice of Structure: The Local Elites' Behaviors in Lahat Regency, South Sumatra." *Antropologi Indonesia* 26 (Special Volume): 44–55.
Amann, Peter
  1975. *Revolution and Mass Democracy: The Paris Club Movement in 1848.* Princeton, NJ: Princeton University Press.
Ananta, Aris, ed.
  2003. *The Indonesian Crisis: A Human Development Perspective.* Singapore: ISEAS.
Andaya, Barbara
  1993. *To Live as Brothers: Southeast Sumatra in the Seventeenth and Eighteenth Centuries.* Honolulu: University of Hawai'i Press.
Anderson, Benedict, ed.
  2001. *Violence and the State in Suharto's Indonesia.* Ithaca, NY: Cornell University SEAP.
Anderson, Ivan, Ifran Imanda, and Muhnandar
  1999. "Vegetation Fires in Sumatra, Indonesia: The Presentation and Distribution of NOAA-Derived Data." European Union Ministry of Forestry and Estate Crops (Forest Fire Prevention and Control Project), Jakarta.
Antlov, Hans
  2004. "*Demokrasi Pancasila* and the Future of Ideology in Indonesia." In *Elections in Indonesia: The New Order and Beyond*, ed. Hans Antlov and Sven Cederroth. London: RoutledgeCurzon.
Antlov, Hans, and Tak-Wing NGO, eds.
  2000. *The Cultural Construction of Politics in Asia.* Richmond, Surrey: Curzon.
Arghiros, Daniel
  2001. *Democracy, Development and Decentralization in Provincial Thailand.* Richmond, Surrey: Curzon.

Arndt, H. W., and Hal Hill, eds.
  1999. *Southeast Asia's Economic Crisis: Origins, Lessons, and the Way Forward.* Singapore: ISEAS.
Ascher, William
  1998. "From Oil to Timber: The Political Economy of Off-Budget Development Financing in Indonesia." *Indonesia* 65: 37–61.
The Asia Foundation
  2004. *Indonesia Rapid Decentralization Appraisal, Laporan ke-4 (February 2004).* Jakarta: USAID.
Aspinall, Edward
  2005. *Opposing Suharto: Compromise, Resistance, and Regime Change in Indonesia.* Stanford, CA: Stanford University Press.
Aspinall, Edward, and Greg Fealy, eds.
  2003. *Local Power and Politics in Indonesia: Decentralisation and Democratisation.* Singapore: ISEAS.
Aziz, Abdul, Imam Tholkhah, and Soetarman
  1989. *Gerakan Kaum Muda Islam Mesjid Salman* [The Islamic Youth Movement in Salman Mosque]. In *Gerakan Islam Kontemporer di Indonesia* [Contemporary Islamic Movements in Indonesia]. Jakarta: Pustaka Firdaus.
Azra, Azyumardi
  1994. *Jaringan Ulama Timur Tengah dan Kepulauan Nusantara Abad XVII dan XVIII: Melacak Akar-akar Pembaruan Pemikiran Islam di Indonesia.* [Networks of *Ulama* in the Middle East and the Islands of the East Indies in the 17th and 18th Centuries: Tracing the Roots of the Islamic Renewal Movement in Indonesia]. Bandung: Mizan.
Barr, Christopher
  1998. "Bob Hasan, the Rise of Apkindo, and the Shifting Dynamics of Control in Indonesia's Timber Sector." *Indonesia* 65: 1–36.
  2000. "Profits on Paper: The Political Economy of Fiber, Finance, and Debt in Indonesia's Pulp and Paper Industries." WWF Macroeconomic Program Office and Center for International Forestry Research (CIFOR). Bogor, Indonesia.
  2001. *Banking on Sustainability: Structural Adjustment and Forestry Reform in Post-Suharto Indonesia.* www.cifor.org/publications/
Bello, Walden, and Shea Cunningham
  1994. "North South View: The World Bank and the IMF." Z Magazine Online, http://www.zmag.org/zmag/articles/july94bello.htm/.
Boudreau, Vincent
  2001. *Grass Roots and Cadre in the Protest Movement.* Manila: Ateneo de Manila University.
  2004. *Resisting Dictatorship: Repression and Protest in Southeast Asia.* Cambridge: Cambridge University Press.
Bowie, Alasdair, and Danny Unger
  1997. *The Politics of Open Economies: Indonesia, Malaysia, the Philippines, and Thailand.* Cambridge: Cambridge University Press.

Bresnan, John
  1993. *Managing Indonesia: The Modern Political Economy*. New York: Columbia University Press.
Brown, David W.
  1999. "Addicted to Rent: Corporate and Spatial Distribution of Forest Resources in Indonesia, Implications for Forest Sustainability and Government Policy." www.geocities.com/davidbrown_id/.
  2001. "Why Governments Fail to Capture Economic Rent: The Unofficial Appropriation of Rain Forest Rent by Rulers in Insular Southeast Asia between 1970 and 1999." http://www.geocities.com/davidbrowh_id/.
  2002. FWI/GWF 2002. "The State of the Forest: Indonesia." Bogor, Indonesia: Forestwatch Indonesia, and Washington, DC: Global Forest Watch.
Brown, Robert, ed.
  1995. *Southeast Asia: A Past Regained*. Alexandria, VA: Time-Life Books.
Brownlee, John Malcolm
  1997. "Scripturalism and Religious Liberalism on Yogyakarta Campuses." M.A. thesis, Ohio University.
Budiman, Arief, ed.
  1990. *State and Civil Society in Indonesia*. Clayton, Australia: Centre of Southeast Asian Studies, Monash University.
Budiman, Arief, Barbara Hatley, and Damien Kingsbury, eds.
  1999. *Reformasi: Crisis and Change in Indonesia*. Clayton, Australia: Monash Asia Institute.
Callahan, William A.
  1998. *Imagining Democracy: Reading "The Events of May" in Thailand*. Singapore: ISEAS.
Chapman, Cameron
  1999. "Agriculture and the WTO." University of Washington, UW Gateway to the World Trade Organization. http//www.washington.edu/wto/issues/agriculture.html/.
Carrere, Ricardo, and Larry Lohmann
  1996. *Pulping the South: Industrial Tree Plantations and the World Paper Economy*. London: Zed Books Ltd.
Case, William
  2002. *Politics in Southeast Asia: Democracy or Less*. London: RoutledgeCurzon.
Casson, Anne
  2000. "The Hesitant Boom: Indonesia's Oil Palm Sub-Sector in an Era of Economic Crisis and Political Change." *CIFOR Occasional Paper No. 29*.
Chua, Amy
  2003. *World on Fire: How Exporting Free Market Democracy Breeds Ethnic Hatred and Global Instability*. New York: Doubleday.
Clark, T. J.
  1973. *The Absolute Bourgeois: Artists and Politics in France 1848–1851*. Princeton, NJ: Princeton University Press.

Cleary, Mark, and Peter Eaton
    1996. *Tradition and Reform: Land Tenure and Rural Development in Southeast Asia.* Kuala Lumpur: Oxford University Press.
Collins, Elizabeth Fuller
    1996. "(Re)negotiating Gender Hierarchy in the New Order: A South Sumatran Field Study." *Asia Pacific Viewpoint* 37 (2):127–138.
    2001. "Multinational Capital, New Order 'Development,' and Democratization in South Sumatra." *Indonesia* 71:111–134.
    2003. "Islam Is the Solution: Dakwah and Democracy in Indonesia." *Kultur* 1:151–181.
    2004. "Islam and the Habits of Democracy: Islamic Organizations in Post–New Order South Sumatra." *Indonesia* 78:1–28.
Collins, Elizabeth, and Ernaldi Bahar, M.D.
    2000. "To Know Shame in Malay Societies." *Crossroads* 14:35–70.
Colombijn, Freek
    2003. "The Volatile State in Southeast Asia: Evidence from Sumatra, 1600–1800." *The Journal of Asian Studies* 62 (2):469–530.
Cribb, Robert
    2000. *Historical Atlas of Indonesia.* Richmond, Surrey: Curzon Press.
Damanik, Ali Said
    2002. *Fenomena Partai Keadilan: Transformasi 20 Tahun Gerakan Tarbiyah di Indonesia* [The Justice Party Phenomenon: Transformation over 20 years of the Tarbiyah Movement in Indonesia]. Jakarta: Teraju.
Darlington, Susan M.
    2003. "Buddhism and Development: The Ecology Monks of Thailand." In *Action Dharma: New Studies in Engaged Buddhism,* ed. Christopher Queen, Charles Prebish, and Damien Keown, 96–108. London: RoutledgeCurzon.
Dauvergne, Peter
    2001. *Loggers and Degradation in the Asia-Pacific: Corporations and Environmental Management.* Cambridge: Cambridge University Press.
De Janvry, Alain, et al., eds.
    2001. *Access to Land, Rural Poverty, and Public Action.* Oxford: Oxford University Press.
De Soto, Hernando
    1989. *The Other Path: The Economic Answer to Terrorism.* New York: Basic Books.
    2000. *The Mystery of Capital: Why Capitalism Triumphs in the West and Fails Everywhere Else.* New York: Basic Books.
Dick, Howard, Vincent J. H. Houben, J. Thomas Lindblad, and Thee Kian Wie
    2002. *The Emergence of a National Economy: An Economic History of Indonesia, 1800–2000.* NSW Australia: Allen & Unwin and University of Hawai'i Press.
Dijk, Kees van
    2001. *A Country in Despair: Indonesia between 1997 and 2000.* Leiden: KITLV Press.

Directorate General of Estate Crops
1999. "The Report of NES Projects Development." Jakarta.

Dohner, Robert S., and Ponciano Intal
1989. "Debt Crisis and Adjustment in the Philippines." In *Developing Country Debt and the World Economy*, ed. Jeffrey D. Sachs, 169–192. Chicago: University of Chicago Press.

Dove, Michael R., ed.
1988. *The Real and Imagined Role of Culture in Development.* Honolulu: University of Hawai'i Press.

Duveau, Georges
1967. *"1848: The Making of a Revolution."* New York: Random House.

Eldridge, Philip J.
1995. *Non-Government Organizations and Democratic Participation in Indonesia.* Kuala Lumpur: Oxford University Press.

Emmerson, Donald K., ed.
1999. *Indonesia beyond Suharto: Polity, Economy, Society, Transition.* New York: M. E. Sharpe.

Environmental Justice Foundation
2003. *Smash and Grab: Conflict, Corruption and Human Rights Abuses in the Shrimp Farming Industry.* London: Environmental Justice Foundation in partnership with Wild Aid.

Evans, David, and Nurimansjah Hasibuan
1989. "South Sumatra: Dualism and Export Orientation." In *Unity and Diversity: Regional Economic Development in Indonesia since 1970,* ed. Hal Hill, 455–471. Singapore: Oxford University Press.

Feillard, Andrée
1996. "Traditionalist Islam and the Army in Indonesia's New Order: The Awkward Relationship." In *Nahdlatul Ulama, Traditional Islam and Modernity in Indonesia,* ed. Greg Fealy and Greg Barton, 42–67. Clayton, Australia: Monash Asia Institute.

Forrester, Geoff, ed.
1999. *Post-Soeharto Indonesia: Renewal or Chaos.* Singapore: ISEAS, and The Netherlands: KITLV Press.

Forrester, Geoff, and R. H. May
1999. *The Fall of Soeharto.* Singapore: Select Books.

Fox, Jonathan A., and L. David Brown, eds.
1998. *The Struggle for Accountability: The World Bank, NGOs, and Grassroots Movements.* Cambridge, MA: MIT Press.

Frey, Marc, Ronald W. Pruessen, and Tan Tai Yong, eds.
2003. *The Transformation of Southeast Asia: International Perspectives on Decolonization.* Armonk, NY: East Gate.

Fuad, Muhammad
2002. "Civil Society in Indonesia: The Potential and Limits of Muhammadiyah." *Sojourn* 17 (2): 133–163.

Gellert, Paul

1998. "A Brief History and Analysis of Indonesia's Forest Fire Crisis." *Indonesia* 65:63–85.

Girling, John

1996. *Interpreting Development: Capitalism, Democracy, and the Middle Class in Thailand.* Ithaca, NY: Cornell University SEAP.

Hadiwinata, Bob S.

2003. *The Politics of NGOs in Indonesia: Developing Democracy and Managing a Movement.* London: RoutledgeCurzon.

Hadiz, Vedi R.

1997. *Workers and the State in New Order Indonesia.* London: Routledge.

2001. "Capitalism, Oligarchic Power and the State in Indonesia." *Historical Materialism: Research in Critical Marxist Theory,* no. 8 (Summer): 119–152.

2003. "Decentralisation and Democracy in Indonesia: A Critique of Neo-Institutionalist Perspectives." Hong Kong: Southeast Asia Research Center Working Paper No. 47.

2004. "Indonesian Local Party Politics: A Site of Resistance to Neoliberal Reform." *Critical Asian Studies* 36 (4): 615–636.

Hasbullah, Jousairi

1996. *Mamang dan Belanda: Goresan-goresan Wajah Sosial-Ekonomi dan Kependudukan Sumatera Selatan Zaman Kolonial dan Refleksinya pada Hari Ini* [Uncle and the Dutch: Sketches of the Society and Economy of South Sumatra under Colonial Rule and Reflections]. Palembang, South Sumatra: Sriwijaya University (UNSRI).

Hedman, Eva-Lotta E.

2006. *In the Name of Civil Society: From Free Election Movements to People Power in the Philippines.* Honolulu: University of Hawai'i Press.

Hefner, Robert W.

1993. "Islam, State, and Civil Society: ICMI and the Struggle for the Indonesian Middle Class." *Indonesia* 56:1–36.

2000. *Civil Islam: Muslims and Democratization in Indonesia.* Princeton, NJ: Princeton University Press.

Hertz, Noreena

2004. *The Debt Threat.* New York: HarperBusiness.

Hewison, Kevin, ed.

1997. *Political Change in Thailand: Democracy and Participation.* London: Routledge.

Hill, Hal, ed.

1994. *Indonesia's New Order: The Dynamics of Socio-Economic Transformation.* Honolulu: University of Hawai'i Press.

Hill, Hal

1996. *The Indonesian Economy since 1966.* Cambridge: Cambridge University Press.

1999. *The Indonesian Economy in Crisis: Causes, Consequences and Lessons.* Singapore: ISEAS.

Hill, Hal, and Andrew MacIntyre

1994. *Indonesia's New Order: The Dynamics of Socio-economic Transformation.* Honolulu: University of Hawai'i Press.

Hochchild, Adam

1999. *King Leopold's Ghost: A Story of Greed, Terror, and Heroism in Colonial Africa.* Boston: Mariner Books.

Humaidi, Ahmad H.

1997. *Kebangkitan Pers Daerah: Sepuluh Tahun Perjalanan Harian Umum Sriwijaya Post 1987–1997* [The Rise of a Regional Press: Ten Years of the Daily Newspaper *Sriwijaya Post* 1987–1997]. Palembang, South Sumatra: Jasa Jurnalis Molimedia.

Human Rights Watch

2003. "Indonesia: Paper Industry Threatens Human Rights." http://hrw.org/.

International Labor Organization

2000. *World Employment Report (2000.)* www.ilo.org/.

Jaspan, M. A.

1967. "Tolerance and the Rejection of Cultural Impediments to Economic Growth: The South Sumatran Case." *Bulletin of Indonesian Economic Studies* (June), 38–59.

Johnson, Chalmers

2000. *Blowback: The Costs and Consequences of American Empire.* 2nd ed. New York: Henry Holt.

Kamis, Abdul Aziz

2002. *Menggugat Transparansi APBD di Sumsel* [South Sumatra Operating Budget Accused of Not Being Transparent]. Palembang, South Sumatra: Forum Indonesia Untuk Transparansi Anggaran (FITRA) Palembang (February).

2003. *Perjuangan Hukum Atas Pengalihan Dana APBD: Kasus Tempur Vs DPRD Sumsel* [The Legal Struggle over Changes in the Operational Budget: The Case of TEMPUR against DPRD Sumsel]. Palembang, South Sumatra: Forum Indonesia Untuk Transparansi Anggaran (FITRA) Palembang (February).

Kerkvliet, Benedict J., and Resil B. Mojares, eds.

1991. *From Marcos to Aquino: Local Perspectives on Political Transition in the Philippines.* Honolulu: University of Hawai'i Press.

Kingsbury, Damien, and Harry Aveling, eds.

2003. *Autonomy and Disintegration in Indonesia.* London: RoutledgeCurzon.

Kingsbury, Damien, and Arief Budiman, eds.

2001. *Indonesia: The Uncertain Transition.* Adelaide: Crawford House Publishing.

Kinnvall, Catarina, and Kristina Jonsson, eds.
  2002. *Globalization and Democratization in Asia: The Construction of Identity.*
    London: Routledge.
Kraince, Richard
  2000. "The Role of Islamic Student Groups in the *Reformasi* Struggle: KAMMI
    (Kesatuan Aksi Mahasiswa Muslim Indonesia)." *Studi Islamika* 7:3–50.
  2002. "The Role of Islamic Student Activists in Divergent Movements for Reform
    during Indonesia's Transition from Authoritarian Rule, 1998–2001." Ph.D.
    diss., Ohio University.
Kurzman, Charles, ed.
  1998. *Liberal Islam: A Sourcebook.* Oxford: Oxford University Press.
Laffan, Michael
  2003. *Islamic Nationhood and Colonial Indonesia: The Umma below the Winds.*
    London and New York: RoutledgeCurzon.
Laird, John
  2000. *Money Politics, Globalization, and Crisis: The Case of Thailand.* Singapore:
    Graham Brash Pte. Lte.
Lev, Daniel S.
  1987. *Legal Aid in Indonesia.* Working Paper 44. Clayton, Australia: Centre of
    Southeast Asian Studies, Monash University.
  2000. *Legal Evolution and Political Authority in Indonesia: Selected Essays.* The
    Hague: Kluwer Law International.
  2005. "Memory, Knowledge and Reform." In *Beginning to Remember: The Past
    in the Indonesian Present,* ed. Mary Zurbuchen, 195–208. Singapore: Sin-
    gapore University Press.
Liddle, William
  1996. "*Media Dakwah* Scripturalism: One Form of Islamic Political Thought
    and Action in New Order Indonesia." In *Toward a New Paradigm: Recent
    Developments in Indonesian Thought,* ed. Mark Woodward, 323–356.
    Tempe: Arizona State University.
Lindsey, Timothy
  1998. "Square Pegs and Round Holes: Fitting Modern Title into Traditional
    Societies in Indonesia." *Pacific Rim Law and Policy Journal,* 699–719.
Lloyd, Grayson, and Shannon Smith, eds.
  2001. *Indonesia Today: Challenges of History.* Singapore: ISEAS.
Lubis, Todung Mulya
  1993. *In Search of Human Rights: Legal-Political Dilemmas of Indonesia's New
    Order 1966–1990.* Jakarta: Gramedia.
Lucas, Anton, and Arief Djati
  2000. *The Dog is Dead So Throw It in the River: Environmental Politics and
    Water Pollution in Indonesia: An East Java Case Study.* Clayton: Monash
    Asia Institute.

Macintyre, Andrew
  1991. *Business and Politics in Indonesia.* St. Leonards, NSW, Australia: Allen & Unwin.
Madjid, Nurcholish, Abdul Qadir Djaelani, Ismail Hasan Metareum, and H. E. Saifuddin Anshari
  1970. *Pembaharuan Pemikiran Islam* [The Renewal of Islamic Thought]. Jakarta: Islamic Research Centre.
Madrid, Robin
  1999. "Islamic Students in the Indonesian Student Movement, 1998–1999." *Bulletin of Concerned Asian Scholars* 31 (July–September): 17–32.
Magallanes, Catherine, J. Iorns, and Malcolm Hollick
  1998. *Land Conflicts in Southeast Asia: Indigenous Peoples, Environment and International Law.* Bangkok: White Lotus Press.
Mahruf, Kamil, Nanang S. Soetadji, and Djohan Hanafiah
  1999. *Pasemah Sindang Merdika 1821–1866* (A History of the Conquest of Pasemah). Palembang: Paguyuban Masyarakat Peduli Musi.
Marx, Karl
  1963. *The Eighteenth Brumaire of Louis Bonaparte* (1852). New York: International Publishers.
  1974. *The Revolution of 1848: Political Writings.* Vol. 1. Ed. David Fernbach. New York: Vintage Books.
  1978. "The Class Struggles in France, 1848 to 1850." In *The Marx-Engels Reader,* ed. Robert C. Tucker. New York: W. W. Norton & Co.
McMichael, Philip
  2004. *Development and Social Change: A Global Perspective.* 3rd ed. Thousand Oaks, CA: Pine Forge Press.
McVey, Ruth, ed.
  1992. *Southeast Asian Capitalists.* Ithaca, NY: Cornell University, SEAP.
  2000. *Money and Power in Provincial Thailand.* Honolulu: University of Hawai'i Press.
Ministry of Agriculture, Government of Indonesia
  1985. *Petunjuk Umum Pelaksanaan Proyek Perusahaan Inti Rakyat Perkebunan* [General Guidelines for Nucleus Estate and Smallholder Plantations]. No 668/Kpts/KB.510/10/1985.
Miranda, Felipe B., ed.
  1997. *Democratization: Philippine Perspectives.* Quezon City: University of Philippines Press.
Mobini-Kesheh, Natalie
  1999. *The Hadrami Awakening: Community and Identity in the Netherlands East Indies, 1900–1942.* Ithaca, NY: Cornell University, SEAP.
Mohamad, Goenawan
  2005. *Sidelines: Thought Pieces from Tempo Magazine.* Trans. Jennifer Lindsay. Jakarta: Equinox Publishing.

Naipul, V. S.
   1982. *Among the Believers: An Islamic Journey.* New York: Vintage Books.
   1998. *Beyond Belief: Islamic Excursions among the Converted Peoples.* London: Little Brown & Co.
Neher, Clark D., and Ross Marlay
   1995. *Democracy and Development in Southeast Asia: The Winds of Change.* Boulder, CO: Westview Press.
Nuh, Jamila
   2004. "Environmental Politics in Indonesia: Water Pollution along the Musi River in South Sumatra." Project report, MAIA Program, Ohio University.
Nuh, Jamila, and Elizabeth Collins
   2001. "Land Conflict and Grassroots Democracy in South Sumatra." *Antropologi Indonesia* 25, no. 64 (January–April): 41–55.
Nur Kholis
   2005. *Wajah Bantuan Hukum di Sumatera Selatan: Seperempat abad LBH Palembang* [A Portrait of Legal Aid in South Sumatra: Twenty-five Years of LBH Palembang]. Palembang, South Sumatra: LBH Palembang.
Ockey, James
   2004. *Making Democracy: Leadership, Class, Gender, and Political Participation in Thailand.* Honolulu: University of Hawai'i Press.
O'Rourke, Kevin
   2002. *Reformasi: The Struggle for Power in Post-Soeharto Indonesia.* St. Leonard's, NSW, Australia: Allen & Unwin.
Otsuka, Kejiro, and Agnes R. Quisumbing
   2001. "Land Rights and Natural Resource Management in the Transition to Individual Ownership: Case Studies from Ghana and Indonesia." In *Access to Land, Rural Poverty and Public Action,* ed. Alain De Janvry, Gustavo Gordillo, Jean-Philippe Platteau, and Elisabeth Sadoulet, 97–128. Oxford: Oxford University Press.
Padoch, Christine, and Nancy Lee Peluso, eds.
   1996. *Borneo in Transition: People, Forests, Conservation, and Development.* New York: Oxford University Press.
Peeters, Jeroen
   1995. "Space, Religion, and Conflict: The Urban Ecology of Islamic Institutions in Palembang." In *Issues in Urban Development: Case Studies from Indonesia,* ed. Peter J. M., 143–163. Nas. Leiden: Research School CNWS.
   1997. *Kaum Tuo–Kaum Mudo: Perubahan Religius Di Palembang 1925–1935* [Generational Conflict: Religious Change in Palembang]. Jakarta: INIS.
Perkins, John
   2004. *Confessions of an Economic Hit Man.* San Francisco: Berrett-Koehler.
Phongpaichit, Pasuk, and Chris Baker
   1998. *Thailand's Boom and Bust.* Chiang Mai, Thailand: Silkworm Books.

2002 (1995). *Thailand: Economy and Politics.* New York: Oxford University Press.

Phongpaichit, Pasuk, and Sungsidh Piriyarangsan

1994. *Corruption and Democracy in Thailand.* Chiang Mai, Thailand: Silkworm Books.

Polyani, Karl

1944. *The Great Transformation: The Political and Economic Origins of Our Time.* 2nd ed. Boston: Beacon Press

Porter, Donald J.

2002. *Managing Politics and Islam in Indonesia.* London: RoutledgeCurzon.

Price, Roger, ed.

1975. *1848 in France.* Ithaca, NY: Cornell University Press.

Raillon, François

1993. "The New Order and Islam, or the Imbroglio of Faith and Politics." *Indonesia* 57:197–217.

Rais, Amien

1985. "International Islamic Movements and Their Influence upon the Islamic Movement in Indonesia." *Prisma* 35:27–49.

Ramage, Douglas E.

1995. *Politics in Indonesia: Democracy, Islam and the Ideology of Tolerance.* London: Routledge.

Rasyid, Tarech

1997. *Menggugat Intellektual.* [I Accuse the Intellectuals]. Palembang, South Sumatra: Himpunan Pengarang Indonesia Aksara.

1998. *Kembalikan Daulat Rakyat.* [Return Sovereignty to the People]. Palembang, South Sumatra: LP3HAM.

Ricklefs, M. C.

1993. *A History of Modern Indonesia since c. 1300.* Stanford, CA: Stanford University Press.

Rifai, Amzulian

2002. *Pola Politik Uang Dalam Pemilihan Kepala Daerah* [Pattern of Money Politics in District Elections]. Jakarta: Ghalia Indonesia.

2004. "Socio-legal Aspects of Land Disputes in Relation to Oil Palm Plantation Activities: The Case of South Sumatra." Ph.D. diss., Monash University.

Robertson, Priscilla

1952. *Revolutions of 1848: A Social History.* New York: Harper & Row.

Robison, Richard

1986. *Indonesia: The Rise of Capital.* Sydney: Allen & Unwin.

1990. *Power and Economy in Suharto's Indonesia.* Manila: Journal of Contemporary Asia Publishers.

2002. "What Sort of Democracy? Predatory and Neo-liberal Agendas in Indonesia." In *Globalization and Democratization in Asia,* ed. Catarina Kinnvall and Kristina Jonsson. London: Routledge.

2004. "Neoliberalism and the Future World: Markets and the End of Politics." *Critical Asian Studies* 36 (3):405–423.

Robison, Richard, and David S. G. Goodman

1996. *The New Rich in Asia: Mobile Phones, McDonald's and Middle-class Revolution.* London: Routledge.

Robison, Richard, and Vedi R. Hadiz

2004. *Reorganising Power in Indonesia: The Politics of Oligarchy in an Age of Markets.* London: RoutledgeCurzon.

Rodan, Garry, Kevin Hewison, and Richard Robison, eds.

1997. *The Political Economy of Southeast Asia: An Introduction.* Melbourne: Oxford University Press.

Rosihan Arsyad H.

1998. *Revitalisasi Pembangunan Sumatera Selatan Melalui Pemberdayaan Masyarakat* [Revitalizing Development in South Sumatra by Empowerment of Society]. Palembang, South Sumatra: n.p.

Ross, Michael L.

2001. *Timber Booms and Institutional Breakdown in Southeast Asia.* Cambridge: Cambridge University Press.

Rosser, Andrew

2001. *The Politics of Economic Liberalisation in Indonesia: State, Market and Power.* Richmond, Surrey: Curzon.

2004. "Indonesia: The Politics of Inclusion." IDS Working Paper 229. Brighton, Eng.: Institute of Development Studies.

Sachs, Jeffrey D., ed.

1989. *Developing Country Debt and the World Economy.* Chicago: University of Chicago Press.

Sachs, Jeffrey D.

2005. *The End of Poverty: Economic Possibilities for Our Time.* New York: The Penguin Group.

Sachsenroder, Wolfgang, and Ulrike E. Frings, eds.

1998. *Political Party Systems and Democratic Development in East and Southeast Asia: Volume I: Southeast Asia.* Aldershot, Hants, Eng., Brookfield, VT: Ashgate.

Said, Abi Hasan

1992. *Bumi Sriwijaya Bersimbah Darah: Perjuangan Rakyat Semesta Menegakkan Republik Indonesia di ujung Selatan Sumatera.* [The Land of Sriwijaya Drenched in Blood: The Semesta Struggle to Establish the Republic of Indonesia in the Southern Tip of Sumatra]. Jakarta: Yayasan Krama Yudha.

Sakai, Minako

2002. "Land Dispute Resolution in the Political Reform at the Time of Decentralization in Indonesia." *Anthropologi Indonesia* (Special Volume), 40–56.

Sastra, Nikilanta K. S.
  1949. *History of Sri Vijaya.* Madras: University of Madras.
Sato, Yuri
  2004. "Corporate Governance in Indonesia: A Study on Governance of Business Groups." In *The Role of Governance in Asia,* ed. Yasutami Shimomura. Singapore: Institute of Southeast Asian Studies.
Schaffer, Frederic Charles
  2001. "Clean Elections and the 'Great Unwashed': Electoral Reform and Class Divide in the Philippines." Paper delivered at the American Political Science Association Annual Meeting, San Francisco.
Schnitger, F. M.
  1989. *Forgotten Kingdoms in Sumatra.* 1st ed. 1939. Singapore: Oxford University Press.
Schwarz, Adam
  1999 (1994). *A Nation in Waiting: Indonesia's Search for Stability.* 2nd ed. St. Leonard's, NSW, Australia: Allen & Unwin.
Schwarz, Adam, and Johathan Paris, eds.
  1999. *The Politics of Post-Suharto Indonesia.* New York: Council on Foreign Relations Press.
Scott, James C.
  1998. *Seeing Like a State: How Certain Schemes to Improve the Human Condition Have Failed.* New Haven, CT: Yale University Press.
Scott, Margaret
  1998. "Indonesia Reborn?" *New York Review of Books,* August 13, 43–48.
Sen, Amartya
  2000. *Development as Freedom.* New York: Anchor Books.
Sewell, William
  1980. *Work and Revolution in France: The Language of Labor from the Old Regime to 1848.* Cambridge: Cambridge University Press.
Shigetomi, Shinichi, ed.
  2002. *The State and NGOs: Perspective from Asia.* Singapore: ISEAS.
Shimomura, Yasutami, ed.
  2003. *The Role of Governance in Asia.* Singapore: ISEAS.
Sidel, John
  1999. *Capital, Coercion, and Crime: Bossism in the Philippines.* Stanford, CA: Stanford University Press.
Silliman, Sidney, and Lela Garner Noble, eds.
  1998. *Organizing for Democracy: NGOs, Civil Society, and the Philippine State.* Honolulu: University of Hawai'i Press.
Simanjuntak, Togi, ed.
  2000. *Premanisme Politik.* Jakarta: Institut Studi Arus Informasi.
Situmorang, Abdul Wahib, ed.
  2005a. *Pembangunan di Sumatera Selatan: Masalah dan Jalan Keluarnya* [Devel-

opment in South Sumatra: Problems and the Way Forward]. Palembang, South Sumatra: Yayasan Pustaka Indonesia.

Situmorang, Abdul Wahib
  2005b. *The Toba Batak: Fighting for Environmental Justice (1988–2003).* Jakarta: Walhi.

Soeripto, et al.,
  1996. *Nucleus Estate and Smallholders in Plantation.* Jakarta: Yayasan Agrimedia.

Soesastro, Hadi, Anthony L. Smith, and Han Mui Ling, eds.
  2003. *Governance in Indonesia: Challenges Facing the Megawati Presidency.* Singapore: ISEAS.

Soros, George
  1998. *The Crisis of Global Capitalism: Open Society Endangered.* New York: BBS/Public Affairs.

Stiglitz, Joseph E.
  2002. *Globalization and Its Discontents.* New York: W. W. Norton.

Strauss, John, Kathleen Beegle, et al.
  2004. *Indonesian Living Standards: Before and After the Financial Crisis: Evidence from the Indonesia Family Life Survey.* Singapore: Center for the Study of the Family in Economic Development, ISEAS, and University of Gadjah Mada.

Sumarto, Sudarno, Asep Suryahadi, and Alex Arifianto
  2004. "Governance and Poverty Reduction: Evidence from Newly Decentralized Indonesia." SMERU Working Paper, www.smeru.or.id/.

Tocqueville, Alexis de
  1949 (1850). *The Recollections of Alexis de Tocqueville.* New York: Columbia University Press.
  1986. *Selected Letters on Politics and Society,* ed. Robert Boesche. Berkeley: University of California Press.

Traugott, Mark
  1985. *Armies of the Poor: Determinants of Working-Class Participation in the Parisian Insurrection of June 1848.* Princeton, NY: Princeton University Press.

Trocki, Carl A., ed.
  1998. *Gangsters, Democracy, and the State in Southeast Asia.* Ithaca, NY: Cornell University SEAP.

Tsing, Anna Lowenhaupt
  2005. *Friction: An Ethnography of Global Connection.* Princeton, NJ: Princeton University Press.

Uhlin, Anders
  1997. *Indonesia and the "Third Wave of Democratization": The Indonesian Pro-Democracy Movement in a Changing World.* New York: St. Martin's Press.

United Nations Development Program
1999. *Human Development Report.* Oxford: Oxford University Press.
Upaya, Ganda
2002. "Two Bupati Elections in South Sumatra." M.A. thesis, Ohio University.
US State Department
1997. Report on Human Rights: Indonesia. www.state.gov/.
Utami, Ayu
1998. *Saman.* Jakarta: Kepustakaan Gramedia Populer.
Vatikiotis, Michael
1998. *Indonesian Politics under Suharto: The Rise and Fall of the New Order.* New York: Routledge.
Wah, Francis Loh Kok, and Joakim Ojendal, eds.
2005. *Southeast Asian Responses to Globalization: Restructuring Governance and Deepening Democracy.* Singapore: ISEAS.
Whitten, Tony, Sengli J. Damanik, Jazanul Anwar, and Nazaruddin Hisyam
2000. *The Ecology of Sumatra.* Singapore: Periplus.
Wijaya, Taufiq
2005. *Juaro* [Hooligan]. Bandar Laumpung, Lampung: Pustaka Melayu.
Wilson, Ian Douglas
2005. "The Changing Contours of Organised Violence in Post New Order Indonesia." Working Paper 118, Asia Research Centre, Murdock University, Perth, Western Australia.
Winters, Jeffrey A.
1996. *Power in Motion: Capital Mobility and the Indonesian State.* Ithaca, NY: Cornell University Press.
Wolters, Oliver W.
1967. *Early Indonesian Commerce.* Ithaca, NY: Cornell University Press.
1970. *The Fall of Sriwijaya in Malay History.* Ithaca, NY: Cornell University.
Woodward, E. L.
1963 (1929). *Three Studies in European Conservatism: Metternich, Guizot, The Catholic Church in the Nineteenth Century.* 2nd ed. Hamden, CT: Archon Books.
World Bank, http://worldbank.org/wdr/2000/fullreport.html/.
1999. *World Development Report 1999/2000.* New York and Oxford: Oxford University Press.
2000. *Indonesia: Accelerating Recovery in Uncertain Times.* World Bank: East Asia Poverty Reduction and Economic Management Unit.
2001. *Indonesia: Environment and Natural Resource Management in a Time of Transition.* Washington, DC: World Bank.
2003. *Indonesia Environment Monitor.* http://wbln0018.worldbank.org/eap.nsf/Attachments/o62403-EnvMonitor2003/.
World Wildlife Fund
2002. *Oil Palm Plantations and Deforestation in Indonesia.* WWF Germany in collaboration with WWF Indonesia and WWF Switzerland.

Ya'kub, A., and Dadan Afrdian [sic]
  n.d. *Kembalikan Lebak Lebung Kepada Rakyat* [Give the Lebak Lebung Back to the People]. n.p.
Yamamoto, Tadashi
  1995. *Emerging Civil Society in the Asia Pacific Community: Nongovernmental Underpinnings of the Emerging Asia Pacific Regional Community.* Singapore: ISEAS and Japan Center for International Exchange.

Newspapers, Magazines, and Other Sources

Asia Times Online, www.atimes.com/
  1999. February 23, "Gajah Tunggal to Restart Shrimp Farming with $114m."
  2002. August 16, Bill Guerin, "Indonesia's First Man."
Asia Week, www.asiaweek.com/
  1997. August 15, Keith Loveard, "The Dark Side of Prosperity: A World Bank Critic Alleges Waste and Graft."
Alliance of Independent Journalists (Aliansi Jurnalis Independen or AJI), http://ajindonesia.org/id/
  1999. February 4, "Atas Pelecehan dan Ancaman oleh Aparat Terhadap Wartawan Lampung Post" [Harassment and Intimidation of Lampung Post Reporter by Security Forces].
  2001. August 27, "Subowo: 'Saya Dipenjara Karena Memperjuangkan Hak'" [Subowo: I was Jailed Because I Fought for My Rights].
Berita Pagi (Palembang), newspaper (owned by Alex Noerdin)
  2005. July 23, "Lumbung Energi Untuk Rakyat" [Energy Storehouse for the People]; July 25, "Menolak Dipindah Hari Ini PKL Gelar Demo" [Street Vendors to Demonstrate against Relocation Today].
Business Intelligence Online, www.geocities.com/realestatefundmanager/cguba_indonesians.html/
  2004. March 12, "Troubled Indonesian Tycoons Pump Billions into China."
Detikcom, www.detik.com/
  2002. August 5, "Antara Syahrial Oesman, Taufik Kiemas, dan Ponco Sutowo" [Between Syahrial Oesman, Taufik Kiemas, and Ponco Sutowo].
  2003. July 5, "Rapor Merah Lingkungan Buat 5 Perusahaan di Sumsel" [5 Factories in South Sumatra Receive Red Environmental Rating].
Down to Earth, http://dte.gn.apc.org/
  1997. June, "Pulping the People: Barito Pacific's Paper Pulp Factory and Plantations in South Sumatra"; September, "Suharto Fiddles While Indonesia's Forests Burn."
  1998. December, "PT Tanjung Enim Lestari Pulp and Paper, South Sumatra, Indonesia: Comments on the Official Environmental Impact Assessment Documents."
  1998. February (no. 36), "World Bank's Forest Policy Review."
  1999. January, "Paper Pulp Development in South Sumatra, Indonesia: Tanjung

Enim Lestari (PT TEL) and Musi Hutan Persada (PT MHP), A Down to Earth Campaign Update"; [n.d.], "Bank of Scotland Investment in Controversial Indonesian Paper Pulp Project PT TEL/MHP in South Sumatra: Brief Notes from Frances Carr, Campaigner Down to Earth, Following Her Visit in March 1999"; August (no. 42), "Sumatra Pulp Plant Protestors Fight On"; October (Special Issue), "Poverty in the Midst of Plenty."

2000. February (no. 44), "Protests at PT TEL Pulp Plant"; March, "The Challenges of World Bank Involvement in Forest: Indonesia Case Study"; May (no. 45), "Communities Confront Loggers," "Displaced Villagers Win Back Land," and "Coastal Resources in Crisis."

2001. February (no. 48), "Paper and Pulp Heading for Trouble"; May (no. 49), "Export Credit Finances Destructive, Debt-laden Projects"; November (no. 51), "The Shrimp Industry."

2002. November (no. 55), "Green Light for Mining in Forests."

2003. November (no. 59), "Protests over Fatal Collapse at Freeport/Rio Tinto West Papua Mine."

Economic Justice Now, www.economicjustice.org (Oakland, CA)

2004. September, Nadia Martinez, "World Bank Backs Big Oil: Refuses to Implement Recommendations of Extractive Industries Review."

Far Eastern Economic Review (Hong Kong), www.feer.com/

1993. December 9, John McBeth, "Lottery Lament."

1999. August 7, "Megawati's Husband Fends off Cronyism Charges."

2000. June 1, Dan Murphy, "Deeper into the Morass: The Collapse of the World's Largest Shrimp Farm, Once Valued at $2.5 Billion, Sounds Alarm Bells over the Fate of Indonesia's Bank-Restructuring Efforts."

Fortune Magazine

2001. September 3, "Indonesia's First Husband."

Forum Keadilan (Jakarta), weekly news magazine

2000. October 29, "Amoniak Berujung Pidana" [Ammonia Ends in Court Case].

Gatra (Jakarta), weekly news magazine

1996. March 16, "Huru-hara THR Kebun Sawit: Sekitar 2,000 buruh perkebunan PT Musi Banyuasin Indah mengamuk. Mereka main bakar" [Riot at THR Oil Palm Plantation: 2,000 workers of PT Musi Banyuasin Indah Go Amok and Set Fires].

1998. May 16, "Kami tak menyulut kerusuhan" [We Don't Ignite Riots].

2001. June 23, "Senjata Makan Pamflet: Gara-gara berdemo saat sidang berlangsung, Direktur LSM WCC Palembang ganti diajukan ke mega hijau" [Guns Eat Pamphlets: The Next Act a Demonstration at the Court with the Director of WCC in the Defendant's Chair].

Guardian Unlimited, www.guardian.co.uk/

2003. June 25, John Aglionby, "Indonesia Told to Clean Up"; July 16, Joseph Stiglitz, "Don't Trust Technocrats."

2004. March 26, "Suharto, Marcos and Mobutu Head Corruption Table with $50 bn Scams."

2005. January 17, Edith Lederer, "U.N. Report Urges Aid to Poor Countries"; August 6, John Aglionby, "Gold Mining Giant Faces Pollution Test Case."

Human Rights Watch, www.hrw.org/

1999. February 12, "Rights Group Demands Release of Indonesian Shrimp Farmer."

Indonesian Business on the Web, ibonweb.com/

2000. October 21, "Save the Company, Catch the Crooks."

Indonesian Observer, www.indoexchange.com/indonesian-observer/

1999. October 22, "Shrimp Workers Protest in Indonesia."

2001. April 19, "Sacked Secretary Unveils Prayoga's List of Graft Cases"; May 14, "AGO to Quiz Prajogo Tomorrow for Graft."

Inside Indonesia (Melbourne, Australia), quarterly, www.insideindonesia.org/

2004. October/December, Andrew Steele, "Peripheral Problems: Indonesia's Decentralisation Law Is Causing Headaches in Dusun Belido."

International Crisis Group, www.crisisweb.org

2002. August 8, "Al-Qaeda in Southeast Asia: The Case of the Ngruki Network in Indonesia"; December 11, "Indonesia Backgrounder: How the Jemaah Islamiyah Terrorist Network Operates."

2003. August 26, "Jemaah Islamiyah in South East Asia: Damaged But Still Dangerous."

International Herald Tribune, www.iht.com/

1996. July 29, "Action Dashes Hope for Change."

2003. May 8, "Worldwide Shrimp Surplus Threatens Industry."

Inter Press Service, www.ips.org/

2001. March 17, Richard Dursin, "Shrimp Farming Destroying Mangroves."

Jakarta Post, daily newspaper

1998. October 20, "Two Firms Guilty of Forest Fires."

1999. July 29, "Cronyism Not Gone from Forestry Business."

2000. February 17, "Big Names Probed for Alleged Abuse of Forestry Funds"; April 25, "Half of Mangrove Forests Destroyed"; April 26, "Jakarta, National Dialogue on the Impact of the Shrimp Industry on Indonesia's Mangroves and Coastal Communities"; August 29, "Kwik Vows to Continue Fight against 'Black' Conglomerates."

2001. January 8, "IMF Questions Delay of Legal Action"; February 20, "Analysis of Muslim Student Groups"; March 29, "PT Pupuk Sriwijaya Denies Dumping Ammonia into Musi"; April 6, "Regions Ask for Reforestation Funds"; April 8, "Dissolve the Current Legislature"; April 19, "Documents on Alleged Graft by Prajogo Submitted."

2002. January 16, "Taufik Kiemas Goes Back Home"; August 29, "Autonomy Benefits Officials But Not People"; September 10, "Shrimp Farmers Seek Debt Relief"; October 7, Rendi Witular, "Six Mining Firms Can Resume Operations in Forest Areas"; December 19, "Gajah Tunggal Clarifies."

2003. January 2, "Taufik Kiemas' Role Set to Grow"; January 21, "Hutan Habis, Habislah Kita" [When the Forest Is Gone, We Are Finished]; March 1, "Amien's Sister Pays Back 'Hot Money'"; March 8, "Soeharto Family Members Implicated in Pertamina Corruption Cases"; August 22, Aan Suryana, "AGO Cancels Probe into High-profile Graft Cases."

2004. January 28, "Despite Some Decent Progress, Autonomy Remains Big Problems" [sic]; July 23, Fabiola Desy Unidjaja and Abdul Khalik, "Sjamsul Repays Rp 10.1t Debt to Government"; December 8, Ridwan Max Sijabat, "Indonesia's Labor Indicators Deteriorate: ILO Report."

2005. March 17, "Government Completes Blueprint on Aceh, Allocates Rp 45 Trillion"; July 30, "RI Inks US$ 7.5b in Deals with China."

Jaringan Advokasi Tambang (JATAM) [Mining Advocacy Network], www.jatam .org/

2000. May 17, "Dukung Protes atas Kekerasan Aparat thdp buruh PT SMJ" [Support Protests against Police Violence toward PT SMJ Workers].

Jaringan Gerakan Petani Indonesia dan Reform Agraria, e-mail list managed by JJ Polong

1999. May 24, "Pokok Pikiran LBH Palembang Terhadap Kebijakan Tambak Inti Rakyat (PIR)" [LBH Proposal for People's Shrimp Farms].

2000. February 11, "Hapuskan Lelang Lebak Lebung" [End Auction of the Lebak Lebung], Serikat Petani Sumatera Selatan (SPSS) press release; September 19, "SPSS Persoalkan Lelang Lebak Lebung" [SPSS Raises the Issue of the Lebak Lebung Auction]; November 7, "Semua Lebak-Lebung Dilelang" [All Lebak Lebung Auctioned]; November 12, "Perda Lelang Lebak Lebung Penyebab Kericuhan Nelayan di OKI" [Regulations for the Auction of the Lebak Lebung Cause Turmoil among OKI Fishermen].

Jaringan Advokasi Masyarakat Urban (JAMUR) (Palembang)

2001. February 15, "Pedagang tak Ingin Bentrok dengan Aparat" [Vendors Don't Want Clash with Police]; February 22, "Pencabutan Perda Tunggu Berita Daerah" [Withdrawal of Regulation Waits for Regional News].

Kompas (Jakarta), daily newspaper

1996. February 1, "Mulai Besok Sriwijaya Post untuk Sementara tidak Terbit" [Beginning Tomorrow Publication of *Sriwijaya Post* Suspended]; February 2, "Pembaca Menyesalkan Sriwijaya Post tak Terbit" [Readers Frustrated Sriwijaya Post Not Published].

2000. February 17, "Kasus Tanah di Sumsel 3000 Warga Berkemah" [Land Cases in South Sumatra: 3000 People Sit In]; October 4, "Yahli Gugat PT Pupuk Sriwijaya" [Yahli Accuses PT Pupuk Sriwijaya]; October 8, "Warga Minta PT Pusri Bebaskan Lahan Sekitar Pabrik" [People Request PT Pusri Release Land around Factory]; October 10, "Amoniak PT Pusri Bocor Lagi" [Another Ammonia Leak at PT Pusri]; October 13, "PT Pusri Digugat Secara Pidana" [PT Pusri Charged with Criminal Offense]; October 20, "Untuk Srinivasan, Prayogo, dan Syamsul Presiden Tunda Tuntutan Hukum" [President Delays Srinivasan, Prayogo, and Syamsul Prosecution]; November 3, "Kasus Pencemaran PT Pusri Terhambat Penelitian Bapedalda" [Case of Pollution by PT Pusri Obstructed by Bapedalda Investigation].

2001. April 18, "Subowo Tengah Menanti Hukum" [Subowo Awaits Sentence]; June 10, "Warga Tuntut Janji Ganti Rugi PT Pusri" [The Residents Demand Compensations from PT Pusri]; August 24, "Warga Sekitar Pusri Sesalkan Kelambanan Tim Bapedalda" [Residents Complain about Bapedalda's Failure to Act].

2006. March 23, "Riau Masuk Lima Provinsi Terkorup" [Riau Is among the Five Most Corrupt Provinces]; July 15, "Perkara yang Ditangani Komisi Pemberantasan Korupsi" [Cases Accepted by the Commission to Eradicate Corruption].

Kompas Online, www.kompas.com/
1998. February 9, "Moslems Called to Face Traitors of the Nation."

Koran Tempo (Jakarta), daily newspaper, www.korantempo.com/
2002. January 10, "KPKPN Akan Panggil Taufik Kiemas" [Corruption Commission Will Summon Taufik Kiemas]; November 5 (1), "Mendagri pastikan Syahrial Oesman Menjadi Gubernur Sumatra Selatan" [Home Affairs Minister Confirms Syahrial Oesman as Governor of South Sumatra]; November 5 (2), "Jalan Panjang Syahrial" [Syahrial's Long Journey].

Kyodo News Service, Japan, www.kyodo.co.jp/
2001. April 18, Christine T., "Commission Unveils Wahid, Megawati Wealth."

Laksamana.net/. (This Web site can no longer be accessed.)
2001. September 20, "Prajogo Pangestu Quizzed in Corruption Case"; October 2, "Doubts over South Sumatra Officials' Wealth"; November 2, "Mega Man: A Look at Taufik Kiemas."

2002. August 11, "Oil and Gas: Taufik Kiemas under Fire."

2003. February 9, "Kiemas Takes the Initiative"; April 7, "Megawati: Expel Corrupt Party Members"; May 2, "Rais Slams Taufik Kiemas"; June 27, "Srinivasan Family Dogs Yet Another President"; September 10, "Soewandi, Sukhois and the US Connection."

2004. January 3, "The Kiemas Political Agenda"; July 23, "Anti-Graft Watchdog Rejects Tycoon's Reprieve"; August 6, "Kiemas Win in South Sumatra"; October 8, "Nepotism in South Sumatra?"

LBH-Palembang
1998. November 19 (1), "Ribuan Petani Tambak Ngamuk PT Wachyuni Mandira Dibakar di Desa Bumi Pratama Mandira, Kec. Pembantu Pematang Panggang, Ogan Komering Ilir, Sumatera Selatan" [Thousands of Shrimp Farmers Riot at PT Wachyuni Mandira, Desa Bumi Pratama Mandira in Pembantu Pematang Panggang District Burned Down]; November 19 (2), "Konflik antara petani plasma dengan PT Wachyuni Mandira" [Conflict between Contract Farmers and PT Wachyuni Mandira].

1999. February 8, "Protes Keras Tentang cara-cara penangkapan Sdr. Endang Suparmono" [Protest at Manner of Arrest of Endang Suparmono]

2000. (1) "Jumlah Kasus Tanah di Sumatera Selatan" [Land Cases in South Sumatra]; (2) "Kasus Buruh PT SMJ (sub PT Bukit Asam): Kronologi" [PT SMJ Workers' Case (Sub PT Bukit Asam): Chronology]; May 5, "Aksi Penyanderaan Kendaraan PT SMJ" [PT SMJ Vehicles Taken Hostage].

2001. "Matriks pengkriminalisasian dan tindakan Kekerasan terhadap Petani Sumatera Selatan" [Farmers in South Sumatra Face Criminalization and Violence]; February 9, "Penertiban Pedagang Kaki Lima" [Controlling Street Vendors].

2002. February 9, "Penggusuran Pedagang Kaki Lima" [Eviction of Street Vendors]; February 13, "Pedagang: Pemkot Pembohong" [Vendors: City Government Lies]; March, "Sengketa Pengelolaan Gua Sarang Burung Walet antara CV Agung Putra and Forum Tiga Desa (Desa Lubuk Mabar, Sukajadi dan Tanjung Raya)" [Conflicts over Management of Swallows' Nest Caves between CV Agung Putra and the Forum of Three Villages, Desa Lubuk Mabar, Sukajadi and Tanjung Raya].

Lembaga Kemasyarakatan Tanjung Raja OKI (Grassroots Organization, Tanjung Raya, OKI, South Sumatra)

1999. May 25, press release: "39 Eks Petani Plasma Tambak Udang Windu PT Wachyuni Mandira Yang Ditahan" [39 Former Contract Shrimp Farmers PT Wachyuni Mandira Held].

2000. September 30, "Kasus PT. Wachyuni Mandira Serobot Tanah: Warga Tuntut Hak dan Ganti Rugi" [PT Wachyuni Mandira Seizes Land: People Demand Rights and Compensation].

Lembing KAYU (Lembar Informasi Gerakan Lingkungan), newsletter of the Environmental Movement [*kayu* is Indonesian for "wood"], publication of WALHI Sumsel, Palembang.

2000. January (1), "Palembang dan Prabumulih Terancam Racun" [Palembang and Prabumulih Threatened by Poison]; January (2), "Banjir Menghantui Wilayah Sumatera Selatan" [Floods Haunt South Sumatra]; January (3), "Faktor Penyebab Konflik Sumber Daya Alam di Sumatera Selatan" [Factors Causing Conflict over Natural Resources in South Sumatra].

Media Indonesia, www.mediaindo.co.id/

1999. September 3, "Thousands of Farmers in Muara Enim Ask Prajogo to Return Their Land."

2003. November 13, Keluarga Gubernur Sumsel Borong Proyek Fasilitas PON XVI 2004" [Family of South Sumatra Governor Takes Over Contracts for Facilities for PON XVI 2004].

NorWatch, www.justmake.no/kunder/norwatch/

1999. April (no. 6), "4,500 people's land has been stolen."

Oxfam Community Aid Abroad Website, Australia, www.oxfam.org.au/

2000. March 8, Jeff Atkinson, National Policy Coordinator and Mining Ombudsman for Community Aid Abroad, "Case 3: Barisan Gold Mine."

Oxfam International, www.oxfam.org/en/
   2004. June, "The Rural Poverty Trap: Why Agricultural Trade Rules Need to Change and What UNCTAD XI Could Do about It."
   2005. March, "Food Aid or Hidden Dumping? Separating Wheat from Chaff."
Palembang Pos, daily newspaper
   1999. December 19, "PT TEL Masih Mencekam" [PT TEL Still Taken Over]; December 20, "Pabrik PT TEL Lumpuh Total" [PT TEL Factory Totally Stopped]; December 22, "5 Pembunuh Mahasiswa IBA" [5 Kill IBA Student]; December 23, "Kasus pembunuhan Mahasiswa IBA: Pangdam Tak ada garis komando dalam hal itu" [Murder of IBA Student Commander: No Tie to Military].
   2000. February 16, "Pemda Bingung, Ratusan Tukang Becak Tolak Ditertibkan" [Local Government Perplexed, Hundreds of Becak Drivers Refuse Regulations]; March 30, "Serikat Becak Palembang Segera Dideklarasikan" [Palembang Becak Union Formed]; July 9, "Limbahnya Resahkan Warga: PT Pusri di Panggil Gubernur" [Pollution Disturbs People: Governor Summons PT Pusri]; October 5, "PT Pusri Akan di Ikutkan: Soal Amoniak, Komisi D Panggil Bapedalda" [PT Pusri Will Follow Up: Commission D of DPRD Calls upon Bapedalda in Regard to Ammonia Leak]; October 6, "Buntut Kebocoran Gas Amoniak: Komisi D Tugaskan Bapedalda Teliti Pengelolaan Limbah Pusri" [Aftermath of Ammonia Leak: Commission D Orders Bapedalda to Examine PT Pusri Waste Management]; October 7, "Soal Kebocoran Amoniak: Dirut Pusri: Tak Benar Terjadi Berulang Kali" [Executive Director of PT Pusri Denies Ammonia Leaks Are Frequent]; October 13, "Buntut Bocornya Gas Amoniak: Warga 3 Ilir laporkan PT Pusri ke Polda Sumsel" [Ammonia Leak: People of Ilir 3 Report PT Pusri to South Sumatra Police]; October 15, "Soal Bocornya Gas Amoniak, PT Pusri Hormati Proses Hukum" [Ammonia Leak Problem, PT Pusri Respects the Law]; October 16, "Atas laporan warga, PT Pusri bakal kembali dipanggil Polda" [Due to People's Report, PT Pusri Once Again Summoned by Provincial Police]; October 19, "Terkait Bocornya Gas Amoniak PT Pusri" [In Connection with Ammonia Leak at PT Pusri]; October 23 (1), "Terkait dugaan mark up dana PON Sumsel TGPTPK bakal turunkan tim Satgas Investigasi" [In Connection with Accusation of Markup in PON Expenses TGPTPK Will Send Investigation Team]; October 23 (2) "Soal Bocornya Gas Amoniak PT Pusri: Walau PT telah beri bantuan, proses hukum tetap jalan" [Problem of the Ammonia Leak at PT Pusri: While Help Is Given, Legal Process Proceeds]; November 6 (1), "Kinerja Bapedalda Dinilai Lamban, DPRD dan Bapedalda Sumsel saling bantah" [Bapedalda Efforts Said to be Sluggish, DPRD and Bapedalda Deny]; November 6 (2), "Terkait Bocornya Gas Amoniak PT Pusri: LSM Pendamping Pertanyakan Penelitian Bapedalda" [In Connection with Ammonia Leak: NGOs Inquire about Bapedalda Investigation].
   2001. February 13, "Saksi: Gubernur izinkan warga panen kelapa sawit" [Wit-

ness: Governor Gave Farmers Permission to Harvest Oil Palm]; February 20, "Terdakwa: Saya memanen atas izin Gubernur" [Accused: I Harvested with Governor's Permission]; April 11, "Subowo dipukuli hingga pingsan, puluhan pengacara datangi Rutan" [Subowo Beaten Unconscious, Dozens of Lawyers Come to Detention Center]; April 14, "LSM protes pemukulan terhadap Subowo" [NGOs Protest Beating of Subowo]; April 15, "Subowo dipukuli karena tradisi, retorika semata" [Subowo Beating Traditional, Only Rhetoric]; April 20, "Apapun alasannya, Rutan harus bertanggung jawab" [Detention Center Must Take Responsibility]; September 21, "Pengalihan kasus Subowo bernuansa politis" [Shift in Subowo Case Smells of Politics].

2002. March 30, "Produksinya 18 ton/hari dan Warga Sungai Angit Tambang Minyak Secara Ilegal" [People of Sungai Angit Illegally Produce 18 Barrels a Day].

2003. March 6, "Warga Bingin Rupit demo PT DMIL" [People from Bingin Rupit Demonstrate at PT DMIL].

2004. February 16, "Pemda bingung, Ratusan Tukang Becak Tolak Ditertibkan" [Government Confused: Hundreds of Becak Drivers Reject Regulations]; February 21, "Rakyat diminta ngerti, Pemda harus tebas" [People Asked to Understand: Local Government Must Clear (the Roads)]; March 30, "Serikat Becak Palembang Segera Dideklarasikan" [Palembang Becak Drivers' Union Established].

Panji Masyarakat (Jakarta), Yayasan Nurul Islam, trimonthly news magazine

1999. July 28, Dodi Kusmajadi, "Demi Sawit, Warga Diusir: Sengketa Tanah" [Citizens Evicted for Oil Palm: Conflict over Land].

Pemerintah Kabupaten Musi Banyuasin [Musi Banyuasin District Government]

2001. "Perencanaan Strategik: Dinas Pemberdayaan Masyarakat Desa Kabupaten Musi Banyuasin Tahun Anggaran 2001–2005" [Strategic Plan: Village Empowerment in Musi Banyuasin 2001–2005].

2003. *Muba Randik: Majalah Informasi Kabupaten Musi Banyuasin* [Beautiful MUBA: Magazine with Information about Musi Banyuasin].

petani@e-groups.com/

2000. May 4, "12 Unit Mobil Disandera Mantan Karyawan PT SMJ" [12 Vehicles Taken Hostage by Former PT SMJ Employees]; May 5, "Peningkatan Aksi Buruh PT SMJ" [PT SMJ Workers Escalate Protest Action]; May 16, "Penembakan ibu-ibu, anak-anak dan buruh PT SMJ di PT Tambang Batubara Bukit Asam" [The Shootings of Women, Children, and PT SMJ Workers in PT Tambang Batubara Bukit Asam]; May 17, Jaringan Advokasi Tambang (JATAM) [Mining Advocacy Network]: "Dukung Protes atas Kekerasan Aparat thdp buruh PT SMJ" [Support Protests against Police Violence toward PT SMJ Workers].

Republika (Jakarta), daily newspaper

1999. November 19, "Tanah tak Kembali, Massa Bakar 26 Unit Base Camp PT

Multrada" [Land Not Returned: Mass Burns 26 Units of PT Multrada Base Camp].

2000. February 19, "Ribuan Warga Masih Menginap di Kantor Gubernur" [Thousands Stay Overnight at the Governor's Office]; February 24, "Pertemuan Tertunda, Warga Tetap Nginap di Kantor Gubernur" [Meeting Delayed, People Remain at Governor's Office Overnight].

2001. March 27, "Limbah PT Pusri Diduga Cemari Sungai Musi" [PT Pusri Accused of Polluting Musi River].

Republika online, www.republika.co.id/

2002. February 12, "LSM Protes Gaji Anggota DPRD Sumsel Rp 19,5 Juta" [NGOs Protest Salaries of Provincial Legislators].

Serikat Pedagang Radial (Palembang), grassroots organization

2003. February 12, press release: "Suara Pedagang Jl Radial" [Voice of Radial Vendors].

Sriwijaya Post (Palembang), daily newspaper

1994. July 19, "Warga Eks Marga Benakat Tuding PT MHP Serobot Hutan Larangan" [Ex-Marga Benakat Farmers Accuse PT MHP of Seizing Protected Forest]; July 21, "Hutan Rimba Sekampung, Riwayatmu Dulu" [Rimba Sekampung Forest Traditions]; July 25, "Kegiatan MHP di Benakat Ditunda Sementara Waktu" [MHP Activities in Benakat Temporarily Suspended]; July 26, "Lestarikan Hutan Bukan Slogan" [Forest Preservation Not Simply a Slogan]; September 22, "Menhut Serius Tangani "Rimba Sekampung'" [Forestry Minister Serious about Dealing with Rimba Sekampung].

1995. September 11, "Soal Sengketa Tanah di Kundi. Bupati Akan Pertaruhkan Jabatan Jika Penggusuran Tanpa Ganti Rugi" [Land Conflicts in Kundi: Bupati Will Resign If Evicted Are Not Compensated]; September 14, "Sengketa Tanah Desa Kundi Dirjenbun Akan Tinjau Kembali Izin Lokasi" [Kundi Land Conflict: Plantations Director General Considers Revoking Permit]; September 20, "Ratusan Warga Kundi Lakukan Unjuk Rasa. Bupati: Ini Sudah Kriminal" [Bupati: Kundi Villagers Protests Are Criminal].

1996. February 1 (1), "Perjalanan 'Sriwijaya Post' dan Kronologi Munculnya Kemelut" [Account of the *Sriwijaya Post* and Chronology of the Crisis]; February 1 (2), "Ringkasan Berita Acara Rapat Direksi PT Sriwijaya Perdana" [Summary of Official Report of Sriwijaya Perdana Board of Directors].

1998. February 7, "Pembakar Gudang Pupuk Diadili" [Fertilizer Warehouse Arsonists Tried]; February 14, "Sidang Pembakaran Gudang" [Trial of Warehouse Arsonists]; March 5, Silvester Sarjoko SCJ and Jamilah, "Relevansi Peran DPR terhadap Kasus Tanah di Sumsel" [Provincial Legislature's Role in South Sumatra Land Cases]; May 16, "Palembang Masih Mencekam" [Palembang Still Gripped]; May 19, "Aksi Unjuk Rasa Mahasiswa Palembang" [Palembang Students Demonstrate]; September 24,

"Kembalikan Hak Rakyat" [Return People's Rights]; October 13, "Warga histeris di depan Gubernur" [Citizens Hysterical in Front of Governor]; December 8, "Camp PT MMM Masih Dijaga Aparat" [Security Forces Still Guarding PT MMM Camp].

1999. November 13, "Massa Bakar Sebelas Basecamp PT Multrada" [People Burn Eleven PT Multrada Basecamps]; December 22 (1), "Meyer Ardiansyah Dikukuhkan Sebagai Pahlawan Reformasi" [Meyer Ardiansyah a Hero of *Reformasi*]; December 22 (2), "Denpom Ringkus Pembunuh Meyer" [Military Police Capture Meyer's Killer]; December 23, "Ayah Meyer Pertanyakan Jati Diri Pelaku Utama" [Meyer's Father Asks: Who Is the Real Killer?]; December 26, "Kasus Meyer: Rekonstruksi Dijaga Ketat" [Meyer Case: Reconstruction Closely Guarded].

2000. January 26, "KSKP Ajukan Kriteria Balonbup MURA" [KSKP Proposes Criteria for MURA Bupati Election]; January 28 (1), "Aman Ramli Teratas Cabup OKU" [Aman Ramli Foremost OKU Bupati Candidate]; January 28 (2), "Klan Ramli 'Come Back'" [Ramli Clan 'Come Back']; February 9, "Pedagang K-5 Ditampung di Pasar Tradisional" [Street Vendors to Be Accomodated in Traditional Markets]; February 15, "Penarik Becak Ancam Datangi Walikota" [Becak Drivers Threaten to Go to Mayor]; February 17, "Wakil Ketua DPRD Disodori Jok Becak" [Provincial Legislature Vice Chairman Mockingly Given Becak Seat]; February 22, "Walikota Dituntut Cabut Perda No 3" [Demand Mayor Withdraw Regulation No. 3]; February 23, "Pedagang K-5 Inginkan Lokasi Percontohan" [Street Vendors Want Example of Location]; February 24, "Sosialisasi Penertiban Diperpanjang" [Campaign for Orderliness Extended]; February 28, "Becak di IP, Pilihan Sulit" [Becak at IP: Difficult Choice]; February 29 (1), "Pemda Cabut Surat Edaran Penertiban" [Government Withdraws Circulation Regulations]; February 29 (2), "Warga Sandera 3 Mobil MHP" [Residents Seize 3 MHP Vehicles]; March 3, "Aksi Brutal di Tambak Udang Dipasena" [Brutality in Dipasena Shrimp Ponds]; March 4, "Korban PT Dipasena" [Victim of PT Dipasena]; March 18, "'Money Politik' Kembali" ['Money Politics' Returns]; March 20, "Suhu Politik di Mura Memanas: LBH Punya Bukti Transfer Rp. 90 Juta" [Political Climate in Mura Heats Up: LBH Has Proof of Transfer of Rp. 90 Million]; March 24, "Soeprijono Joesep Bupati MURA Uang Suap 30 Juta Dikembalikan" [30 Million Bribe Returned to MURA Bupati Joesep Soepriyono]; April 1, "Kasus PT SMJ 'Deadlock'" [SMJ Case Deadlocked]; April 2, "Ratusan Pekerja PT SMJ Ancam Bakar Mess" [Hundreds of PT SMJ Workers Threaten to Burn Down the Mess]; April 14, "Kikim Masih Mencekam" [Unrest Continues in Kikim]; April 28, "Sekjen Dephutbun Putuskan 12 Ribu Ha Lahan MHP Dikembalikan" [Secretary General of Forestry and Plantations Decides 12,000 Hectares MHP Land to Be Returned]; May 2 (1), "PDI-P Goyang Kursi Ketua DPRD MURA" [PDI-P Shakes the Chair of the Chairman of MURA Legislature]; May 2 (2), "Kapolda Tantangi Tersangka

'Money Politik' MURA" [Provincial Police Seize Accusor of 'Money Politics' in MURA]; May 5, "Muaraenim Masih Diramaikan Demonstrasi" [Demonstrations Continue in Muaraenim]; May 10, "Karyawan PT BA Bentrok dengan Demonstran PT SMJ" [PT BA Employees Clash with PT SMJ Demonstrators]; May 13 (1), "Aparat Tembaki Eks Pekerja PT SMJ" [Security Forces Shoot Ex-Workers of PT SMJ]; May 13 (2), "17 Kendaraan PT SMJ Dilepas: Terima Transfer Pembayaran" [17 Vehicles Returned to PT SMJ: (Severance) Pay Transferred]; June 6, "Warga Rambangdangku Tuntut Tanah PT MHP" [Rambangdangku Villagers Protest MHP Concession]; June 10, "Warga Rambangdangku Ancam PT MHP" [Rambangdangku Villagers Threaten PT MHP]; June 29, "Perundingan Ganti Rugi Warga Rambanglubai" [Rambanglubai Villagers' Compensation Negotiations]; June 29, "Terpaksa Gunakan Kain Basah" [Forced to Use a Wet Cloth]; July 10, "Ratusan Petambak Plasma WM Tersingkir" [Hundreds of WM Contract Shrimp Farmers Purged]; July 14, "Atasi Bau Limbah Dengan Penghijauan" [Green Belt to Suppress the Smell of Waste]; July 28, "Warga Satu Ilir Keluhkan Limbah PT Pusri" [People in Ilir 1 Complain about PT Pusri Waste]; August 31, "Manajer Lingkungan PT BTM Enggan Komentari Protes" [BTM Environmental Manager Balks at Commenting on Protest]; September 29, "Gas Amoniak Pusri Bocor, 28 Keracunan" [Ammonia Leak at Pusri, 28 Poisoned]; October 6, "Dewan Desak Pusri Atasi Amoniak" [DPRD Demands PT Pusri Deal with Ammonia Leak]; October 9, "Warga 3 Ilir Resah Amoniak Bocor Lagi" [People in Ilir 3 Nervous about Another Ammonia Leak]; October 10, "Atasi Kebocoran Amoniak PT Pusri: Gubernur Perintahkan Bapedalda Bergerak Cepat" [Governor Orders Bapedalda to Take Immediate Action on Ammonia Leak at PT Pusri]; October 13, "PT Pusri Dilaporkan ke Polda Sumsel" [PT Pusri Reported to Sumsel Police]; October 17 (1), "SSCW: Soal dana PON, Negara dirugikan Rp 800 juta lebih" [SSCW: Nation Suffers Loss of More Than Rp 800 Million Due to Problems with PON Funds]; October 17 (2), "Soal Kebocoran Gas Amoniak, Harus Didukung Data Akurat" [Problem of Ammonia Leak Must Be Supported with Accurate Data]; October 19 (1), "Akibat Bocornya Gas Amoniak: Pusri Diminta Ganti Rugi Biaya Pengobatan" [Result of Ammonia Leak: PT Pusri Asked to Pay Compensation for Treatment]; October 19 (2), "Operasi Pabrik Urea Pusri IV Dihentikan" [Operations of Pusri Urea Factory No. 4 Stopped]; October 21 (1), "Buntut Bocornya Amoniak: PT Pusri Didesak Penuhi Tuntutan Warga" [Outcome of Ammonia Leak: PT Pusri Urged to Respond to People's Demands]; October 21 (2), "WALHI: Silahkan itu Hak Warga" [WALHI: Go Ahead, That Is the Residents' Right]; October 21 (3), "Yahli: Sebaiknya Koordinasi Dulu" [Yahli: Best to Coordinate]; November 10, "Atasi Kebocoran Amoniak PT Pusri: Gubernur Perintahkan Bapedalda Bergerak Cepat" [Governor Orders Bapedalda to Take Quick Action to

Deal with the Ammonia Leak at PT Pusri]; November 13, "PT Pusri Akhirnya Bantu Masyarakat" [PT Pusri Finally Helps Residents].

2001. January 24, "Pemuda MUBA Minta Cabup Sipil Murni" [MUBA Youth Call for Civilian Bupati Candidate]; February 5, "Pengelolaan Limbah Buruk, Denda Rp 5 Juta" [Bad Waste Treatment, Fined 5 Million Rupiah]; March 1, "Cabup MUBA harus lolos uji kemampuan" [MUBA Bupati Candidate Must Pass 'Fit and Proper' Test]; March 13, "Proses Suksesi Bupati MUBA, Pansus Minta Pendapat Masyarakat" [Election Commission Request Input from People on Selection of MUBA Bupati]; March 21, "Tata Tertib Pilbup MUBA diserahkan, Pansus dan Ketua DPRD Beda Pendapat, Panitia 'Polling' Dinilai Ilegal" [MUBA Bupati Election Rules Submitted: Election Commission and Chairman of Legislature Differ, Polling Committee Considered Illegal]; April 14, "97 Persen Tanah Warga Prabumulih tak Bersertifikat" [97 Percent of People's Land in Prabumulih Has No Certificate]; May 10, "Tes Kelayakan 29 Balonbup MUBA, Daftar Nama-nama Balonbup MUBA" [Fit and Proper Test for 29 Prospective MUBA Bupati Candidates]; May 12, "Delapan Nama berpeluang: Disinyalir terjadi Perang Politik Uang" [Eight People Named: Pointing to a War of Money Politics]; May 21, "Politik Uang Harus Dibuktikan dengan Pengakuan Dewan" [Money Politics Must Be Proven with Approval of the Legislature]; June 15, "Suplemen Tatib Tak Perlu Diperdebatkan" [Not Necessary to Debate Additional Rules]; July 6, "MMBA Ancam Mosi Tidak Percaya" [MUBA Student Forum Threatens Petition of Distrust]; July 14, "KPMM tolak keputusan Dewan" [MUBA Youth Communication Forum Rejects Decision of Legislature]; July 17, "Warga Minta Pilbup-Wabup Dipercepat" [People Request Bupati Election Be Speeded Up]; August 1, "Soal Pilbup-Wabup MUBA, MPM Desak DPRD Revisi Tatib DPRD" [MPM Pushes DPRD to Revise Rules on MUBA Bupati Election]; August 30, "FKPMM Menilai Kelompok 22 Tidak Representatif" [MUBA Youth Communication Forum Considers Group of 22 Not Representative]; November 29, "LSM dan Mahasiswa Kecam Sikap Empat Calon Bupati" [NGO and Students Criticize the Attitude of Four Bupati Candidates]; November 30, "Proyek PON XVI dan KKN Baru" [PON XVI and New Corruption]; December 12, "Politik Jangan Dibawa ke Muhammadiyah" [Don't Bring Politics into Muhammadiyah]; December 20, "Pemilihan Bupati-Wabup tidak melanggar" [Bupati Election Not Against the Law].

2002. January 29, "Pertambangan dan Energi Andalan MUBA Tarik Investor" [MUBA Relies on Mining and Energy to Attract Investors]; February 28, "Massa Boikot Sidang DPRD" [Boycott of Provincial Legislature]; February 29, "Massa Bongkar Tenda Kaki Lima" [Mob Tears Down Vendor Stalls]; March 6, "Rakyat Miskin di Sumsel 1,8 Juta Jiwa" [1.8 Million Poor People in South Sumatra]; March 28, "Persoalan Pedagang Kaki Lima: Dilematis Antar Kepentingan" [Problem of Street Vendors: A Dilemma of

Priorities]; September 11, "Pedagang K-5 Demo Pol PP" [Street Vendors Demonstrate at Police Station]; September 25, "BPN OKU Serahkan 297 Sertifikat"[OKU Land Agency Distributes 297 Certificates]; September 26 (1), "Petani vs. Investor" [Farmers vs. Investors]; September 26 (2), "Bela Hak Dianggap Kriminal" [Defending One's Rights Considered Criminal]; September 26 (3), "Kepala BPN Salahkan Masa Lalu" [Head of National Land Agency Blames the Past]; September 26 (4), "Jadi Buruh di Tanah Sendiri" [Becoming a Laborer on One's Own Land]; October 3, "Tuntut Plasma ke PT Pinago: Warga Babattoman Datangi Dewan" [Plasma Protest to PT Pinago: Babattoman People Go to Legislature]; October 5, "Hanya 14.95 Persen Tanah Punya Sertifikat" [Only 14.95 Percent of Land Has Been Titled]; October 31 (1), "Wachyuni Mandira Bangun Tambak 30,000 Ha" [Wachyuni Mandira to Build 30,000 Hectares of Ponds]; October 31 (2), "Pedagang K5 'makanan" oknum POL PP" [Street Vendors "Food" for Police]; November 1, "Warga Tujuh Desa Protes Sikap PT Pinago" [People of Seven Villages Protest against PT Pinago]; November 2, "Gubuk Liar Terminal Karyajaya Dibongkar" [Wild Stalls at Karyajaya Terminal Torn Down]; November 5, "45 Pedagang K-5 Disidang Yustisi" [45 Street Vendors Tried]; November 23, "Lelang Lebak Lebung Masih Berpihak ke Pemodal" [Lebak Lebung Auction Still Favors the Capitalist]; December 13, "Penarik Becak Sekeluarga Berdemo" [Becak Drivers All Demonstrate].

2003. January 6, "Ada 100 Ribu Penganggur di Sumsel" [100 Thousand Unemployed in South Sumatra]; January 10, "Ratusan Pedagang K-5 tolak pemindahan" [Hundreds of Street Vendors Refuse to Move]; January 11, "PBB Sumsel: Serahkan Dana Operasional ke Rakyat" [Partai Bulan Bintang: Distribute Operational Funds to the People]; January 14, "Tak puas; Ratusan PK-5 Datangi Kantor Pemkab" [Not Satisfied, Hundreds of Street Vendors Go to Government Offices]; January 17, "Santai Saja" [Simply Relaxed]; January 20, "600 Warga Portal Jalan PT GPI" [600 People Block Road to PT GPI]; January 21, "Tak Ada Kendala" [There Is No Constraint]; January 24, "40 Warga Muba Tuntut Ganti Rugi PT MBI" [40 Muba People Protest Compensation by PT MBI]; February 5, "Pengelolaan Limbah Buruk, Denda Rp 5 Juta" [Bad Waste Treatment, Fined 5 Million Rupiah]; February 7, "Mahasiswa Serbu Gedung DPRD" [Students Attack the Provincial Legislature]; February 10, "PT WM Perluas Areal Tambak 30 Ribu Ha" [PT WM Increases Area of Ponds by 30 Thousand Hectares]; February 11, "Ketua PKB Sumsel: Kembalikan Rp 100 Juta" [Partai Kebangkitan Bangsa Chairman: Return Rp. 100 Million]; February 13, "Giliran PAN Kembalikan Rp 100 Juta" [Partai Amanat Nasional's Turn to Return Rp. 100 Million]; February 14, "Dana Operasional Dibekukan" [Operational Funds Frozen]; February 18, "Ada yang Ditelepon Keponakan" [One Received a Call from His Nephew]; February 19, "Uangnya Satu Tas Penuh" [A Purse Full of Money]; February 20 (1), "Kas DPRD

Sumsel akan Lebihi Kapasitas Jika Pengembalian Dana Diterima" [DPRD Sumsel Treasury Will Be Over Capacity If Funds Taken Are Returned]; February 20 (2), "Dana Operasional DPRD: Sulit Berkomentar" [DPRD Operational Funds: Difficult to Comment On]; February 24, "Mekanisme Pengembalian Dana Operasional" [Mechanism to Return Operational Funds]; February 27, "Pengembalian Dana Operasional Dicicil" [Operational Funds to be Returned in Installments]; March 7, "Dana Operasional Balik Kas Rp 1.2 M" [Rp. 1.2 Billion Returned to the Operational Budget Account]; March 8, "Rakyat Awasi Pengembalian Dana" [The People Watch Out for the Return of Funds]; March 10, "Siap Diperiksa" [Ready to Be Questioned]; March 12, "Pengembalian Dana 42 Anggota Dewan Ditunggu" [Waiting for 42 Legislators to Return Funds]; March 13, "Kejati Masih Menghimpun Data" [Sumatra Selatan High Court Still Collecting Data]; March 18, "Pembangunan di Muba Belum Merata" [Development in Muba Not Yet Equal]; March 21, "30 Persen Warga Palembang Miskin" [30 Percent of Palembang Residents Are Poor]; March 25, "Anggota DPRD Sumsel harus Dipidanakan" [Legislators Must Be Tried]; April 14, "97 Persen Tanah Warga Prabumulih tak Bersertifikat" [97 Percent of People's Land in Prabumulih Has No Certificate]; April 15, "Usut Dana Operasional tak Perlu Petunjuk" [Handling of Operational Funds (Case) Does Not Require Guidance]; April 16, "Keluarga Miskin Dapat Askes Perdana" [Poor Families Receive Assistance]; April 23, "Anggota DPRD Sumsel Jadi Tersangka" [Legislators Accused]; April 24 (1), "Baru 33 Anggota Dewan Lunasi Dana Operasional" [Only 33 Legislators Paid Off Operational Funds Debt]; April 24 (2), 2003; "Silakan kejati Tetapkan Dewan Sebagai Tersangka" [Let the High Court Carry Out Accusation of the Legislature]; April 28, "TK: Tidak disiplin tak Usah Dipilih" [TK: If You Are Not Disciplined, Don't Run for Election]; June 4, "Islamic Centre Cetak Generasi Islami" [Islamic Center Shapes an Islamic Generation]; July 3, "Warga Pesta Ikan Mabuk" [Residents Celebrate Dead Fish]; July 9, "Perda Becak Terus Jalan" [Becak Regulations to Be Enforced]; July 21, "Rakyat Miskin Muba Akan Diberi Kebun" [Poor People in Muba to Be Given Land]; September 25, "19,095 Sertifikat Tanah Bagi Warga Miskin" [Poor Receive 19,095 Land Certificates]; October 7, "Nazaruddin Kiemas Pimpin PDI-P Sumsel" [Nazaruddin Kiemas Leader of PDI-P South Sumatra].

2004. January 6, "Ada 100 Ribu Pengangur di Sumsel" [100 Thousand Unemployed in South Sumatra]; January 23, "Tim Penelitian Walet Dipermanenkan" (Swallows'-Nest Inspection Teams Made Permanent); March 21, "30 Persen Warga Palembang Miskin" [30 Percent of Palembang Residents Are Poor].

Suara Merdeka, www.suaramerdeka.com/

1999. October 4, "Warga Betawi Long March Semanggi-Bundaran HI Dijaga Barisan Pendukung Habibie" [The Long March of the *Betawi* from Semanggi to Hotel Indonesia in Support of Habibie].

Suara Pembaruan, www.suarapembaruan.com/

1997. December 18, "Gubernur Sumsel akan cabut Izin Investor yang gusur tanah warga" [South Sumatra Governor to Withdraw Permits of Investors Who Take Over People's Land].

1999. January 2, "Soeharto's Land Should Become Object of Land Reform"; January 4, "Tutut's Land in South Sumatra Has Not Paid Tax"; August 7, "Forest Management Licenses Owned by Former President Soeharto Family, Foundation, or Partners."

Sumatera Ekspres (Palembang), daily newspaper

1996. January 29, "Diamuk, Kantor Sriwijaya Post Beberapa Wartawannya Dipukuli" [Sriwijaya Post Office Ransacked, Several Reporters Beaten]; February 2, "Ansel da Lopez: Penutupan Sripo Terpaksa, Mohon Maaf" [Ansel da Lopez Apologizes: Forced to Close Sripo].

1997. March 26, "Digelar, Unjuk Rasa Antikekerasan terhadap Wartawan" [Protest against Attack on Reporter].

1998. January 14, "Petani Desa Wonorejo ngadu ke Komnas HAM" [Wonorejo Farmers Appeal to Human Rights Commission]; March 29 (1), "PT MMM ganti rugi RP 500 ribu/hectare" [PT MMM Offers Compensation of 500 Thousand Rupiah/Hectare]; March 29 (2), "Aksi demo warga dari 6 desa terus berlanjut" [6 Villages Continue Demonstrations]; May 26, "Mahasiswa unjuk rasa bela petani" [Students Demonstrate in Defense of Farmers]; July 29, "PT MMM dan PP serobot tanah warga" [PT MMM and PP Seize People's Land]; September 24, "Ratusan Warga Kikim Nginap di Gedung Dewan" [Hundreds from Kikim Overnight at Legislature]; September 25, "Tanggapi tuntutan warga Kikim, Bupati bentuk tim" [Bupati Forms Team to Investigate Kikim Farmers' Protests]; December 5, "Warga blokir kawasan perusahaan" [Farmers Blockade Factory].

1999. February 11, "Seluruh karyawan terpaksa mengungsi" [All Employees Forced to Leave]; March 29, "Aksi Demo Warga dari 6 desa terus berlanjut" [Demonstrations by People of 6 Villages Continue]; May 4, "Warga nekat memanen sawit" [Farmers Determined to Harvest Oil Palm]; May 25, "Eks Petani WM Menuntut Pembebasan 39 Temannya" [Former WM Farmers Demand 39 Friends Be Freed]; November 12, "Warga unjuk rasa, 10 pelaku tangguhkan penahanannya" [People Protest: Arrest of 10 postponed]; November 13, "Warga ngamuk, bakar basecamp PT MMM" [People Riot, Burn PT MMM Basecamp]; November 15, "Bupati sesalkan pembakaran basecamp" [Bupati Regrets Basecamp Burning]; November 25, "Gubernur: Warga bakar PT MMM akan ditindak" [Governor: Measures to Be Taken against Those Who Burned PT MMM Basecamp]; December 2, "Kasus tanah di Kikim, bagai memperbaiki benang kusut" [Land Cases in Kikim: Repairing a Tangled Knot]; December 22, "Tersangka pembunuh Meyer ditangkap" [Accused Killer of Meyer Arrested]; December 23 (1), "Saya Memang Menusuk Meyer" [Yes, I Stabbed Meyer]; December 23 (2), "Pangdam masih harus bertanggung jawab" [Commander Must

Take Responsibility]; December 26, "Meyer dihajar, sebelum ditikam 2 tusukan" [Meyer Beaten and Stabbed Twice].

2000. February 26, "Nur Azhari, Pemilik 120 Becak: Kalau sebebas-bebasnya, malah bisa kacau" [Nur Azhari, Owner of 120 Becak: If There Are No Rules, There Will Be Disorder]; February 29, "Wali Kota Akhirnya Penuhi Tuntutan Penarik Becak" [In the End Mayor Fills Demands of Becak Drivers]; March 2, "Asal Serentak, PK-5 Siap Pindah" [So Long as Vendors Move All Together, They Are Ready to Move]; May 25, "Plasma, solusi terbaik mencapai penyelesaian" [*Plasma*, Best Solution]; June 16, "Pencurian sawit di PT MMM masih berlanjut" [Theft of Oil Palm at PT MMM Continues]; June 21, "Camat Kikim: Pencuri sawit banyak orang luar" [Kikim Camat: Many Outsiders Steal Oil Palm]; June 28, "Warga Ngeluh Limbah, PT Pusri Membantah" [People Complain about Waste, PT Pusri Denies Responsibility]; October 3, "Gas Amoniak Pusri Bocor, 28 Keracunan" [Ammonia Leaks at PT Pusri, 28 Residents Poisoned]; October 6, "Bapedalda Diminta Audit Limbah Pusri" [Bapedalda Asked to Audit PT Pusri Waste]; October 17, "Soal pH Limbah Cair, Dewan dan Pusri Tak Sepakat" [Legislature and Pusri Do Not Agree on the pH of Liquid Waste]; October 20, "LBH, WALHI dan YAHLI Protes Bapedalda" [LBH, WALHI, YAHLI Protest Bapedalda]; December 7, "Warga Sekitar Merasakan Getaran dan Bunyi Ledakan" [People Nearby Feel the Earth Rumble and the Sound of an Explosion]; December 27, "Soal Limbah, Warga Masih Tuntut PT Pusri" [Residents Still Protest PT Pusri about Pollution].

2001. February 13, "Saksi: Gubernur beri izin panen" [Witness: Governor Granted Permission to Harvest]; March 13, "Aktivis KSKP dituntut 2 tahun penjara" [KSKP activists protest 2-year sentence]; March 23, "Tiga pencuri TBS dibekuk" [Three Who Stole Oil Palm Arrested]; April 6, "Subowo kembali ditangkap" [Subowo Arrested Again]; April 20, "TAPS minta rutan proaktif" [TAPS Request Authorities Take Action]; May 8, "Bertentangan, Kejati Sumsel dan TBPTPK: Tujuh bulan kasus dugaan mark up PON gantung" [Clash between South Sumatra Public Prosecutor and TGPTPK: Case of PON "Markup" Still Hanging].

2002. March 2, "Asal Serentak, PK-5 Siap Pindah" [So Long as All Together Street Vendors Are Ready to Move]; March 13, "Aktivis KSKP dituntut 2 tahun penjara" [Two-Year Sentence Demanded for KSKP Activist]; March 23, "Tiga pencuri TBS dibekuk" [Three Who Stole Oil Palm Captured]; March 30, "Puluhan Sumur Minyak Ditambang Liar oleh Masyarakat" [Tens of Wild Oil Wells Illegally Managed by Local People]; April 6, "Subowo kembali ditangkap" [Subowo Rearrested]; December 27, "Soal Limbah, Warga Masih Tuntut PT Pusri" [Residents Still Protest PT Pusri Pollution]; April 22, "48.9% Warga Muba Miskin, Pemkab Lakukan Upaya Tingkatkan Kesejahteraan" [48.9% of People in Muba Poor: Kabupaten Government Trying to Improve Welfare].

250   Bibliography

2003. April 23, "Abang Becak Minta Perda No. 39 Dicabut" [Becak Drivers Request Regulation No. 39 Be Withdrawn].

2005. June 1, "Hampir 50 persen gedung SD di Muba rusak berat" [Almost 50 percent of elementary school buildings in Muba are falling down].

Sydney Morning Herald, www.smh.com.au/

2001. July 25, "Power Behind the Presidential Throne."

Taufiq Wijaya, reporter for the *Lampung Post*. His articles were reposted on many Web sites, particularly ISAI and Laksamana.net.

1998. (1) retrieved December 7, "Kasus PT Wachyuni Mandira: Kerusuhan yang Direkayasa Dua Bulan Sebelumnya" [PT Wachyuni Mandira: Engineered Riot Two Months before It Happened]; (2) retrieved December 7, "Izin Diberikan Sesudah Dua Tahun Beroperasi" [Permission Granted Two Years after Operations Began]; (3) retrieved December 7, "Boleh Dipukul Asal Tak Dibunuh" [Beating OK, But Don't Kill]; (4) retrieved December 7, "Enam Protes Untuk Empat Menteri" [Six Protest to Four Ministers]; (5) retrieved December 7, "Kamp Konsentrasi Pertambakan Terbesar Se-Asia Tenggara" [The Largest Shrimp Farms in Southeast Asia a Concentration Camp]; December 15 (1), "Pabrik PT Tanjung Enim Lestari Hanya Menguntungkan Investor" [PT Tanjung Enim Lestari Factory Only Benefits Investors]; December 15 (2), "Kasus Pabrik Kertas Siti Hardiyanti Rukmana: Pabrik Penebar Klorin dan Cap Komunis" [The Case of Siti Hardiyanti's Paper Factory: Factory Disperses Chlorine and the Label of Communist]; December 17, "51 Petambak PT Wachyuni Mandira Dipaksa Mengundurkan Diri" [51 PT Wachyuni Mandira Shrimp Farmers Forced to Retire Themselves]; December 31, "Perusahaan Tambang Emas Milik Setiawan Djody Mencemari Warga Musirawas" [Gold Mining Company Owned by Setiawan Djody Pollutes the People of Musirawas].

1999. January 13, "Petani Muara Enim Menolak Jadi Karyawan PT Milik Siti Hardiyanti Rukmana" [Muara Enim Farmers Refuse to Become Workers in Company of Siti Hardiyanti Rukmana]; January 25, "Diputuskan Secara Sepihak, Petambak Aksi ke Pemda Sumsel" [Unilateral Decision: Shrimp Farmers Protest to South Sumatra Government]; January 26, "Tidak Puas, Datangi Lagi Kantor Pemda" [Not Satisfied: Protest Again at Government Offices]; January 27, "PT WM: Mereka Mengundurkan Diri Secara Baik-baik" [PT WM: They Retired Voluntarily]; February 8 (1) "Setelah Memberikan Keterangan Kepada Human Rights Watch Aktifis Petambak Diculik Aparat Polres OKI" [Shrimp Farmer Kidnapped by OKI Police after Interview with Human Rights Watch Activist]; February 8 (2), "450 Petambak Plasma dibuang PT WM" [450 Contract Shrimp Farmers Expelled by PT WM]; February 10, "Human Rights Watch Protes Soal Penangkapan Endang" [Human Rights Watch Protest Arrest of Endang]; February 16, "Ribuan Petani Aksi ke PT TEL, Menuntut Agar Proses Pembebasan Tanah Diulang" [Thousands of Farmers Demonstrate at PT TEL, Protest the Expropriation of Land]; March 17, "Francis Carr: PT TEL Harus Dihentikan" [Francis Carr: PT TEL Must be Stopped]; April 4, "Perang Kepentingan Soal PT TEL" [PT TEL: Conflict of Interest]; April 29, "Minuman dan Pelacur Marak di PT TEL" [Alcohol and Prostitution Flare Up at PT TEL]; May 5, "Aparat Militer Bubarkan Aksi Petani di PT TEL" [PT TEL Demo Broken Up by Security Forces]; May 24, "39 Eks Petambak Plasma PT Wachyuni Mandira Mogok Makan" [39 Former PT Wachyuni Mandira Contract Shrimp Farmers on Hunger Strike]; December 19, "PT TEL Masih Mencekam" [PT TEL: Still Taken Over]; December 20, "Pabrik PT TEL Lumpuh Total" [PT TEL Factory Totally Paralyzed].

2000. September 30, "Lagi, Warga Menuntut Pertambakan Milik Syamsul Nursalim" [Protest at Contract Shrimp Farming of Syamsul Nursalim].

2003. August 11, "Suksesi Gubernur Sumsel Dinilai Matikan Demokrasi" [Succession of South Sumatra Governor Means Death of Democracy].

Tempo (Jakarta), weekly news magazine (English and Indonesian editions published)

2001. May 22–28 (1), "Prajogo Pierces the Clouds Robbing 'Hoods'?"; May 22–28 (2) "More Drama at the Round House"; June 17, "Prajogo Pangestu dan Hutan Kita yang Meranggas" [Prajogo Pangestu and Our Disappearing Forests]; August 21–27, "I Honestly Swear."

2002. May 7–13, "Para Pesuap dari Senayan: Banyak anggota DPR kaya mendadak" [The Bribers of Senayan: Many DPR Members Are Suddenly Rich]; October 15, "Bartering Worthless Assets for Cash Debt"; December 23, "Heavenly Freedom for Sjamsul."

2003. April 7, "Ticket Home for Sjamsul?"; May 5, "Legislators Implicated"; August 4, "Dipasena: Half-hearted Cooperation"; August 26, "Prajogo Cleared."

Tempointeractive, www.tempo.co.id

2000. October 20, "Withdraw the Police from PT Dipasena"; October 26 (1), "Ratusan Petambak Datangi Mapolda Lampung" [Hundreds of Contract Farmers Go to Lampung Police]; October 26 (2), "Pemerintah Tak Serius Selesaikan Konflik" [Government Not Serious about Ending Conflict]; November 4, "Polisi Tambah Pasukan Pengamanan Bumi Dipasena" [Police Increase Security Force at Bumi Dipasena]; November 10, "Workers Demand Security Guarantees."

2001. February 25, "Aksi Itu Dibiayai Fuad Bawazier" [Demonstration Funded by Fuad Bawazier]; June 18, "AGO to Hunt Down Indonesian Tycoon Prajogo Pangestu"; June 29, "AGO Not Yet Able to Extradite Prajogo from Singapore."

Time Asia, weekly news magazine

2002. July 15 (1), "I Have Become the Target," interview with Taufik Kiemas; July 15 (2), Simon Elegant, "Looming Large—Taufik Kiemas, Husband of Indonesian President Megawati, Might Be the Country's Most Powerful Man."

Transparan (Palembang), biweekly newspaper
  2000. October 2, "28 Warga 3 Ilir Masuk RS Akibat Amoniak PT Pusri" [28
       people from Ilir 3 Hospitalized Due to Ammonia from PT Pusri]; October
       9, "Warga Resah, Bau Amoniak PT Pusri Tercium Lagi" [The Residents
       Are Nervous, They Smell Ammonia Again from PT Pusri]; October 16,
       "150 Warga Dipekerjakan PT Pusri, Tuntutan Pidana Jalan Terus" [150
       People Hired by PT Pusri, Protest Criminal Charges]; November 11, "PT
       Pusri Bersedia Beri Ganti Rugi kepada Warga" [PT Pusri Ready to Give
       Compensation]; November 24, "Kasus Kebocoran Amoniak: PT Pusri
       Bersedia Beri Ganti Rugi kepada Warga" [Ammonia Leak Case: PT Pusri
       to Compensate the Residents]; December 8, "Buntut Meledaknya Tower
       UOP PT Pusri II: Amoniak Menebar, Warga Resah" [Explosion of UOP
       Tower of PT Pusri II: Ammonia Dispersed, People Nervous].
  2001. March 6, "Bantuan PT Pusri Tak Tepat Sasaran" [PT Pusri Aid Fails to
       Meet Target]; September 13, "Semua Industri Kimia Cemari Lingkungan"
       [All Chemical Industries Pollute Environment]; December 12, "Protes
       Warga terhadap PT Pusri di Duga Ada Maksud Tertentu" [Residents' Pro-
       test against PT Pusri Has Hidden Agenda].
  2002. February 29, "4 Maret, PK-5 Jenderal Sudirman Harus Pindah" [Vendors
       on Jenderal Sudirman Must Move on March 4]; September 11, "Preman
       Ikut Razia, PK5 Demo ke Kantor Pol PP Kota" [Gangsters Join Raid: Street
       Vendors Demostrate at Police Station].
  2003. April 24, "Bupati OKU Dinilai Paling Berhasil Laksanakan Otonomi
       Desa" [OKU Bupati Recognized as Most Successful in Implementing Vil-
       lage Autonomy].
Transparency International, London, www.transparency.org
  2004. March 25, *Global Corruption Report 2004.*
USINDO Brief, The United States–Indonesia Society, www.usindo.org/
  2003. June 25, Ross H. McLeod, "Dead on Arrival: A Post-Mortem on the IMF
       Program in Indonesia."
Van Zorge Report, Van Zorge, Heffernan & Associates, www.vanzorgereport.com/
  1998. December, "The Islamist Movement."
WALHI National Executive (Jakarta)
  2000. April 26, Raja Siregar, "Konsep Pertambakan Inti-Plasma Dalam Pertam-
       bakan Udang Skala Besar" [Concept of Inti-Plasma in Industrial Shrimp
       Farming]; April 28, "Perkebunan Besar" [Plantation Agriculture].
WALHI Sumsel (Palembang)
  1997. June 20, "Analisis Dokumen AMDAL Industri Pulp and Paper PT TEL
       P&P" [Analysis of the PT TEL P&P Environmental Impact Report].
  1999. May 25 (1), "Aksi Mogok Makan Petani Plasma Petambak Udang" [Hun-
       ger Strikes of Contract Shrimp Farmers].
  2000. January 22, "Hentikan Eksploitasi Sumber Daya Mineral oleh PT BRM/PT
       BSM di Bumi Silampari" [Stop Exploitation of Mineral Resources by PT

BRM/PT BSM in Bumi Silampari]; September 30, "Kasus PT Wachyuni Mandira Serobot Tanah: Warga Tuntut Hak dan Ganti Rugi" [Case of PT Wachyuni Mandira Seizing Land: People Demand Rights and Compensation].

Wall Street Journal, www.wallstreetjournal.com/

1998. August 19, Glenn R. Simpson, "World Bank Memo Depicts Diverted Funds, Corruption in Jakarta."

2002. March 19, "Power of Megawati's Husband Raises Concerns."

World Rainforest Movement, www/wrm/org.uy/

1999. March (no. 21), "Indonesia: Opponents to Shrimp Farming Industry under Arrest."

2005. April (no. 93), "Investing in Disaster: The IFC and Palm Oil Plantations in Indonesia"; June (no. 95), "The World Bank," "International Financial Institutions," and "The Destructive Role of Export Credit Agencies."

Index

Note: Page numbers in **bold** refer to illustrations.

Abdullahi, Malan, 168
ABRI. *See* Indonesian military
accountability, 192
Action Committee of Indonesian Muslim Students (KAMMI), 160–161, 163, 165, 168, 170
adat (customary law), 53, 66, 118
Advocacy Network for the Urban Poor (JAMUR), 112
agriculture, 20, 22–23, 53–54, 174, 175, 192. *See also* industrial forestry; land rights/land ownership; oil palm plantations; shrimp farming
Al Arqam, 159
Alliance of Independent Journalists (AJI), 46
All-Indonesia Workers' Union (SPSI), 98
al-Palimbani, 13
Amnesty International, 185
Ardiansyah, Meyer, 45
Arsyad, Rosihan: and collusion, 75; and corruption, 122, 124, 129, 130; election (2004), 147–148, 149; and land conflicts, 44, 64, 65, 73–74; and Wachyuni Mandira versus shrimp farmers, 105, 108; and workers versus PT TEL, 80, 83, 85
Asian Development Bank, 9, 31, 184
Asian Economic Crisis (1997): and debt, 20, 182; NGOs and, 124–125; *reformasi* movement and, 37–39;

and shrimp farmers, 107–108; in Thailand, 181–182; and unemployment, 98, 111–112
Asinar, Syamsul, 36, 46, 137
Asnawi, Azimi, 168
Aspinall, Ed, 11, 12, 197n.18
Association for Pesantren and Community Development (P3M), 153
Association of Muslim Intellectuals (ICMI), 49, 157, 161
Atkinson, Jeff, 88, 89

Bakara, Arnold, 84
Bandung Institute of Technology (ITB), 137
Bangka, 54, 58–61
Bank Dagang Nasional Indonesia, 103, 110–111
bankruptcy, 2, 5, 98, 111, 189
Bapedal. *See* National Environmental Agency
Bapedalda. *See* Provincial Environmental Impact Management Agency
Barisan Sumatra Mining (BSM), 89
Barisan Tropical Mining (BTM), 85–90
Barito Pacific Group, 19, 20, 67, 72, 76, 79, 109, 182
Basic Forestry Law (1967), 18, 54
Basri, Ramli Hasan: and bus accidents, 33; and corruption, 30, 79, 81, 144, 149; and land conflicts, 63, 69–70
Baswedan, Anies Rasyid, 158
Bawazier, Fuad, 148, 163
Bayu, Anwar Putra, 7, 31
becak drivers, 111–113

beking (backing), 25, 117, 126–130
biodiversity, 77, 175, 192
bribery, 116, 121–122, 125–126, 133,
    144. *See also* money politics *(politik
    uang)*
bridge funding, 176
Brown, David, 185
Budiman, Arief, 11–12
Bukit Asam. *See* Tambang Batu Bara
    Bukit Asam (Bukit Asam)
bupati elections, 135–136, 143–144
bureaucratic capitalism, 116–117
bus station land dispute, 168–169, **169**

camat, 19, 62, 66, 69
Campus Normalization Act (1978), 28
Cendana Group, 19, 81. *See also*
    Suharto family
Center for Strategic and International
    Studies, 38
China, 13, 23, 98, 111, 150, 181
Chinese-Indonesians, 38, 39, 43, 189
Chua, Amy *(World on Fire),* 189
clear cutting, 20, 67–68, 69, 72, 83, 85
coffee, 7, 8, 17, 22–23, 37, 39, 177
collusion, 75, 97, 116, 122, 133
Commission on the Environment, 94
Commission to Eradicate Corruption,
    138
Communication Forum for the Envi-
    ronment (FKPL), 94–95
Communication Forum of the Sons
    and Daughters of the Indonesian
    Military, 129, 148
Communication Union of Fishermen
    (IKAN), 84–85
Community Forest Management, 74–75
community forestry, 53
Community Recovery Program, 112
Conoco-Philips, 136
conservation forests, 141, 142–143
corruption, 116–133; bribery, 116,
    121–122, 125–126, 133, 144; collu-
    sion, 75, 97, 116, 122, 133; develop-
    ment funding and, 180–181; and
    Good Governance, 186–187; and
    harvest of swallows' nests, 119–120;

judicial system, 25, 122, 125–126;
KKN *(korupsi, kolusi, nepotism),* 37,
    116–117; in land acquisition, 79–81;
    and *lebak lebung* harvest, 118–119;
    money politics *(politik uang),* 66,
    117, 120–122, 134, 135, 144,
    148–150; in MUBA, 138; National
    Sports Games (Pekan Olahraga
    Nasional, PON), 123–124; and New
    Order, 116–118; and NGOs, 124–
    125; Palembang Mafia, 130–133;
    and *preman* gangs, 126–133; and
    Provincial Legislature, 122–123;
    and *reformasi* movement, 116–118
Council of Indonesian Mujahidin
    (MMI), 165
Crescent Moon and Star Party (PBB),
    72
cronyism, 37
cycle rickshaws. See *becak* drivers

dakwah movement, 153–155, 164–165
Dakwah School Forum (FORDS), 164
DDII (Indonesian Council for Dak-
    wah), 154, 155
debt, 14, 15, 16, **17,** 18, **18,** 20, 76,
    114–115, 176–178
decentralization, 134, 150–151
deforestation, 20, 77, 85, 111, 181
democracy: and decentralization, 134,
    150–151; and Islam, 152, 154–155,
    161, 163, 170; and justice, 172,
    190–192; and myth of the danger-
    ous masses, 191–192; transition to,
    11–12
Democrat Party, 149
de Soto, Hernando, 174–175, 187
development: and debt, 176–178; and
    environmental damage, 77–78;
    funding, 150, 179–181; militariza-
    tion and, 181; neoliberal economic
    policies, 187; and poverty, 20, 54,
    173–175, 180; priority of corporate
    interests, 97, 143, 147, 172, 185,
    186–187; sustainable, 187
Dipasena Citra Darmaja, 103, 109–110
Djodi, Setiawan, 85

Down to Earth, 81, 82, 85, 86
Dual Function *(dwifungsi)*, 44, 161
Dusun Belido, 141–143

ECAs (export credit agencies), 179–181
Eldridge, Philip, 29
elections: *bupati*, 135–136, 139, 143–
    144, 151; direct, 25, 147, 151, 169,
    186; gubernatorial (2004), 147–150,
    151; money politics *(politik uang)*,
    66, 117, 120–122, 134, 135, 144,
    149–150; New Order, 15, 16
El Niño drought (1997), 35, 62–63, 108
empowerment, 151, 185, 192
Environmental Impact Assessment
    (EIA), 81
Environmental Impact Management
    Agency. *See* National Environmen-
    tal Impact Management Agency;
    Provincial Environmental Impact
    Management Agency
environmental laws, 78, 96
ethnic conflicts, 189–190
Expan Nusantara, 127–128
export credit agencies (ECAs), 179–181
Export Import Bank (Ex-Im; U.S.), 179
Export Import Bank (Japan), 103
export orientation, 5, 11, 54, 103,
    176–177, 181–182

Farmers' Prosperity and Welfare Union
    (KSKP), 60, 62, 66, 71, 120, 128
Fealy, Greg, 12
fertilizer industry, 90–97
fishing and fishermen, 83–84, 87,
    118–119, 146
FITRA (Indonesia Forum for Budgetary
    Transparency), 122, 130
FKPL (Communication Forum for the
    Environment), 94–95
FKPPI (Communication Forum of the
    Sons and Daughters of the Indone-
    sian Military), 129, 148
floating masses, 16, 172
FOLSIP (Palembang Community
    Forum on Industrial Environment),
    94–95, 96

Food for Peace, 174
Ford Foundation, 175
FORDS (Dakwah School Forum), 164
forest fires (1997), 35–37, 63, 66, 70
Forestry Acts (1999), 71, 89
forests: clear cutting, 20, 67–68, 69,
    72, 83, 85; concessions to foreign
    and Indonesian companies, 19–20,
    67; deforestation, 20, 77, 85, 111,
    181; fires (1997), 35–37, 63, 66, 70;
    Forestry Acts (1999), 71, 89; illegal
    logging, 85, 129, 141–143, 149; open
    pit mining and, 89; ownership of,
    18–19, 53–56; and shrimp farming,
    111. *See also* industrial forestry; oil
    palm plantations
FORMAD (Student Forum for Civil
    Society), 160
Foundation for Environmental Advo-
    cacy (YALHI), 77, 93, 94
Foundation for Village Social Welfare
    (KEMASDA), 30
Fox, Jonathan, 185
FPI (Islamic Defenders Front), 165
free-market economics, 12, 181–182,
    188–190
Friends of the Earth, 81, 184

Gajah Tunggal Group, 20, 103, 104,
    109–111, 180, 182
Gemuis (Young Islamic Generation),
    160, 163
George, Susan, 187
Gie, Kwik Kian, 20, 109
globalization, 12, 170, 173, 178
Global Trends 2015, 190
GMNI (Indonesian Nationalist Stu-
    dents Movement), 131
gold mining, 85–90
Golkar, 15, 129, 130, 135, 139, 143–
    144, 147–148, 149
Good Governance, 182, 186, 192
Green Revolution, 175
Gunung Sawit Bina Lestari (PT GSBL),
    58–61
Gus Dur. *See* Wahid, Abdurrahman
    "Gus Dur"

Habibie, B.J., 11, 44, 71, 72, 79, 80–81, 157, 161, 165
Hadiz, Vedi R., 12, 20, 99, 150, 187
Hadrami, 152, 165
Hafidz, Wardah, 112
Halim, Haji, 149
Hanafiah, Djohan, 15
Hefner, Robert, 11, 154
Hertz, Noreena, 187
Hill, Hal, 117
HMI (Islamic Students Association), 124, 148, 153, 154, 156, 158–160, 161–163, 165, 170
HMI Alumni Association (KAHMI), 158–159, 161–162, 163
HMI-*progresif*, 162
Human Development Report (1999), 175
Human Rights Commission, 59, 60, 63, 72, 105, 132
human rights NGOs, 35, 107–108, 115, 185
Human Rights Watch, 107, 185

IAIN Raden Fatah (State Institute for Islamic Studies), 157, 160, 167–168
ICMI (Association of Muslim Intellectuals), 49, 157, 161
IKAN (Communication Union of Fishermen), 84–85
illegal logging, 85, 129, 141–143, 149
Imaduddin, 155, 156, 157
Indonesia Forum for Budgetary Transparency (FITRA), 122, 130
Indonesian Bank Restructuring Agency (IBRA), 76, 109, 110
Indonesian Center For Environmental Law, 83
Indonesian Committee for World Muslim Solidarity (KISDI), 38–39, 154
Indonesian Communist Party (PKI), 14, 15, 62
Indonesian Corruption Watch (ICW), 123, 124
Indonesian Council for Dakwah (DDII), 154, 155

Indonesian Council of Ulama (MUI), 159
Indonesian Democracy Party (PDI), 15, 34–35, 60, 71, 131, 158, 159
Indonesian Democracy Party-Struggle (PDI-P), 120–122, 131, 139, 143–144, 147–148
Indonesian Development Bank, 34
Indonesian government: Department of Manpower, 100–101; Department of Public Works, 150; Human Rights Commission, 59, 60, 63, 72, 105, 132; Ministry of Conservation, 142; Ministry of Forestry and Plantations, 18, 62, 68, 70–71, 73, 74, 75, 142; Ministry of Home Affairs, 123, 144, 149–150; Ministry of Mines, 88–89; Ministry of Religion, 157, 167; Ministry of the Environment, 96; National Environmental Agency, 83; Supreme Court, 126
Indonesian military (TNI, ABRI): coup attempt, 14–15; intimidation and violence, ix, 24, 30, 32, 34, 38, 46, 56, 58, 59, 60, 69, 80; Kopassus (Special Forces Command), 127–128, 132; and land disputes, 58, 145; and politics, 15, 39, 44–45, 103, 135, 148, 161; sons and daughters of, 127, 129; Sriwijaya Corps, 15, 31–32, 35, 44–45; ties to gangs, 41, 45, 130
Indonesian Nationalist Students Movement (GMNI), 131
Indonesian National Youth Committee (KNPI), 130, 135, 160
Indonesian Nature Conservancy, 86
industrial forestry, 179–180, 181; compensation to farmers, 79–81; environmental damage from, 77–78, 81–85; Musi Hutan Persada (MHP), 67–75; Tanjung Enim Lestari Pulp & Paper (PT TEL), 78–85
informal economy, 111, 174
Institute for Campus Dakwah (LDK), 158, 160
Institute for the Free Flow of Information (ISAI), 26, 86, 107

International Finance Corporation, 67, 180

International Labor Organization, 98

International Monetary Fund (IMF), 67, 176–177, 181, 182, 185

inti/plasma schemes, 56–58, 65, 74–75, 103–104, 140, 145

Iranian Revolution, 176

IRM (Union of Mosque Youth), 157–158

ISAI (Institute for the Free Flow of Information), 26, 86, 107

Iskandar, Ian, 33

Islam, 152–170; *dakwah* movement, 153–155, 164–165; and democracy, 152, 154–155, 161, 163, 170; after fall of Suharto, 164–168; Hadrami, 152; influence of, 8–9, 13; jihad, 155; KISDI, 38–39, 154; modern, 152; and New Order, 38–39, 153–159, 211n.16; NGOs, 153, 162; *pesantren*, 49, 51, 52, 167; and politics, 139, 151, 154–155, 158–159, 161–163, 166–167; radical, 154, 159, 165; and *reformasi* movement, 44, 52, 159–161, 163, 168–170; separatist rebellions (1957), 14–15

Islamic Defenders Front (FPI), 165

Islamic Law (sharia), 154, 165, 166, 169, 172

Isma'il, Nur Mahmudi, 73

ITB (Bandung Institute of Technology), 137

Jafar, Pak, 140–143

JAMUR (Jaringan Advokasi Masyarakat), 112

Japan, 14, 179, 180

Japanese Overseas Economic Cooperation Fund, 81–82

JATAM (Jaringan Advokasi Tambang), 86

Javanese settlers, 51, 61–62, 140–141

jihad, 155, 163

Jones, Sidney, 107–108

judicial system, 25, 122, 125–126

justice, concept of, 170–171, 190–192

Justice and Prosperity Party (PKS), 139, 168–170

Justice Party, 168

KAHMI (HMI Alumni Association), 158–159, 161–162, 163

Kamis, Azis, 122, 130, 148

KAMMI (Action Committee of Indonesian Muslim Students), 160–161, 163, 165, 168, 170

Kedung Ombo Dam, 29–30, 68

KEMASDA (Foundation for Village Social Welfare), 30

Keraf, Sonny, 78

Kerinci-Sebelat National Park, 89

Keterbukaan ("Openness"), 10, 31

Kiemas, Nazaruddin, 132, 148, 207n.33

Kiemas, Taufik "TK," 110, 130–133, 144, 148

Kingsbury, Damien, 11–12

KISDI (Indonesian Committee for World Muslim Solidarity), 38–39, 154

KKN *(korupsi, kolusi, nepotism)*, 37, 116–117. *See also* corruption

KNPI (Indonesian National Youth Committee), 130, 135, 160

Komando Jihad, 165, 211n.16

Komar, Junial, 71–75

Komnas Ham. *See* Human Rights Commission

KONTRAS (Commission on the Disappeared and Victims of Violence), ix, 107

Kopassus (Special Forces Command), 127–128, 132

krismon (krisis moneter). See Asian Economic Crisis (1997)

KSKP (Farmers' Prosperity and Welfare Union), 60, 62, 66, 71, 120, 128

Kuala Merdeka, 30, 125

Kundi, 58–61

Kurnia Musi Plywood Industry, 69

labor disputes, 100–114; contract shrimp farmers, 103–111; police violence, 102–103; street vendors

and *becak* drivers, 111–114; Tambang Batu Bara Bukit Asam (Bukit Asam), 100–103
labor unions, 98–100, 203n.4
Lahat: swallows' nests harvest, 119–120; Wonorejo farmers versus MMM, 61–66
Lampung Post, 46, 82, 86, 107
land conflicts: Desa Pelawe versus MHP, 68–71; farmers versus oil palm plantations, 56–67; Marga Benekat versus MHP, 67–68; in MUBA, 139–143; OKU villages versus Mitra Ogan, 145–147; Palembang bus station land dispute, 168–169, **169**
land rights/land ownership, 53–56, 75–76. *See also* land conflicts
Laverton Gold NL, 85
LBH-Palembang, 10, 32; Bukit Asam/SMJ, 100–103; bus station land dispute, 168–169, **169;** cases handled, overview, 54–56; and corruption, 122; Dusun Belido village land dispute, 140–143; establishment of, 29; intimidation of, 39–40; and Islam, 168–170; Kundi versus GSBL, 59–61; Nur Kholis, 51; in OKU, 144; Pelawe versus MHP, 70–71; and PT TEL, 79–80, 82; and Pusri, 93–94, 96, 97; Rambang Lubai versus MHP, 74; and shrimp farmers, 104–106; and street vendors, 113; Wonorejo versus PT Multrada Multi Maju (MMM), 62–65, 66; and workers, 99–100; Yeni Roslaini's libel prosecution, 126
LDK (Institute for Campus Dakwah), 158, 160
lebak lebung, 118–119, 146
Lee, Gavin, 89
Lev, Daniel, 190
local autonomy, 120, 134, 150–151
Local Environmental Impact Control Agency, 88
logging. *See* forests; industrial forestry
London Sumatra (Lonsum), 71, 142
Lopa, Baharuddin, 75–76

LP3ES (Social and Economic Research, Education, and Information Institute), 153
LSM *(lembaga swadaya masyarakat),* 29, 125
Lubis, Todung Mulya, 29, 171, 182
Lustrilanang, Pius, 132

MacIntyre, Andrew, 117
Makmud, Emil, 37–38
Malari Affair, 28
Malley, Mike, 150
marga, 13–14, 18–19, 53, 67–68, 118
Marga Benakat, 67–75
Marx, Karl, 4, 191
Masyumi, 152, 155
MHP. *See* Musi Hutan Persada (MHP)
middle class: expansion of, 8, 17–18, 177–178; fear of lower classes, 2–3, 6, 42, 44, 114, 191; and Islam, 8, 153; and neoliberalism, 12, 186; and *reformasi,* 5, 10, 37, 52, 190, 191
minimum wage, 99
mining, 180, 185–190
MMI (Council of Indonesian Mujahidin), 165
MMM (PT Multrada Multi Maju), 61–67
Mohamad, Goenawan, 171
money politics *(politik uang),* 66, 117, 120–122, 134, 135, 144, 149–150
motorcycle theft, 128–129
Muara Enim, 68, 71–75, 79, 100–103
Muhammadiyah (organization), 50, 52, 152, 153, 160, 164, 165, 166, 170
Muhammadiyah University, 17, 44, 149, 158, 162, 166
MUI (Indonesian Council of Ulama), 159
Multrada Multi Maju (MMM). *See* MMM
Munarman, 106
Murod, Dudy Makmun, 132, 149
Murod, Makmun, 144
Murtopo, Ali, 28, 211n.16
Musi Banyuasin (MUBA): Dusun Belido village land dispute, 140–143;

economic conditions, 136, 137–139; *lebak lebung,* 118–119; Noerdin as *bupati* of, 134, 135–139, 143; resources, 136–137
Musi Hutan Persada (MHP), 19, 67–75, 81, 128; forest fires of 1997, 36–37; versus people of Marga Benakat, 67–68; versus people of Pelawe, 68–71; versus people of Rambang Lubai, 71–75
Musi Rawas (MURA), 69, 88, 120–122
Musi River, 68, 82, 90–97
Muslim-Christian conflict, 163, 165, 189–190
Muslim Student Association. *See* HMI (Islamic Students Association)

Nahdlatul Ulama (NU), 152, 153, 157, 166–168
National Environmental Agency, 83
National Human Rights Commission, 59, 60, 63, 72, 105, 132
National Land Agency, 75
National Legislature, 89, 120, 131, 133
National Sports Games (Pekan Olahraga Nasional, PON), 123–124, 137
native son *(putra daerah)* candidates, 121, 135, 144
Natsir, Muhammad, 155
Neklikesabe, Tamin, 77, 84
neoliberal economic policies, 12, 176–177, 178, 181, 182, 187, 188–189
nepotism, 37, 115, 116. *See also* Suharto family
NES. *See* Nucleus Estate and Smallholder Scheme (NES)
Network of Indonesian Non-Governmental Organizations for Forest Conservation (SKEPHI), 111
New Order (1966-1998): corruption, 116–118; development, 15–20; end of, 5–6, 10–11, 39–44; era of "Openness" *(Keterbukaan),* 10, 31; Golkar, 15, 129, 130, 135, 139, 143–144, 147–148, 149; and Islam, 153–159; labor and, 98; land concessions, 54; and NGOs, 182–183; and *preman* gangs, 129; response to student

protests, 31–32, 33, 34–35; youth organizations, 129
NGOs, 29–30; and corruption, 117, 122–123, 124–125; development-oriented, 30, 182–186; environmental, 81–85, 93–94, 97, 111, 185; funding of, 185–186; government-linked, 130; human rights issues, 35, 50, 107–108, 115, 185; and international financial institutions, 182–186; Islamic, 153; New Order and, 182–183; in Philippines, 172–173; red plate, 124–125; in Thailand, 172–173
NICs (newly industrializing countries), 175
Noerdin, Alex, 134, 135–139, 143, 149, 151
nongovernmental organizations. *See* NGOs
Nopianto, 135–136
NorWatch, 81, 82
Nucleus Estate and Smallholder Scheme (NES), 56. *See also inti/ plasma* schemes
Nuh, Jamila, **47,** 47–50, **92;** intimidation of, 36; in Kundi, 59, 61; and land conflicts, 54; and Pusri, 96; at Sriwijaya University, 10, 32–33, 34, 49; and street children, 35, **48;** in U.S., 36, 50
Nurcholish, Madjid, 154, 157, 171
Nur Kholis, **48,** 51, **55;** case against MHP, 36–37; on fall of Suharto and oppression, 46; intimidation of, 37, 40; Palembang bus station land dispute, 168–169, **169;** and PT TEL, 79, 80, 83–84; and Pusri, 93; and shrimp farmers, 105, 106; and TEMPUR, 123; on vote buying, 135; and Wonorejo farmers, 63
Nursalim Syamsul, 20, 103, 107–109, 110–111, 132, 182

Oesman, Syahrial, 130, 134, 151; as *bupati* of Ogan Komering Ulu (OKU), 143–147; as governor of South Sumatra, 147–151

Ogan Komering Ilir (OKI), 118–119, 126–127
Ogan Komering Ulu (OKU), 134, 143–147
oil and gas industry, 14, 15, 16–18, 136–137, 138, 176, 177–178, 180
oil palm plantations, 56–58; compensation to farmers, 56–57, 62, 64, 66; environmental damage from, 35, 77–78; funding, 180; Kundi versus GSBL, 58–61; land converted to, 66–67; land disputes, 57–58; Mitra Ogan, 145–147; Wonorejo versus MMM, 61–67
OPEC (Organization of Petroleum Exporting Countries), 176
"Openness" (Keterbukaan), 10, 31
O'Rourke, Kevin, 11
Oxfam, 87, 88, 89, 177, 187

packet, 57. See also inti/plasma schemes
Pagaralam riot, 37–39
Palembang: bus station land dispute, 168–169, **169**; Islam in, 152–153, 158, 159–163, 165, 167; May 1998 riots, 41–44, **43**; and New Order, 8–10; and oil industry, 17–18; population, 21; poverty, 20, 112, 114–115; preman gangs, 114; street vendors and becak drivers, 112–114; violence at Police Headquarters, 102–103
Palembang Becak Union, 112–113
Palembang Community Forum on Industrial Environment (FOLSIP), 94–95, 96
PAN (Partai Amanat Nasional), 148, 166
Pancasila, 16, 39–40, 156, 196n.12
Pangestu, Prayogo: and corruption, 72, 73, 75–76, 109; debts of, 20, 182; industrial forestry, 19, 67, 79, 180; and Taufik Kiemas, 131, 132
paper and pulp production. See industrial forestry
Partai Keadilan, 163
Partai Kebangkitan Bangsa (PKB), 168

Pasemah, 7, 21–23, 39
patronage, 117, 124, 133, 139, 169, 197n.18
PBB (Islamic Crescent Moon and Star Party), 72
pedagang kaki lima (street vendors), 111–112, 113–114
Pekan Olahraga Nasional (PON), 123–124
Pelawe, 68, 71
Pembaruan (Renewal Movement), 154
Pemuda Panca Marga, 45
Pemuda Pancasila, 129
Pertamina, 16–17, 95, 137, 174
pesantren, 49, 51, 52, 167
Petro MUBA, 137, 138
Philippines, 172–173, 181, 182–185
PII, 156, 160
PKB (Partai Kebangkitan Bangsa), 168
PKI (Indonesian Communist Party), 14, 15, 62
PKS (Justice and Prosperity Party), 139, 168–170
pollution: fertilizer industry and Musi River, 90–97; mining, 86–89; palm oil industry, 146; pulp and paper industry, 81–85; shrimp farming, 111
Polong, JJ, 34, 35
Polyani, Karl, 53, 188–189, 190
PON (Pekan Olahraga Nasional), 123–124
poverty, 20, **21**, 213n.15; and development, 173–175, 180, 187–188; in MUBA, 139; in OKU, 144; and unemployment in Palembang, 114–115
preman gangs, 126–133; and anti-corruption campaigns, 124; and local politics, 129–130; May 1998 riots, 42; and New Order, 129; and police and security forces, 61, 114, 117, 127–130; and street vendors, 113, 114; ties to military, 45; types of, 126–127
press, freedom of, 3, 10, 28, 31, 34, 46, 91, 92
Pribumi, 38, 42, 43

Project Underground, 86
"Prosperous MUBA in 2006," 136–139, 142, 143
Provincial Environmental Impact Management Agency, 93–94, 95–96
Provincial Legislature, 122–123
PSPKL (Street Vendors Solidarity Union), 113
P3M (Association for Pesantren and Community Development), 153
PT Multrada Multi Maju (MMM). *See* MMM
PT TEL, 34, 78–85, 179
Puruhita, Robby, 162
Pusri, 17, 90
Putra, Eddy Santana, 148

Qutb, Sayyid, 156

Rachmat, Jalalluddin, 155–156
Ramage, Douglas, 11
Rambang Danku, 71, 73
Rambang Lubai, 71–75
Ramli, Rizal, 155
Rasyid, Tarech, 34, 35, 44, 45
Rawas Mine, 85–90
red plate NGOs, 124–125
reformasi movement, 31–52; and Asian Economic Crisis, 37–39; beginnings of, 9–10; compared to French Revolution, 5–6; and corruption, 116–118, 122–124; cultural movement for democracy, 31; and elections, 144; and environmental issues, 91, 92; after the fall of Suharto, 44–46; and forest fires of 1997, 35–37; former activists and Palembang Mafia, 132; and intimidation, 33, 34, 35, 36–37, 39–40; and Islam, 52, 159–161, 163, 168–170; Islamists versus pro-democracy groups, 44; kidnapped and "disappeared," 40, **40;** and labor, 99, 104; and land conflicts, 70; May 1998 riots, 41–44; and middle class, 5, 10, 37, 52, 190, 191; profiles of four activists, 47–52; student protests, 31–35
Remaja Masjid, 164

rescue packages, 67, 176
reverse flow of wealth, 177, **178**
rice, 21, 53, 62, 137, 175
rickshaw drivers. See *becak* drivers
Rifai, Amzulian, 57
Right of Forest Exploitation (HPH), 18–19
road pirates *(bajing loncat),* 136
Robison, Richard *(Indonesia: The Rise of Capital),* 12, 20, 116, 187
Romli, AS, 166
Roslaini, Yeni, 34, 35, **46,** 50–51, 112, 115, 125–126
rubber, 23, 35, 53, 54, 62
Rukmana, Siti Hardiyanti (Tutut), 19, 54, 73, 180
rule of law, 30, 171
Ryacudu, Ryamizard, 132, 148, 150, 207n.33

Sabowo, Pak, 62, 63, 64, 65–66
Sachs, Jeffrey *(The End of Poverty),* 188
Said, Usman, 164–165
Saip, Adjis, 131, 144
Salim, Emil, 90, 112
Salman Mosque, 155–156
Sanit, Arbi, 35
Saparuddin, 70, 71
SAPs (structural adjustment programs), 176–177
Saputra, Untung, 145
Sarekat Islam, 152
Sasono, Adi, 35
Schwarz, Adam, 11
Sen, Amartya, 187
Setiawan, Benny, 94–95
sharia, 154, 165, 166, 169, 172
Shari'ati, Ali, 156–157
shrimp farming, 103–111; contract agreement, 103–104; debt, 108–111; environmental damage, 111; farmer's demands and demonstrations, 104–105; involvement of human rights groups, 107–108; negotiations, 105–106; press coverage, 107; rioting, 106–107
Situmorang, Abdul Wahib "Ucok," **47,** 52; director of WALHI, 71, 79,

83–84, 85, 87, 93; on 1997 fires, 36;
on *reformasi* split, 44; on Suharto
resignation, 42
SKEPHI (Network of Indonesian Non-
governmental Organizations for
Forest Conservation), 111
Social and Economic Research, Educa-
tion, and Information Institute
(LP3ES), 153
Sohe, Prana, 121–122
Soros, George, 187
South Sumatra: districts, xi *(see also
specific districts);* ethnic groups,
13–14; governor (*see* Arsyad, Rosi-
han; Basri, Ramli Hasan; Oesman,
Syahrial); gubernatorial election
(2004), 147–150; history, 13–15;
Islamic heritage of, 152–153; map, **9**;
under New Order, 15–20
South Sumatra Corruption Watch
(SSCW), 123–124, 165
South Sumatra Farmers and Workers
Resistance Movement, 102
South Sumatra High Court, 123
South Sumatra Youth Front (BPS),
129–130
SPSI (All-Indonesia Workers' Union),
98
Sri Melamin Rezeki, 96
Sriwijaya Corps, 15, 31–32, 35, 44–45
Sriwijaya Post, 30, 37, 41, 49, 60, 95,
124, 144
Sriwijaya University, 9–10, 31–33, 82,
157
Stiglitz, Joseph, 187
street vendors *(pedagang kaki lima)*,
111–112, 113–114
Street Vendors Solidarity Union
(PSPKL), 113
structural adjustment programs (SAPs),
176–177
Student Forum for Civil Society (FOR-
MAD), 160
Subianto, Prabowo, 39, 42
Sudjana, Eggi, 154
Suharto, 10–11, 31, 39–40, 42, 157,
181, 197n.18. *See also* New Order

Suharto, Tommy, 34, 85
Suharto family, 19, 54, 73, 79, 81
Suharyono, 80
Sukarno, 15, 58, 131
Sukarnoputri, Megawati, 34–35, 76,
110, 130–131, 133, 148, 150
Sumargono, Ahmad, 38, 39
Sumatera Ekspres, 41, 139
Sumber Mitra Jaya (SMJ), 100–103
Suparmono, Endang, 107, 108
Supriyono, Joesep, 121–122
Suripto, 73, 74, 75
Suryosumarmo, Yapto, 129, 132
Sutowo, Ibnu, 14–15, 16–17, 149
Sutowo, Ponco, 149
swallows' nests, 119–120
Syah, Chairil, 32, 34, 42, 68, 102

Talang Ubi, 127–128
Tambang Batu Bara Bukit Asam (Bukit
Asam), 100–103, 150
Tanjung Enim Lestari Pulp & Paper
(PT TEL), 34, 78–85, 179
Tarto, Surah (Pak Tarto), 59, 60, 61
Team of Advocates to Save the People's
Money (TEMPUR), 122, 123
Tempo, 34, 46
Temporary Contract Shrimp Farmers
Negotiation Team, 105
Thailand, 172–173, 180, 181–186, 191
Thalib, Munir Said, ix–x, 107
Thamrin, Soleh, 30
TNI. *See* Indonesian military
Tocqueville, Alexis de, 1, 2–3, 4, 191
transmigration projects, 56–57, 140,
180, 185
Transnational Corporations (TNCs),
187
Transparency International, 19,
180–181

Uhlin, Anders, 11, 154
ulama, 139, 152, 167
unemployment, 98, 111–112, 114–115
Union of Mosque Youth (IRM),
157–158
United Development Party (PPP), 15

urban migration, 21, 174–175
USAID (US Agency for International Development), 185
usroh, 155, 156

Wachyuni Mandira, 103–108, 109–110, 162
Wahid, Abdurrahman "Gus Dur," 71, 72, 75, 109, 157, 163, 167, 168
WALHI (Indonesian Environmental Forum), **47;** and BTM, 86–89; and Desa Pelawe versus MHP, 70; establishment of, 30; forest campaign, 77, 78; forest fires of 1997, 36; and Islam, 168–170; and Marga Benakat versus MHP, 68; Nur Kholis, 52; and PT TEL, 79–80, 82, 83–84; and Pusri, 93, 94, 95, 96, 97; and rights to harvest swallows' nests, 119; and shrimp farming, 105, 106; Situmorang, Abdul Wahib "Ucok," 52
Wijaya, Taufiq, 34, 46, 82, 86, 107
Women's Crisis Center (WCC), 50, 125–126
Wonorejo, 61–66
World Bank, 173–174; Good Governance, 186; *Human Development Report* (1999), 175; on Indonesian pollution, 77–78; on loss of Indonesian forests, 77; NGOs and, 182, 184, 185, 186; promotion of plantations, 54, 56, 66–67, 76; rescue packages and bridge funding, 67, 176–177; shrimp farming loans, 103; on smallholder agriculture, 192; support for mining projects, 89–90; transmigration projects, 180; and U.S. firms, 179
World Rainforest Movement (WRM), 184
World Trade Organization (WTO), 182, 185

YALHI (Foundation for Environmental Advocacy), 77, 93, 94
Yayasan Kesejahteraan (DPRD), 122
Young Islamic Generation (Gemuis), 160, 163
Yudhoyono, Susilo Bambang, 35, 142–143

Zen, Hasan, 79, 81
Zulkifli, Hilda, 87

About the Author

ELIZABETH COLLINS teaches in the Department of Classics and World Religions and the Southeast Asian Studies Program at Ohio University. She is the author of *Pierced by Murugan's Lance: Ritual, Power, and Moral Redemption among Malaysian Hindus* (1997) and has written articles on Islam and democratization in Indonesia. She is also one of the founders of an Indonesian NGO, Yayasan Nurani Dunia, which helps victims of natural and social disasters and conducts participatory development projects in many parts of Indonesia.

Production Notes for *Collins / Indonesia Betrayed*

Designed by the University of Hawai'i Press production staff with text in Cordelia and display in Optima

Composition by Josie Herr

Printing and binding by Edwards Brothers, Inc.

Printed on 60# Text White Opaque, 426 ppi